MATOAKA, POCAHONTAS, REBECCA

EARLY AMERICAN HISTORIES

Douglas Bradburn, John C. Coombs, and S. Max Edelson, Editors

MATOAKA, POCAHONTAS, REBECCA

Her Atlantic Identities and Afterlives

EDITED BY
KATHRYN N. GRAY AND AMY M. E. MORRIS

UNIVERSITY OF VIRGINIA PRESS
Charlottesville and London

The University of Virginia Press is situated on the traditional lands of the Monacan Nation, and the Commonwealth of Virginia was and is home to many other Indigenous people. We pay our respect to all of them, past and present. We also honor the enslaved African and African American people who built the University of Virginia, and we recognize their descendants. We commit to fostering voices from these communities through our publications and to deepening our collective understanding of their histories and contributions.

University of Virginia Press
© 2024 by the Rector and Visitors of the University of Virginia
All rights reserved
Printed in the United States of America on acid-free paper

First published 2024

9 8 7 6 5 4 3 2 1

LIBRARY OF CONGRESS CATALOGING-IN-PUBLICATION DATA
Names: Gray, Kathryn N., editor. | Morris, Amy M. E., editor. | Wood,
    Karenne, honoree.
Title: Matoaka, Pocahontas, Rebecca : her Atlantic identities and afterlives /
    edited by Kathryn N. Gray and Amy M. E. Morris.
Description: Charlottesville : University of Virginia Press, 2024. | Series:
    Early American histories | Includes bibliographical references and index.
Identifiers: LCCN 2024027752 (print) | LCCN 2024027753 (ebook) |
    ISBN 9780813952420 (hardback) | ISBN 9780813952437 (paperback) |
    ISBN 9780813952444 (ebook)
Subjects: LCSH: Pocahontas, -1617. | Powhatan Indians—Biography. |
    BISAC: HISTORY / Indigenous Peoples in the Americas | HISTORY /
    United States / Colonial Period (1600–1775) | LCGFT: Biographies.
Classification: LCC E99.P85 M37 2024 (print) | LCC E99.P85 (ebook) |
    DDC 975.501092—dc23/eng/20240809
LC record available at https://lccn.loc.gov/2024027752
LC ebook record available at https://lccn.loc.gov/2024027753

Cover art: Engraving of Pocahontas by Simon van de Passe, 1616. (National Portrait Gallery, Smithsonian Institution)
Cover design: Cecilia Sorochin

Engraving of "Matoaka Als Rebecca," Simon van de Passe, created in 1616 during her visit to London, and published in *Baziliωlogia: A Booke of Kings* (London, 1618). The Latin inscription identifies her as the daughter of Powhatan of Virginia. (National Portrait Gallery, Smithsonian Institution)

CONTENTS

A Tribute to Karenne Wood   ix
    Amy M. E. Morris

Introduction   1

Part I. Colonial Archives and Colonial Entanglements

Knowledge Gained and Knowledge Withheld in Early Virginia   21
    Karen Ordahl Kupperman

Pocahontas in Both English and Indian Eyes   45
    Helen C. Rountree

Prisoners of History: Pocahontas, Mary Jemison, and the
Poetics of an American Myth   62
    Karenne Wood

Part II. Reassessing Methodology

Tracing the Auto/Biographical in Paula Gunn Allen's
Pocahontas: Medicine Woman, Spy, Entrepreneur, Diplomat:
Or Lessons on Story, Sources, and the Archive   73
    Lucinda Rasmussen

The Pocahontas Pattern: Intermarriage as a Political Strategy
for Native American Women in Early Virginia   95
    Camilla Townsend

Part III. Engagements with Englishness

Pocahontas's Trip to England: The View from London, 1616–1617   117
E. M. Rose

Why Rebecca? Calvin and Indigenous Women   151
James Ring Adams

Part IV. Visual and Sensory Records and Reclamations

Visual Constructs and Indigenous Character in American
Origin Myths: Pocahontas, George Washington, and the
Parental Structure of Nationhood, 1820s–1870s   173
Graziella Crezegut

Pocahontas Chic   204
Cristina L. Azocar and Ivana Markova

Old and New Visual Cultures: An Interview   224
Stephanie Pratt and Kathryn N. Gray

"Listen to the Atlantic": Archives and Memory   242
Sarah Sense and Kathryn N. Gray

Selected Bibliography   257
Notes on Contributors   267
Index   271

A TRIBUTE TO KARENNE WOOD

Karenne Wood (1960–2019) was a Monacan writer, activist, scholar, and teacher. She received many accolades in her all-too-brief life, including the Schwartz Prize in 2009 from the Federation of State Humanities Councils for her work on Virginia Indian Programs and being recognized as one of the "Virginia Women in History" by the Library of Virginia in 2015. Wood earned an MFA from George Mason University in 2000. She published her first book of poetry, *Markings on Earth*, that same year and won the North American Native Authors Award for Poetry. From 2009 she served as director of Virginia Indian Programs at the Virginia Foundation for the Humanities. As she expanded the archive to include Indigenous perspectives, her goal was "to demonstrate that Native people have their own ways of seeing their participation in what's become a shared story." This simple, powerful message speaks out from her poetry, essays, and the historical resources that she created, including the *Virginia Indian Heritage Trail* (2007) which she edited for the 400th anniversary celebrations and subsequently the digital treasure trove of documents, images, and audiovisual material that is the *Virginia Indian Archive*. Through her work with the Virginia Department of Education and with textbook publishers, Wood revised the way history was taught in schools to "redress the historical omission of Native peoples from the story of Virginia and our nation in general." She put in place changes that will enable the next generation of schoolchildren to learn that "the past goes back 18,000 years. It does not begin in 1607, and there is no vanishing into the mist after that."[1]

With a characteristic blend of seriousness and good humor, Wood's essays open up an Indigenous perspective for a non-Native reader. In "Prisoners of History," reprinted in this volume, for instance, she points out the bias so often lurking in bland museumspeak, a bias that is stingingly apparent if it's you that is being marginalized. Wood points out how the disrespect shown to Indigenous people in the text of commemorative signs reinscribes past wrongs in the present. Captions are themselves historical texts, part of the curation of the historical archive that has to be scrutinized. Through the autobiographical reflections that thread through her research, she gives us a glimpse into the balancing act demanded of a Native American public historian. Her educational projects included working with the heritage and tourism industry, and she shouldered the burden of tirelessly engaging with a popular mythic history that implicitly endorsed white supremacy. What should she say when invited to speak at an event in Los Angeles commemorating the marriage of John Rolfe and Pocahontas, organized by descendants of Jamestown colonists? Wood responded with grace and openness, and she treated such invitations as educational opportunities.

"Almost all of my work is about history, memory, identity, our place in the natural world, and the connections between other living beings and ourselves," Wood explained. Her research, poetry and teaching all aimed to make those connections better, even if her task involved pointing out uncomfortable differences of perspective. She became an anthropologist, earning her PhD from the University of Virginia in 2016, but confessed that she turned to this discipline when she "got tired of other people studying us and telling us who we were. My people know who they are. They've just not been asked—until recently—to speak." This determination to overturn and move "past" an unjust historical silencing is eloquently expressed in Wood's meditative manifesto, "Past Silence," reprinted below. "Past Silence" is also the title of a subsection within Wood's second poetry collection, *Weaving the Boundary* (2016) that comprises a chronological series of historical poems. The section opens with Native American creation stories. Then follow poems about the colonial period, including one on Bartolomé de las Casas and several written in the first person featuring Native Americans whose stories became entangled with the history of colonization: "Paquiquineo, 1570," "Amonute, 1617," and "De-he-wä-mis." These people's stories (the latter two are more commonly known by the names of Pocahontas and Mary Jemison) were written down by white settlers, but Wood reconstructs their subjective points of view. The ensuing poems treat violence and war in the nineteenth century, and the last biographical poem tells the story of Ira Hayes, the Pima man who participated in the flag raising at Iwo Jima in 1945, which became immortalized in the Pulitzer-prize winning photo, and who died of alcoholism at the age of thirty-two. Each poem tells a more personal and painful story than would sit comfortably in the national narrative. And yet, as part of a shared past, they belong in that narrative.

Both "Amonute, 1617" and "De-he-wä-mis" were first published with the essay "Prisoners of History" in *SAIL*. We are grateful to Wood's editors and publishers for the opportunity to reprint some of her work here. By including it in this volume, we aim to celebrate Wood's legacy and to hold on a little longer to her voice in an ongoing conversation that she helped begin. The London conference took place in March 2017, four hundred years after Pocahontas died at Gravesend, at the start of her homeward journey. Wood's poem "Amonute, 1617" marks the date of her death. The title serves as a memorial that gives Pocahontas back the name that was neither her English name, nor her funny nickname, nor the sacred name (Matoaka) that she relinquished at baptism, but her ordinary name. It tells the story of the arrival of the English at Tsenacomoco, evoking the landscape, describing children playing at the water's edge, and imagining how the English looked to Native eyes ("a squatty short man, face sprouting red fur"). Yet at the end we realize the further significance of the date. The images of the poem are a deathbed memory, a nostalgic yearning for a precolonial moment that the speaker knows is lost forever, not just to her, but to all her people. The second line of the poem alludes to the passage at the end of Fitzgerald's *The Great Gatsby,* in which Nick Carraway imagines the Dutch sailors' wonder at "the fresh, green breast of the new world" (a passage that Wood referenced directly in her poem on Roanoke). Amonute remembers "Tsenacomoco . . . heart of all hearts, / our center, that lime-green breast of a world." Through this allusion and the "fevered dream" at the end of the poem, Wood turns the American Dream idea on its head. The dream for Amonute and her people is not a vision of an exciting new world but the remembrance of a once loved homeland about to vanish.

Wood's poem weaves its own myths too: Pocahontas realized when she met Smith in London "that more of them would always come to us." Then, when the time came to return to Tsenacomoco, she "felt weak" and "stumbled." It is as if she falls ill because she can't bear to return and see what she now knows will happen. She identifies in herself a biblical type, not the young bride Rebecca who submissively left her people to marry Isaac, but the older Rebecca, who helped trick Esau, her "red" firstborn, out of his inheritance. Wood's Amonute incorporates historical material, but she is shaped to a poetic purpose of unravelling and rewriting colonial myths to express resistance and show how the story can be retold from an opposing point of view.

In the documentary archive, Pocahontas utters few words. Little of her speech was recorded, and then only by male English writers who were probably inventing her words for their own purposes. So it is fitting that Wood's Amonute is hungry for more words. The language exchange in the poem also nicely highlights the historical irony that Pocahontas must have learned to *speak* English very well, though she left no written legacy, so that, in a sense, her "silence" is a result of Western academia's privileging of text over oral culture. The poem includes the Algonquian words that passed into American English as *raccoon* and *moccasin*, but it also reminds us of how much was lost by listing many more unfamiliar words, words for domestic, homely things: *yehakin* (house), *ponap* (bread), *matchcore* (garment).

As a first-person poem with a blended subjectivity, "Amonute, 1617" expresses some of Wood's own passions and concerns, her love of nature and community, but perhaps most poignantly, her sense of the loss of tribal languages, including that of her own Monacan people. A later poem in her "Past Silence" series begins:

> Around us, charged
> particles of sound:
> Languages lost, every
> Word for what matters.

Entitled "What It Is," the poem slips from lost language to lost land: "Fenced / out, we turn away but cannot / let go." In Wood's experience, these losses went hand in hand. As she explains in her doctoral dissertation, "For Monacan people, the inability to express themselves in the language of their ancestors is felt, by many members, not only as the loss of ethnolinguistic conventions and the intellectual wealth encoded therein, nor as the loss of their history embodied in orally transmitted narratives. It is felt, I believe, as the loss of relationships—relationships with one another, with their ancestors, and with the natural world." According to Wood's spiritual tradition, the living beings with whom she expected to communicate included not only people, but also the sky, water, plants, animals, and her ancestors. These interlocutors were lost when the language was lost.

As she explains in her dissertation, Tutelo, the closest linguistic relative of Monacan, a Sioux-group language, died out in Canada in the mid-twentieth century. Consequently, the language can only be reconstructed from academic lexicons. Wood was interested in pursuing a language reclamation project and took the initial step, in her dissertation, of analyzing Monacan attitudes toward the language. She theorized that the presence of a "language ghost" united the community in a shared sense of "lost sacred relationships." Wood has Amonute recall and cherish Algonquian words, reciting them in her final delirium like a catechism or a spell, to carry her back home. Yet Wood, a scholar-poet, garnered these words from a colonizer's lexicon. As she rehomed them in Amonute's voice, she retained their recognizable vocabulary list format and managed to evoke, in a skillful act of poetic transparency, both the speaker's oral memory and the writer's textual source. Although the poem brings Algonquian momentarily into a meaningful dialogue with the present, it also portrays the start (and end) of a linguistic exchange that culminated in the loss of Virginia's Indigenous languages and in English being the language in which Wood wrote. As Wood summed up in her dissertation, the problem of accurately representing an Indigenous historical figure is compounded by language loss and by the privileging of a culture of writing that marginalized Native people: "There is an understanding, among Monacan people, that the voices of their ancestors have been lost, that the ancestors are not correctly represented in history and are unable to speak for themselves, partly because they were unable to write their own histories and partly because the language has shifted to the language of the colonizers." In "Amonute, 1617," Wood deploys the resources of English to express her speaker's Indigenous identity, borrowing from the Bible, American literature, and an Algonquian lexicon. But she also voices through Amonute her own hunger for more words, for the dream of a heart-language, a mother tongue of her own: "Tsenacomoco. A place like no other, heart of hearts, / our center, that lime-green breast of a world. / We were of it. Belonged . . ."

Karenne, we hope you have found your way home. Thank you for your words.

Amy Morris

Note

1. Anna Kariel, "A Conversation with Karenne Wood," Virginia Humanities, November 19, 2013, https://virginiahumanities.org/2013/11/a-conversation -with-karenne-wood/.

AMONUTE, 1617*

Tsenacomoco. A place like no other, heart of all hearts,
our center, that lime-green breast of a world.
We were of it. Belonged to its waters, which spread west
like fingers from Chesapioke, where saucer-sized oysters
stacked themselves on underwater shelves and shad teemed upriver
when trees budded, such as grew a hundred feet or higher:
cypress, sycamore, chestnut, crowding out the understory. Where,
at forest's edge, white dogwood blossoms shimmered like stars.
Where our women dug *tuckahoe* tubers, pounded out bread, and
planted their corn, beans and pumpkins with songs, according to the moon.

My father, Powhatan, our *mamanatowick*, holiest of chiefs,
who in his dreams entered all realms seeking our futures
              and who spoke with our priests the secret holy words,
called me Pokahuntas, little Mischief. A nickname. He knew my name,
Amonute.

Wind from the east, with what portent, the day runners brought word
of more ships with sails, pale strangers with hair on their faces like dogs?
Watch them, Powhatan said. We heard tales: they tried
to catch fish with flat pans, built a wall around their huts.
Could not feed themselves.

Opechancanough, our war chief, captured and brought us their leader.
A squatty short man, face sprouting red fur. No one had seen
such a man or heard his talk. My father exchanged boys with him.
The white boy
would stay in our town. He and I traded words. I learned "house," *yehakin*.
              "Bread," *ponap*. "Garment," *matchcore*. "Arrows," *attonce*.
Aroughcun, I taught him, that one with the black-striped tail.
Mockasin, supple buckskin, scent of woodsmoke.

I wanted more words. Went to their fort, to the redheaded man.
Chawnsmit, his name. He became my father's son, called him Father, said
what was his would be ours. I learned to speak to him.

---

* "Amonute, 1617" and "Past Silence" from Weaving the Boundary by Karenne Wood, © 2016
Karenne Wood. Reprinted by permission of the University of Arizona Press.

Ka ka torawincs yowo?

"What do you call this?"

And my father's question:

Casacunnakack, peya quagh acquintan vttasantasough?

"In how many days will there come more English ships?"

Then he left. Chawnsmit, our son. We were told he was wounded. He had
died, they said.

That Anglo tongue, my undoing. Years passed.
Oftentimes, we were fighting the strangers.

My husband Kocoum disappeared,
and his Patawomeck people sold me to Captain Argall for a copper kettle.
I was to be ransomed. Was sent to Henricus
where the Reverend Whitaker, a dour man hunched like a buzzard,
    instructed me in their words, their religion, and where
John Rolfe came to love me. Our people were at war. Would I marry him,
he asked.

Would my father make peace? We said yes. I gave up my sacred name,
Matoaka, she who kindles,

and I became Rebecca,
a biblical woman who left homeland for Canaan, married Abraham's Isaac,
        brought peace between enemies,
bore twins: the red Esau, who emerged first; and Jacob,
        who through his mother's treachery inherited the land.

A few years of calm. We planted tobacco. I bore a son, Thomas.
Then another question: would I cross the sea, go to London, be their
emissary?

Yes, my father said. Go. We need to know more.
I saw Plymouth, then London. Felt its crowds press upon me, knew its
    stench.

I saw that Chawnsmit.

He still lived. No son of ours. Heard their lies in his words.
Knew then that more of them would always come to us.

At last, when spring came and the winds turned, our ship left for home.
I felt weak. I stumbled. We must stop, my husband said.

She is too ill to go on.

He cupped the bones of my face. Wiped my brow when delirium
swallowed me. Spoke gently.
Words.

>   Black words swirling like London's murmurations of starlings that
>   clouded the sky at dusk.

At home, my sisters pat out corn cakes and laugh. The elder calls to a
>   child
who splashes at river's edge, where the sand wears each stone smooth.
>   *Crenepo,* woman. *Marowanchesso,* boy. *Sukahanna,* water.

On the shore, men scrape dugouts with oyster shells.

>   *Acquintan,* canoe.
Words. As though nothing had changed.

It is but the fevered dream of one who sleeps an ocean away.
Tsenacomoco.

>   We thought it the center of the world.

PAST SILENCE

>   *homage to Michel-Rolph Trouillot (1949–2012)*

Stories are made of silences. We know this. What matters becomes
narrative; what is thought not to matter is excluded. Some call it history,
which is one kind of story, with this distinction: in the Western manner,
the pretense to exclusive truth. We had other kinds of stories: to show how
we came into the world, how to behave—as one among many, to remember
holy places that distinguish the land, places touched by spirit—how to
avoid mistakes of all kinds, how to find beauty, how to reciprocate, how
to think in balance. We knew time as a series of cycles: that we do not
progress but repeat. We called ourselves human beings. The People. We
were related. We had orators: keepers of wisdom, traditions, faith, law,
who were careful not to omit. Who gave us the stories in winter, when the
animals were silent, and we gathered near our fires. It was a good system.
It worked well for thousands of years.

>   *We*

The unthinkable happened. Disaster. Which defied definition. Defied even the words with which our questions were phrased. We had no instruments for imagining this. Others entered our world. They named things that had names. Created fields of power. Semantic, transformative power. They named us. The silences began when they "discovered" us, when we became Other. Homeland became wilderness; land virgin (read: *empty*). Inhabited land. They could own it. Doctrine of Discovery. They could take it. Degrees of humanity. We were now not quite human. Our past appeared in museums of natural history, with dinosaurs, insects, and rocks. Not in history museums, with stories of human beings. The illusion of dichotomy; i.e., history begins when they arrive, is preceded by prehistory. Thousands of years of pre-history, excluded. Because they were not here. *Ipso facto.* Palimpsest: the covering of an ancient text by writing over it. In archaeology, the burial of a site by building on top of it. Call it the Americas.

We are

"Is it really inconsequential that the history of America is being written in the same world where few little *boys* want to be Indians?" How do we recognize a bottomless silence? We became invisible. Passive voice: no one was responsible. Words were manipulated. Words like *extinct. Disappeared. Vanished.* Mists of history obscuring the gaze. Words like *authentic. Full-blood.* No real Indians remained. A language of euphemism: discovery, not conquest. Battles, not massacres. Language of simplification: villages, not towns. Gardens, not agriculture. Survival skills, not science. Legends or myths, but not history. Language of interpretation. Words like *savage.* Like *lore.* Past tense. Lived in tipis. Hunted buffalo. Wore feathers. Like *dead.* We began to believe this story. Became imprisoned in invisibility. Because it did not matter whether we fought or surrendered. Words like *culture.* Like *traditional.* The bottomless argument: Who is an Indian? We became self-destructive.

We are still

And all the commemorations. Four or five hundred years of this or that. Others decide what is momentous and why, as though their imagined destiny foreshadowed the sequence of events. Archival power. Retrospective significance. Primary sources. Marching bands, Knights of Columbus. Plymouth Rock, Santo what's-his-name. Packaged history. Pocahontas, Thanksgiving: American myths for public consumption. Heritage Tourism: What is it worth? Who wrote this story? Who imposed silence on neglected events, filled that silence with new stories (read: *about power*). How they invented democracy, free enterprise, cultural plurality. As though these did not already exist. As though it was a New World.

We are still here

The past is not history. It is all of what happened, not some of what some have said happened. Truth lies not in being faithful to a view of what mattered but in confronting the present as it re-presents the past. In examining current injustices. We create and recreate the past in the present. Only then can we participate. Revise narratives, insert absent voices. Seek words that resist erasure.

MATOAKA, POCAHONTAS, REBECCA

INTRODUCTION

Overview

In her 2016 article, Karenne Wood, to whom this volume is dedicated, comments that the daily lives and beliefs of Native people, especially women, were of no real interest to the colonial explorers and settlers.[1] The early American colonial archive of books, manuscripts, letters, and collected and consolidated volumes, offers only partial accounts and glimpses of Indigenous experiences. Jean O'Brien notes that these primary materials, as we're used to calling them, practice a logic of elimination, effacing and erasing Indigenous experience in favor of a settler-colonial perspective.[2] The imperative of this collection is to explore the enduring presences of the woman who came to be known as Pocahontas. More than four hundred years since her all too premature death in England, this collection seeks to establish a sense of the worlds that she occupied in North America and London. The collection is interested in the ways that an image was created and perpetuated, in the seventeenth century and beyond, and how that might be challenged by new archival research, a multidisciplinary methodology, comparative analysis, and contemporary creative practice.

The collection navigates the narratives of exploration and national mythologies, it traces the complex work of identity construction in the past and present, and it seeks to follow Wood's instincts and "look for the Native voices, to try to learn more about them as people."[3] By contextualizing the Eurocentric bias of the colonial mindset within a growing body of new knowledge about Indigenous practices and traditions, this collection aims to establish a generative space where old and new ways of "knowing" this elusive, yet seemingly ubiquitous, historical figure are productively aligned and debated: from the told and retold narratives of the early modern and early American archive, to representations in art and fashion, and in relation to contemporary debates about feminist, and Indigenous feminist discourse. As such, the collection is self-consciously varied in its content, with the traditional essay sitting alongside creative practice, collaborations, and interviews, each contribution situated within its own methodology. Contributors to the collection approach their analysis through different sets of priorities, practices, and assumptions. Collectively, the contributions produce generative debate, sometimes in productive disagreement, and each contributor poses and responds to different sets of intellectual and cultural questions. While the scope and range of the contributions demonstrate a breadth of scholarly engagement, this is not an exhaustive account of the woman known as Pocahontas. There are, no doubt, more accounts to be uncovered and more books to be written. Rather, by bringing together scholars from different fields and areas of expertise, the collection is intended to engender the expansive possibilities of the ongoing work of historical analysis and cultural production that coheres around the traces of Pocahontas in the archive and afterlives.

Contexts and Constructs

Though a familiar historical figure, the woman we call Pocahontas can often seem more mythological than real. Her voice in the historical record exists only as ventriloquized by English colonials, and her story is controversial and contested among Native American groups and non-Native historians alike. Academic histories and Mattaponi oral history, diverge, for example, over whether Pocahontas was raped during her captivity or experienced "kind handling," and whether her death in England in 1617 was a result of illness or of poisoning.[4] Within the academy, there is disagreement over the extent to which John Smith invented or misinterpreted Pocahontas's words and actions, and many scholars question his well-known account of her saving him from execution by her father. Smith narrated the rescue episode in his 1624 *Generall Historie of Virginia* and vaguely alluded to it in *New Englands Trials and Present Estate* (1622), but he did not mention it in his earlier reports (from 1608 and 1612) nor do other contemporary accounts.[5] Scholars of early America, including Philip Barbour and Karen Ordahl Kupperman, have puzzled over Smith's description and suggested ways in which it might have misinterpreted a likely Powhatan practice such as an adoption ritual.[6] Others, including Camilla Townsend and Helen C. Rountree, have concluded from the persistent discrepancies that

Smith simply invented this incident. They note that bludgeoning was not the Powhatan method of executing an enemy, and they concur with the Mattaponi view that young girls would not have been present at political meetings.[7] Townsend points out that Smith referred to an adoption ritual that took place two days later. "Can it be true that this story, still running, began with a lie?" asks Neil Rennie at the conclusion of his study of Pocahontas in literature from Smith to the twentieth century.[8] The story of Smith's rescue bears a striking similarity to Smith's description of being saved by the Lady Tragabigzanda in Turkey before he traveled to the New World. It also echoes a tale in the *Gesta Romanorum* and later found in the folksong "Lord Beichan" (or sometimes Baker or Bateman). The rescue of a European man by a high-ranking Native woman, who, against the wisdom of her own people, recognized his superior worth, was a recurrent orientalist motif.[9] Even the early documentary accounts of Pocahontas were crafted from Eurocentric myth.

The later development of the Pocahontas myth is well known. The scenario of Pocahontas's rescue of Smith was recycled in many forms in the Indian romance genre that flourished in the United States from the early nineteenth century onward. Although Pocahontas's heroism, defying her father in order to save a young stranger, contributed to its popularity, the cultural message of the story was clearly flattering to the dominant elite. In Robert Tilton's analysis: "Pocahontas chose to save Smith, and, by extension, all white Americans."[10] The story, as Philip Young observed, "will work for any culture, informing us, whoever we are, that we are chosen or preferred."[11] Yet this is also the kind of exclusive, self-serving myth that is unraveled by historical investigation. Pocahontas's own captivity among the English in 1613–14, however, has featured little in popular retellings, despite its being much longer, better documented, and more consequential. The documentary record is silent about the reasons for Pocahontas's decisions during this period, and historians have come to different conclusions: some say she was "brainwashed" (Mattaponi), others posit Stockholm syndrome (Rountree), and others, while acknowledging her limited options, interpret the decision to cement her relationship with the English through marriage as thoughtful, mature, and, in some ways, heroic (Townsend, Allen).

To give a brief recap of some key events in Pocahontas's short life: She was born circa 1597 to one of the many wives of paramount chief Wahunsenacah, also known as Powhatan. Her names are recorded as Amonute and Matoaka, but her father nicknamed her Pocahontas, which has been translated as "little

Mischief."[12] John Smith believed her to be about ten years old when he met her in 1608 in the course of his efforts to trade with and coerce the Powhatans to supply the ailing colony with food.[13] Accounts by William Strachey and John Smith present Pocahontas as a lively child who seemed to enjoy meeting the English.[14] Smith has it that she sometimes defied her father in order to help them, but it is more likely, given her age, that she was sent to accompany his delegations and with food gifts as a sign of goodwill. Sometime between 1609 when Smith returned to England and 1612, Pocahontas married a warrior, Kocoum. Mattaponi oral history adds that they had a child and that Kocoum was murdered by the English at the time of her abduction.[15]

In 1612, Captain Samuel Argall found her staying in a Potowomac village and took her captive. She was held at Jamestown and then upriver at Henrico. Reports conflict over whether her father paid the ransom demanded by the English, but, either way, she was not released. The stalemate ended when, following intensive instruction by the colony's chaplain, Alexander Whitaker, Pocahontas converted to Christianity in April 1614, took the name Rebecca, and, with her uncle present to represent the Powhatan people, married the twenty-nine-year-old John Rolfe. Rolfe had petitioned the governor for permission to marry her. At that time he was also attempting to establish commercial tobacco growing in the Chesapeake. After her marriage, Pocahontas bore a son, Thomas. In 1616, she traveled with husband and child as part of a delegation to England. There, she was presented at the court of King James I and Queen Anne and attended Ben Jonson's masque, *The Vision of Delight*. While in London, Pocahontas sat for the portrait engraved by Simon van de Passe, and she met and exchanged a few words with John Smith. In March 1617, at the start of her return journey to Virginia, Pocahontas sickened and died. She was buried at St. George's Church in Gravesend. After her death, Rolfe returned to Virginia. Thomas was brought up by his English relatives and returned to Virginia in 1635, aged about twenty.

Even a brief account like this cannot avoid stumbling through some of the controversial disagreements over the facts within and between oral, documentary, and anthropological accounts. But these divergences pale in comparison to the gaps between serious historiographical versions and the story as told in popular fictionalizations. Since the nineteenth century, possibly because of concerns about "miscegenation," fictionalized accounts have emphasized and romanticized Pocahontas's relationship with John Smith, invariably needing to alter Pocahontas's age in order to make this possible.[16] As the scholar Helen Rountree observed, the 1995 Disney movie was entirely about the legendary and not the historical figure of Pocahontas, and it "clouded the issue further with female dependency, teenage angst, and doomed interracial love."[17] Terrence Malick's *The New World* (2005) incorporated fascinating background reconstructions of daily life at Jamestown and in the Powhatan settlements, created through impressive collaborations between the filmmakers and archaeologists, linguists, and Virginia tribal groups. But the film ultimately retained as its centerpiece the counterfactual and deeply unsettling love story and its allied Eurocentric myth of the potential for a "new" start. The film's final scenes, as Monika Siebert has pointed out, seem to erase the traumatic history that it has already portrayed, as the film circles back to show the Virginia landscape once again as it appeared in the opening: apparently unpeopled, viewed from the water by arriving Englishmen.[18]

Because Pocahontas and her story continue to be instrumentalized to serve a colonial or nationalistic agenda, it is important to contextualize current historiographical studies by placing them alongside scholarship that addresses her cultural legacy. Examining Pocahontas's evolving role in mythology about the origin and meaning of the United States highlights how much is at stake, culturally and politically, in historians' ongoing efforts to enhance our understanding of the seventeenth-century cultural encounter, and of the experience of the figure who remains the most well-known and yet least-well understood Native American woman in US history. Accordingly, this volume includes essays that offer new insights into the life experience of the woman known as Pocahontas and the political relations between her, the Powhatan people, and the English in the early seventeenth century. In addition to original historical research, the collection also includes new scholarship addressing the afterlife of Pocahontas in the form of visual iconography; the reception of her story in the nineteenth and twentieth centuries; and cultural appropriation, consumerism, and contemporary representations of Indigenous identities and heritage.

This collection is the offspring of a conference that was held in London in March 2017 to mark the four hundredth anniversary of the death of Pocahontas. Using her visit to England and her death and burial in Kent as an entry point, scholars from both sides of the Atlantic, representing a wide range of academic disciplines and perspectives, gathered at the Eccles Centre for American Studies at the British Library and at the Institute of Historical Research.

We explored the breadth, sophistication, and political engagement of current work on Pocahontas, her transatlantic life and times, and her ongoing legacy. The essays in this collection continue the work of the conference, showcasing different approaches to Pocahontas as a subject of study, but they move beyond that focus to consider issues of gender and Indigeneity more broadly. The essays draw on a vast amount of published research from different disciplines and gather together perspectives and material that would otherwise be scattered across different fora and publication venues. The research on Pocahontas's "afterlife" gives an indication of the complex cultural context in which current scholars, historians, and artists are pursuing their efforts to understand her historical role and milieu. Contemporary scholars and artists engaging with early modern materials work to reorient the story of a historical figure who has a persistent alternative presence in cultural mythology and whose significance is entangled with local and national identities, gender politics, and the ongoing consequences of settler colonialism.

As a collection, the essays, interviews, and poems reflect the fractured and refracted nature of their subject: at times there seems little connection between the historic woman and the cultural myth, but sometimes a clear alignment emerges, as the colonial dynamics of the historic encounter reappear with a surprising vividness in the modern age. The scandalous scale of the disappearance and violent death of Indigenous women in North America in recent years was on several speakers' minds as they considered Pocahontas's legacy. Mishuana Goeman notably addressed it in her keynote lecture, which formed the basis of her recent book on film and "settler aesthetics."[19] Since Rayna Green's seminal essay on the "Pocahontas Perplex," scholars have highlighted the troubling connection between the gendered imagery of colonization in this story of US origins and the marginalization of Native American women in mainstream culture.[20] S. Elizabeth Bird has argued that the influence of the Pocahontas myth can be seen in the stereotypical roles given to Native American women in film and television, roles that follow the bifurcated pattern of Indigenous princess or submissive "squaw."[21] More recently, Missing Matoaka, an online resource that seeks justice for missing Indigenous women, makes a causal connection between sexist stereotypes and violence against Indigenous women, identifying Matoaka as "one of the first documented Missing & Murdered Indigenous Women—the first of many sisters."[22] As an Indigenous "princess" who submits to a European man, the Native American woman confers legitimacy on white male supremacy and the colonial project. As a "squaw," the

Pocahontas figure exists to serve the colonials' sexual and physical needs and has no agency or subjectivity.

Shades of this meaning persist in consumer advertising in mainstream US culture today, as Cristina Azocar shows in this volume. Indigenous North American artists, including Rebecca Belmore (Canadian Anishinaabe) and Cannupa Hanska Luger (who is of Mandan, Hidatsa, Arikara, Lakota, and European descent) have created powerful works that protest the abuse of Native American women, and some of these can be interpreted as responses to the popular iconography of Pocahontas. In her street performance piece, *Vigil* (2002), for instance, Belmore began with the menial task of scrubbing the sidewalk.[23] Donning a red dress, she shouted out the names of missing women, then repeatedly nailed her dress to a post and struggled to rip herself to freedom. These acts, performed in front of passersby, presented sexual commodification and violence as hauntingly sad, but also, through the symbolic reenactment in the performer's body, as a cycle that is relentless and exhausting. Hanska Luger's "Every One" (2018) recreated an image of an anonymous Indigenous woman from a tin-type photograph ("Sister," by Kali Spitzer) on a large scale in clay beads, assembled into the form of a curtain.[24] Luger dyed and arranged the beads, which were all originally handmade by different communities of Indigenous women: the work embodied Indigenous craftwork, solidarity, and protest. These artworks both use the Indigenous female body, but they put forward an alternative representation that challenges the colonialist icon of Pocahontas, the submissive princess who betrayed her people.

The continuing relevance of Pocahontas and her story was evident in the controversies over Senator Elizabeth Warren's ancestry, and in Donald Trump's use of the name "Pocahontas" as a mocking slur in 2018. Participants in environmental political conflicts also feel the long shadow of the Pocahontas myth. Reflecting on the Indigenous and environmental protests over the Dakota Pipeline in 2017, the Cheyenne and Arapaho filmmaker Chris Eyre commented that "Pocahontas is alive at Standing Rock."[25] Not only does the mythology of Pocahontas continue to damage social relations in the USA, but her name has become a familiar part of the rhetoric of conflict and is invoked by different groups for different and sometimes opposing purposes. In such a situation, research into the complexity of Pocahontas's historical experience and what it reveals about early American intercultural encounter has a vital role to play by offering rich, many-sided accounts, and counternarratives. Bringing together innovative historical research, dialogue, and creative practice with reflective analysis of Pocahontas's "afterlife," this transatlantic volume hopes to provide stimulating opportunities for discussion in the ongoing scholarly and artistic effort to inform, rethink, and reshape this part of the US national imaginary.

The essays in this volume highlight key issues in current scholarship on Pocahontas and address the academic challenges that scholars face in attempting to reconstruct her story. Here is one of the central problems, as outlined by another of our keynote speakers, Karenne Wood: "As both a Native poet and a historical researcher, I am often caught in this dilemma, aware that the mainstream stories of our people are deeply flawed but unable to find more authentic accounts, usually because the American Indians remain voiceless or were deliberately silenced. This is particularly true for Native women—their daily activities and beliefs were of no interest to the colonial explorers and settlers whose accounts form the 'primary sources' dear to American historians and teachers."[26] Where Pocahontas's voice is not silent in the historical record, her words are formulated to serve the interests of those telling her story. It is possible to read a strategic resistance into some of Pocahontas's silences. Her cool reserve compared with Smith's almost embarrassed garrulousness in his account of their London meeting has been interpreted by Karen Robertson, for instance, as part of a strategy of reproachful silence.[27] But the fact that Pocahontas left "no verifiable words of her own" has ironically facilitated the "contrasting representations" and "multifarious narratives" of the many fictionalized accounts, which, as Tilton has shown, offer "cumulative power" but little historical clarity.[28]

Monique Mojica memorably dramatized the problem of Pocahontas's stilted words in her surreal and darkly comic play, Princess Pocahontas and the Blue Spots (1990). Mojica has "Lady Rebecca" speak verbatim the words ascribed to her by Smith, but as a character who is in the process of being "caught, stuck, girdled," as she gradually steps into a gilt picture frame and fits herself into her ruff and cuffs "as if being put into stocks and pillory." Mojica gives Pocahontas the freedom to be herself only in a flashback scene, showing her as Matoaka, her younger self, anticipating with solemn excitement a ritual celebrating her transition from child to woman. For Mojica, Pocahontas had to be rescued from the confines of masculine colonial history, and performance enabled this by reconnecting her story with Indigenous traditions and the shared rhythms of the female body: "Dark skies, the moon is mine / stars travel / woman's time."[29] Mojica identified in Pocahontas a mythic aspect of womanhood but not the colonialists' version. In focusing on Pocahontas's coming of age, Mojica turned to a notable gap in the historical record (between 1609 when Smith left and 1612 when Pocahontas was abducted) and took the opportunity to give this period a symbolic importance. Mojica portrayed Pocahontas's incipient sexuality not as a prequel to the doom of her race but as a moment of transformation that marked the possibility of adaptivity, of openness to the future, of the potential to negotiate and survive colonization. Although Mojica highlighted the legacy of struggle that resulted from colonization, in the women's refrain, "No map, no trail, no footprint, no way home," she pointed to the creation of the métisse—literally interracial children, but symbolically a hybrid, adaptive, bicultural identity—as a source of hope and potential. In this, Mojica took inspiration from the feminist writer and poet Gloria Anzaldúa who celebrated hybrid identities as peculiarly creative, empowering and open to the future.[30]

Toward the end of the twentieth century, as academics and thinkers caught up with Anzaldúa and began to share her positive view of border crossings, historical scholarship on colonial America was also becoming more adaptive. Academic framings of Native Americans as victims were increasingly replaced with the idea of the "middle ground," meaning relationships of exchange and negotiation that emphasized the historical agency of Indigenous peoples.[31] Daniel Richter's *Facing East from Indian Country: A Native History of Early America* and Karen Ordahl Kupperman's *Indians and English: Facing Off in Early America* illustrate how academic historians found new ways to research and reconstruct Indigenous perspectives from the period of Contact and sought to rebalance the record. The integration of information from the related disciplines of archaeology and anthropology, plus the benefit of a transnational and hemispheric perspective, have enabled scholars such as Camilla Townsend, Jace Weaver, and Caroline Dodds Pennock to foreground Indigenous perspectives in their historiographical work. Complementing these broader developments in historiography, and building on Philip Barbour's mid-twentieth-century seminal work on Smith and his narratives, Helen Rountree's extensive anthropological research into Powhatan culture has infused recent research on Pocahontas with a new level of depth, detail, and intercultural respect.

It seems no coincidence that many of the recent and contemporary scholars who have taken on the challenge of trying to explore the situation from Pocahontas's point of view are women. As Wood and Robertson have underlined, an intersection of ethnicity and gender led to the silence, and, as this volume illustrates, an intersection of scholarliness and gender has helped drive recuperative research. But this acknowledgment brings with it new methodological questions about the relationship between Indigeneity, feminism, and gender studies. In "Theorizing Indigeneity, Gender, and Settler Colonialism," Shelbi Nahwilet Meissner and Kyle Whyte draw on the perplexing use of Pocahontas mythos in documenting Virginia's historic legislation in defining citizenship and identity: "In 1924, Virginia passed the Racial Integrity Act. The act enforced the one-drop rule, which made it so that someone was either white or colored, and one drop of non-white meant someone was colored. The only exception to the one-drop rule occurred in cases where white people claimed to be descendants of any Indigenous women, which included Pocahontas. While white people who claimed an often-fictional Indigenous great-grandmother were classified as white, actual Indigenous people were homogenized as 'colored,' their Indigenous ancestry omitted from public records."[32] The deeply flawed and problematic set of legal assumptions about Indigenous and white identity, specifically as it relates to Indigenous female ancestry, encapsulates the continued and often uneasy relationship between feminist and Indigenous methodologies and discourses. Underscoring the challenge in their influential special edition of the *Wicazo Sa Review,* "Native Feminisms: Legacies, Interventions, and Indigenous Sovereignties," Mishuana Goeman and Jennifer Nez Denetdale confront "strains of liberal-feminist thought that continue to contain racial hierarchies and imperial intent." Alternatively, their approach is to secure an enabling Native feminist methodology that allows for "multiple definitions and layers of what it means to do Native feminist analysis."[33] Other scholars, reiterating the complexity of defining Native feminism, address "mainstream, or 'whitestream' feminism," and challenge the "multiple ways that the condition of being white, and enjoying the often nationalist privileges of that whiteness, is made to seem neutral and inviting or inclusive of racial, sexual, and other minorities."[34] From this growing body of work emerged the necessary acknowledgment that strains of liberal-feminist discourse that fail to recognize the limits of western ontological and epistemological assumptions will only restate the asymmetrical power dynamics of settler colonialism.

Joanne Barker and Aileen Moreton-Robinson offer rich and comprehensively theorized assessments of Indigenous feminisms, each noting that Indigenous feminist scholarship begins with the dismantling of western histories and logic. By way of setting the scene, Barker notes with searing clarity: "Indigenous feminisms are predicated on two assumptions. One is that Indigenous life matters. The other is that feminism cannot mean the same thing as it has in those modes of analysis and organizing that have failed—even unwittingly—to undo the empire's logic."[35] And Moreton-Robinson, in positioning the debate in an issue of *Australian Feminist Studies,* notes that her concern, with respect to "Gender and Indigeneity . . . is with ontological (ways of being) and epistemological (ways of knowing) matters that differentiate Indigenous gender from White Western feminism's conceptualisations."[36] Both Barker and Moreton-Robinson acknowledge the need to disentangle Indigenous feminist discourse from its white counterpart, and both acknowledge that this is not a straightforward task. In relation to the United States, Barker assesses the critical heritage of Indigenous feminisms with a summary overview of responses to early Indigenous feminist writers, like Paula Gunn Allen, who were, at times, challenged as "many Indigenous scholars (and) activists pushed back, particularly against the universalism and civil rights of feminists politics," while insisting on "a fundamental divide between Indigenous sovereignty and self-determination and the mainstream women's or feminist movement's concerns for civil rights."[37] Within these contexts, a cautionary note is struck, and the challenges of defining an Indigenous methodology become clear, especially when Barker describes the experience of Indigenous women's rights campaigners who "were criticized for inviting alliances with feminists" and accused of "being complicit with a long history of colonization and racism that imposed, often violently, non-Indian principles and institutions on Indigenous people."[38] In this scenario, feminism sits in conflict with Indigeneity. A growing and burgeoning body of work, from Barker, Moreton-Robinson, Goeman, and many others, consciously works through these conflicts and confrontations, and, as Barker summarizes: "grapples with the demands of asserting a sovereign, self-determining, Indigenous subject without reifying racialized essentialisms and authenticities."[39]

The hope for this collection is that it sits in productive conversation with these theoretical and intellectual challenges. We do not presume to set a theorized agenda around the complex relationship between gender and Indigeneity. Some of our contributors are Indigenous women (Azocar, Pratt, Sense, Wood); most are not. The purpose of the collection is to enable generative discussions, from multiple disciplinary perspectives, modes of engagement, and subject positions, to widen the possibilities for understanding and interpretation in a non-totalizing and expansive way.

Overview of Contributions

The collection is separated into four sections, conceptualizing different aspects of research, recovery, image-making, and expression. The first section, with contributions from Karen Ordahl Kupperman, Helen C. Rountree, and Karenne Wood, offers new insights into the early American and colonial archive, and this is followed by a reassessment of methodological assessments of gender and Indigeneity in section 2. Section 3 sees a return to the seventeenth century with historical analysis of the political, mercantile, and religious contexts of marriage, specifically Pocahontas's "English" marriage to John Rolfe. In the final section, visual and sensory culture, including fashion and contemporary art, demonstrate the evolving nature of image-making practices about and by Indigenous artists.

More broadly, in the essays by Kupperman, Rountree, and Camilla Townsend, we see how historians with long experiences of working with colonial and Indigenous sources use their expertise to piece together the evidence. They show how the English authors, despite their biased viewpoints, documented more information than they could have understood at the time about the inhabitants of Tsenacomaco. Kupperman traces the untold life stories of the English and Native American boys who, like Pocahontas, were co-opted to serve as mediators and who learned to survive within both cultures. Rountree expertly pulls together what the colonial archive provides on Pocahontas's life in Virginia and London. The limitations of the colonial archive are clearly drawn, and contextual information about Indigenous diplomacy and decision-making offer illuminating re-readings of key events and their implications. Townsend shows how the names of Powhatan's wives can be unlocked to reveal how kinship worked in Pocahontas's Indigenous community, making it possible to envisage the similarities and differences Pocahontas perceived between the rival cultures. E. M. Rose's focus is London, but her approach also involves drawing lateral connections through the documentary record in order to build a new and composite picture. Rose reinterprets the significance of Pocahontas's visit to London through a mesh of contingent details, including rumors that the king was about to call a new Parliament, a map of the London houses where Native Americans lived in 1617, the troubles of the Virginia Company, and even the state of health of the governor's wife.

The ways in which the colonial archive and the visual archive of Pocahontas narratives enable an inflected debate about Anglo-American religious and political identities are addressed by James Adams, and his assessment of Alexander Whitaker's part in Pocahontas's religious conversion, and Graziella Crezegut, with her account of the artwork in the US State Capitol that secured an image of Pocahontas as a "mother" of the nation. In the eighteenth-century accounts, such as that included in Robert Beverley's *History and Present State of Virginia* (1705), Pocahontas's religious conversion to Christianity and marriage with John Rolfe and the line of descendants it produced through their son Thomas was given central place, and the lack of subsequent intermarriage even nostalgically lamented as the inverse of the bloodshed that ensued. An inherited connection with Pocahontas continued to be a source of pride among Virginia's leading families, even though interracial marriage was banned in the late 1600s. Yet, while views hardened into the taboo of "miscegenation," pride in the region's connection with Pocahontas contributed to Virginians' sense of their American identity. Despite her having quite a different claim to Americanness, Pocahontas was co-opted into the contest for American primacy between the South's Jamestown (founded in 1607) and the North's Puritan settlements of Plymouth (1620) and Boston (1630). Although campaigns of cultural eradication against Native American groups were more or less official federal policy in the nineteenth century, Pocahontas was held up as a proto-national heroine because she had chosen the settlers over her own people. When John Gadsby Chapman depicted her in a mural in the Capitol Building (in 1840), his choice of her baptism was therefore key. It showed her submissively assimilating and thereby symbolically representing the "choice" that many in the United States wished to impose on Indigenous inhabitants.

The white European dress worn by Gadsby's Pocahontas is a sign of her acceptance of Anglo-American manners, beliefs, and sovereignty. In the twentieth and twenty-first centuries, however, the fashion and advertising industries have capitalized on a reverse trend: the cultural appropriation of Native American dress. In an essay that twines together two voices, Cristina Azocar and Ivana Markova examine the allure of the fringe in US fashion and contrast this "Pocahontas chic" with the pre-Contact history of textiles and Indigenous women's clothing. Markova offers restorative historical knowledge and shows how Indigenous textile practices anticipated current research into sustainable fibers, while Azocar draws on her own experience and research to underline the connection between popular fashion advertising and the continuing marginalization and mistreatment of Indigenous women.

By way of exploring the limits of the written and visual archival record, and, in part, the limits of our own expectations as researchers in the humanities, contributions from Lucinda Rasmussen, Karenne Wood, and Stephanie Pratt help reconfigure the debate in relation to Pocahontas, historically and mythically, but methodologically too. Rasmussen's essay focuses on Pocahontas scholarship, reflecting on issues of agency and control. Pocahontas was certainly not silent or passive much of her life—we just don't know precisely what she said and did because, like most people's lives, it went unrecorded. Filling in agency that was entirely obscured and overwritten by the discourses of English patriarchal colonialism is a problematic task. As Rasmussen explains, Paula Gunn Allen recovered Pocahontas's agency by stepping beyond the bounds of documentary evidence and drawing deeply on Native forms of knowledge, including patterns of behavior and shared customs, in order to offer a plausible reconstruction. Allen's portrayal of Pocahontas as a dynamic medicine woman, spiritual leader, and spy restored her agency but was judged to fall short of standards of credibility based on the customary western emphasis on written evidence. This apparently no-win situation, as Rasmussen points out, is important to analyze because it illustrates how the legacy of colonialism functions within mainstream US culture today and how we, in the academy, are implicated in it. Paula Gunn Allen, in addition to the short and ironic monologue poem ("Pocahontas to John Rolfe"), contributed a major biography of Pocahontas, portraying her as a mediator and medicine woman. Yet, as Rasmussen explains later in this volume, Allen's work received a cool academic reception that evidenced the continuing difficulty of bridging the gulf between Native and non-Native cultural perspectives.

The collection closes with a focus on visual art and creative practice: two interviews, one with a leading scholar in the field of Indigenous portraiture, Stephanie Pratt, and another with contemporary artist Sarah Sense, expand the conversation, bringing to the fore the vitality of the contemporary Indigenous art scene as it confronts the legacies of settler colonialism.

Where this collection has accepted the limits of the traditional archive, it has challenged its received wisdom and opened up debates about intellectual modes of inquiry, methods, and practices that unsettle the prevailing dominance of Eurocentric worldviews and expectations. With a focus on just one, practically unknowable woman, whose "real" name is barely known, this collection re-opens a seemingly familiar historiography and, from multiple perspectives and methodologies, endeavors to relocate this woman's presence in the colonial archive in a bid to foreground urgent contemporary debates about the implications of the settler-colonial past and present. This collection begins with a recent poem by Wood and ends with an interview with Sense on contemporary Indigenous visual culture, highlighting the revisions, re-imaginings, and redress made possible through agency and creative means. These two contributions from Wood and Sense frame the collection and hopefully indicate the wider contemporary, creative, and scholarly space within which traditional archival scholarship operates.

Notes

1. Karenne Wood, "Prisoners of History: Pocahontas, Mary Jemison, and the Poetics of an American Myth," reprinted in this volume from *Studies in American Indian Literatures* 28, vol.1 (2016): 73.
2. Jean M. O'Brien, "Tracing Settler Colonialism's Eliminatory Logic in *Traces of History*," *American Quarterly* 69, no. 2 (2017): 249–55.
3. Wood, "Prisoners," 73.
4. Helen C. Rountree, "Pocahontas: The Hostage Who Became Famous," in *Sifters: Native American Women's Lives,* ed. Theda Perdue (New York: Oxford University Press, 2001), 22, 25; cf. Linwood "Little Bear" Custalow and Angela L. Daniel "Silver Star," *The True Story of Pocahontas: The Other Side of History* (Golden, CO: Fulcrum, 2007), 62, 85. According to Mattaponi oral history, Pocahontas's mother was Mattaponi. Tribal historians and scholars agree that her father, leader of the Powhatan confederacy at the time the English arrived, was Pamunkey.
5. Alden T. Vaughan, *Transatlantic Encounters: American Indians in Britain, 1500–1776* (Cambridge: Cambridge University Press, 2006), 81, 287, n. 11–12. For close comparison of Smith's accounts as they "grow" the myth, see Neil Rennie, *Pocahontas, Little Wanton: Myth, Life and Afterlife* (London: Quaritch, 2007), 5–30.
6. Karen Ordahl Kupperman, *The Jamestown Project* (Cambridge: The Belknap Press of Harvard University Press, 2007), 228; Philip Barbour, *The Three Worlds of Captain John Smith* (Boston: Houghton Mifflin, 1964), 167.
7. Rountree, "Pocahontas: The Hostage Who Became Famous," 18; Camilla Townsend, *Pocahontas and the Powhatan Dilemma* (New York: Hill and Wang, 2004), 52–59.

8. Rennie, *Pocahontas*, 155.

9. John Smith, *True Travels* (1630), in *Complete Works of Captain John Smith*, ed. Philip Barbour 3:145; Philip Young, "The Mother of Us All: Pocahontas Reconsidered," *The Kenyon Review* 24 (1962): 409–12; Rennie, *Pocahontas*, 41–43.

10. Robert Tilton, *Pocahontas: The Evolution of an American Narrative* (Cambridge: Cambridge University Press, 1994), 178.

11. Young, "The Mother of Us All," 13.

12. *Amonute* and *Pochahuntas* are in William Strachey, *The Historie of Travell into Virginia Britania* (1612), ed. Louis B. Wright and Virginia Freund (London: Hakluyt Society, 1953), 113. *Matoaka* and *Matoaks* are on the engraving by Simon van de Passe and found in other sources (Rennie, *Pocahontas*, 72). According to Rountree, Amonute was a public name, Matoaka "a private, very personal name" (Rountree, "Pocahontas: The Hostage Who Became Famous," 15–16).

13. For estimates of Pocahontas's age, see Townsend, *Pocahontas*, 180n4. Strachey put her at eleven or twelve in 1609. Her engraved portrait inscribes her as twenty-one in 1616.

14. Smith, *True Relation*, in Barbour, *Complete Works*, 1:93, 95. Strachey passed on the story of her cartwheeling in the fort, *Historie*, 72.

15. Strachey, *Historie*, 62; Custalow and Daniel, *The True Story of Pocahontas*, 51.

16. Tilton, *Pocahontas*, 3.

17. Rountree, "Pocahontas: The Hostage Who Became Famous," 27.

18. Monika Siebert, "Historical Realism and Imperialist Nostalgia in Terrence Malick's *The New World*," *The Mississippi Quarterly* 65, no. 1 (2012): 139–55.

19. Mishuana Goeman, *Settler Aesthetics: Visualizing the Spectacle of Originary Moments in the New World* (Lincoln: University of Nebraska Press, 2023).

20. Rayna Green, "The Pocahontas Perplex: The Image of Indian Women in American Culture," *Massachusetts Review* 16, no. 4 (1975): 698–714.

21. S. Elizabeth Bird, "The Burden of History: Representations of American Indian Women in Popular Media" in *Women in Popular Culture: Representation and Meaning*, ed. Marian Meyers (Cresskill, NJ: Hampton Press, 2008), 185–207.

22. Missing Matoaka: The True Story of Pocahontas, accessed May 7, 2024, https://www.missingmatoaka.ca/.

23. Rebecca Belmore, "Vigil," accessed November 3, 2023, https://www.rebecca belmore.com/video/Vigil.html.

24. Cannupa Hanska Luger, accessed November 3, 2023, https://www.cannupa hanska.com/every-one.

25. Gregory D. Smithers, "The Enduring Legacy of the Pocahontas Myth," *The Atlantic*, March 21, 2017, https://www.theatlantic.com/entertainment/archive/2017/03/the-enduring-legacy-of-the-pocahontas-myth/520260/.

26. Wood, "Prisoners," 73.

27. Karen Robertson, "Pocahontas at the Masque," *Signs* 21 (1996): 551–83.

28. Tilton, *Pocahontas*, 186.

29. Monique Mojica, *Princess Pocahontas and the Blue Spots* (Toronto: Women's Press, 1991), 29, 30, 35.

30. Mojica, 19. See also 31.

31. The term "middle ground" found its way into historiographical discourse following Richard White, *The Middle Ground: Indians, Empires, and Republics in the Great Lakes Region, 1650–1815* (Cambridge: Cambridge University Press, 1991). Clara Sue Kidwell and Alan Velie, *Native American Studies* (Edinburgh: Edinburgh University Press, 2005), 42–43.

32. Shelbi Nahwilet Meissner and Kyle Whyte, "Theorizing Indigeneity, Gender, and Settler Colonialism," in *The Routledge Companion to Philosophy of Race*, ed. Paul C. Taylor, Linda Martin Alcoff, and Luvell Anderson (New York and London: Routledge, 2018), 152. Meissner and Whyte cite E. Tuck and K. W. Yang, "Decolonization Is Not a Metaphor," *Decolonisation: Indigeneity, Education and Society* 1, no. 1 (2012): 13. The consequences of Virginia's Racial Integrity Act (1924) are also noted by Karenne Wood, "Prisoners of History" (included in this volume) as well as Helen Rountree, *Pocahontas's People: The Powhatan Indians of Virginia through Four Centuries* (Norman: Oklahoma University Press, 1990), 221.

33. Goeman and Denetdale go on to argue that: "While acknowledging these strains of feminism that work at odds with Indigenous sovereignties and understanding the debates among Native women about the usefulness of the term and its application to our intellectual labors, and applications to our Native nations and communities, we affirm the usefulness of Native feminism's analysis and, indeed, declare that Native feminist analysis is crucial if we are determined to decolonize as Native peoples." Mishuana R. Goeman and Jennifer Nez Denetdale, "Guest Editors' Introduction: Native Feminisms: Legacies, Interventions, and Indigenous Sovereignties," *Wicazo Sa Review* 24, no. 2 (Fall 2009): 10.

34. Maile Arvin, Eve Tuck, and Angie Morrill, "Decolonizing Feminism: Challenging Connections between Settler Colonialism and Heteropatriarchy," *Feminist Formations* 25, no. 1 (2013): 10. For more comprehensive accounts of the Indigenous feminist research and methods, see Linda Tuhiwai Smith, *Decolonizing Methodologies: Research and Indigenous Peoples* (London and New

York: University of Otago Press, 1999); Emma Lee and Jennifer Evans, eds. *Indigenous Women's Voices: 20 Years on from Linda Tuhiwai Smith's "Decolonizing Methodologies"* (London: Zed Books, 2021).

35. Joanne Barker, "Indigenous Feminisms," in *The Oxford Handbook of Indigenous Peoples Politics,* ed. Jose Antonio Lucero, Dale Turner, and Donna Lee VanCott. Oxford Handbooks Online (Oxford: Oxford University Press, 2015): 1, https://doi.org/10.1093/oxfordhb/9780195386653.013.007.

36. Aileen Moreton-Robinson, "Introduction: Gender and Indigeneity," *Australian Feminist Studies* 35, no. 106 (2020): 315.

37. Joanne Barker, ed., introduction to *Critically Sovereign: Indigenous Gender, Sexuality, and Feminist Studies* (Durham: Duke University Press, 2017), 20.

38. Barker, introduction to *Critically Sovereign,* 20.

39. Barker, "Indigenous Feminisms," 1.

PART I

COLONIAL ARCHIVES AND COLONIAL ENTANGLEMENTS

KNOWLEDGE GAINED
AND KNOWLEDGE WITHHELD
IN EARLY VIRGINIA

KAREN ORDAHL KUPPERMAN

When the first Jamestown-bound ships entered the Powhatan flu, later called the James River, they were following lore gained from earlier expeditions. That knowledge stemmed largely from partnerships with Native people.[1] The first Roanoke colony (1585–1586) on an island within the Carolina Outer Banks, had sent an expedition to explore Chesapeake Bay, looking for a site that could host a permanent settlement. Manteo, a young coastal Carolina Algonquian man, accompanied the English and paved the way for them as they explored.

English colonization relied on Native knowledge to a great extent, but colonial leaders and backers rarely acknowledged how essential that knowledge was. Manteo, along with another young man named Wanchese, was taken from the Carolina Outer Banks by a reconnaissance expedition in 1584. The records say nothing about how or why they joined the English party. They may just have been taken by force, but it is more likely that they embarked on a knowledge-seeking expedition themselves. Countless European ships had traveled along North America's east coast and American leaders wanted more information about the land the ships came from. It made sense to send young men who could adapt to new conditions, learn, and report back.

The 1584 reconnaissance ships had been sent out by Sir Walter Ralegh to find a site that could become a base for privateering ships. The new Anglo-Spanish War meant that English captains could secure licenses for privateering and, if they were lucky, could make themselves and their nation wealthy while wounding the national enemy. Richard Hakluyt, who would go on to make his career collecting and publishing accounts of overseas voyages, wrote his *Discourse of Western Planting*, encouraging Ralegh's colonization scheme. He argued that the Spanish Empire was weak and, if it were confronted by determined English men, would fall to the ground. The American Natives "hated the proude and bluddy governement of the Spaniarde," and English attacks could easily bring the Spanish regime down.[2]

Manteo and Wanchese spent the winter and spring of 1584–1585 in Ralegh's home in Durham House on the Strand in London with a young scientist recently come down from Oxford named Thomas Harriot. Harriot learned their coastal Carolina Algonquian language and Manteo and Wanchese learned English during that winter, and all three traveled to Roanoke Island, the site selected for the new colony and base, with the hundred-plus men who went to establish it.[3]

Another member of the team was John White, a "gentleman limner."[4] Ralegh's plan was that the four would create a complete natural history of the land and its people. Most colonial promoters of this period wanted precious metals and a way through North America to the rich trades in the Pacific. Ralegh wanted these, but he was also a Renaissance scientist and he wanted to know as much as possible about the newly revealed lands and people, and he understood that only with Native guidance could that information be gained.

Europeans in America needed practical knowledge: What can you touch and eat? How do you navigate the rivers and whom will you meet as you travel? How can you tell a friendly from an unfriendly village?[5] Capt. Ralph Lane, who was governor of the new colony, affirmed in the most dramatic way the colonists' utter dependence on Native knowledge. When he feared that the Roanoke chief Wingina might refuse to plant corn for the English and move away from contact with them, he wrote, "which if he had done, there had bene no possibilitie in common reason (but by the immediate hand of God) that we could have bene preserved from starving out of hand. For at that time wee had no weares for fish, neither could our men skill of the making of them, neither had wee one grayne of corne for seede to put into the ground."[6]

We know this perception of the colonists' extreme dependence on Indigenous knowledge took hold in England, because it appeared in Shakespeare's *The Tempest* in 1611. When Caliban rebelled against the colonizer Prospero who had enslaved him, his declaration was, "No more dams I'll build for fish."[7]

As well as practical information necessary to survival, intellectuals like Ralegh also wanted more profound understanding. Europeans assumed that God had revealed these two previously unknown continents so that the Americans could be converted to Christianity and also so that all the knowledge that had been lost when people scattered over the earth could be recovered. They wanted to know as much as they could about Native life: how they lived and composed their families and government; their religion and knowledge of their own history; and their understanding of nature.

As Manteo, Wanchese, Harriot, and White set out on their scientific quest, we have a pretty good idea of Ralegh's directives to them because we have instructions for such a knowledge-gathering expedition a couple of years earlier. That voyage, which was to have been in 1582 or 1583, did not actually happen, but the planning documents survive. Thomas Bavin was to be the artist and cartographer on this expedition, and the instructions for him and his companions were extremely detailed.

Bavin was to carry "good store of parchments, Paper Ryall, Quills, and Inck, black powder to make yncke, and of all sorte of colours to drawe all thinges to life, gumme, pensyll, a stone to grinde Colours, mouth glue, black leade, 2 Payres of brazen Compasses. And other Instruments to draw cardes and plottes." With these he was "to drawe to life all strange birdes beastes fishes plantes hearbes Trees and fruictes and bring home of eache sorte as nere as you may. Also drawe the figures and shapes of men and women in their apparell as also of their manner of wepons in every place as you shall finde them differing." Servants accompanying Bavin were to carry various forms of compasses, and "Another to attend him alweis when he draweth with all his marckes written in parchment to oversee him that he mistakes not any of the sayd marckes in his plottes."[8] Although the instructions do not acknowledge this, Bavin, like Harriot and White, could have done nothing without Native guides to make the connections necessary for his research and show him the way to go.

The Manteo-Harriot-White collaboration culminated in *A Briefe and True Report of the New Found Land of Virginia* (Frankfort, 1590), which became a huge best seller across Europe. It was lavishly illustrated with engravings from White's paintings and was published in four languages, including Latin, so it sold everywhere in Europe. Nothing like it came from any other English colony, so it became *the* book on America's environment, products, and people.[9]

None of this would have been possible without Manteo. Wanchese did not stay with the English and, as far as they knew, they never saw him again. Presumably, with his insider's knowledge, he stayed near and monitored the Englishmen's activities. Manteo remained and worked with Harriot and White. He controlled what they saw and whom they met, and he made it possible for them to see coastal Carolina life up close and to understand American strategies and meanings. His presence meant that the two Englishmen saw mothers and their children, people cooking and eating, and, even more impressive, religious leaders and their ceremonies.

The *Briefe and True Report* had a second purpose: in addition to informing Europeans about America and its people, it was also intended to keep Roanoke present in the public mind. After the 1585–1586 group returned to England, Ralegh had sent a second colony comprising families in 1587 and then, because of complications at home, including preparations for the Spanish Armada in 1588, failed to send supplies for three years. By 1590 the families had left Roanoke Island and no English saw them again. So Harriot's 1590 publication with engravings from White's paintings was meant to convince potential investors that North America represented a good place to put their money. Rather than touting gold and silver, Harriot focused on practical products that would enhance English life. Doctors hoped America would furnish previously unknown medicines for diseases common in Europe, new and old. Harriot argued from his own experience that *Winauk*, Carolina sassafras, "a wood of most pleasant and sweete smel; and of most rare vertues in phisick for the cure of many diseases," was superior to the "*Guaiacum* or *Lignum vitae*" used in England. He referred readers to the work of the Spanish doctor Nicolas Monardes to learn about how to prepare it and "the manifold vertues thereof."

Among the many medicines Harriot recommended, *Uppówoc* or tobacco was, he wrote, a "sovereign remedy." Coastal Algonquians were said to use tobacco to sustain themselves on long voyages, but it was mainly used in worship: "they think their gods are marvelously delighted therewith." They would create a fire and put tobacco into it so the smoke would rise up to heaven. If caught in a storm they cast some on the waters and celebrated an "escape from danger" by dancing and throwing tobacco into the air.

Harriot, reasoning from the medical consensus of his day, believed that smoking tobacco would cure diseases prevalent in Europe by clearing the body of foul humors. Good health depended on proper balance between the four humors—blood, black bile, yellow bile, and phlegm—in the body. If the humors became corrupted or unbalanced, sickness ensued. Harriot reasoned that taking smoke into the body "purgeth superfluous fleame & other grosse humors, openeth all the pores & passages of the body . . . wherby their bodies are notably preserved in health & knoweth not many greevous diseases wherewithall wee in England are oftentimes afflicted."

Harriot wrote of how the coastal Carolina Algonquians dried the leaves, crushed them to a powder, and then took "the fume or smoke thereof by sucking it through pipes made of claie," and he said the colonists "during the time we were there used to suck it after their manner, as also since our return, & have found many rare and wonderful experiments of the virtues thereof." To detail all tobacco's healthful qualities, he wrote, would require a whole book in itself.

Harriot described the abundance of foods America offered, and how the Natives grew or gathered, prepared, and ate them. A one-pot dinner he described as a "gallimaufrye" cooked in a large clay pot over the fire. He also offered hopes of good "merchantable" commodities such as fabric made of "silke-grasse" and dyes, pearls in their oysters, wine from the abundant grapevines, furs and deerskins, and even copper or other metals in the interior.

Manteo controlled what the English observed and Harriot also knew that knowledge was a valuable commodity and should only be shared with the appropriate people. The *Briefe and True Report*, with its circulation across Europe, argued that some of the land's rich resources remained to be discovered, and Harriot said he had deliberately omitted description of some "commodities of great value" and had also limited his information on those he did describe "because others then welwillers might be therewithall acquainted, not to the good of the action."[10] His caution indicated another reason for the English to act quickly lest they be preempted by other Europeans.

Harriot withheld some information deliberately, but he and John White were also deprived of much of the knowledge they had gathered by the circumstances of the colonists' hasty departure in 1586, even though Manteo went back to England with them. Conflict with their Native neighbors had risen to the point that they needed to leave. When Sir Francis Drake arrived hoping to inaugurate Roanoke as a privateering base, Gov. Ralph Lane insisted he take everyone back to England. A storm was impending so the mariners needed to lighten the load; as Lane wrote, "the weather was so boysterous . . . that the most of all wee had, with all our Cardes, Bookes and writings, were by the Saylers cast over boord."[11]

Manteo, Harriot, and White were part of a much larger search for knowledge in lands previously unknown to Europeans. Sending young men away on ships was common practice in the early modern Atlantic, and both Europeans and American leaders did it. A decade after Manteo and Wanchese joined the English, Ralegh turned his attention to the more promising Guiana. For this

1595 voyage, which Ralegh led in person, Thomas Harriot drew up detailed instructions for navigation and taught the seamen how to use the sophisticated instruments they needed and the charts he had created for the voyage.[12] Elated by his belief in the voyage's success, Ralegh left "one Frauncis Sparrow . . . (who was desirous to tarry, and coulde describe a cuntrey with his pen) and a boy of mine called Hugh Goodwyn to learne the language" and Topiawari, "the lord of Aromaia, . . . freelie gave me his onelie sonne to take with me into England." Topiawari's son was named Cayowaroco, and Ralegh called him Gualtero. He lived in Ralegh's household with other Natives brought from Guiana and the Caribbean. Ralegh's lieutenant, Lawrence Keymis, went to Guiana again in 1596 and reported that Topiawari asked about Cayowaroco. That same summer Lady Ralegh wrote to Sir Robert Cecil that Topiawari was dead and his son returned.[13] Neither Sparrow (Sparrey) nor Goodwyn (Goodwin) was in Guiana when Ralegh finally returned in 1618, and their fates are unclear.

Virginia Company leaders had read the Roanoke reports as they planned for their colony twenty years later, although apparently they had not learned much. They did not bother to interview Thomas Harriot until 1609.[14] Ralegh, looking at the record of the 1585–1586 colony, had instituted the only colonial design that ever worked in an English American colony—families with land of their own—in his 1587 Roanoke venture. Possibly because of the 1587 colonists' disappearance or because of investors' fears, the Virginia Company reverted to the military model. The first group was just over a hundred men whose leaders were veterans of the religious wars in Europe. None of them were prepared to grow food. So poorly trained were the rank and file that the Virginia Company determined to withhold that information from the Powhatans. In their initial instructions, they ordered the colony's leaders not to allow any Natives see the men practicing with their muskets, "for if they See your Learners miss what they aim at they will think the Weapon not so terrible and thereby will be bould to Assaillt You."[15]

Capt. John Smith, the only person who was put on the colony's governing council because of what he knew rather than who he was, decided to go exploring up the James River rather than sit in the fort and complain as the others did. As his small party moved upriver, they were captured by Pamunkey; Smith's companions were killed and he was paraded around to several villages. At one village, the "King" decided to find out exactly how impressive English guns really were. He "intreated me to discharge my Pistoll, which they there presented me with a mark at six score to strike therwith." Smith was acutely aware of his pistol's inaccuracy, so "to spoil the practise I broke the cocke, wherat they were much discontented though a chaunce supposed."[16]

His captors took him to the great Powhatan's capital at Werowocomoco on the York River north of the James. Several days of religious ceremonies ensued until, finally, Smith was taken into the great Powhatan's presence.[17] Smith was forced to "two great stones" and, with his head pressed down on them, he saw men with clubs who, he thought, were about to "beate out his braines." All of a sudden, young Pocahontas came forward and "got his head in her armes, and laid her owne upon his to save him from death." Smith estimated that she was about ten years old, and the Powhatan's "dearest daughter." Two days later, Powhatan presented Smith with a list of items he wanted the captain to send him, including two "great gunnes," probably ship's cannons, and a grindstone. In return, Powhatan said that he would give Smith "the Country of Capahowosick, and forever esteeme him as his sonne Nantaquoud."[18] Because Powhatan now addressed him as a dependent relative, it is possible that Pocahontas had not, as Smith asserted, risked her life to save his, but rather acted as the principal in some kind of adoption ceremony.

Just as Powhatan told Smith that he now considered him his son, often these early relationships were framed in kinship terms. A thirteen-year-old English boy named Thomas Savage arrived on the first supply fleet in January, 1608, and the admiral, Capt. Christopher Newport, presented him to Powhatan, describing him as his son.[19] In return, Powhatan gave Newport a young man named Namontack, "his trusty servant and one of a shrewd, subtill capacity."[20] The English and the Powhatans both expected the boys to learn the language and secrets of the other side in the hope that their knowledge would be useful in the future. Powhatan later said that he "purposely sent" Namontack to "King James his land, to see him and his country, and to returne me the true report thereof."[21]

And shortly after Smith's captivity, Pocahontas began visiting the Jamestown fort; she always came accompanying her father's emissaries, and her presence indicated that the mission was peaceful. Colonist William Strachey wrote of how her visits lifted the spirits within the fort. He thought she was eleven or twelve when he saw her in 1610, and she taught the English boys to turn cartwheels—she would "gett the boyes forth with her into the markett place, and make them wheele, falling on their handes turning their heeles upwards, whom she would follow, and wheel so herself naked as she was all the

Fort over." Her nakedness was another indication of her youth. Strachey said that when girls reached the age of twelve, they put on a leather apron and were very ashamed to be seen naked.[22]

Language was crucial if the English were to establish working relationships and explore, so Smith included a list of Chesapeake Algonquian words and their English equivalents in one of his early books. The list ended with a sentence that showed how much Pocahontas's presence had come to mean. "*Kekaten pokahontas patiaquagh ningh tanks manotyens neer mowchick rawrenock audowgh.* Bid Pokahontas bring hither two little Baskets, and I wil give her white beads to make her a chaine."[23]

Pocahontas's role as an intermediary continued. Capt. Newport, on his second trip to Virginia, carried Namontack, and presents and a crown for Powhatan. He sent Smith to bring Namontack back to Werowocomoco and to invite Powhatan to come to Jamestown to be crowned as a vassal of King James. Powhatan refused to come to Jamestown, but Pocahontas put on a ceremony of welcome to invite the English visitors to a feast. At first the little group of English men were afraid because of the "hydeous noise and shreeking" they heard coming from the woods. Pocahontas came to Smith and told him to relax, and then thirty young Powhatan women came from the woods and put on their show, which Smith described as a "Virginia maske." Masques were part of the lavish ceremonial at the English court, and Pocahontas would experience a Twelfth Night masque, *The Vision of Delight*, when she was in London.[24]

Soon Smith made another visit to Werowocomoco, responding to an invitation that Powhatan had sent with Thomas Savage. The English visitors quickly found that the invitation had been a setup and Powhatan no longer welcomed them. Virginia was in the depths of the worst drought in the previous 770 years and the colonists' constant demands for food had become intolerable. In Smith's telling, Pocahontas came in the middle of the night to warn him and his companions to depart immediately, and she refused to take the presents Smith offered her because she said she did not dare to be seen with them.[25]

Colonial leaders were forced to widen their search for food, ultimately finding people on the Potomac who were willing to sell corn in exchange for English goods. But obtaining food was just the start; you needed to know what was safe to eat and how to prepare it. From the beginning, colonists made no secret of their complete dependence on Chesapeake Algonquians for their food. Archaeologists have found plentiful evidence that some Powhatan women lived in Jamestown and prepared food for the English.[26] We do not know what information they conveyed back to the Powhatans.

Chesapeake Algonquians depended on roots, especially in the terrible drought. One that grew in the swamps was *Tockawhoughe* (tuckahoe), which Smith said tasted like potatoes. He wrote that Powhatan women covered "a great many of them with oke leaves and ferne" and then put dirt over the top "in manner of a colepit." On the sides they built fires, which they kept going for 24 hours "before they dare eat it. Raw it is no better than poyson, and being roasted, except it be tender and the heat abated, or sliced and dried in the sun, mixed with sorrell and meale or such like, it will prickle and torment the throat extreamely, and yet in sommer they use this ordinarily for bread." Smith also described another root "which they call *Wighsacan:* as th'other feedeth the body, so this cureth their hurts and diseases. It is a small root which they bruise and apply to the wound." In his account, Smith included *Ocoughtanamnis,* a berry like capers. "These they dry in sommer. When they eat them they boile them neare halfe a day; for otherwise they differ not much from poyson." He described how they made acorns safe to eat. "The Acornes of one kind, whose barke is more white, then the other, is somewhat sweetish, which being boyled halfe a day in severall waters, at last afford a sweete oyle, which they keep in goards to annoint their heads and joints. The fruit they eate made in bread or otherwise." Long boiling in several changes of water extracted the tannic acid that makes acorns poisonous. Smith and William Strachey wrote extensively of other food sources and medicines and of how to recognize when they were ripe and how the Powhatans prepared and used them.[27]

No one had learned about the hallucinogenic properties of Jimsonweed (Jimson is a contraction of Jamestown) when a group of soldiers up the James River apparently consumed some with bad effects. Overnight they heard voices around their camp, saying "hup hup" and "Oho Oho" and saw a Native man leap over their fire. In the darkness and fearing they were under attack, they picked up their muskets and started hitting each other. "[S]udenly as men awaked out a dream they began to search for their supposed enemies, but findeing none remained ever after quiett."[28] Such wild hallucinations were not reported among the English again, so presumably someone taught them to recognize the plant.

Smith returned to England soon after being warned by Pocahontas, having been badly injured when his powder bag exploded in his lap as he traveled down the James. Back in England, he published an extremely detailed map of the Chesapeake Bay and the rivers that flow into the bay from the west with all the Native towns marked on the land. All the citations referred to Indigenous names for places and waterways, and clearly Smith could not have produced such a record without substantial Native guidance. In his *A Map of Virginia. With a Description of the Countrey, the Commodities, People, Government and Religion,* he gave detailed descriptions of the land and the rivers, including distances with the names. His barge carried English people with technical skills, and he did refer obliquely to his Native guides. He wrote that he put "little Crosses" on the published map to show the limits of his own exploration, and, he added, "the rest was had by relation of the Savages, and are set downe, according to their instructions." The engraved map borrowed images from John White's work to illustrate the description.[29]

Meanwhile, Powhatan moved farther away from the English. He shifted his capital from Werowocomoco to Orapax, at a location much harder for the English to access.[30] Thomas Savage, who did not control his own life, accompanied Powhatan to the new location, and Pocahontas quit visiting the English. Powhatan soon sent Thomas to Jamestown with a gift of venison accompanied by a party of Powhatan's men. When they had completed their mission, Thomas pleaded not to be sent back alone. Jamestown's leaders decided that Henry Spelman, a recently arrived fourteen-year-old boy, should go with him back to Orapax. As Henry wrote, "which I the more willingly did, by Reason that vitals were scarse with us, carriing with me sum copper and a hatchet with me which I had gotten. And Cumminge to the Great Powetan I presented to him such thinges as I had which he tooke, using me very kindly."[31] Although he had been there only a few weeks, Henry had already learned how relationships were conducted in America.

Life was uncomfortable for the boys at Orapax, and they did not know what to expect. Powhatan seemed to be manipulating them. As Henry reported, "After I had bin with him About 3 weekes he sent me backe to our English bidding me tell them, that if they would bring ther Ship, and sum copper, he would Fraught hir backe with corne." Actually, it was a trap and the Powhatans attacked the English who came in response to this invitation.[32]

Soon Iopassus, a Patawomeck chief from the Potomac, visited Orapax and invited the boys and some others to go north with him. It was a welcome invitation, as it offered the chance to escape the tensions at Orapax. Both

Thomas and Henry accepted, but after they had gone a short way, Thomas thought better of it and returned to Orapax. Powhatan then sent men to pursue the absconders and one man, a German carpenter named Samuel, was killed with an axe, but Henry did make it up to the Potomac; Capt. John Smith later said that Pocahontas had intervened to save Henry's life. As in the previous instance where she warned Smith, we cannot know whether this was true and, if so, if she acted on her own, or if Powhatan had sent her to save Henry, either because of his affection for him or because he thought Henry could be of use to him in the future.

Powhatan now cut off relationships with the soldiers in the fort at Jamestown. He sent Thomas back, and Pocahontas married a "private captain" named Kocoum.[33] However he had felt about the boys and Pocahontas's relationship with them, he wanted nothing more to do with the colony and its leaders. And William Strachey recorded a Powhatan song mocking the colonists, saying they could kill the English whenever they wanted to. One stanza was dedicated to Thomas: "*Mattanerew shashashewaw erowango pechecoma Thom. Newport inoshashaw neir in hoc nantion monocock Whe whe etc.*" Because Christopher Newport had introduced Thomas Savage as his son, the Powhatans called him Thomas Newport. Strachey's translation was that they could hurt Thomas Newport, "for all his Monnacock that is his bright Sword." The refrain "*whe, whe*" was the sound of the English crying as they died.[34]

Henry Spelman had accumulated a vast store of knowledge about Chesapeake Algonquian life when Capt. Samuel Argall, on the perpetual search for food in 1611, heard that "ther was an english boy named Harry" with Iopassus on the Potomac. Henry wrote that Argall gave Iopassus "some copper for me, ??? *which he receyved*. Thus was I sett free *at libertye* and brought into England."[35]

While he was in England, Henry Spelman wrote a detailed memoir of his life both with the Powhatans and the Patawomecks, and it contained a great deal of knowledge about the land and the people's life, customs, and beliefs. He, like Harriot, was one of the few reporters who made clear that his knowledge was entirely from Native sources. His youth and the friendship offered by Iopassus, who told Henry that he loved him, meant that he could describe family relationships, and marriage, child naming, curing rituals, and burial. He told of how Native people conducted meals and grew food. He especially emphasized the great respect shown the leader, even though he did not dress or live differently from his people. Henry also witnessed battles and described relationships among tribes. He ended with a short chapter on "The Pastimes."[36] Henry's memoir was left unfinished and unpublished.

William Strachey returned to London in 1611, and his much larger account, based on countless interviews including one with Henry about Patawomeck beliefs about the world's origins and the afterlife, also remained in manuscript.[37] The Virginia Company was in financial trouble in 1612 and its leaders were prepared to sacrifice the knowledge contained in both accounts in order to control the flow of information. But it was common for unpublished books and papers to circulate among interested people and we know Strachey's book did just that. We cannot know how many people with an interest in Virginia saw Henry Spelman's unfinished manuscript.[38] Sir Henry Spelman, probably because of the Virginia Company's campaign to control knowledge about what was going on in Virginia, was desperate to get his nephew back on a Virginia-bound ship. Finally, he arranged the rank of captain and a salary for young Henry to incentivize his return.[39]

Despite his life in Iopassus's household and his intimate knowledge of Chesapeake Algonquian life, even Henry's access to knowledge was controlled. His *Relation of Virginia* contained a description of an annual ceremony, which later reports proved to be inaccurate. He wrote,

> onc in the yeare, ther preests which are ther conjurers with ye ~~people~~ *men*, weomen, and children doe goe into the woods, wher ther preests makes a great cirkell of fier in ye which after many observanses in ther= conjurations they make offer of 2 or 3=children to be given to ther god if he will apeare unto them and shew his mind whome he ~~will have~~ *desier*. Uppon which offringe they heare a noyse out of ye Cirkell Nominatinge such as he will have, whome presently they take bindinge them hand and footte and cast them into *the circle of* the fier, for be it the Kinges sonne he must be given if onc named by ther god, After ye bodies ~~which are offered~~ are consumed in the fier and ther cerimonies performed the men depart merily, the weomen weaping.[40]

Colonists soon realized that Henry's and other reports of this ceremony were inaccurate, because, as Samuel Purchas wrote, it was conducted in a place "where they would not suffer our men to see." Native leaders "by false reports might delude our men, and say they were sacrificed when they were not." Colonists "found a woman mourning for yong Paspiha, sacrificed at the towne of

Rapahanna: but this Paspiha is now alive as Mr. Rolph hath now related to me." This ceremony actually marked the boys' transition to adulthood, and mothers wept because they had lost their close relationship with their children.[41]

Powhatans and allied people had been in and out of the fort from the beginning, but Native expertise returned to Jamestown in a special way in 1613. Capt. Samuel Argall, looking for food as always, entered the Potomac and learned that Pocahontas was visiting there. He forced Iopassus to collaborate in her capture and returned to Jamestown with her. The original plan to exchange her for English men being held by Powhatan was transformed when Gov. Sir Thomas Dale learned that she was being instructed in Christianity by Rev. Alexander Whitaker and that the highly religious puritan John Rolfe had fallen in love with her and wanted to marry her. Dale realized that she was much more valuable as the "first fruits" of Virginia, the highly prized first convert.[42]

Pocahontas's baptism did not lead to mass conversion of her people, but her marriage to John Rolfe brought Chesapeake Algonquian knowledge to the English in the most dramatic way: Pocahontas taught John Rolfe how to grow tobacco. By 1614 the colonists knew that locating a source of gold or some other precious metal was a long way off, as was their other principal goal—finding a way through the continent to the rich products of the East. Virginia was costing a fortune and not making any money, so everyone feared the Virginia Company would just give up on the effort, as Ralegh had abandoned Roanoke after 1587.

Colonists had tried to grow tobacco from the beginning, but all their efforts failed. Women took care of the agriculture in Chesapeake Algonquian society, and growing and curing tobacco was a long and painstaking effort, and very different from European agriculture. Now, with Pocahontas to instruct him, John Rolfe produced a crop that customers across the ocean would buy. Although many in England were concerned about building the colony on such an ephemeral product, tobacco became Virginia's gold. Tobacco smoking, or drinking as they called it, spread quickly in England, along with specialized shops where everyone could buy it as the price went from several pounds to a few pennies over the next few years.[43]

Pocahontas's son, Thomas, was born in 1615, and the Virginia Company decided to bring the Rolfes to England to show how much had been accomplished and to inspire pious investors. The party, comprising Pocahontas's friends and relatives, including her sister Mattachanna and the Powhatans' chief priest,

Uttamattomakin, arrived in late spring of 1616. Henry Spelman came along as interpreter. They lodged at the Belle Sauvage Inn on Ludgate Hill near St. Paul's Cathedral. Ludgate Hill becomes Fleet Street as it moves west and finally the Strand, so Pocahontas was lodged not far from where Manteo and Wanchese had had their London experience.

Londoners were eager to see Pocahontas, who was presented as an English gentlewoman, but intellectuals wanted access to Uttamattomakin's knowledge. Colonists had gathered practical knowledge about how to travel and grow and prepare food, but scholars wanted to understand the Americans' spiritual life and beliefs. John Rolfe told Samuel Purchas, who was Hakluyt's successor in collecting and publishing travel narratives, that the Powhatans used various techniques to keep colonists in the dark. He said they were "inconstant" in their descriptions of their religion, "one denying that which another affirmeth, and either not knowing, or not willing that others should know their divellish mysteries."[44]

English scholars did have sources of knowledge, however. Thomas Harriot, in the Roanoke colony, recorded what he had learned about the coastal Carolina Algonquians' creation story and their beliefs about life after death. He wrote that because of his language skills, he had had "special familiarity with some of their priestes." Harriot recounted that the Natives believed there are many gods, collectively called *Mantoac*. The "one onely chiefe and great God, which hath bene from all eternitie" first created lesser gods to help in shaping the creation. The sun, moon, and stars were such "petty gods." On earth the waters were made first, and then creatures "visible or invisible." Images of the gods were called *Kiwasa,* collectively *Kiwasowak*. The first human being was a woman "which by the working of one of the goddes, conceived and brought foorth children."

He learned about two men who had had near-death experiences and could therefore tell about what happened when people died. One had been in hell, *Popogusso,* and had been allowed to return to tell his people how to avoid that terrible place by living good lives. The other, a good man, had traveled along a highway bordered by fruit trees until he reached a town of "most brave and faire houses," where he encountered his father, who instructed him to return and describe this paradise so the people would change their ways and "enjoy the pleasures of that place" after death.[45]

Henry Spelman described what he had learned about the Patawomecks' creation story and their beliefs about the afterlife in his interview with William

Strachey when they were both back in England in 1611–1612. It all happened when Capt. Samuel Argall had discovered Henry with Iopassus on the Potomac. On Christmas eve, Iopassus and Henry came aboard Argall's ship where "one of our men was reading of a Bible, to which the Indian gave a very attent eare and looked with a very wish't eye upon him as if he desired to understand what he read." Argall "tooke the booke, and turned to the Picture of the Creation of the world, in the beginning of the book, and caused a Boy one Spilman, who had lived a whole yeare with this Indian-King and spake his language, to shew yt unto him, and to enterprett yt in his language which the boy did, and which the king seemed to like well of." Then Iopassus asked Argall if he would like to hear,

> the manner of their begynning, which was a pretty fabulous tale indeed: We have (said he) 5. godes in all our chief god appeares often unto us in the likewise of a mightie great Hare, the other 4. have no visible shape, but are (indeed) the 4. wyndes, which keepe the 4. Corners of the earth (and then with his hand he seemed to quarter out the scytuation of the world) our god who takes upon this shape of a Hare conceaved with himself how to people this great world, and with what kynd of Creatures, and yt is true (said he) that at length he divised and made divers men and women and made provision for them to be kept up yet for a while in a great bag, now there were certayne spirritts, which he described to be like great Giants, which came to the Hares dwelling place (being towards the rising of the Sun[)] and hadd perserveraunce of the men and women, which he had put into that great bag, and they would have had them to eate, but the godlike Hare reproved those Caniball Spirritts and drove them awaie. . . . the old man went on, and said, how that godlike hare made the water and the fish therein and the land and a greate deare, which should feed upon the land, at which assembled the other 4. gods envious hereat, from the east the west from the north and sowth and with hunting poles kild this deare drest him, and after they had feasted with him departed againe east west north and sowth, at which the other god in despight of this their mallice to him, tooke all the haires of the slayne deare and spredd them upon the earth with many powerfull wordes and charmes whereby every haire became a deare and then he opened the great bag, wherein the men and the women were, and placed them upon the earth, a man and a woman in one

Country and a man and a woman in another country, and so the world tooke his first begynning of mankynd.

Iopassus also told,

> that after they are dead here, they goe up to the toppe of a highe tree, and there they espie a faire plaine broad pathe waye, on both sydes whereof doth grow all manner of pleasant fruicts, as Mulberryes, Strawberryes, Plombes etc. In this pleasant path they run toward the rysing of the sun, where the godlike hares howse is, and in the midd waie they come to a howse, where a woman goddesse doth dwell, who hath alwaies her doores open for hospitality and hath at all tymes ready drest greene *Uskatahomen* and *Pokahichary* (which is greene Corne bruysed and boyld, and walnutts beatten smale, then washed from the Shells, with a quantety of water, which makes kynd of Milke and which they esteeme an extraordinary dainty dish) togither with all manner of pleasant fruicts in a readines to entertayne all such as do travell to the great hares howse, and when they are well refreshed, they run in this pleasant path to the rysing of the Sun, where they fynd their forefathers living in great pleasure in a goodly feild, where they doe nothing but daunce and sing, and feed on delicious fruicts with that great Hare, who is their great god, and when they have lived there, untill they be starke old men, they saie they dye there likewise by turnes and come into the world againe.[46]

Scholars had read Harriot's and Spelman's accounts, but now they had the real thing, the Powhatan priest who could speak directly of his own knowledge and answer questions. Over a series of evenings, Dr. Theodor Goulston hosted salons at his home in the parish of St. Martin's Ludgate, and they were recorded by Samuel Purchas, who was the rector of St. Martin's. The intellectuals gathered there watched and listened raptly as Uttamattomakin described his people's beliefs and enacted their ceremonies, with Henry Spelman interpreting. Purchas acknowledged at the outset that Uttamattomakin, like Namontack and others before him, had been "sent hither to observe and bring newes of our King and Country to his Nation." But the English had the opposite goal: they wanted to learn as much as they could of the Powhatans' spiritual beliefs.

Purchas wrote that "Of Him . . . I learned, that their *Okeeus* doth often appeare to them in His House or Temple." Uttamattomakin told how this was managed. "First foure of their priests or sacred persons (of whom he said he was one) goe into the House, and by certaine words of a strange language (which he repeated roundly in my hearing, but the Interpreter understood not a word, nor doe the Common-people) call or conjure this Okeeus, who appeareth to them out of the aire." Okeeus came into the house and walked up and down talking in a strange language with weird gestures. Okeeus then called eight more leading men into his presence and told the twelve men "what he would have done." After this discourse, he disappeared into the air again. Purchas wrote that the Powhatans believed that it was "hee which made Heaven and Earth, had taught them to plant so many kinds of Corne, was the author of their good; had prophesied to them before of our mens comming; knew all our Country." Although he spoke directly only to the chosen twelve, through signs Okeeus indicated his will to the commons, and directed them to game when they went hunting.

Uttamattomakin had informed Okeeus of his intention to go to England but said he would soon return. Okeeus replied that he would be gone longer than he anticipated, "neyther at his return must he goe into that house till Okeeus shall call him." Purchas also recorded that Uttamattomakin was "very zealous in his superstition, and will heare no persuasions to the truth."[47]

English scholars were also learning that the coastal Algonquians, like the English, embedded knowledge in their names and titles. The name Pocahontas does not appear on her engraved portrait done while she was in London. The legend around her picture says, "*Matoaka als Rebecca Filia Potentiss: Prince: Powhatani Imp: Virginia.*" Below the portrait is the translation, "Matoaka als Rebecka daughter to the Mighty Prince Powhatan Emperour of Attanoughkomouck als Virginia, converted and baptized in the Christian faith, and wife to the worth. Mr. Joh Rolff." When she was baptized, her people revealed that Pocahontas was nothing more than a nickname. Rev. Alexander Whitaker, the man who educated her in Christianity, wrote home of her conversion and identified her as Matoa. Later, when she was in England, Purchas learned that her real name was Matoaka, which the Powhatans had kept hidden "in a superstitious feare of hurte by the English if her name were knowne."[48]

Names were powerful and had meaning and knowledge embedded in them. William Strachey said that children were given many names "according to the severall humour of their parents." He reported that Pocahontas was a nickname meaning "Little-wanton," but that "she was rightly called Amonute." He also said that Powhatans were given names "yf so be yt be Agility, Strangth or any extraordinary Strayne of of witt, he perfourmes any remarkeable or valorous exployt in open act of Armes, or by Stratagem," and he compared this practice to "the auncyent warlick encouragement and order of the Romains to a well deserving and gallant young Spirritt."[49]

Name changes could also advertise intentions. Wingina, chief of the Roanokes, signalled his purpose to form a coalition to resist the English by changing his name to Pemisapan, and Opechancanough became Mangopeesomon just before the Powhatans attacked the Virginia plantations in 1622.[50]

Some actors who joined the English may have chosen new names that echoed the names of the deities who appeared to Native priests when they were called. By adopting a name that echoed the supernatural Mantoac, Manteo may have conveyed to the coastal Carolina Algonquians his intention to learn about and control the English. One particularly vivid example is Squanto or Tisquantum. Squanto, having been kidnapped from New England and sold in Spain, had made his way to London and was there at the same time as Pocahontas and her entourage.[51] He returned to New England in 1619 and joined the separatist puritans known as the Pilgrims after they arrived in 1620. He did not change his name even though the English knew, as Francis Higginson wrote, "their evill God whom they feare will doe them hurt, they call Squantum."[52] Manteo was baptized with the name Manteo; presumably colonial leaders, knowing of the power embedded in names like Squanto and Manteo, wanted that power to act in their interest. In the case of Pocahontas, it was more important that she, as Rebecca Rolfe, take on the role of a Christian gentlewoman and a harbinger of success to come.

Knowledge, sought by Americans and English, and sometimes granted and sometimes withheld, made colonization possible. One knowledge transfer had particularly fateful consequences. Pocahontas died as she and her party were embarking on their return journey, so she never understood the great catastrophe she had unwittingly helped to bring on her own people through her willingness to share knowledge of agricultural techniques with her husband. While she was in London, tobacco was still a controversial product. Although people such as Thomas Harriot praised tobacco as a bringer of health, others, including King James, considered smoking filthy and dangerous. Many scoffed at the idea that you could build an empire on a product that vanished in smoke.

Nonetheless, tobacco was catching on and, as the price dropped, more and more people were "drinking" it. Once tobacco became established as a crop among the English, the Virginia Company and its investors opened the possibility of profitable land ownership to Englishmen broadly. They arranged to ship many young boys and girls over as servants to work on that land and do the painstaking labor that tobacco required. They also sent respectable young women as wives for the planters, thus ensuring that English men would take up the offered land and establish homes for their families. As the Virginia Assembly, another invention of this period, wrote home, the only way to "tie and root the Planters' minds to Virginia" was through "the bonds of wives and children."[53]

With this huge influx of young colonists, most sent by investors, the plantations spread over the region, especially along the rivers, Virginia's highways. At the same time, slave traders sold the first Africans in Virginia, initiating the slavery system that would facilitate massive plantation growth. Powhatans were pushed inland and off the land they had cultivated for countless generations. As Helen Rountree writes, 1619 was "the year of a real explosion of incursions onto the [Native] people's farmland." The English incomers "took over all the of the prime corn-growing land, where the naturally fertile Pamunkey loams occur." Settlements on both sides of the rivers and creeks meant their use as natural highways by Pocahontas's people was constrained or ended for good.[54]

All this happened much too suddenly. Arrangements that had been in place for generations were overturned with no time to work out new partnerships and alternative ways to sustain life. In a very short time, the English went from a small number of people who could be controlled through their dependence on Native sources of food and their need for Native expertise to an overwhelming number who were imposing their own agricultural regimes on the land and their own social arrangements on the people. Pocahontas had had no inkling of this future as her short life ended in Gravesend.

Young Thomas Rolfe, left behind in England to be raised by his father's relatives after his mother died, returned in 1635 to a very different Virginia from the one he left as a baby. In this new reality, the English outnumbered the Powhatans and their allies. Although he made one effort to contact his mother's relations, he had no choice but to live as an English man on his father's lands.[55]

Notes

1. The English applied the name *Virginia* to the entire east coast.
2. Richard Hakluyt, *Discourse of Western Planting*, 1584, ed. David B. Quinn and Alison M. Quinn (London: Hakluyt Society, 1993), 40–44.

3. On the Roanoke colonies, see David Beers Quinn, *Set Fair for Roanoke: Voyages and Colonies, 1584–1606* (Chapel Hill: University of North Carolina Press, 1985), Karen Ordahl Kupperman, *Roanoke: The Abandoned Colony*, 2nd ed. (Totowa, NJ: Rowman and Littlefield Publishers, 2007), Michael Oberg, *The Head in Edward Nugent's Hand: Roanoke's Forgotten Indians* (Philadelphia: University of Pennsylvania Press, 2011).

4. Kim Sloan, "Knowing John White: The Courtier's 'Curious and Gentle Art of Limning,'" in *A New World: England's First View of America*, ed. Kim Sloan (Chapel Hill: University of North Carolina Press, 2007), and Katherine Coombs, "'A Kind of Gentle Painting': Limning in Sixteenth-Century England," in *European Visions, American Voices*, ed. Kim Sloan (London: British Museum, 2009).

5. Karen Reeds, "Don't Eat, Don't Touch: Roanoke Colonists, Natural Knowledge, and Dangerous Plants of North America," in Sloan, *European Visions, American Voices.*

6. Ralph Lane, *An Account of the Particularities of the Imployments of the English Men Left in Virginia*, 1586, in *The Roanoke Voyages, 1584–1590*, ed. David Beers Quinn (London: Hakluyt Society, 1955), 1:276.

7. William Shakespeare, *The Tempest*, act 2, scene 2, line 186.

8. "Instructions for a voyage of reconnaissance to North America in 1582 or 1583," *New American World: A Documentary History of North America to 1612*, ed. David B. Quinn, Alison M. Quinn, and Susan Hillier (New York: Macmillan, 1979), 3:239–245.

9. Peter Stallybrass, "Admiranda Narratio: A European Best Seller," in Thomas Harriot, *A Briefe and True Report of the New Found Land of Virginia*, 1590 Theodor de Bry Latin edition (Charlottesville: University of Virginia Press, 2007), 9–30; David B. Quinn, "Thomas Harriot and the New World," in *Explorers and Colonies: America, 1500–1625*, ed. David B. Quinn (London and Ronceverte: The Hambledon Press, 1990), 239–256.

10. Thomas Harriot, *A Briefe and True Report of the New Found Land of Virginia*, in Quinn, *Roanoke Voyages*, 1:325–46 (Winauk, 329; tobacco, 344–46; wine, 331; copper and pearl, 332–34; silke-grasse, 325–26; furs and skins, 330–31; The description of gallimaufrye is in Harriot's caption for John White's painting of a cooking pot over a fire, Harriot, 437–38).

11. Lane, *Account of the Particularities*, in Quinn, *Roanoke Voyages*, 1:293.

12. E. G. R. Taylor, "Hariot's Instructions for Ralegh's Voyage to Guiana, 1595," *The Journal of Navigation* 5 (1952): 345–350.

13. Walter Ralegh, *Sir Walter Ralegh's Discoverie of Guiana*, ed. Joyce Lorimer (London: Ashgate for the Hakluyt Society, 2006), 176–77. See Alden T.

Vaughan, "Sir Walter Ralegh's Indian Interpreters, 1584–1618," *William and Mary Quarterly*, 3rd ser., 59, no. 2 (April 2002): 341–76.

14. Richard Hakluyt, Dedication to Virginia Company, 1609, in Quinn, *Roanoke Voyages*, 1:388; See Quinn, "Thomas Harriot and the New World," in Quinn, *Explorers and Colonies*, 255.

15. Virginia Company, "Instructions Given by way of Advice," 1606, in *The Jamestown Voyages under the First Charter, 1606–1609*, ed. Philip L. Barbour (Cambridge: Cambridge University Press, 1969), 1:52.

16. John Smith, *A True Relation of Such Occurrences and Accidents of Noate as Hath Hapned in Virginia*, 1608, in *The Complete Works of Captain John Smith*, ed. Philip L. Barbour (Chapel Hill: University of North Carolina Press, 1986), 1:51.

17. Wahunsenacah was the name of the paramount chief, and his title was the Powhatan; his people were collectively known as Powhatans.

18. Smith, *True Relation*, 1:43–61; John Smith, *The Generall Historie of Virginia, New-England and the Summer Isles*, 1624, in Barbour, *Complete Works*, 2:146–51.

19. Karen Ordahl Kupperman, *Pocahontas and the English Boys: Caught between Cultures in Early Virginia* (New York: New York University Press, 2019), 25–33.

20. John Smith, *The Proceedings of the English Colony in Virginia*, 1612, in Barbour, *Complete Works*, 1:216.

21. Ralph Hamor, *A True Discourse of the Present Estate of Virginia* (1615; repr. Richmond: Virginia State Library, 1957), 38

22. William Strachey, *The Historie of Travell into Virginia Britania*, 1612, ed. Louis B. Wright and Virginia Freund (London: Hakluyt Society, 1953), 72.

23. John Smith, *A Map of Virginia. With a Description of the Countrey, the Commodities, People, Government and Religion*, 1612, in Barbour, *Complete Works*, 1:136–39.

24. Smith, *Generall Historie*, 2:182–84; Samuel Purchas, *Purchas His Pilgrimage*, 2nd ed. (London, 1614), 764–65.

25. Smith, *Generall Historie*, 2:195–199.

26. Jeffrey L. Shelter, "Rethinking Jamestown," *Smithsonian Magazine*, Jan. 2005.

27. For these observations of plants and foods, see John Smith, *The Description of Virginia*, 1612, in Barbour, *Complete Works*, 1:151–59; Strachey, *Historie of Travell*, 17–24. On digging and preparing tuckahoe, see Helen C. Rountree, "Powhatan Indian Women: The People Captain John Smith Barely Saw," *Ethnohistory* 45, no. 1 (Winter 1998): 1–29.

28. Alexander Whitaker to Mr. Crashawe, August 9, 1611, in *The Genesis of the United States*, ed. Alexander Brown (1890; rpt. Bowie MD: Heritage Books,

1994), 1:498. Ivor Noël Hume conjectures that the fantasy may have been induced by ingestion of jimsonweed, *The Virginia Adventure: Roanoke to James Towne—An Archaeological Odyssey* (New York: Knopf, 1994), 301–3.

29. Smith, *Map of Virginia*, 1:131–77, quote on p. 151; Helen C. Rountree, Wayne E. Clark, and Kent Mountford, *John Smith's Chesapeake Voyages, 1607–1609* (Charlottesville: University of Virginia Press, 2007). For the modern project to place markers at the site of the crosses led by Edward Wright Haile and Connie Lapallo, see Kelsey Everett, "Trail Cross Markers," Chesapeake Conservancy, https://chesapeakeconservancy.org/what-we-do/explore/find-your-chesapeake/about-the-trail/trail-cross-markers/.

30. Martin D. Gallivan, *The Powhatan Landscape: An Archaeological History of the Algonquian Chesapeake* (Gainesville: University Press of Florida, 2016).

31. Henry Spelman, *Relation of Virginia: A Boy's Memoir of Life with the Powhatans and Patawomecks,* transcribed and edited by Karen Ordahl Kupperman (New York: New York University Press, 2019), 17 (221v in original manuscript). Henry's own crossed-out words are retained.

32. Spelman, 52–55 (221v–222).

33. Strachey, *Historie of Travell,* 62.

34. Strachey, 85–86; Hamor, *True Discourse,* 37.

35. Spelman, *Relation of Virginia,* 24 (224v). Insertions above the line are in italics. Henry's own crossed-out words are retained.

36. Spelman, 32 (228 in ms), 78–80 (237 in ms).

37. Spelman, 56 (223 in ms); Strachey, *Historie of Travell,* 101–3.

38. Michelle O'Callaghan, *The English Wits: Literature and Sociability in Early Modern England* (Cambridge University Press, 2006; Cambridge Books Online, 2009), 17; Harold Love, *The Culture and Commerce of Texts: Scribal Publication of Seventeenth-Century England* (Amherst: University of Massachusetts Press, 1998).

39. Sir Henry did not keep his promise. See Henry Spelman, "To my honored and most esteemed uncle Sir Henry Spelman Kt: at his house in Cow Lane near Smiths Field in London," volume 74, folio 49, Tanner Manuscripts, Bodleian Library, Oxford University.

40. Spelman, *Relation of Virginia,* 24 (224v in ms). Insertions above the line are in italics. Henry's own crossed-out words are retained.

41. Samuel Purchas, *Purchas His Pilgrimage,* 3rd ed. (London, 1617), 952. 955.

42. Alexander Whitaker, *Good Newes from Virginia* (London, 1613), 25–26; John Rolfe, "The coppie of the Gentle-mans letters to sir Thomas Dale, that after maried Powhatans daughter, containing the reasons moving him thereunto," in Hamor, *True Discourse,* 61–68. The Virginia Company edited the letter for

publication. For the full text from the surviving manuscript, which is in the Bodleian Library, MS Ashmole 830, fols. 118–19, see Edward Wright Haile, ed., *Jamestown Narratives: Eyewitness Accounts of the Virginia Colony* (Champlain, VA: Roundhouse, 1998), 850–56.

43. Melissa N. Morris, "Tobacco and Indigenous Agricultural Knowledge" (paper presented at the Pocahontas and After Conference, London, Institute of Historical Research, March 17, 2016); Jean B. Russo and J. Elliott Russo, *Planting an Empire: The Early Chesapeake in British North America* (Baltimore: Johns Hopkins University Press, 2012), 55–58; James D. Rice, *Nature and History in the Potomac Country: From Hunter-Gatherers to the Age of Jefferson* (Baltimore: Johns Hopkins University Press, 2009), 110–13; T. H. Breen, *Tobacco Culture: The Mentality of the Great Tidewater Planters on the Eve of Revolution* (Princeton: Princeton University Press, 2001), chap. 2.

44. Purchas, *Purchas His Pilgrimage*, 3rd ed., 952.

45. Harriot's description of coastal Carolina Algonquian religion and his interaction with religious leaders is in his *Briefe and True Report*, in Quinn, *Roanoke Voyages*, 1:345, 372–78, and in his captions to the de Bry engravings, in Quinn, *Roanoke Voyages*, 1:425–27, 430–32, 442–43.

46. Strachey, *Historie of Travell*, 101–3.

47. Purchas, *Purchas His Pilgrimage*, 3rd ed., 952–55.

48. Purchas, *Purchas His Pilgrimage*, 3rd ed., 943; Alexander Whitaker, "To my verie deere and loving Cosen M. G. Minister of the B. F. in London," in Hamor, *True Discourse*, 59–60.

49. Strachey, *Historie of Travell*, 113–14.

50. Lane, *Account of the Particularities*, 1:265; Council in Virginia to the Virginia Company, January 1622, in *Records of the Virginia Company of London*, ed. Susan Myra Kingsbury (Washington, DC: Government Printing Office, 1906–1935), 3:584. On the significance of name changes see Rountree, Clark, and Mountford, *John Smith's Chesapeake Voyages*, 40.

51. On the coincidence of Pocahontas and Squanto being in London at the same time see Kupperman, *Pocahontas and the English Boys*, 126–28, and the essay by E. M. Rose in this volume.

52. Francis Higginson, *New-Englands Plantation* (London, 1630), sig. C4v.

53. Virginia Company, "A Coppie of the Subscription for Maydes," July 16, 1621, Ferrar Papers, Magdalene College, Cambridge, partially reprinted in David R. Ransome, "Wives for Virginia, 1621," *William and Mary Quarterly* 48, no. 1 (1991): 3–18, quote on 7. Company discussions of the need to send women colonists are in Kingsbury, *Virginia Company Records*, 1:256, 268–69, 391, 566; 2:394; 4:82, 265, 521.

54. Kupperman, *Pocahontas and the English Boys*, 109–10; Helen C. Rountree, *Pocahontas, Powhatan, Opechancanough: Three Indian Lives Changed by Jamestown* (Charlottesville: University of Virginia Press, 2005), 198–201.

55. Conway Robinson, "Notes from the Council and General Court Records, 1641–1659," *Virginia Magazine of History and Biography* 13 (1906): 394–95; Rountree, *Pocahontas, Powhatan, Opechancanough*, 186, 226.

POCAHONTAS IN BOTH
ENGLISH AND INDIAN EYES

HELEN C. ROUNTREE

Much of what we know—or more accurately, think we know—about Pocahontas is a series of myths that grew up around her name after her death in 1617. In the following pages, we will examine what the English actually thought of her at various stages of her life, where she stood in her own Native country among her own people, and what her father thought about her relations with the English.

In addressing these matters, we must move from the historical records left by the English themselves, through ethnographic reconstruction of the Virginia Algonquian speakers' culture to find Pocahontas's position in it, and on to educated speculation about Powhatan's thinking. That speculation is a necessity here. He and his people did not have writing: living in a smaller population with a less complex social life, they did not need writing. Technically, they were nonliterate, rather than illiterate. Several speeches were put into Powhatan's mouth by English writers, but they were not literal transcriptions of what he said. Instead they were a literary device, acceptable in the early seventeenth century, to bring the narrative to life for the readers. That is why we have to use indirect methods, based upon the writings of foreigners, to deduce what the Indian side of things may actually have been like.

The writings in question are of varying usefulness. John Smith set down most of what was written about Pocahontas; he wrote seven years after her death, by which time nearly all the English colonists who had ever met her in person were also dead and unable to lodge protests about inaccuracies. The rest of the records, aside from a few embellishments by still later writers, were set down by the early Jamestown colonists, including John Smith himself. These early records, in turn, vary in usefulness. None were written immediately after events occurred; there was always a time lag in which details could be forgotten and interpretations shifted and simplified. We must also consider the writers themselves because as reporters on Indian behavior and customs, most of them were less than adequate, being thoroughly English and much more interested in advancing the English enterprise than in learning about the local people who might hinder it. Altogether, trying to see the Indian world of 1607 is like peering through two pairs of dirty spectacles: Englishmen, whose culture four centuries ago differs significantly from ours today, writing about people they themselves only partially understood.

There were three colonists that we have to rely upon for glimpses into the Indian world, and each one was flawed. John Smith spent some time as a captive of Powhatan but otherwise saw Indian people only on military and diplomatic occasions. Obsessed with military matters and with rising from yeoman to gentleman status at home, even his earliest account (1608) is skewed, and his 1624 account is full of bravado and self-promotion. Henry Spelman, writing around 1613 for friends in London, was in his early teens when he lived first with Powhatan (fall of 1608) and then with the Patawomeck chief (1609–10). He admitted that though he learned the language, his youth made him uninterested in many things he saw while living among the Native people as a guest. William Strachey had diplomatic experience in Constantinople and a classical education that made him knowledgeable about the cultures of ancient Rome and Greece. He was interested in trying to fathom Pocahontas's people's world for its own sake. But he had only a year in Virginia, and that was during the First Anglo-Powhatan War (1610–1613), so he had only meetings, not living-in experience, with the Native people, and some of those meetings were battles. Yet he had a good interpreter available, and he interviewed a brother-in-law of Powhatan who was then living among the English, so his account of Indian customs has more understanding and depth than either Smith's or Spelman's.

The Native American person we are concerned with in this chapter happened to be female, which presents us with another obstacle in understanding her and her surroundings. All the English writers were men, and they came from a society that ranked men as far more important than women, who unless they were the daughters of kings and nobles, were irrelevant to things political, military, and diplomatic. And those things were the ones worth writing about. Thus our three best record-makers were handicapped: Smith was obsessed with military matters, and Spelman had not, in modern parlance, "discovered girls." Strachey comes out best: he was married, missing his wife back in England, and at least taking an interest in the Indian women's world.

Altogether, it is not entirely surprising that so few records about Pocahontas were made by the people who saw her face-to-face. Their sum total of documents is dismally small, and we can produce figures to demonstrate it. In 1998, Edward Haile made an inestimable contribution to Virginia colonial scholarship by publishing, in one fat volume, all of the accounts made by Jamestown colonists (not by people back in London) in 1607–1617. The passages about Pocahontas, all put together, make up *a little over one page* out of 831 pages of text, exclusive of introductions, bibliography, and the like. That fact should help to explain why the picture of Pocahontas that will emerge in this chapter will still not have as much detail as we would like, and it will be a picture that differs significantly from the cardboard cutout–like image that mythology has bequeathed to us.

The Jamestown colonists took little interest in Pocahontas in the first few years of the settlement. For one thing, she was only a child, not the woman the movies make her out to have been. For another thing, she was not a princess. She rarely behaved like a European noble during her childhood, and her father was not a king in the European sense, as the English found out as soon as they acquired some decent interpreters.

The first record we have of her, written in the spring of 1608, is John Smith's "True Relation." In it, he says she was "a child of ten years old, which for feature, countenance, and proportion, much exceeds any of the rest of his people, but for wit, and spirit, the only nonpareil of his country."[1] William Strachey, using reliable hearsay, adds to Smith's account by describing the attire of prepubescent girls among the Native people: they wore nothing or next to it. His example is "Pocahontas, a well featured but wanton [seventeenth-century meaning of mischievous and bawdy] young girl, Powhatan's daughter, sometimes resorting to our Fort [in 1608], of the age then of 11 or 12 years, [she would] get the boys forth with her into the marketplace and make them [turn cart]wheels, falling on their hands turning their heels upwards, whom she would follow, and wheel so herself, naked as she was, all the fort over, but being past once 12 years they [females] put on a kind of semicinctum leather apron."[2] Strachey's example of someone that age who donned such an apron was Pocahontas, who two years before his writing (in 1612) had reached menarche, changed her attire, and married (more on that below).[3] Thus in the first years of the Jamestown colony, the future celebrity usually dressed and acted like a little girl when she visited the English fort. Not only that, but she brought with her a group of rowdy youngsters ("her wild train") just as eager as she was to gawk at the funny-looking bearded aliens. The one and only time she visited the fort in a different role, which has led some modern writers to label her a "diplomat," I will address when we consider her position in her own society.

Because of her liveliness and wit, Pocahontas was her father's favorite daughter. She would be supplanted by a half sister only after her marrying and going to live among the English, out of reach.[5] But how much social prominence did that favorite position actually bestow upon her in the eyes of the English? In the colony's early years, not much, for they considered her father to be a "savage" and did not respect him very much. They feared him, but they did not defer to him unless forced to do so in a diplomatic meeting. We shall explore the matter further when we turn to Powhatan Indian society and Pocahontas's place in it. For now, we can state that nobody in Jamestown during Pocahontas's lifetime regarded her as a princess. Nobody even used the term for her until much later in American history. She seems to have been regarded only as a minor character for the colonists to deal with.

There is a good example of that attitude in writings from the colony's first year, namely the famous "rescue" incident from December 1607. At the very first meeting, Powhatan supposedly tried to have the captive John Smith's brains knocked out—before ever interviewing him about English intensions—and Pocahontas supposedly prevented it at the risk of her own life. Such a rescue would in reality have been unnecessary, given Powhatan's eagerness to question an Englishman in person. Smith's "True Relation," written the next June, says nothing about a rescue, instead giving details of the interview. Nor did any other writer at Jamestown mention a rescue in any of the letters sent back to England. Even the 1612 narrative written by Smith's friends with his encouragement omit Smith's visit, his alliance-making, and his release by Powhatan. But Smith's 1624 "Generall Historie," written not only after Pocahontas's death but also during the Second Anglo-Powhatan War (1622–1632), talks of her rescuing him, and not long after, of her doing other things as a power-wielding sympathizer with the English.[6] That late account is the only one, up to that time, that had painted her in such a light.

Another example of the rescue narrative could come from January 1608, when the Jamestown fort had burned down, taking the colonists' supplies with it. The Native people kept their new allies from starving, and the Pocahontas myth would have us believe that she, by herself, was the moving force behind that "rescue." However, the eyewitness records about her involvement are more a matter of observation than of interpretation, so we will delay considering them until we deal with the young lady's position in her Native society, for that is what those records tell us about more directly.

There are no other references to Pocahontas in the Jamestown accounts before early 1609. By then, even the pretense of an alliance had ended and Powhatan—and all his family, including his favorite daughter—had moved far up the Chickahominy River, where even the shallowest-draft English watercraft could not reach. Her visits to the English fort therefore came to an end. John Smith had to leave Virginia the next fall. Distrust and hostilities continued building up between the two peoples until real war began in mid-1610.[7]

Lacking records, there is one assumption we can safely make about the English attitude toward Pocahontas during that war: known to be her father's favorite, she would be an extremely valuable hostage, if the English could lay hands on her. Through the man whom William Strachey interviewed, English leaders knew that she had married and her place of residence might not be in her father's capital anymore. But where she did live, they knew not.

An English ship captain, Samuel Argall, had the luck to find her in April 1613, visiting in a village up on the Potomac River. The reason for her visit was not recorded, but she was the guest of the brother of the Patawomeck chief, the same man who had hosted Henry Spelman until his retrieval, by Argall, back in 1610. Argall pressured the village leader, and the capture was made. Pocahontas was taken back to Jamestown and kept there as a hostage for a year while negotiations went on with her father. We have several accounts of the capture,[8] but only the skimpiest ones of the captivity, which presumably took place in the Jamestown fort. We know only that the governor there, Sir Thomas Dale, saw that Pocahontas was evangelized, and once she converted to Christianity, he and other Englishmen were highly pleased.[9] She was now a "good Indian" and, they hoped, an example to her people.

Powhatan called a truce when the English abducted his daughter, but his stubbornness in negotiating an exchange—his daughter for all the English weapons his people had captured—meant that there was enough time not only for evangelizing Pocahontas successfully but also for an English gentleman, John Rolfe, to fall in love with her.[10] John Smith asserted later that she reciprocated Rolfe's feelings.[11] We have no details of the courtship and only the skimpiest mentions of their marriage in April 1614.[12] Further, nobody recorded where the couple lived after the wedding—several localities in Virginia claim that honor today—nor is there any indication of where or when their son Thomas was born.

That marriage resolved the stalemate between the two peoples, and a period of peace followed. Pocahontas, now baptized Rebecca, has since been credited with bringing about the peace, but that is the mythologizing done by nineteenth-century writers. Ralph Hamor's eyewitness description of the last negotiations before the peace shows plainly that Pocahontas played only a passive role in them. In addition, the "ancient planters" wrote in 1623 about the peace without mentioning her at all.[13] Her contemporaries (English and, probably, Indian) saw her only as a useful hostage at the time. Yet it is evident that Powhatan ceased stonewalling the negotiations once he knew that his favorite daughter wanted to marry an Englishman. Women in his world had a say about whom they married.[14] To that extent, then, Pocahontas's wishes brought about a peace.

In the spring of 1616, the Rolfes were taken to England and shown off at the expense of the Virginia Company of London. That private organization, rather than the English Crown, was supporting the Jamestown colonization effort, and the members hoped to do some major fund-raising that used the now-Christianized Rebecca as a promising figurehead. That did not mean that she led the enterprise, however, only that she played a part in it. John Smith later claimed not only that he had visited her,[15] which is quite possible, but also that he had written a letter introducing her to the queen of England and speaking of how Pocahontas had rescued him years earlier.[16] The original letter, if it ever existed, has never been found, and his writing it would have been unnecessary in any case: gentlemen members of the Virginia Company of London were already taking their guest into far more exalted circles than Smith could ever have managed to do. As a piece of self-promotion, however, his claims in that "letter" did the trick—he gained a reputation as a major figure in the history of the early colony that has lasted down to the present day.

We have other records written closer to the events that tell us about the Rolfes' stay in England. Rebecca's father sent with them an entourage of a dozen or so Indian people, of both sexes and various ages. One of them was a senior priest named Uttamatomakkin, who was under orders to escort her and make careful observations about the English in London.[17] Rebecca was taken to meet high-ranking people such as the Bishop of London.[18] Though she seems not to have been presented to the king, she and the priest ("her father councilor") were "graciously used" by him and were "well-placed at the Twelfth Night Masque" at the palace.[19] Seating at such events was based upon genealogical precedence, so some credence was obviously given to her father's position at home. Among the bored aristocracy, she was something of a nine days' wonder. It is doubtful, though, whether members of the nobility viewed her as a fellow aristocrat, as later Virginia writers would allege. One member of the gentry, John Chamberlain was not impressed with her at all. Upon seeing a copy of the portrait of her that Simon van de Passe had engraved shortly before, he wrote to a friend in February 1617 that she struck him as being neither pretty nor a "lady" in spite of the fine clothes provided by the Virginia Company (and not by her husband).[20]

Rebecca/Pocahontas made a sufficiently impressive appearance in English society that on 10 March, the Virginia Company made a very substantial grant of £100 to enable the Rolfes to set up a mission to Native people back in Virginia.[21] Rebecca was to hold the key position not only as an exemplary Indian convert but also as interpreter and house-mother. She was apparently willing to take on those roles, but her death a week and a half later put an end to the project.

The Rolfes boarded a ship named the *George*[22] and embarked upon their return to Virginia soon after the grant was made, but Rebecca took sick and was taken ashore to die at Gravesend. Her contemporaries did not mention the malady she died from, only that she had made a "good" Christian death, which in the early seventeenth century was of greater concern than medical observations. There is circumstantial evidence, however, that she died in a shipboard epidemic of bloody flux—a hemorrhagic form of dysentery, which in later retellings mutated into something milder—that was brought on by inadequate sanitation in crowded conditions. Her son Thomas was sick as well, and by the time the ship reached Plymouth he had to be taken ashore as well and left behind in someone else's care. His father wrote on June 8, 1617, that he had been afraid to proceed across the Atlantic with the child for "fear and hazard of his health, being not fully recovered of his sickness and lack of attendance [care-takers]—for they who looked to [after] him had need of nurses themselves."[23] That sounds like an epidemic which had gone on for some time among the travelers. The *George* having left, John Rolfe boarded another Virginia-bound vessel and both ships reached Virginia that summer, after which an epidemic recorded specifically as bloody flux broke out in the colony.[24]

On March 10, 1617, Rebecca Rolfe was buried in St. George's Church in Gravesend. Significantly, her grave was in the chancel of the church, not the churchyard outside.[25] Only high-status people were buried in such places, so that tells us how the last people to see her alive regarded her.

Pocahontas's conversion and visit to England, with considerable embellishment by John Smith and later writers, has established her in a prominent place in Virginia history, among both Europeans and Euro-Americans. But did that celebrity correspond in any way to how her own people in the Indian towns thought of her? Not much, in all probability.

Pocahontas was the daughter of a paramount chief, Powhatan. His domain covered most of the James and York River drainages east of the fall line[26] in Virginia; his sphere of influence was wider, reaching to the Eastern Shore and to the south bank of the Potomac River. His power, even in the center of his territory, was limited. He was a chief, not a king.[27] It was only on diplomatic and military occasions, when representing his people to foreigners, that he and his subordinate chiefs had absolute power, a fact that misled some of the English into using the term "king." Chiefs did not hold court, or "keep state," all day, every day. Their power was not backed by a standing army or their orders carried out by a bureaucracy. A chief's standard of living was higher than that of others, who had to pay him tribute. But the tribute was spent on diplomatic and military purposes, and chiefs needed somewhat larger houses and multiple wives for the elaborate hospitality required when important people came to call. On ordinary days, chiefs and their families did the same work as other folk. Henry Spelman and John Smith both tried to set the record straight: "The king is not known by any difference from other of the chief [i.e., better] sort in the country but only when he comes to any of their houses they . . . show much reverence to him,"[28] and "the King himself will make his own robes, shoes, bows arrows, pots [we doubt this], plant [crops], hunt, or do any things so well as the rest [of his people]."[29] Pocahontas would therefore have grown up learning to do ordinary women's work, such as digging-stick farming and collecting wild foods and materials for making household implements. Like her female relatives, she would have had jobs to do both in and out of the towns, and being accustomed to such frequent coming and going,[30] her captivity in the Jamestown fort must have been very hard to bear at first.

Even on important occasions, and even though she was known to be her father's favorite daughter,[31] she would not have been anywhere near the forefront. There were far too many people around her, all of them wanting the attention of the paramount chief. Aside from the comings and goings of councilors and priests, her father had many wives—a revolving-door policy on wives, actually—and her mother, about whom nothing whatsoever was recorded, was only one of a raft of women Powhatan had married and divorced during his life. It was a custom with political reasoning behind it. The wives came from various parts of his domain and, likely, adjacent regions whose leaders were friendly. A wife would be picked out of lineup, married, and kept with Powhatan, along with a dozen or so other wives at the time, until she had a child. She and the child would then be sent back home, and Powhatan would acquire a new wife. When the child reached a certain age, probably about eight years old, its mother would be divorced and remarried to someone else, and the child would be sent to live with Powhatan—and join a horde of half brothers and sisters.[32] In 1610, William Strachey learned that Powhatan had "then living" twenty sons and ten daughters.[33] Pocahontas's wit and liveliness had gotten her busy father's attention at times, but once she married and moved away, he made another daughter his favorite.[34] And being a preferred child was not the same, in that world, as being a princess-for-life. Everyone in the Indian towns knew that any prominence she enjoyed would evaporate when her father died because inheritance in Powhatan Indian chiefly families, if not the bulk of the people, was matrilineal.

Powhatan had inherited his position from his mother, not his father. None of his children could be his successors. Instead his successors were his siblings: his brothers in order of age, then any surviving sisters in order of age, and then the sons and daughters of his eldest sister (or the next eldest, if the eldest had had no children).[35] Pocahontas would therefore, if she lived long enough, become the niece of the paramount chief, then the first cousin of one, and eventually the first cousin once removed of one—and she hadn't possessed a great deal of power even while she was the paramount chief's daughter. Such an unglamorous future is indicated by the fact that when Pocahontas did marry within her own people, she did not make a politically advantageous match or even marry a prominent man who was socially equal to her half brothers. In 1610, she married Kocoum, whom Strachey described as a "private captain," or ordinary warrior.[36] History is silent about where the couple lived and whether they had any children before the marriage ended with her capture and remarriage.

We now return to the question of whether or not Pocahontas, aged ten or so, saved the English colony from starvation in January 1608. Somebody sent the food. But was it Pocahontas who did that? No, because she couldn't. For one thing, it wasn't her food—it was her father's food, gathered in the form of tribute from his people and intended for political and military uses. For another thing, aiding the English newcomers fitted both those uses, and in the Native American world, chiefs and their councilors made the decisions in those matters, not little girls. Pocahontas could and did wrangle permission for herself and her friends to go along, but that is the only part she played. The colonists' records are indicative: two 1608 accounts give us details from eyewitnesses. Powhatan sent gifts and messages once or twice a week, and half the food was for John Smith and half was for the ship's captain Christopher Newport. (An account from 1612 says that the other half was for others in the fort.) Powhatan also sent along people to teach weir-making (men's work, to get fish) and farming (women's work, though men knew how to do it) to the English newcomers.[37] Strachey added the previously mentioned part about Pocahontas turning cartwheels with the boys in the central plaza. It is only in Smith's 1624 "Generall Historie" that we see Pocahontas herself organizing supplies—in a drought year, no less[38]—and bringing food that she gave solely to Smith.[39] Smith twisted the facts to make himself look more important.

Later that spring, Pocahontas did make a visit to the fort in which she played a prominent role and behaved with great dignity. But she was not the one dickering with the English on that occasion. John Smith committed details of the event to paper a month or two later:

> Powhatan, understanding we detained certain [men of his], sent his daughter . . . ; this he sent by [with] his most trusty messenger, called Rawhunt, as much exceeding in deformity of person, but of a subtle wit and crafty understanding. He [Rawhunt] with a long circumstance[long-winded oratory] told me how well Powhatan loved and respected me, and in that I should not doubt [in] any way of his kindness, he had sent his child, which he most esteemed, to see me . . . [she] not taking notice at all of the Indians that had been [our] prisoners three days, till that

morning that [when] she saw their fathers and friends come quietly [peacefully], and in good terms to entreat their liberty.[40]

In other words, Pocahontas came as a figurehead, representing her father's good faith; she was not a negotiator—Rawhunt was. It was in later accounts that Smith inflated her importance further: Smith agreed to release the prisoners but first "gave them what correction he thought fit," held them "a day or two after, and then delivered them to Pocahontas, for whose sake only he fained [pretended] to save their lives, and gave them liberty."[41] Even in Smith's later version, she does not appear as a negotiator, still less as a diplomat. She did, nevertheless, appear as a potential hostage for the English, at least in her suspicious father's view.

In January 1609, myth has it that Pocahontas saved John Smith again. He and his people had broken the alliance made during his captivity a year before, and a face-to-face meeting with Powhatan had broken down in anger, followed by an attempted ambush of the English after the women and children in the town had fled (a bad sign). Worse, Smith and his men had been foiled in making their getaway from Powhatan's capital thanks to the low tide that made their pinnace, out in the river, unreachable.[42] Smith was no dummy; he had more than enough military savvy to know that he could expect another attack while waiting for the tide to come back in, so he put his men on guard. Once again, though, in the 1624 "Generall Historie" version, he has Pocahontas doing something unnecessary that saved him: she somehow remained with her father, rather than evacuating, and then she sneaked out to warn Smith of a planned attack. And Smith writes as if it was news to him. (He must have thought his readers were credulous fools; these contradictions all appear on the same page!)[43] Would Pocahontas really have stepped so far out of a role appropriate to a little girl, daughter of a chief or not, to deliver a warning to Smith? Probably not. Again, the position she was in did not have either diplomatic or military clout, and she was supposed to let adult males take care of such matters. She also did not have immunity from consequences. Warning Smith would have made a fool of her father, whom she was said to love, and would have drawn her father's wrath, which would rapidly have had fatal consequences once he found out. She would have been guilty of mutiny on a military occasion, and Powhatan Indian chiefs had life-and-death power over their people in military and diplomatic matters, if not in other areas of life.

As to what Powhatan thought about his daughter's later relations with the English, the evidence is scanty but indicative. We do have an eyewitness account of his opinion of her marriage to Rolfe, though being voiced during a diplomatic visit, it may only have been for show. Ralph Hamor visited Powhatan in the spring of 1615. "I resolved him [assured him] that . . . his daughter [was] so well content that she would not change her life to return and live with him, whereat he laughed heartily, and said he was very glad of it."[44] Powhatan's personal feelings of regret may have been assuaged by the ease with which she and John Rolfe could have come to see him, for it was peacetime. He, on the other hand, was not free to visit her. Hamor heard that tidbit directly during their conversation, for he had been sent to ask for the hand of one of Pocahontas's sisters on behalf of Sir Thomas Dale. "His answer hereunto was that he loved his daughter as dear as his own life, and though he had many children, he delighted in none so much as in her, whom if he should not often behold, he could not possibly live, which she living [coming to live, as Pocahontas had done] with us he knew he could not, having with himself resolved upon no means whatsoever to put himself into our hands or come amongst us; and therefore entreated me to urge that suit no further."[45] Above all, as an astute politician, Powhatan knew that Pocahontas's marriage to an Englishman was extremely useful to him and his people, for it helped to keep what was already becoming a difficult peace.[46]

His thoughts, public or private, on her conversion to Christianity were not recorded. He may have felt the same way that his priest Uttamatomakkin did. The Reverend Samuel Purchas talked with Uttamatomakkin at length during his London stay, apparently with Henry Spelman interpreting. When Purchas tried to convert him, the priest replied that he would "hear no persuasions to the truth [Christianity], bidding us teach the boys and girls which were brought over from thence, he being too old now to learn."[47] It would seem that Uttamatomakkin did not accept the idea of being obliged to worship one all-powerful God. Instead he remained rooted in a more tolerant polytheism that allowed people's reverence to be paid to whatever deities they needed to appease at a given time. To him, the English minister was pressing conversion to a different god (small "g"), the Christian one, which would simply involve shifting attention to a deity that meant little to this priest. In his—and possibly Powhatan's—view, it was Pocahontas's right to shift to Christianity if she wanted to.

Powhatan very likely viewed his daughter's junket to England as precisely that: another person going out, observing, and reporting back, as Namontack had done in 1608[48] and Uttamatomakkin would do in 1617. He also probably viewed her accompanying her husband over there as proper wifely behavior, so long as she went voluntarily, which she presumably did. As a girl, she seemed to always have had a lively curiosity; she may have kept it in adulthood, and her father continued to respect it.

Her death, and her son having to be left behind in England (where he would become a thorough Englishman) undoubtedly grieved him. Samuel Argall wrote to the Virginia Company a year later, on March 10, 1618, after the news had been carried to Powhatan, that the bereaved father "lamented his daughter's death, [and] was glad her son was alive."[49] The paramount chief had had other worries in the interim—there was a serious famine in his country in the summer of 1617[50]—and in his old age he also knew that young women died all the time of disease, if not in childbirth (a worldwide fact of life at the time). He had already had other terrible griefs. He had told John Smith back in 1608 that he had "seen the death of all [his] people thrice," which more likely referred to famines during droughts, for which there is dendrochronological evidence,[51] than to epidemics, for which there is no evidence before the bloody flux episode of 1617. Times of mass suffering like that had very likely hardened him.

As for Pocahontas's son, her father would have understood why the boy had been left in England and would have hoped to see him. It is sad to reflect that neither Powhatan nor the boy's father lived to see him again. Powhatan died in April 1618,[52] and John Rolfe died, apparently of natural causes rather than in the newly begun war, in 1622.

The mythology about Pocahontas as the savior of the English colonists, and as "the only good Indian" amid "savages," is mostly inaccurate. She was friendly and curious about the newcomers, but she seems to have remained very much a member of her own society, and a loyal daughter to her father. Her father, in turn, was a powerful chief and a fine politician, which kept him very busy. But toward Pocahontas, when time permitted him to pay attention to her doings, he behaved like a loving father, not a cold-hearted villain. It is time to cast off the cardboard cutout images that most of us have of both of them.

Notes

1. John Smith, "A True Relation" (1608), in *The Complete Works of Captain John Smith, 1580–1631,* ed. Philip L. Barbour (Chapel Hill: University of North Carolina Press, 1986), 1:93; Edward W. Haile, ed., *Jamestown Narratives: Eyewitness Accounts of the Virginia Colony; The First Decade, 1607–1617* (Champlain, VA: RoundHouse, 1998), 181.

2. William Strachey, *The Historie of Travell into Virginia Britania* (1612), ed. Louis B. Wright and Virginia Freund (Cambridge: The Hakluyt Society, 1953), series 2, 103:72; Haile, *Jamestown Narratives,* 630–31.

3. Strachey, *Historie of Travell,* 62; Haile, *Jamestown Narratives,* 619.

4. John Smith, "The Generall Historie of Virginia, New England, and the Summer Isles, 1624," in *The Complete Works of Captain John Smith,* 2:257; Haile, *Jamestown Narratives,* 962.

5. Ralph Hamor, *A True Discourse of the Present State of Virginia* (1615; repr. Richmond: Virginia State Library, 1957), 42; Haile, *Jamestown Narratives,* 834.

6. Smith, "True Relation," 53; Smith, "Generall Historie," 2:150–51; Haile, *Jamestown Narratives,* 160–61, 239.

7. Helen C. Rountree, *Pocahontas's People: The Powhatan Indians of Virginia through Four Centuries* (Norman: University of Oklahoma Press, 1990), chap. 2.

8. Samuel Argall, "A Letter of Sir Samuel Argall Touching His Voyage to Virginia, and Actions There: Written to Master Nicholas Hawes" (1613), in *Hakluytus Posthumus or Purchas His Pilgrimes,* ed. Samuel Purchas (Glasgow: James MacLehose and Sons, 1904–1906), 19:93–95; Haile, *Jamestown Narratives,* 753–55, 802–4; Hamor, *True Discourse,* 4–6; Smith, "Generall Historie," 2:243–44. The Smith account, of course, has her showing the most emotion, crying bitterly as the Indian party left her aboard the ship.

9. Alexander Whitaker, letter of 18 June 1614, in Hamor, *True Discourse,* 59–60; Haile, *Jamestown Narratives,* 848, 845; Dale letter, in Hamor, *A True Discourse,* 55–56.

10. John Rolfe, letter to Sir Thomas Dale, in Hamor, *True Discourse,* 61–68; Haile, *Jamestown Narratives,* 850–56.

11. Smith, "The Generall Historie," 2:245.

12. Samuel Argall, letter to Nicholas Hawes, in Purchas, *Hakluytus Posthumus,* 19:90–95; Haile, *Jamestown Narratives,* 753–56, 802–9, 843–45; Hamor, *True Discourse,* 4–10; Sir Thomas Dale, letter of 18 June 1614, in Hamor, *True Discourse,* 52–54.

13. Hamor, *True Discourse*, 9–10; Haile, *Jamestown Narratives*, 808, 903. Ancient Planters, letter, 1623, in *Journal of the House of Burgesses*, comp. H. R. McIlwaine (Richmond: Virginia State Library, 1915), 1:33.

14. Helen C. Rountree, *The Powhatan Indians of Virginia: Their Traditional Culture* (Norman: University of Oklahoma Press, 1989), chap. 5; Helen C. Rountree, "Powhatan Indian Women: The People Captain John Smith Barely Saw," *Ethnohistory* 45 (1998): 1–29.

15. Smith, "Generall Historie," 2:261; Haile, *Jamestown Narratives*, 263–64.

16. Smith, "Generall Historie," 2:258–60; Haile, *Jamestown Narratives*, 861–83.

17. For an account of the entourage, see Sir John Chamberlain, letter to Dudley Carleton, 3 June 1616, in *Letters of John Chamberlain*, ed. Norman E. McClure (Philadelphia: American Philosophical Society, 1939), 2:12; George Lord Carew, letter to Sir Thomas Roe, June 1616, in W. Noel Sainsbury, J. W. Fortescue, and Cecil Headham, comp., *Calendar of State Papers, Colonial Series* (Washington, DC: Library of Congress, 1860–1926), 1:18; Smith, "Generall Historie," 2:261; Haile, *Jamestown Narratives*, 885.

18. Samuel Purchas, comp. and ed., *Purchas His Pilgrimes* (London, 1617), 954; Purchas, *Hakluytus Posthumus*, 19:118; Haile, *Jamestown Narratives*, 883–84; McClure, *Letters of John Chamberlain*, 2:50.

19. John Chamberlain, letter, 18 Jan. 1617, in McClure, *Letters of John Chamberlain*, 2:50.

20. John Chamberlain, letter to Dudley Carleton, 22 Feb. 1617, in McClure, *Letters of John Chamberlain*, 2:56–57.

21. Farrar Papers (1992 ed.), microfilm reel 1, item 72; pub. in Haile, *Jamestown Narratives*, xviii.

22. Smith, "Generall Historie," 2:262

23. On accounts of her death, see McClure, *Letters of John Chamberlain*, 266; Purchas, *Hakluytus Posthumus*, 19:118; Haile, *Jamestown Narratives*, 884. On cause of sickness, see John Rolfe, letter to George Sandys, 8 June 1617, in *Records of the Virginia Company of London*, ed. Susan Myra Kingsbury (Washington, DC: Library of Congress, 1935), 4:372; Haile, *Jamestown Narratives*, 889; plus speculation by the author, based on Pocahontas's ship being the *George*, which is known to have arrived in Virginia carrying bloody flux, which became an epidemic there: Helen C. Rountree, *Pocahontas, Powhatan, Opechancanough: Three Indian Lives Changed by Jamestown* (Charlottesville: University of Virginia Press, 2005), 183–84.

24. McIlwaine, *Journal of the House of Burgesses*, 1:28; Haile, *Jamestown Narratives*, 905.

25. Burial register of St. George's Church, Gravesend, Kent.

26. "Fall line" is a term used by geologists and geographers in the region. It is an imaginary line drawn, northeast–southwest, between the places on the rivers where tidal waters end and rocky channels are the rule upriver. In later colonial times, those were the places where shipping ended and transportation upriver was by foot, horseback, or wagon. Numerous cities in the American Southeast grew up at such depot points; the ones in Virginia are Richmond (James River), Fredericksburg (Rappahannock River), and Washington, DC (Potomac River).

27. For a cross-cultural discussion of chiefs in general and Powhatan's power in particular, see Helen C. Rountree, "Who Were the Powhatans and Did They Have a Unified 'Foreign Policy?,'" in *Powhatan Foreign Relations, 1500–1722*, ed. Helen C. Rountree (Charlottesville: University Press of Virginia, 1993), 1–19.

28. Henry Spelman, *Relation of Virginia: A Boy's Memoir of Life with the Powhatans and Patawomecks,* transcribed and edited by Karen Ordahl Kupperman (New York: New York University Press, 2019), which contains Spelman's relation, 13–48, quotation on 42; Haile, *Jamestown Narratives*, 493–94.

29. Smith, "Generall Historie," 151; Haile, *Jamestown Narratives*, 239.

30. For the full list of jobs and their implications, see Rountree, "Powhatan Indian Women."

31. John Smith, "A Map of Virginia" (1612), in Barbour, *Complete Works of Captain John Smith*, 1:93; Haile, *Jamestown Narratives*, 1:181.

32. Spelman, *Relation of Virginia*, 28, 29; Haile, *Jamestown Narratives*, 488–89, 618–19; Strachey, *Historie of Travell*, 61–62.

33. Strachey, *Historie of Travell*, 61–62; Haile, *Jamestown Narratives*, 619–20.

34. Hamor, *True Discourse*, 42; Haile, *Jamestown Narratives*, 834.

35. Smith, "A Map of Virginia," 1:174; Strachey, *Historie of Travell*, 77; Haile, *Jamestown Narratives*, 634.

36. Strachey, *Historie of Travell*, 77; Haile, *Jamestown Narratives*, 634.

37. For accounts of gifts of food, see Smith, "True Relation," 1:61; Smith, "Map of Virginia," 1:215; Haile, *Jamestown Narratives*, 165, 243. For teaching skills, see Francis Perkins, "Letter of March 18, 1608," in *The Jamestown Voyages under the First Charter,* ed. Philip L. Barbour (Cambridge: Hakluyt Society, 1969) 136:160; Haile, *Jamestown Narratives*, 164.

38. David W. Stahle et al., "The Lost Colony and Jamestown Droughts," *Science* 280 no. 5363 (1998): 565 and fig. 3-B.

39. Smith, "Generall Historie," 152; Haile, *Jamestown Narratives*, 241.

40. Smith, "True Relation," 91; Haile, *Jamestown Narratives*, 181.

41. Smith, "Map of Virginia," 220–21; Smith, "Generall Historie," 160; Haile, *Jamestown Narratives,* 250.
42. Smith, "Map of Virginia," 245–50; Haile, *Jamestown Narratives,* 297–303.
43. Smith, "Generall Historie," 198–99; Haile, *Jamestown Narratives,* 303.
44. Hamor, *True Discourse,* 40; Haile, *Jamestown Narratives,* 832.
45. Hamor, *True Discourse,* 42; Haile, *Jamestown Narratives,* 834.
46. The English used the peace to expand their settlements rapidly into Powhatan's James River territories. Compare the maps on pp. 152 and 188 in Rountree, *Pocahontas, Powhatan, Opechancanough.*
47. Purchas, *Purchas His Pilgrimes,* 954; Haile, *Jamestown Narratives,* 881.
48. Smith, "True Relation," 69, 91; Smith, "Map of Virginia," 216, 236; Haile, *Jamestown Narratives,* 168, 179, 245.
49. Kingsbury, *Records,* 3:92.
50. Kingsbury. The famine hit the Indians harder than the English, according to Argall.
51. Stahle et al., "The Lost Colony and Jamestown Droughts."
52. John Rolfe letter, quoted in Smith, "Generall Historie," 265.

PRISONERS OF HISTORY

Pocahontas, Mary Jemison, and the Poetics of an American Myth

KARENNE WOOD

Anyone interested in history will admit that it's risky to take on the personas of historical characters—to impute motives to their actions, to "speak" for them, reimagining them as human beings apart from the narrative thread that delivers them to us. And yet what do we receive in most histories of Native people in the Americas during colonial times—characters pulled out of cultural context because those who wrote about them seldom knew or even tried to understand what it meant to be Native then? In popular culture, we receive worse: characters that have been manipulated to suit the agendas of media and marketing agencies, bearing little resemblance to their origins beyond their names.

As both a Native poet and a historical researcher, I am often caught in this dilemma, aware that the mainstream stories of our people are deeply flawed but unable to find more authentic accounts, usually because the American Indians remain voiceless or were deliberately silenced. This is particularly true for Native women—their daily activities and beliefs were of no interest to the colonial explorers and settlers whose accounts form the "primary sources" dear to American historians and teachers. And so it seems only right to go back to those accounts and to look for the Native voices, to try to learn more about them as people.

I've always found the story of Pocahontas troubling and avoided writing about her for that reason. In 2006 I visited Kent County, England, with a group of more than fifty Virginia Indians, and we saw the church at Gravesend where she is buried. In 2014 I was asked to speak about Pocahontas to the Jamestowne Society in Los Angeles, because that year marked the four-hundredth anniversary of her marriage to John Rolfe. I chose to speak about the roles of

Native women at that time in our region, an attempt to add cultural depth to her story. It seemed then that perhaps I had something to say about her life and the situation in which she found herself from the perspective of a Virginia Indian woman, and so I wrote a poem. But first I researched what we know about her and her people, turning to recent books and articles by reputable scholars, ignoring stories from earlier times, which cast her as that Indian girl who saw English culture as inherently superior to her own and who "helped the white man" because she loved him.

I also found myself drawn to another Native woman, born 150 years or so later, known to American "frontier history" as Mary Jemison but not nearly as well known as Pocahontas. Interestingly, Mary Jemison was born white. And so I wrote about her, too. This essay is the story of these two women as I see it and the story of two poems that emerged from their experiences.

Not Quite the Fairy-Tale Princess

In the summer of 2015 the Pamunkey Indian Tribe of Virginia received notice from the U.S. Department of the Interior, Bureau of Indian Affairs, that their efforts to obtain federal acknowledgment had finally met with success—permitting tribal members, for the first time in nearly four hundred years, to officially assert their claim as the descendants of the paramount chief Powhatan and his famous daughter, Pocahontas. All two hundred of them. In contrast, the non-Native Americans who also claim to descend from Pocahontas now number more than twenty thousand.[1] Many of them belong to an elite club that calls itself the FFV, the Founding Families of Virginia, as though no families lived here when the colonists arrived. Their grandparents and great-grandparents proclaimed descent from Pocahontas even during the period when anti-Indian sentiment was most virulent, when Virginia passed an antimiscegenation law known as the 1924 Racial Integrity Act. That law defined anyone with a drop of "Negro" blood as "colored" and felonized marriage between whites and persons of color. An exception was made, however, for those whose only non-Caucasian blood was one-sixteenth or less American Indian, to accommodate those wealthy and well-placed Virginians descended from Pocahontas.[2]

Pocahontas has long been the stuff of legend, dating back to Captain John Smith's adventurous account of his visit to what is now Virginia in 1607. A year later he was gone, back to England, never to return to the mid-Atlantic region.

The year of publication of his account, 1624, is significant, as the majority of the other participants in his Virginia exploits had by then died; his earlier accounts do not mention the story that made Pocahontas famous. According to the 1624 account, Smith was captured by Powhatan's war chief, Opechancanough, taken on a tour of Powhatan's lands, and subjected to several rituals and perceived threats. He was then transported to Powhatan's capital, Werowocomoco, where he was suddenly forced to put his head on a stone. When warriors raised clubs to smash his head, Pocahontas leaped in, laying her head on his and pleading for his life.[3] Scholars generally now agree that if the event occurred at all, it was probably a ritual adoption, intended to bring Smith and the English colonists into the Powhatan polity to strengthen the Powhatans' power and protect them from enemy tribes. Scholars and tribal members agree that Pocahontas was likely not present, because she was a child and would not have been permitted in council.

Smith departed for England, and Pocahontas went on with her life. She married a Patawomeck warrior named Kocoum and is thought to have had a child. Kocoum disappeared from the historical record, though, and Pocahontas was kidnapped by Samuel Argall with the help of Patawomeck people. Argall took her to Jamestowne and then to another colonial settlement, Henricus, where she learned to dress and speak like an Englishwoman. Although her father paid the ransom the English demanded, they refused to return her. Her options were limited, and when the English gentleman John Rolfe declared his desire to make her his wife, she agreed. They were married in 1614, and she had one child, named Thomas. They visited England, where she died of an unknown disease. She was about twenty years old.[4]

An Original American Myth

The Pocahontas rescue story was popularized by English expatriate John Davis and gained momentum following the War of 1812 as Americans began to explore and develop a nascent history of their country. With the Indians of the East no longer a threat, the easterners were free to develop nostalgia, such as that evident in James Fenimore Cooper's *The Last of the Mohicans*. Poems and plays based on the Pocahontas rescue emerged, popularizing an attitude evident from one introduction: "Pocahontas is one of those characters, rarely appearing on the theatre of life, which no age can claim, no country appropriate. She is the property of mankind, serving as a beacon to light us on our way.

In Pocahontas we view the simple child of nature, prompted by her own native virtues alone, discharging the most generous acts of self-devotion."[5] Pocahontas came to embody those virtues idealized for Christian white women of the time—an American mother figure, a myth, decontextualized from her culture and her community, her personal circumstances ignored or transfigured. Even her name, Amonute, disappeared, along with her sacred name, Matoaka, and her Christian name, Rebecca, though those two last were noted on the only image made of her in her lifetime (see frontispiece). She remains Pocahontas, a nickname given to a child by her father that meant "wanton" or "mischievous."

At the same time, she emerged in the American mindset as a beautiful, exotic female Other, desired by white men, a sexual model. In her article "The Pocahontas Perplex," Rayna Green deftly traces the art history of this model from images of Caribbean queens published in 1575 to the emergent American Indian princess that represented Liberty before the image of Columbia supplanted her. As Camilla Townsend suggests, those models gave European men notions that America was a land waiting to be ravished and that Native women were available for the taking. Pocahontas was thus cast both as a demure, motherly figure and as an object of desire, a confounding notion that Green correctly characterizes as dysfunctional. In many of the later paintings representing her, Pocahontas's skin appears white.

Even more confounding is the misperception most Americans have that it was John Smith, and not John Rolfe, whom Pocahontas loved and wished to marry. There is no evidence to substantiate any physical relationship between Pocahontas, a child of about eleven at the time, and Smith, who was a commoner and thus not permitted to consort with those he perceived as royalty.[6] The "love story" between them has continued to thrive as American legend, however. It emerged in 1958, when Peggy Lee covered "Fever," an R&B tune that refers to a love affair between the two, and most notably in 1995, when Disney released its *Pocahontas* film, which featured John Smith as a tall blonde Ken-doll and Pocahontas as a willowy Asian-looking Native, clearly older than eleven. The love myth has continued to emanate from Hollywood, most recently in Terrence Malick's boring film, *The New World* (2006), which starred Colin Farrell as Smith and Q'orianka Kilcher, age fourteen, as Pocahontas. It's been profitable: the majority of American children know of Pocahontas through Disney's film, and she remains their only contact with Virginia Indians of the past and present. Not only is she legendary, but she's been commodified, animated into an indigenous object of sexual desire that pervades American mindsets and Halloween costumes long after elementary school.[7]

"A Mission to Preserve"

All of this points to a disconcerting truth: while, until recently, American society has remained uncomfortable with the idea of race mixing through marriage, and some states, like Virginia, even outlawed that practice, the interracial union of Pocahontas and John Rolfe (or even Pocahontas and John Smith) is beyond question. Why is that? How did it happen that the four-hundredth anniversary of Pocahontas and Rolfe was publicly commemorated at Historic Jamestowne in 2014[8] and celebrated by those Jamestowne Society members as far away as Los Angeles?

Drew Lopenzina points out that colonial history, which is rooted in various forms of violence and oppression, often cloaks itself in the language of a benign and uncontestable destiny. In this case, Historic Jamestowne—a site jointly owned by the National Park Service and the Association for the Preservation of Virginia Antiquities—states that its mission is "to preserve, protect and promote the original site of the first permanent English settlement in North America and to tell the story of the role of the three cultures, European, North American and African, that came together to lay the foundation for a uniquely American form of democratic government, language, free enterprise and society." On the surface, the mission statement may seem innocuous—except that the order of "the three cultures" is chronologically flawed, and continents are not singular cultural groups. Embedded in it, however, is the notion that colonial institutions and cultural beliefs are inherently privileged, ignoring tribal removals, terminations, cultural suppression, language loss, even slavery and the Racial Integrity Act, which denied Virginia's Native peoples a separate identity and cast them in the "colored" category—except for Pocahontas and those mostly Caucasian descendants of hers who are not Pamunkey tribal members.

Mary Jemison: A Happier Ending

In contrast to the persistent legend and reframing of Pocahontas as an animated rather than a historical character, the story of De-he-wä-mis has vanished from mainstream American consciousness. She was born in 1743 as Mary Jemison to Irish parents on a ship en route to America. The story of her life, which she told to Reverend James Seaver as an elderly woman, was published as a "captivity narrative" and was immensely popular for decades afterward.

Mary grew up near what is now Marsh Creek, Pennsylvania, on land where her parents had squatted without the permission of the Haudenosaunee, or Iroquois, tribes whose homelands these were. In 1755, as tensions escalated between the French and British in what is erroneously called the French and Indian War, a party of French and Shawnee raiders captured Mary, then twelve, and her family. Mary and her younger brother were spared; the others were killed and scalped.

Two Seneca women adopted Mary; she married a Delaware man named Sheninjee and had a son she called Thomas, after her father. Her husband died, and she married Hiakatoo, a Seneca warrior, with whom she had six children. She helped to negotiate terms for the Seneca following the Revolutionary War, when they were forced to cede land because they had supported the British. When the Seneca left the Genesee Valley in 1823, they reserved a parcel of land for Mary's use. She remained there until 1831, when she sold it and returned to her Indian people, among whom she died at the age of ninety.[9] Initially buried in the Seneca community at Buffalo Creek where she died, her remains were removed at the request of her descendants and relocated to the site of a Seneca council house on the estate of James Letchworth, today the site of a New York state park, where a bronze statue commemorates Jemison's life.

Given the opportunity several times to return to the world of white settlers, De-he-wä-mis chose to remain with her Indian family. Her name, however, appears in Seaver's 1824 narrative as Mrs. Mary Jemison—a conflated reflection that casts her status as a white woman who, although married to an Indian husband for decades, retains her first name and her maiden Irish surname rather than the Seneca name by which she was known. While there is evidence indicating that she chose to keep Jemison as a surname, the "Mrs." is interesting: Was that English convention her choice or Seaver's cultural assumptions at play?

Captivity narratives were popular in the nineteenth century and earlier because they detailed a traumatic lived experience that exposed violent confrontations between settlers and Native peoples, casting the former as victims and the latter as predators and obstacles to civilization. Originating with the story of "Mrs. Mary Rowlandson," who was captured by Pequots in Puritan times, the genre typically presented lurid details of grisly encounters between whites and Indians. "The Indian of the captivity narrative was the consummate villain, the beast who hatcheted fathers, smashed the skulls of infants, and carried off mothers to make them into squaws."[10] These stories cast American women as pure and virtuous and their contact with "savages" as irreversible defilement, most likely through rape, because, according to cultural perspective, they would never have participated willingly. This condition was clear to Jemison, who states in her narrative that she could not endure the thought of herself and her children being ignored or despised by her own relatives if she were ever to return to them. She also states that she loved her husband.

Although Jemison's story was initially published and presented to American readers as a captivity narrative, her voice is that of a Seneca woman. Susan Walsh and Karen Oakes argue persuasively that that voice stands in opposition to some of Seaver's editorializing, favoring Native practices and beliefs even when they conflict with those of colonial settlers and privileging the perspective of a female "cultural conservator," creating an autobiography that is quintessentially Native in nature.

In examining the circumstances of these two women, I was struck by some basic similarities: they were smart, resourceful, strong women who made the best of the difficulties they encountered. Both were abducted as teenagers, were married twice, named their first son Thomas. Both negotiated complicated circumstances during wartime, adapting to new languages and societies, and won the regional custom for captives of any race. Both were aware of their positions as outsiders and used their status to broker terms of peace for the Native people with whom they were affiliated.

Neither of these stories can be read in simple terms or as a "captivity narrative." Both women accepted their situations and managed to fit into their new societies. Neither renounced her origins, however: Pocahontas kept a circle of Native women around her even while living with Rolfe on a colonial farm; Jemison continued to practice speaking English and gave her children English names. Each seemed to have done the best she could. As such, perhaps we should consider them not as captives but as pioneers in the truest sense: those who went before us, endured difficulties, raised children, and helped to lead their people during times that, to us, remain unimaginable.

Notes

Reprinted with permission from *Studies in American Indian Literatures.*

1. Frederic W. Gleach, "Pocahontas: An Exercise in Mythmaking and Marketing," in *New Perspectives on Native North America: Cultures, Histories, and Representations.* Ed. Sergei A. Kan and Pauline Turner Strong (Lincoln: University of Nebraska Press, 2005), 449.
2. Helen C. Rountree, *Pocahontas's People: The Powhatan Indians of Virginia through Four Centuries* (Norman: University of Oklahoma Press, 1990), 221.
3. Captain John Smith, *The Generall Historie of Virginia, New-England, and the Summer Isles. The Complete Works of Captain John Smith, 1580–1631.* Vol. 2. Ed. Philip L. Barbour (Chapel Hill: University of North Carolina Press, 1986 [1624]), 150–51.
4. Drew Lopenzina, "The Wedding of Pocahontas and John Rolfe: How to Keep the Thrill Alive after Four Hundred Years of Marriage." *Studies in American Indian Literatures* 26.4 (2014): 59–77; Rountree, *Pocahontas's People*, 1990.
5. Gleach quoting William Watson Waldron, *Pocahontas, Princess of Virginia, and Other Poems* [1841], in "Pocahontas" 2005, 9.
6. Gleach, "Pocahontas" 2005.
7. Kent A. Ono. and Derek T. Buescher, "Deciphering Pocahontas: Unpacking the Commodification of a Native American Woman." *Critical Studies in Media Communication* 18.1 (2001): 23–43.
8. Drew Lopenzina, "The Wedding of Pocahontas and John Rolfe," 2014.
9. James E. Seaver, *A Narrative of the Life of Mrs. Mary Jemison* (New York: American Scenic and Historic Preservation Society, 1922 [1823]).
10. Hilary E. Wyss, quoting Roy Harvey Pearce, *The Savages of America* [1953], in "Captivity and Conversion: William Apess, Mary Jemison, and Narratives of Racial Identity." *American Indian Quarterly* 23.3/4 (1999): 63–82, 58.

PART II

REASSESSING METHODOLOGY

TRACING THE AUTO/BIOGRAPHICAL IN PAULA GUNN ALLEN'S *POCAHONTAS: MEDICINE WOMAN, SPY, ENTREPRENEUR, DIPLOMAT*

Or Lessons on Story, Sources, and the Archive

LUCINDA RASMUSSEN

Pocahontas didn't write reports, at least not in a form that survives in university archives or reissued publications.
—Paula Gunn Allen, *Pocahontas: Medicine Woman, Spy, Entrepreneur, Diplomat*

The use of Roman orthography should not be the start or end point, nor the be-all and end-all of Indigenous literacy, intellectualism, or stories.
—Niigaanwewidam James Sinclair, "Responsible and Ethical Criticisms of Indigenous Literatures"

What happens to our conception of literature when we momentarily set aside the literary frameworks of Europe and consider what constitutes Native American writing?
—Lisa Brooks, *The Common Plot*

In the introduction to *Pocahontas: Medicine Woman, Spy, Entrepreneur, Diplo-mat*, Paula Gunn Allen explains her goal to "'Nativize'" her subject's life story, a project she undertakes as a way to move beyond the usual life narrative that "do[es] great injustice to pathfinders such as Pocahontas by . . . considering them as having lived tragic lives, victims of European greed."[1] Allen, who is

Laguna Pueblo, elaborates on those circumstances that motivated her academic work in general in an essay titled "Thus Spake Pocahontas" in which she observed how "the contributions of our peoples to the literatures, philosophies, sciences, and religions of the world are ignored" by those in charge of mainstream institutions.[2] Interestingly enough, the just-cited essay bears traces of having been subjected to a form of institutional interference, with Allen noting in the republished version that her title—"Thus Spake Pocahontas"—had been changed by the Modern Language Association so as to fit with their publishing agenda.[3]

Much of Allen's career was spent addressing the colonial hegemony within the academy, and it is for this reason that Niigaanwewidam James Sinclair identifies her as one of a handful of literary scholars who started an "intellectual movement that marks a range of committed critical responses to the calls throughout the 1980s and early 1990s for Indigenous-centered literary scholarship."[4] As Sinclair explains when introducing this field of study, scholars such as Allen stressed the importance of studying literature in ways that would "illuminate [Indigenous peoples'] intellectual histories, experiences, and knowledge structures available in Native (tribal/pan-tribal) nations' creative and critical expressions."[5] With such scholarship in mind, this essay discusses Allen's work to theorize and present a version of Pocahontas's life story from "a Powhatan worldview."[6] In particular, Allen's text and responses to it invite some deep contemplation of what it means to be a scholar within a system where authority is granted to some voices with the outcome of hindering others who also have important knowledge to share. Located in Allen's representation of Pocahontas are lessons about what it means to reconsider the Eurocentric worldview through which genre, sources, and the archive are commonly understood. Each lesson is rooted in what I describe as small but deeply significant auto/biographical moments that Allen includes within her remarkable text. While none of the observations I wish to touch on are new to conversations about Indigenous literatures or literary studies broadly—genre, citation, and the lifting of Indigenous women's voices—they are ones that are new to conversations about Allen's *Pocahontas* and provide reasons that her work ought to be unquestionably counted among important texts within that body of scholarly works.

Before going further, I should perhaps pause to say something more about my background, particularly since scholars of Indigenous literatures regard it as "good protocol [to] locate[e] oneself, Indigenous or non-Indigenous, in relation to a text."[7] Here, I want to clarify that I approach Allen's text, not with the goal of claiming mastery over the cultural insights needed to fully comprehend all that Allen shares, but as a settler academic who is embroiled in learning how to participate in work that is being done to rethink scholarly practices that have often worked to alienate many members of the academy, Allen included.[8] While many institutions are working toward greater diversity and inclusion of Indigenous peoples—to decolonize, if you will, and in Canada where I am from toward reconciliation—in the work that Allen undertakes in her telling of Pocahontas's life story, those "Western traditional demands for verification"[9] are defined as constraints. This work brings her into conversation with what Linda Tuhiwai Smith refers to as the "'archive' of knowledge and systems, rules and values"[10] that governs western intellectual thought. Smith draws on work by Stuart Hall when setting out what she means by "archive," so as to clarify that this space of which she speaks is yoked to processes geared toward classifying, evaluating, and comparing—processes that ultimately reify hierarchies and that exclude or diminish many Indigenous peoples.[11] For example, as I will discuss in due course, scholars and public intellectuals who want to discuss Pocahontas's life story must cite a particular canon of written works by male colonists if their work is to be viewed as credible.

I discovered Allen's life narrative about Pocahontas while doing research to plan a first-year literature course that deconstructs Eurocentric literary works in which Pocahontas is (mis)represented and which then proceeds to show students how the historical archive as a place of knowledge production is replete with rhetoric that, in the contemporary moment as I will discuss, is related to the problem of violence against Indigenous women. Violence against Indigenous women is a problem of sobering magnitude in North America broadly and Canada in particular.[12] Many of the students I encounter in my first-year classes are non-Indigenous and have little or no experience with Indigenous literatures or histories. Most, however, recognize Pocahontas by name (the Disney film continues to be pervasive in this regard) but, as they have learned the popular narrative surrounding her life, they have also internalized its many stereotypes. I would hasten to add that Indigenous students tend to understand the relationship between stereotypes and lived experience very clearly.

The reason I mention my observations in the classroom is because, in addition to showing how my own scholarly and geographical location brings me to a particular reading of Allen's text, this context has prompted me to observe the extent to which her life has been made to seem familiar within the mainstream, and how, even within the academy and spaces of so-called higher learning, that familiarity needs to be interrupted. It is in this capacity that I have been drawn to engage with Allen's work on Pocahontas—both her poem and her life narrative—for the ways Allen as an Indigenous woman does work that foregrounds conversations about what it would necessarily mean to decolonize Pocahontas's life story and by extension the university and other mainstream institutions.

Critical sources that guide my exploration of Allen's text are primarily by scholars of Indigenous literatures, many of whom self-identify as members of various Indigenous nations, and who connect their work as literary scholars to their cultural backgrounds. In addition, this essay draws very briefly on work that has been done in auto/biography studies, a field in which I did my doctoral research on women's life writing, and which is important for the ways in which its scholars have dedicated themselves to exploring the challenges and possibilities that emerge through writing and reading real life narratives. Certainly, as a field, auto/biography studies is important to this conversation because much of the work done on Pocahontas can be said to be biographical in nature, thereby opening it up to the types of analyses scholars in the field perform as they think through relevant topics like memory, voice, and space.[13] Finally, this essay touches on feminist-oriented discussions about what it means to work for social change within the academy, again with the goal of questioning the circumstances under which knowledge is produced. By considering some moments in Allen's *Pocahontas* where these fields of inquiry intersect, I will suggest that Allen's representation of Pocahontas's life story warrants far more attention than it has received until now, precisely for the way it disrupts the colonial mindset that informs many peoples' understandings about Pocahontas's identity. This approach enables a shift in the conversation about Pocahontas; it reorients the conversation in a direction that does something other than relegate her memory to an unrecoverable past, thereby consigning her to, as Allen puts it, a story in which it is made to seem as if all Indigenous peoples have vanished, or "lived tragic lives."[14]

As already suggested, I was interested in reengaging with Allen's *Pocahontas* because of her commitment to the inclusion of Indigenous women's voices and through previous experiences of teaching other examples of her work, especially "Pocahontas to her English Husband John Rolfe." However, I would soon discover that despite Allen's many contributions to the field of Indigenous literary studies, her work has often been the subject of criticism, and much of it quite unfair. Robert Warrior remarks that, at the time of writing his chapter for inclusion in the co-authored work *American Indian Literary Nationalism,* "he found it amazing . . . that [Allen's] obvious mastery of so much knowledge and so many things could be easily dismissed."[15] This point is acknowledged in the edited collection titled *Weaving the Legacy: Remembering Paula Gunn Allen,* in which Lisa Tatonetti likewise asserts that despite Allen's status as forerunner of Indigenous literary studies, her work remains underappreciated and understudied.[16]

The underappreciation of *Pocahontas* specifically is found, for example, in a review by Donald K. Sharpes, who faults what he perceives as Allen's inexcusable indifference to the institutionally sanctioned body of primary texts. "Key primary texts, like William Strachey's 1612 travelogue, John Smith's own general history of Virginia, and John Rolfe's book *True Relation of the State of Virginia,*" Sharpes explains, "are fleetingly noted in [Allen's] text or endnotes, but unavailable in the references, leaving one who wishes to pursue these primary sources without the benefit of full references."[17] Sharpes also lambasted Allen for what he felt was her insufficient understanding of "historiography" as well as of myth and folklore, while constantly substantiating his own assertions by reference to a canon made up of mostly white men. Elsewhere, John Burch refused to endorse Allen's biography, going so far as to suggest that Allen "flaunts her Native American heritage in order to differentiate her 'biography' of Pocahontas from those written by nonnatives."[18] Burch is critical of Allen for her attempt to discuss Pocahontas's life through a Powhatan worldview since Allen is "of Laguna Pueblo/Metis and Sioux descent."[19] However, at no point does Burch feel a burden to disclose his own cultural background when proclaiming Allen's knowledge as unsatisfactory, and he disregards the fact that Allen does allude to her background and how it differed from Pocahontas's in her text. Instead of correctly identifying Allen's "pan Indigenous" approach[20] as a valid method by which to approach her life story, he presumes she could not write about Pocahontas's life because she is not Algonquin.

It needs to be understood that Allen's *Pocahontas* emerged while scholars of Indigenous literatures held deep anxieties over authorial authenticity and separatism—topics that continue to be raised at the time of this writing as well. A short time after *Pocahontas* was published, Allen was implicated in a particularly wrenching critical conversation regarding authenticity initiated by Elvira Pulitano, a non-Indigenous scholar who was critical of Allen's work (though not her work on Pocahontas specifically) because she felt Allen should not borrow from Western intellectual tradition if her wish was to generate a truly Indigenous-centered approach: she writes "Allen's own strategic location within the discourse of the mainstream academy makes her complicit with the western system with which she wants to be separated."[21] Lest any readers of *Pocahontas* charge Allen with something similar here—since Allen does by her own admission engage with the European archive in this text—I direct them to Lisa Brooks's afterword in *American Indian Literary Nationalism,* which concludes that Pulitano fails to note how all of the authors she critiques "strike out on their own self-determined path, developing methodologies that seek to interpret and read literature of our own choosing based on models drawn from our own, often collective knowledge and experience."[22] Regrettably, Brooks, after reading Pulitano, feels "less hopeful that our [Indigenous] voices will be heard, and fearful that the complexity and depth of what many of us are writing about will be simplified, translated, and tossed back to us in a form that says much less than what we had intended."[23]

For Brooks, what the writer wants to say must be considered within larger contexts. In other words, as part of reading Allen's *Pocahontas* (or any biographical work on Pocahontas), it is vital to consider the author's obligation to engage with narrative conventions already well established by a dominant system that grows out of colonialism. As Allen clarifies, such forces are found in academic publishing houses, which privilege "western modes of discourse" and are thus realities with which she had to deal even as she sought to inscribe Pocahontas's life story in a way that breaks with past representations.[24] And although one could argue that Burch's and Sharpes's reviews are not representative of all the reviews of this text—Allen's *Pocahontas* was, after all, nominated for the Pulitzer—I would suggest that even those reviewers who gave the text a more favorable response often describe it in ways that show the extent to which a western worldview is naturalized within academic circles and the popular realm: Joanne Braxton, for instance, appreciates that all of Allen's sources are not "written, white, or masculinist" but then remarks on Allen's "arrogance" and wonders if many readers won't "put the book down in frustration" for its complex references to Native American ideologies.[25] Laura Mielke praises Allen's work to present a self-determining Pocahontas but suggests that errors "justify reader resistance to [her] alternative history."[26]

It is indeed remarkable that Allen's treatment of source materials be critiqued on such grounds as a failure to complete a thorough bibliography, especially given the extent to which settler culture has appropriated Indigenous intellectual property and treated it without due regard. More ironic still is the number of scholars and public intellectuals who routinely and invariably acknowledge the limitations of findings based on written primary sources when it comes to understanding Pocahontas's life,[27] but then go on to cite those documents extensively when devising an interpretation of Pocahontas's life. A final irony is that many monographs bearing Pocahontas's name in their titles "are not actually about Pocahontas,"[28] an observation that might well speak to the commodification of her identity, not merely in popular media (think Disney), but in the publishing world as well. These examples are why Linda Tuhiwai Smith's point that adherence to standard methods of research often "ensures that Western interests remain dominant" fits well in this conversation.[29]

The point this far has been to affirm the extent to which a particular narrative of Pocahontas's life has been naturalized so as to make it extraordinarily difficult for Allen to credibly reframe the vantage point from which the narrative is to be told. Beyond this observation, one might ask if much of the research done on Pocahontas might be said to justify the ongoing privileging of an archive populated by colonist-authored documents, despite the acknowledged imperfections of those sources. One of the ways this happens is through the tendency to draw a stark line between work that is supposedly imaginative and work that grows out of an unquestioned reliance on a body of knowledge that is material (for instance, primary documents written by colonists). In *Pocahontas and the Powhatan Dilemma*, Camilla Townsend speculates that Paula Gunn Allen wrote her version of Pocahontas's life story in response to "numerous studies of John Smith and Pocahontas . . . [by authors who] often accept uncritically the mythologizing narratives" that diminished Pocahontas and presented her without agency.[30] According to Townsend, where these authors cast Pocahontas as "a good Indian" or as a hapless romantic partner to John Smith, Allen felt motivated to "render [Pocahontas] powerful."[31] On the one hand, this notion that Allen is motivated to invent a narrative whereby she can counter the settler archive makes quite a lot of sense given Allen's past work. In particular, Allen's poem, "Pocahontas to her English Husband John Rolfe," is clearly taking issue with the offensive and paternalizing tone found in primary documents such as John Rolfe's letter. When I have asked undergraduates to read Allen's poem, they are initially quite startled by Allen's acerbic tone, often because it goes against their understandings of her as a romantic heroine. Indeed, within Allen's poem, Pocahontas's anger at John Rolfe for the colonist's patronizing views of her and her community is palatable:

> I'm sure
> you wondered at my silence, saying I was
> a simple wanton, a savage maid,
> dusky daughter of heathen sires
> who cartwheeled naked through the muddy towns.[32]

Of course, once students read excerpts from documents by people like Rolfe and Strachey, they come to understand why Allen's self-aware Pocahontas might well be angry. At this point, students are often startled to observe how those seemingly benign images of Pocahontas cartwheeling in the Disney film can be tied to the offensive language found in settler archives.[33] This discovery becomes very important as students aim to understand the larger implications of colonialism, including the objectification of Indigenous women.

On the one hand, no one would dispute the merits of Allen's poem for what it can teach readers about Pocahontas's resilience in the face of trying circumstances. On the other hand, Townsend's observation that Allen's work as a life narrator is not based on her desire for "accuracy but with providing an alternative telling" is worrisome.[34] There is a danger here that Warrior alerts us to when identifying "a critical attitude through which some people saw Natives as good at creative tasks like fiction, poetry and even essays, but not very astute at criticism."[35] While Townsend locates her assessment of Allen's work in Allen's own words and is paying Allen's work respect, care must be taken not to disregard Allen's theoretical contributions in *Pocahontas* on the grounds that her work is also understood by some as a work of imagination. It is perhaps for such reasons that Daniel Heath Justice emphasizes that Indigenous writers who produce "nonfiction memoir and political commentary" are participating in the construction of important modes of expression, and he cautions that failure to acknowledge these works as such is to "silence generations of writers and obscure their important efforts on behalf of their communities and kin."[36] Here I want to emphasize again that all of Pocahontas's biographers, often through their own admission, are working with imagination and all bring their respective worldviews to texts. The rather important question raised is to what extent Allen's contributions are being overlooked when she expresses Pocahontas's story through an Indigenous worldview that does depend on the same research protocols as the western worldview does.

A way to approach this problem is to consider how some critics of Indigenous literatures understand fiction and nonfiction genres, including the editors of a recently published anthology titled *Read, Listen, Tell: Indigenous Stories from Turtle Island.* The editorial team makes the valuable point that "western notions of genre do not apply to Indigenous texts"[37]; instead, they prefer to think of work as story, which interestingly enough is the term Townsend uses to describe Allen's life narrative about Pocahontas. However, Townsend's observation that Allen's text should be understood as imaginative might be misconstrued to suggest that scholars had not previously undertaken theoretical work. As Thomas King famously conveyed when delivering the Massey Lectures, "the truth about stories is that that's all we are."[38] For King, story, identity, and lived experience are closely interrelated.[39] By way of example, King, who was giving these lectures to a mainstream audience in 2003, tells a brief version of the Christian creation story and a longer version of what he refers to as a Native creation story about Charm. King spends more time telling of Charm, explaining to his audience that he does so because the Christian creation story is ubiquitous. At this point, he wonders if those who "see the world through Adam's eyes" might not be blind to the world that "Charm and the Twins and the animals help to create."[40] King suggests such blindness is probable, and he locates the mainstream's indifference to his Indigenous worldview to the personal difficulties he experienced with his father. Allen's point that "Native tradition can be diagrammed as a series of points that can be connected in an almost endless variety of ways" is helped by King's work.[41] Additionally, the editors of *Read, Listen, Tell* observe that many critical essays and works of nonfiction have stories embedded in them.[42] Their claim that such works are theory is in tandem with Linda Tuhiwai Smith's notes when describing various methods used to decolonize: "the boundaries of poetry, plays, song writing, fiction, and non-fiction," writes Smith, "are blurred as indigenous writers seek to use language in ways that seek to capture the messages, nuances and flavor of indigenous lives."[43] Given these points, it seems vital to observe that Allen's *Pocahontas* is a theoretical work where the distinction between fiction and nonfiction is not relevant when it comes to identifying the truths that are enclosed within the narrative.

It may be helpful to think about Allen's *Pocahontas* in terms of the auto/biographical, a concept that scholars of the life narrative, including Susanna Egan and Gabriele Helms, have used for some time now, in which "writing about the self (auto) to writing about another (biography)" can intersect within a given work to result in a "combining or blending of genres."[44] However, the fluidity that these scholars accept with use of the slash in *auto/*

biography is helpful only as long as it is not used in ways that would privilege the western mode of thought. Sharpes clearly falls into this trap when he writes that "history and biography are not, as Allen claims, a Christian-based capitalistic democracy."[45] Sharpes counters that "historical writing originates with Herodotus . . . and that some of the most stylistic and ingenious historians were . . . Greek and Romans, none of whom were Christian or democratic in thinking or practice."[46] His point is hardly useful since he is still drawing on European intellectual tradition here.

Conversely, Deanna Reder argues for the "Indigenous nature of autobiography" and is interested in ways that the autobiographical can reflect "a communal, collective sense of self, a circular sense of time, and orality, all associated with the Indigenous epistemes."[47] Reder is responding to Arnold Krupat's assumption that "autobiography is distinctly European in origin."[48] While Reder is not commenting on Allen's work, her position bolsters Allen's belief that "in Native traditional life stories, the subject of the biography—or, often, autobiography—is situated within the entire life system: that community of living things, geography, climate, spirit people, and supernaturals."[49] Accordingly, Allen introduces *Pocahontas* by attending to the spiritual so as to elaborate on those connections between disciplines, traditions, and knowledge systems, which are auto/biographical insights she drops into the narrative as proof.

For instance, Allen generally signposts the value of an Indigenous-centered approach to literatures in *Pocahontas* by applying it to works from other intellectual traditions. As a literary scholar with knowledge of both the western canon and of Indigenous ways of knowing, she reads *Sir Gawain and the Green Knight* as "remarkably Algonquin in spirit."[50] By showing how *Sir Gawain and the Green Knight* and *Pocahontas's* life story overlap, Allen demonstrates her understanding of both Anglo and Indigenous cultural traditions as she argues for her interpretation of Pocahontas's life. Allen's use of Indigenous intellectual tradition to interpret a medieval poem about the Green Man is an act that resonates with advice found in *Read, Listen, Tell,* in which the editors encourage recognition of ways that Indigenous-centered methods of reading "may be applied not only to Indigenous writing but stories from many traditions."[51] Brooks touches on this idea as well, writing that she guided her students to "draw [insight] from . . . contemporary [Indigenous] criticism and began to apply them to other literatures, histories, and contemporary issues, [thereby] treating Native American writers as sophisticated intellectuals who have something to say to the world at large, as well as to their tribally specific communities."[52] In *Pocahontas*, Allen is thus modeling an important scholarly process, showing that the Indigenous-centered method through which she reads need not be applied only to Indigenous texts.

Allen also brings together her experiences as a literary scholar and a Laguna Pueblo woman to show how a tension exists between the two. In *Pocahontas*, Allen seems to anticipate resistance to her book when she cites David Bohm to distinguish between the "explicate" (material) and "implicate" (spiritual) worlds, noting that westerners privilege the former whereas Indigenous peoples depend on the latter.[53] Allen follows her overview of these terms by stating that "respectful and highly skilled scholars such as Helen Rountree and Frances Mossiker, who are *impeccable in their documentation and solid academic grounding*, unfortunately miss the basic worldview that characterizes Native thought and that distinguishes it from scholarly and popular modern thought"[54] (italics added). Consequently, Allen has difficulties with these writers for what she perceives as a belittling approach to Indigenous peoples. For instance, Allen states that "the spin Rountree puts on the contrasting systems of belief is [that] the Powhatans have false ideas, while the English *know* the facts of the matter" (italics in original).[55] While Rountree's work is, as Allen notes, remarkable in its adherence to rigorous documentation practices, Rountree also privileges the written archive, and with it, her disciplinary ways of knowing. Rountree's position is stated firmly in later work where she argues that ethnohistorians are best equipped to uncover the truth about Pocahontas and her community.[56] Rountree is sensitive to her audience whom she understands as comprised of both non-Indigenous and Indigenous peoples, and her thirty-plus years of consultation with the Powhatan peoples speaks to her commitment to collaboration. She also correctly understands that "mythologizing is what most books about Pocahontas really discuss, for historical records are scarce."[57] At the same time, she relies on "the primary sources in front of [her]."[58]

Yet Allen is suspicious of critical practice when it is tied to the material realm (e.g., proof in the form of written documentation), and makes a similar point about Mossiker's biography, writing that Mossiker's confusion over why "the Powhatans sent food to the starving English" reveals her lack of awareness regarding the Powhatan people's commitment to their spiritual beliefs.[59] Here Allen explains her interpretation of the Powhatan people's actions by noting that any move to deny care to the starving English would "result in the loss of one's place in the community, both explicate and implicate, village and manito aki [the world or land of the spirits]."[60] Significantly, Allen concludes that both researchers are following a set of rules governing their disciplines—she surmises that neither Rountree nor Mossiker would have been able to "pursue her academic career with the kind of disciplinary respect each has garnered and not be steeped in late twentieth century explicate-think."[61] Consequently, Allen locates deficits within the system to which these scholars belong to show how knowledge production through academic practice that is grounded in material proofs is always partial.

Although Sharpes criticizes Allen for what he witnesses as her failure to interview Powhatan peoples specifically,[62] another way Allen does integrate an Indigenous-centered approach is by referencing conversations with Indigenous peoples, particularly women whom she regards as Knowledge Keepers. Near the beginning of her text, Allen refers to teachings from her mother. "When I was young," writes Allen, "My mother often told me that animals, insects, and plants are to be treated with the kind of respect one customarily accords to people."[63] Allen connects this teaching to ones from Nicolas Black Elk, noting that both teachers taught her "the wholeness and eternity, the constant connectedness, of all that is, was, or will come to be."[64] By speaking of her mother's teachings at the outset—which she then verifies with a reference to another teaching from a different Elder—Allen begins to develop a platform from which to begin her discussion about the dream vision Pocahontas may have had and to think about its significance. Similarly, Allen also discusses her "great-grandmother, Meta Atseye Gunn," who taught Allen during her childhood those traditional stories "about the old gods at Laguna," as well as "[her] late aunt Susie Marmon, Laguna elder," who shared insights that prompted Allen to think through gender roles in Pocahontas's community.[65] After conversing with this aunt, Allen draws the conclusion that "polyandry among the Algonquins was likely" despite "conventional ethnographic wisdom."[66] Here, note that Allen awards her aunt's perspective as much credence as she does a particular disciplinary one. Finally, Allen writes about a Lakota woman named Six Fingers, explaining how the woman's story "opened [her] mind to a new line of inquiry concerning the encounters between Native people and the strangers from across the sea."[67] This latter example, in which Allen begins to articulate how it is that she understands Pocahontas to be a figure who defends and protects her community and who provides "various kinds of sacred knowledge,"[68] is passed on through the stories told between families—in the case of Six Fingers's, the story is passed down to a great-grandson from

Six Fingers's grandchildren, whom Allen refers to as sources.[69] While each of these moments in Allen's *Pocahontas* are seemingly small, they are significant because they locate sources of knowledge about what Pocahontas's life might have been, as Lisa Brooks describes it, "[at] those kitchen-table conversations."[70] Indeed, Allen's conversation with her aunt happened over "peach pie and coffee with Pet milk."[71] This small reference to a personal experience within Allen's family shows that the kitchen table is, for Allen, a place where many voices and perspectives gained through lived experience and teachings can be passed down and that these must be considered legitimate contributions to knowledge production.

The work Allen does to situate the voices of Indigenous women who are connected to cultural teachings should not be thought of as Allen exploiting her Native American identity but rather as part of Allen's legitimate scholarly practice. The reader who seeks what Sinclair identifies as an ethical approach to the reading of Indigenous texts might well observe how Allen includes storytellers and Knowledge Keepers she has known, thereby working to "legitimate a long-standing and wide-ranging Indigenous intellectualism and recognize this intellectual history."[72] Allen's method of inclusions also aligns with what Daniel Heath Justice defines as a foundational question to bring to the reading of Indigenous literatures and to understanding these works' purposes: "How do we become good ancestors?" As Justice elaborates, "How do we create the kind of world and relationships that will nurture those who come after, and give them cause to thank us rather than curse or grief our destructive selfishness? And what does literature do to help guide this work?"[73] It seems appropriate at this juncture to remark that a number of scholars whom Allen mentored now credit her as having influenced their work as writers, thinkers, and academics, and each of who is in turn invested in creating more inclusive spaces of knowledge production.[74] By noting how Allen elevates Indigenous women's voices in her work, and how she has inspired future generations of scholars, we might trace a connection between Pocahontas's life story, as Allen renders it, to work to reform disciplines and academic spaces.

The discussion of Allen's work so far locates *Pocahontas* as part of a larger process to generate knowledge through story, a process Linda Tuhiwai Smith identifies as integral to decolonization: "Story telling, oral histories, the perspectives of elders and of women have become integral parts of all Indigenous research." Smith continues, "These new stories contribute to a collective story in which every indigenous person has a place."[75] The work that Allen does to move the text away from romantic tropes as she foregrounds women's voices and the legitimacy of the spiritual is extraordinarily significant. As Joy Harjo remarks in an online tribute to Allen: "In her last celebrated book, *Pocahontas: Medicine Woman, Spy, Entrepreneur, Diplomat,* Paula flips the Disney Barbie doll image of Pocahontas and renews a female native image of woman to honor the Algonquin Beloved Woman, Pocahontas, and to give an image of empowerment to her descendents. All native women in this country are essentially Pocahontas's descendents."[76]

The type of value Harjo ascribes to Allen's work matters profoundly, given the ways in which Pocahontas's life is often linked to other forms of systemic racism that many Indigenous women experience, as the book titled *#NotYourPrincess: Voices of Native American Women* makes clear. Dedicated by Lisa Charleyboy to "every Indigenous woman who has been called Pocahontas," the work's paratext confirms the ubiquitous nature of a negative stereotype that Pocahontas's name has come to engender. For example, within this collection, Jessica Deer (Mohawk) protests the Pocahottie Halloween costumes as part of a larger system that "normalizes violence against us" (Indigenous women).[77] Like Deer, Lisa Monchalin connects violence against Indigenous women to misrepresentation in the popular media while also showing that it is "imperialism and preconceptions of European settlers, which have permeated institutions and become embedded in today's value systems."[78] When Allen's work to refigure Pocahontas's story is considered in this context, it demonstrates the vital value of her work to write a text in which Indigenous women's roles within their communities are properly acknowledged, because Allen shifts the focus of her life narrative away from a Eurocentric-male-authored archive that many scholars and public intellectuals continue, sometimes inadvertently, to privilege in their works.

The purpose of this essay is not to suggest that Allen's work, or the work of any author, is beyond critique.[79] It is to say, however, that care should be taken to consider the power relations inherent in knowledge production and to consider what is at stake when only one worldview is treated as legitimate over another. In her monograph *Malinche, Pocahontas, and Sacagawea: Indian Women as Cultural Intermediaries and National Symbols,* Rebecca K. Jager regards Allen's work as credible. Jager cites Allen liberally to develop her discussion about Pocahontas while pointing out that Allen's articulation of Pocahontas's life story is unique for its commitment to show that "Native women had powerful roles of consequence and that they exerted social authority, regardless of Europeans' unwillingness to understand or document it."[80] This statement suggests, quite correctly, that Allen's interpretation of the evidence produces a life narrative quite different from others written at the time, an important contribution given the ways in which those understandings achieved through story shape and reflect lived realities such as the violence that touches so many Indigenous women and their families.

However, Allen's worldview, which she explains in her introduction to *Pocahontas*, draws on evidence that is different from what other scholars embroiled in Western ways of knowing would consider credible; for instance, Allen remarks that the real witnesses to Pocahontas's life are "wind, rain, extinct forests, . . . and the like."[81] What this difference in approach has meant, as Jager briefly notes, and I have also discussed, is that Allen's work to "address the more nebulous aspects of the Powhatan spiritual world on which tangible evidence is lacking [has meant] academics have been quick to marginalize her works."[82] Thus Laura Mielke, who admires Allen's *Pocahontas* in some ways, makes the remark that Allen's "use of oral traditions to document the 'implicate order,' . . . literally requires a leap of faith on the part of the reader."[83] While Mielke's tone is ambivalent at this juncture, she perhaps unintentionally raises an important question: what might be lost if the work Allen does to write *Pocahontas* is dismissed because her methods are underpinned by a worldview that does not accord with what is considered to be correct scholarly practice?

Stephanie Sellers recalls Allen's response to her request that Allen supervise her doctoral work in Native American Studies. As Sellers remembers the exchange, Allen had grown weary of what she regarded as failed attempts to have "Indigenous history, experience, and literature" taken seriously by "the most likely misguided and misinformed faculty."[84] Sellers uses the phrase "the wall of ignorance" to describe the barriers Allen and other critics reading through an Indigenous worldview have faced as they sought acceptance in the academy.[85] Her remark is reminiscent of one made by Allen in *Pocahontas* when she predicts her reliance on the implicate will result in "a wall of denial" once the book is published.[86] Both Sellers's and Allen's remarks are striking to read against critical work by Sara Ahmed, who uses a similar metaphor of coming up against a "brick wall" to discuss how scholars doing diversity work in the university encounter systemic constraints.[87] For Ahmed, diversity work is "the work we do [to transform the institution] when we do not quite inhabit [its] norms."[88] The walls are beliefs and practices, like citation, that have been naturalized within the environment so that when a person does not acknowledge their authority in prescribed ways, it appears illogical or suspect—even when that person is actually doing vital work to expand the conversation.

Such frustrations are articulated by other Indigenous scholars as well; for instance, Jo-Ann Episkenew, in an essay titled "Socially Responsible Criticism," writes of her experiences as a student whose professor refused to acknowledge her reading of Leslie Marmon Silko's "Lullaby." The professor gave Episkenew a low grade for her essay about this text because her interpretation differed from his, even though Episkenew's response was reasoned and grew out of cultural knowledge she held as a Métis woman.[89] Had Episkenew's professor been willing or able to accept that different worldviews might produce different interpretations, she would no doubt have written quite a different essay about critical practice. As it sits, the anecdote she shares raises many urgent questions: How might instructors and critics who are non-Indigenous recognize and make sense of the limitations we bring to texts? What would a fair assessment of Episkenew's response to Silko's story have entailed, and how might students and instructors from different cultural backgrounds work together? What are the learning outcomes to be achieved when reading and studying Indigenous texts? Answers to such questions have to do with hiring practices and matters of pedagogy that go beyond the scope of this paper but that are also intimately tied to critical responses to Allen's *Pocahontas*.

As I mentioned at the beginning of this essay, I bring to this text a willingness to acknowledge my status as a novice, not merely in terms of the topics Allen raises but of the critical framework I bring to the reading of her text. For instance, Justice's way of reading, in which he thinks about "relationship, kinship, respect, and responsibility that Indigenous peoples articulate, separately and together," has helped me to appreciate Allen's writing as she works to lift women's voices, but my understanding of those profound relationships remains partial.[90] I would suggest that the discomfort that grows out of such an admission should also be accompanied by a willingness to enter into long-term processes of working toward enhanced understandings but with respect for cultural differences as well as boundaries, while also keeping in mind that not all knowledge exists for the taking. For this reason, I have been finding it helpful to reflect on Rauna Kuokkanen's advice. In her monograph *Reshaping the University*, she argues that academia privileges Eurocentric biases harbored by those "who have the luxury of not being aware of discourses other than their own."[91] In her view, the university can only productively move toward decolonization when it "gives up its control over knowledge and epistemes as well as the colonial mentality of superiority and supremacy."[92] Allen clearly encountered such attitudes as both a critic and a teacher, and she explains that she often felt conflicted over when, and how much, to share with learners when it came to offering information drawn from [Indigenous] ritual or myth.[93] Clearly, Allen felt her responsibilities as a university professor were at odds with those she held to her Laguna Pueblo community whose members safeguard their traditions and she took steps to disrupt presumptions.[94]

I believe Allen does something similar in *Pocahontas*. For instance, Allen provides a brief definition for *manito* in a glossary, which appears at the end of Pocahontas's biography—but follows it by stating that the word's meaning is "complex" and variable "depending on its context."[95] While Allen's approach does not necessarily provide me (a cultural outsider) with an answer that makes sense in the context of my worldview, it is the case that Allen's text is not necessarily for me—and that my tendency to read the text as a response to colonialism or an imperative to decolonize is in its own way an imposition on Allen who should not be required to parse her worldview for outsiders. By reflecting on these matters, and by locating those moments of the auto/biographical in and around Allen's text, it might be possible to shift Pocahontas's life narrative away from the hegemony imposed on it while also including voices historically marginalized by the academy.

Notes

For consistency, this essay maintains Paula Gunn Allen's usage of "Algonquin" for the people often called "Algonquian" in more recent scholarship.

1. Paula Gunn Allen, *Pocahontas: Medicine Woman, Spy, Entrepreneur, Diplomat* (San Francisco: HarperSanFrancisco, 2003), 3, 8. In this essay, the terms *life story* or *life narrative* are used. The latter, in particular, is an acknowledged "general term for acts of self-presentation of all kinds," primarily because it is a democratic term that does not privilege written communication. See Sidonie Smith and Julia Watson, *Reading Autobiography: A Guide for Interpreting Life Narratives*, 2nd ed. (Minneapolis: University of Minnesota Press, 2010), 4.

2. Paula Gunn Allen, "Thus Spake Pocahontas," in *Off the Reservation: Reflections on Boundary-Busting, Border-Crossing Loose Canons* (Boston: Beacon Press, 1998), 164.

3. In the introduction to the collection, *Off the Reservation*, under the subtitle "Pocahontas Looms at Her Loom," Allen remarks that "Thus Spake

Pocahontas" appeared in an earlier collection titled *Introduction to Scholarship in Modern Languages and Literatures,* in which the editors "changed the title of the work to 'Border Studies: The Intersection of Gender and Color' to fit the overall design of the volume" (Allen, *Off the Reservation,* 10).

4. Kristina Fagan et al., "Canadian Indian Literary Nationalism? Critical Approaches in Canadian Indigenous Contexts: A Collaborative Interlogue," *Canadian Journal of Native Studies* 29, no. 1–2 (2009): 40n2.

5. Sinclair's remarks are contained within his section of the jointly authored paper: Fagan et al., "Canadian Indian Literary Nationalism?," 20.

6. Allen, *Pocahontas,* 4.

7. Sophie McCall, Deanna Reder, Devis Gaertner, and Gabrielle L'Hirondelle Hill, eds., *Read, Listen, Tell: Indigenous Stories from Turtle Island* (Waterloo, Ontario, Canada: Wilfrid Laurier University Press, 2017), 4.

8. For a discussion of the term *settler,* see Daniel Heath Justice, *Why Indigenous Literatures Matter* (Waterloo, Ontario, Canada: Wilfrid Laurier University Press, 2018), 14–16.

9. Allen, *Pocahontas,* 14.

10. Linda Tuhiwai Smith, *Decolonizing Methodologies: Research and Indigenous Peoples* (London and New York: Zed Books, 2012), 44.

11. Smith, *Decolonizing Methodologies,* 44–45.

12. It was while I was completing a draft of this paper that the National Inquiry into Missing and Murdered Indigenous Women and Girls was released in Canada. Volume One of the document reports on Jesse Wente's commentary, an Indigenous man and "director of the Indigenous Screen Office [who] highlighted [Disney's] oversexualization of Pocahontas" (389). The report connects the misrepresentation of Pocahontas as part of a system that "legitimize[s] the Canadian government's lack of intervention and inadequate police investigations" and thus ultimately perpetuates violence responsible for the deaths and disappearances of Indigenous women, on scale that is genocidal (391). National Inquiry into Missing and Murdered Indigenous Women and Girls, "Reclaiming Power and Place: The Final Report of the National Inquiry into Missing and Murdered Indigenous Women and Girls, Volume 1A" (Canada, 2019), https://www.mmiwg-ffada.ca/wp-content /uploads/2019/06/Final_Report_Vol_1a-1.pdf.

13. For an overview of the field, please see Sidonie Smith and Julia Watson, *Reading Autobiography.* See also a special issue on Indigenous Biography in *Biography: An Interdisciplinary Quarterly* 39, no. 3 (Summer 2016).

14. Allen, *Pocahontas,* 8.

15. Robert Warrior, "Native Critics in the World," in *American Indian Literary Nationalism*, ed. Jace Weaver, Craig Womack, and Robert Warrior (Albuquerque: University of New Mexico Press, 2006), 196.

16. Menoukha R. Case and Stephanie A. Sellers, "Interview with Dr. Lisa Tatonetti," in *Weaving the Legacy: Remembering Paula Gunn Allen*, ed. Stephanie A. Sellers and Menoukha R. Case (Albuquerque: West End Press, 2017), 211.

17. Donald K. Sharpes, review of *Pocahontas: Medicine Woman, Spy, Entrepreneur, Diplomat*, by Paula Gunn Allen, *American Indian Culture and Research Journal* 28, no. 3 (2004): 162–65, quotation on 164.

18. John Burch, review of *Pocahontas: Medicine Woman, Spy, Entrepreneur, Diplomat*, by Paula Gunn Allen, *Library Journal* 128, no. 16 (2003): 88.

19. Burch, review of *Pocahontas*, 88.

20. Sinclair in Fagan et al, "Canadian Indian Literary Nationalism?," 40n2.

21. Elvira Pulitano, *Toward a Native American Critical Theory* (Lincoln: University of Nebraska Press, 2003), 56.

22. Lisa Brooks, "Afterword: At the Gathering Place," in Weaver, Womack, and Warrior, *American Indian Literary Nationalism*, 236.

23. Brooks, "Afterword," 234.

24. Allen, *Pocahontas*, 3.

25. Joanne M. Braxton, "A Shaman Writes Biography," review of *Pocahontas: Medicine Woman, Spy, Entrepreneur, Diplomat*, by Paula Gunn Allen, *Women's Review of Books* 21, no. 8 (2004): 11.

26. Laura L. Mielke, "A Tale Both Old and New: Jamestown at 400," book reviews, *American Quarterly* 60, no. 1 (2008): 173–82, quotation on 175.

27. Charles R. Larson, *American Indian Fiction* (Albuquerque: University of New Mexico Press, 1978), 20; Robert S. Tilton, *Pocahontas: The Evolution of an American Narrative* (Cambridge: Cambridge University Press, 1994), 389, 391; Helen C. Rountree, *Pocahontas, Powhatan, Opechancanough: Three Indian Lives Changed by Jamestown* (Charlottesville: University of Virginia Press, 2005), 19; Rayna Green, "The Pocahontas Perplex: The Image of Indian Women in American Culture," *The Massachusetts Review* 16, no. 4 (1975): 698–714, 700; Karen Ordahl Kupperman, *Pocahontas and the English Boys: Caught between Cultures in Early Virginia* (New York: New York University Press, 2019), vii.

28. Tilton, *Pocahontas*, 5.

29. Smith, *Decolonizing Methodologies*, 49.

30. Camilla Townsend, *Pocahontas and the Powhatan Dilemma: An American Portrait* (New York: Hill and Wang, 2004), 212.

31. Townsend, *Pocahontas and the Powhatan Dilemma*, 213.

32. Paula Gunn Allen, "Pocahontas to Her English Husband, John Rolfe," in *Skins and Bones: Poems 1979–87* (Albuquerque: West End Press, 1988), 9.

33. See William Strachey's *Historie of Travell into Virginia Britania*, which describes Pokahuntas "wheel[ing] so her self naked as she was all the fort over" (qtd. in Mossiker, 96). While Mossiker defends some of Strachey's language choices, such works nonetheless show the writers of these primary documents contribute to the exoticization of Pocahontas that is perpetuated in popular culture. Frances Mossiker, *Pocahontas: The Life and the Legend* (New York: Knopf, Random House, 1976).

34. Townsend, *Pocahontas and the Powhatan Dilemma*, 213.

35. Warrior, "Native Critics in the World," 195.

36. Daniel Heath Justice, *Why Indigenous Literatures Matter* (Waterloo, Ontario, Canada: Wilfrid Laurier University Press, 2018), 116.

37. McCall, Reder, Gaertner, and Hill, *Read, Listen, Tell*, 6.

38. Thomas King, *The Truth about Stories: A Native Narrative*, The CBC Massey Lectures (Toronto: House of Anansi Press, 2003), 2.

39. King, *The Truth about Stories*, 2.

40. King, *The Truth about Stories*, 77.

41. King, *The Truth about Stories*, 13.

42. McCall, Reder, Gaertner, and Hill, *Read, Listen, Tell*, 6.

43. Smith, *Decolonizing Methodologies*, 250.

44. Susanna Egan and Gabriele Helms, "Auto/Biography? Yes. But Canadian?," *Canadian Literature* 172 (Spring 2002): 7.

45. Sharpes, review of *Pocahontas*, 163.

46. Sharpes, 163.

47. Deanna Reder, "Writing Autobiographically: A Neglected Indigenous Intellectual Tradition," in *Across Cultures, Across Borders: Canadian Aboriginal and Native American Literatures*, ed. Paul Depasquale, Renate Eigenbrod, and Emma Larocque (Peterborough, Ontario, Canada: Broadview Press, 2010), 155, 156.

48. Reder, "Writing Autobiographically," 156.

49. Allen, *Pocahontas*, 2.

50. Allen, *Pocahontas*, 139.

51. McCall, Reder, Gaertner, and Hill, *Read, Listen, Tell*, 10.

52. Brooks, *The Common Pot*, 279.

53. Allen, *Pocahontas*, 169.

54. Allen, *Pocahontas*, 173.

55. Allen, *Pocahontas*, 171.

56. Rountree, *Pocahontas, Powhatan, Opechancanough*, 238.

57. Rountree, 238.

58. Rountree, 5.

59. Allen, *Pocahontas,* 174.

60. Allen, 174.

61. Allen, 173–74.

62. Sharpes, review of *Pocahontas,* 165.

63. Allen, *Pocahontas,* 29.

64. Allen, 29.

65. Allen, 156.

66. Allen, 218.

67. Allen, 96.

68. Allen, 98.

69. Allen, 96.

70. Brooks, "Afterword," 236.

71. Allen, *Pocahontas,* 218.

72. Allen, 308.

73. Justice, *Why Indigenous Literatures Matter,* 28.

74. See various essays in Sellers and Case, *Weaving the Legacy,* especially pp. 210, 115, 77–79.

75. Smith, *Decolonizing Methodologies,* 145.

76. Joy Harjo, "Her Pueblo Round Place: A Remembrance of Paula Gunn Allen," Women's Media Center, June 24, 2009, https://womensmediacenter.com /news-features/her-pueblo-round-place-a-remembrance-of-paula-gunn -allen.

77. Mary Beth Leatherdale and Lisa Charleyboy, eds., *#NotYourPrincess: Voices of Native American Women* (Toronto: Annick Press Ltd., 2017), dedication page; Jessica Deer (Mohawk), "We Are Not a Costume," in Leatherdale and Charleyboy, *#NotYourPrincess,* 61.

78. Lisa Monchalin, *The Colonial Problem: An Indigenous Perspective on Crime and Injustice in Canada* (Toronto: University of Toronto Press, 2016), 178–79.

79. Linwood Custalow and Angela L. Daniel, for instance, disagree with Allen's belief that Pocahontas may have been a spy. Their account, published in 2007, is based on oral history provided from the Mattaponi tribe, one of "few remaining tribes of the great Powhatan nation" (Linwood Custalow and Angela L. Daniel, *The True Story of Pocahontas: The Other Side of History; from the Sacred History of the Mattaponi Reservation People* [Golden, CO: Fulcrum Pub., 2007], 27, 116n3, 1.) Elsewhere, Robert Warrior alludes to the presence of essentialism in some of Allen's work (Warrior, "Native Critics in the World," 196).

80. Rebecca K. Jager, *Malinche, Pocahontas, and Sacagawea: Indian Women as Cultural Intermediaries and National Symbols* (Norman: University of Oklahoma Press, 2015), 238.

81. Allen, *Pocahontas*, 14.

82. Jager, *Malinche*, 238.

83. Mielke, "A Tale Both Old and New," 175.

84. Stephanie A. Sellers, "Writing the Good Fight," in Sellers and Case, *Weaving the Legacy*, 169.

85. Sellers, 170.

86. Allen, *Pocahontas*, 95.

87. Sara Ahmed, *Living a Feminist Life* (Durham: Duke University Press, 2017), 91.

88. Ahmed, 115.

89. Jo-Ann Episkenew, "Notes on Leslie Marmon Silko's 'Lullaby': Socially Responsible Criticism," in McCall, Reder, Gaertner, and Hill, *Read, Listen, Tell*, 320–22.

90. Justice, *Why Indigenous Literatures Matter*, 28.

91. Rauna Johanna Kuokkanen, *Reshaping the University: Responsibility, Indigenous Epistemes, and the Logic of the Gift* (Vancouver: UBC Press, 2007), 77.

92. Kuokkanen, *Reshaping the University*, 153.

93. Paula Gunn Allen, "Special Problems in Teaching Leslie Marmon Silko's *Ceremony*," in *Leslie Marmon Silko's "Ceremony": A Casebook*, ed. Allan Chavkin (Oxford: Oxford University Press, 2002), 83.

94. Allen, "Special Problems," 83.

95. Allen, *Pocahontas*, 334.

THE POCAHONTAS PATTERN

Intermarriage as a Political Strategy for Native American Women in Early Virginia

CAMILLA TOWNSEND

For at least twenty-five years now, historical studies of early America have been reliably multicultural in perspective. Historians regularly seek the perspectives of Indigenous peoples. Sadly, however, due to a paucity of traditional sources, we have often been left to present their thoughts and cultural expectations as probabilities, or even as mere guesswork. We can, for instance, envision the young Pocahontas in her new home with her English husband, the tobacco planter John Rolfe, and imagine the alienation she would have felt at times; but without diaries or letters, we can follow her thoughts no further.[1] In this essay, I would like to suggest that we might be able to do better if we were to widen our search for sources to include *all* that pertain to her Native American context, both broad and local, including linguistic evidence, rather than continuing to depend on narratives generated by Jamestown colonists.

Pocahontas was far from the only Indian woman in colonial Virginia to enter into a relationship with a white man. Archaeologists have uncovered extensive cohabitation even within the fort at Jamestown.[2] Historians have also offered direct evidence. Years before Pocahontas wed John Rolfe, the Reverend Alexander Whitaker chastised his fellow colonists for their sinful habits; he made himself few friends for mentioning the matter.[3] Decades later, in 1661, another pastor continued to lament the situation: "On the Lord's Day, the servants of the Christians Plantations nearest to the [Indians], being then at liberty, oft spend that day in visiting their Indian towns . . . to the great Scandall of the Christian religion."[4] Some of these liaisons were short, and some lasted longer, some even long enough to constitute what we could call common-law marriages.

In the not-so-distant past, historians made ribald jokes or occasionally even scathing commentary about this reality, placing Native American women in the position of being seen as whores. With the advent of the sexual revolution, the tone turned more jocular and celebratory, but it nevertheless remained condescending. "He found the freedoms and customs of aboriginal life irresistible and reverted to the old ways," wrote Carl Bridenbaugh about a "civilized" Indian who took multiple wives despite the pressure placed on him by his straightlaced European advisors.[5] Thankfully, the era of seeing Indigenous women simply as lascivious is finished. As soon as historians began to look at the situation from the Indigenous point of view, it rapidly became clear that Native women made choices regarding sexual and marriage partners according to old cultural custom that placed emphasis on women's serving as intermediaries. In 2001 Daniel Richter succinctly described Pocahontas's probable reasons for agreeing to marry John Rolfe after she had been a captive among the English for a year:

> Through her, the English and the Powhatans became fictive kin, and the ceremonial, political, and economic basis for peace, as people of Tsenacommacah understood that concept, became possible. . . . We need not idealize either the motives of [her father] Powhatan or the unanimity of his people to appreciate the genuine, if fragile, potential that Pocahontas' adoption and marriage represented or the ways in which that potential resonated with traditional Native practices. When Pocahontas took the name Rebecca and went to live among Europeans, she did so not to abandon her culture but to incorporate the English into her Native world, to make it possible for them to live in Indian country by Indian rules.[6]

In the interest of furthering the project of attempting to see the situation from an Indigenous perspective, I would like to suggest here that when an Indian woman in early colonial Virginia chose to have a relationship with a white man, she was not only making him kin, but also, or more specifically, *attempting to set the very terms of that kinship*. That is, Indian women were most certainly trying to bring the foreign men into their people's fold—establishing reciprocal gift giving, reducing the potential for violence, etc.—but they were *also* making more specific statements about what sorts of gifts were to change hands, who was to take advice from whom, and what was to be the fate of the children. The colonists, naturally, were deaf to those statements, but I will argue that the Indian women were making them nonetheless, at least for the first two generations.

We must, of course, be cautious in our assertions. Prior scholars have already offered theories about general efforts by Indigenous people of the Chesapeake to make and cement peace through marriage; they have considered both the double consciousness and mutual misunderstandings potentially produced. "In 1650," wrote Virginia Bernhard, also in the early 2000s, "Giles Brent, a Maryland planter married a young Indian woman named Mary Kitomaquund, the daughter of a Piscataway chief."[7] Many years later, she explained, Mary Kitomaquund's son, Giles Brent Jr., broke away from Nathaniel Bacon's rebel forces at the time they were pillaging Indian communities. "One wonders if Brent's consciousness of his mixed-race status and thoughts of his Indian mother influenced his decision," Bernhard added. One wonders, but one cannot know; there could have been any number of possible reasons for Giles Junior's behavior. Pocahontas's own mixed child would later fight hard alongside the colonists against Virginia Indians. Fortunately, highly responsible scholarship on Mary Kitomaquund and her children, addressing the possible pain the former faced, is now being undertaken, but it will remain difficult to understand their experiences.[8]

The motivations and thought patterns of ordinary Indian women are admittedly largely lost to us. We will probably never be able to know when the average Native woman was exchanging sex for the ability to feed her family in the most immediate sense and when she was trying to establish a long-term relationship that we might translate as a "marriage," in that it involved specific commitments that both she and her partner made to each other. And even in the latter cases, we will be hard put to recognize whether a Native woman was engaging in such a project in order to strengthen trade ties that helped her extended family or her band or her tribe, or in order to stave off attempts on the part of white neighbors to take over her people's farmlands, or in order to render her sons more powerful by giving them blood connections in another culture, or in order to accomplish all of the above, or none.

We can, however, be sure that careful thinking on these subjects was occurring among many women, and that they were attempting to communicate their expectations to the colonists, for one reason: we do have evidence—to be presented here—that it occurred among highborn (or noble) Powhatan women, concerning whom we have more information than we do about most Indigenous women of the era. And given that Algonkian society was relatively egalitarian—in the sense that noble families lived and moved and labored alongside everybody else—it seems likely that their ways of thinking were not so far different from other people's. It seems we can know something about what Pocahontas thought about her marriage to an Englishman: her specific understandings are not utterly lost to us.

James Merrell has addressed the straight-jacketing nature of the English-language terminology and even categories of analysis we have grown to rely on over the years in our scholarly works regarding Indigenous peoples.[9] Numerous others have argued that the very notion of a certain person necessarily belonging within a certain definable "culture" is problematic: the culture concept shifted profoundly in the 1980s and 1990s, in the wake of scholars' recognition that all individuals are embedded within multiple contexts, subject to changing socioeconomic structures, and capable of varied responses.[10] If we are to be accused of a certain lack of imagination, even in this scholarly era valuing complexity and creative thinking, we must consider carefully the nature of the trap in which we sometimes find ourselves, as well as our potential paths out of the difficulties. It would seem that perhaps the heart of the problem is that in our studies of early North America, we are per force reduced to working largely with sources written in English, or occasionally another European language. How can we challenge our own ways of thinking about a subject, or enter into it from a subject's alternate perspective, if we ourselves are working from within a single linguistic frame of reference—or, if our educations did provide us with access to multiple languages, they were generally not that of our subjects?

It is logical that richer analyses of cultural interactions and explorations of possible interpretations of Indigenous actions have been produced for Mesoamerica, where the sources frequently allow us to read Indigenous people's thoughts in texts written for their own posterity in their own languages.[11] We have long assumed that in the vast territories above the Rio Grande, we have little access to sources in Indigenous languages. We have thought that, with very few exceptions, our only hope was to read between the lines of the limited texts left us by Europeans, and we have tried to rise to the challenge. In the case of Pocahontas's story, for instance, there is very little else to read, and we have attempted to make do. The Algonkian family's Powhatan language (a fluid set of mutually intelligible dialects once ranging from the Chesapeake to the Carolinas, sometimes called "Virginia Algonkian") is in fact dead; there have been no speakers since at least the mid-nineteenth century, and no one wrote in it while it was still a living language.[12] An exceptionally large group of loanwords is all that remains in common usage (including *chum, hominy, matchcoat, moccasin, muskrat, opossum, pone, raccoon, terrapin,* and *tomahawk*). However, of the works written by early seventeenth-century Englishmen about the region, at least three include linguistic evidence that is well worth consulting: it may not be enough to reconstitute the language, but it may nevertheless be revelatory of certain aspects of culture and behavior.[13] William Strachey created an especially painstaking vocabulary list, entitled "A Dictionarie of the Indian Language" which he appended to his book manuscript, *The Historie of Travell into Virginia Britania.*[14] The document was once used to create movie dialogue;[15] scholars have yet to plumb its depths or that of other linguistic information offered by Strachey in his text.

It was my study of other Native American culture groups which first alerted me to the fact that Indigenous intermarriage was traditionally about something much more complex than our notion of "alliance." Rather than being statements about "making love, not war," marriages between members of different groups were essentially used to delineate or clarify a power hierarchy and were often the products of intense negotiation and outright conflict. Without digressing from Virginia too extensively, I will offer an illustrative example. In the world of the Nahuas, or Aztecs, we have access to texts written in the mid-sixteenth century that abound in the details of pre-conquest life and thought: young men who had learned the Roman alphabet from the friars used it to transcribe dozens of performances of old-style oral histories and legends. One of the most compelling stories—undoubtedly apocryphal—concerns a fifteenth-century noblewoman from Cuernavaca named Miyahuaxihuitl (Mi-ya-wa-SHEE-wit) or "Corn Tassel Flower." Cuernavaca was (and is) about one hundred miles to the south and west of the city of Mexico, where the Aztecs were then struggling to rise from their former position of weakness to one of great strength. Their high chief or king, Huitzilihuitl (Wee-tzil-EE-wit), was in the process of bringing wives from several locales to live with him, but only his primary wife would be the mother of his heirs. Huitzilihuitl sent emissaries to the high chief of the Cuernavaca region, but he was flatly rejected: "What is Huitzilihuitl saying? What will he give my daughter there on the island [where he lives]? Perhaps he will clothe her with water plant thread, with marsh plants, as he clothes and provides for himself, with breeches made of marsh plants? And what will he give her to eat? Is that place like it is here, where all the various foods have been grown, the fruits and the cotton that one needs for clothing? Do this: Go; tell your ruler Huitzilihuitl, tell him definitely that you are not to come here again."[16] The implied question and comment was, "Will he make her a true queen? Since the answer is 'no,' then get out." The closing words ("*aocmo ceppa anhuallazque nican*") were very strong. They literally translate as, "Not even one more time are you to come here."

The Aztecs, however, whether driven on by the stories of the lovely Miyahuaxihuitl or Cuernavaca's many cotton plants, would not take "no" for an answer. This was in fact the period in which they launched a major war against the cotton region, but what the story goes on to tell us is that the Aztec king made an arrow out of a precious jade, the essence of his royal line, and shot it over the wall into Miyahuaxihuitl's garden. "And when the reed fell in the middle of the courtyard, when the maiden Miyahuaxihuitl saw that the reed came from the heavens, that it fell in the courtyard as if given from the heavens, then she took it up on her hand and marveled at it." She was so spellbound by the lovely gem's shimmering colors that she popped it into her mouth—and thereby became pregnant.[17] Thus did the Aztec king win her as a bride. But, as one historian reminds us, "the conquest was mutual, for when Miyahuaxihuitl internalized the fertile stone, she was power incarnate."[18] Cuernavaca became such an important ally of the Aztecs that Miyahuaxihuitl eventually found herself considered to be the primary wife, not a concubine. It was, in the end, *her* son who inherited the "reed mat" (the throne) from Huitzilihuitl and ruled over tens of thousands.

Anthropologists have provided names for what we are seeing in this story and others like it. Interdynastic *hypogamy* occurs when a subordinate ruler marries the daughter of a superordinate ruler and their son succeeds to the subordinate rulership. This can sometimes work well for the less powerful chieftaincy, rendering their future ruler a close ally of a powerful nation, or it can be particularly painful, especially if the heir is raised in his mother's distant and powerful home and only appears to take up the reins of power in his father's homeland later in his life. Interdynastic *hypergamy* occurs when a subordinate ruler gives his daughter to a superordinate ruler without any understanding that a child of theirs will succeed to anything. It marks an even more pronounced vassalage, as, in our terms, the daughter is considered more a concubine than a wife. Interdynastic *isogamy* occurs between equals. It is understood when one chief gives his daughter to another; in this case their child will be the heir to the father's throne.[19]

These types of relationship are not fixed forever between any two villages but rather are subject to contention—to war and politics. Indeed, the Meso-americans frequently delineated their political arrangements through arguments over what type of intermarriage was at play. If we were to translate the story of Miyahuaxihuitl into the formalized language of anthropologists, the Aztecs were demanding hypergamy, but they got isogamy.

Let us return now to the eastern woodlands of North America, but not yet to the Powhatan region. We should first consider what we know about the Algonkians writ large. Thanks to Ann Marie Plane's meticulous research in New England court cases involving Indians, we now know with certainty what was once only inferred: Algonkians of the eastern seaboard—at least the Narragansetts of New England—resembled other sedentary and semi-sedentary Native Americans in that their culture encompassed a range of marriage practices that were tightly tied to their social hierarchy. The kind of relationship a person was understood to be in depended on numerous specific factors—whether the woman had originally been taken in war, whether her biological or adoptive family approved of the relationship, whether bride wealth had been given, etc. As among the Aztecs, chiefs could marry whomever and whenever they liked, but the children of commoner wives or of certain kinds of foreigners could not *succeed* them.[20]

Many and possibly most of the Virginia Indian tribes were matrilineal—meaning that power passed through the women's line: the chieftaincy and perhaps some property passed not from father to son but from a man to his sister's son. This means that marriage and politics had to be connected somewhat differently than they were among the Aztecs or even the Narragansetts. But they were connected, nonetheless. Pocahontas's father Powhatan clearly used a typical combination of warfare and intermarriage to augment his power, that is, to create his paramount chieftaincy. Indeed, such marriages were probably often offered by less powerful groups in order to end or avert a war. It has long been known that Powhatan married women from various tribes in order to create alliances. After a period of married life, the women returned to their natal villages, though the children were left to grow up with him after the age of four. (It was a startled English boy who had been left among the Indians to learn their language who reported on the exact arrangements: "If any of ye Kings wives have once a child by him, he keeps hir no longer but puts hir from him giving hir suffitient Copper and beads to mayntayne hir and the child while it is younge and then it is taken from hir and maintained by ye King, it now being lawfull for hir beinge thus put away to marry with any other.")[21] Instinctively a number of us have believed that it was most likely that Powhatan married women from other villages' ruling (or noble) families, women whose sons were expected to inherit, so that other villages would not feel that their chiefly line had been destroyed, and yet the heirs would be aligned with Powhatan. In effect, he would have been practicing a sexually reversed version of the Aztecs' hypogamy, in which a subordinate nation accepts the daughter of a more powerful state as a marriage partner for their chief, understanding that the child born to her will be their future monarch and may not even be raised in their homeland. We have known that in at least two cases Powhatan cleverly combined aspects of matrilineality and polygyny to cement his power: he married *werowansquas,* female chiefs who ruled when there were no appropriate nephews available and whose own children were expected to inherit power, as they were the carriers of the line.[22] However, it has not been at all clear who the other wives were. Perhaps randomly selected pretty women whom he wanted, implied some.

I believe I have now found evidence that Powhatan regularly married the sisters of the ruling chiefs of the tribes of his paramountcy—exactly the women we would expect him to marry according to theory, those who were destined to mother political heirs. William Strachey's work proves more illuminating that it first appears, sometimes almost despite himself.[23] In his book, Strachey copied a great deal from John Smith and others, but he also produced a compendium of all the data he was able to collect while living at Jamestown for a year, based largely on his questioning of two Indigenous men, called Kempo and Machumps. As we might expect, he made many errors that are invisible at first glance. For instance, he told one of his interlocutors that he was hungry. The response he got was, "Cuttassamais," and so he recorded it as the word for one who begs; in fact, based on other Algonkian languages, we know that it means, "I will give you food."[24] But he left us important information, nevertheless.

Strachey carefully recorded the names of thirty-two werowances and werowansquas who paid tribute to Powhatan, estimating how many warriors they commanded, and in some cases giving a few sentences of additional information. Among them he listed "Coquonasum," chief of the Appamatuck, and Opussoquonuske, whom he explicitly said was sister to Coquonasum and chief of a neighboring small village of Appamatucks. In the context of Strachey's spelling habits elsewhere, the name *Coquonasum* could have been a rendition of either Kokwonasum or Sokwonasum.[25] The latter is far more likely, given that the sister's name (Oposokwonaske) was thus literally a female rendition of her brother's (Sokwonasum) plus the prefix represented by "Opo" (yielding Opo-sokwonaske). The different ending is easily explained: in numerous Algonkian languages, including Powhatan, the suffix *-sk(wa)* or *-sk(i)* was the feminine marker, with the final vowel, as in many languages, pronounced only when it was phonetically convenient. Indeed, *-skwa-* often functioned as a root word meaning "the quality of being female." Strachey tells us in his Dictionarie, for instance, that the word for "girl" was *usquasens*. Taken together, then, Strachey's information tells us that the prefix *o-* or *opo-* (perhaps *ah-* or *ahpo-*) apparently meant "sister to," or possibly "sibling to."[26]

Elsewhere in his book, Strachey provided a list of the names of Powhatan's wives who currently lived with him, but in the case of this list, he provided no other identifiers or descriptions, just the names.[27] I wondered if any of them were female variants of the names of any of Powhatan's subordinate chiefs. To my surprise, I soon saw that *at least five* of the twelve were (see table 1). Several facts suffice to explain why these common word roots have not been obvious to anyone before: (1) the Powhatan language included extensive dialectical variation in pronunciation and Strachey's sources were apparently from two different villages; (2) Englishmen found it difficult to distinguish Powhatan phonemes—that is, they often could not distinguish what they were hearing; and (3) even the well-educated William Strachey displayed the variations in English spelling so common in his era, and these often mislead us now, masking common roots. But when we reduce the names to their most probable pronunciation, the pattern is striking.

Given the impediments mentioned above to common phonetic roots showing through to modern readers, I think it is probable that there are other pairings in the two lists, hidden to us today. There are several likely candidates, but if we begin to have to change elements as they are given to us by Strachey, we may be entering into the zone of wishful thinking, and thus we should not do it. It is sufficient to say that we have proof that Powhatan was married to female relatives of at least five of his subordinate chiefs. Two of them, whose

TABLE 1. Names of Powhatan's wives that were female variants of names of his subordinate chiefs

CHIEF'S NAME	POWHATAN'S WIFE	CHIEF, PHONETICALLY	WIFE, PHONETICALLY
Amapetough of Nansemond	Amopotoiske	*Amopoto*	*Amopotoisk*(i)
Ashuaquid of Arahateck	Ashetoiske [Ashekwiske][1]	*Ashakwid*	*Ashakwisk*(i) [*Ashetwisk*(i)]
Attossomunk of Paraconos	Attossocomisk	*Atosomunk*	*Atosocomisk*
Pomiscutuck of Youghtenand	Appomosiscut	*Pomoskutuk*	Ah-*pomos*[os]*kut*[2]
Werowough of Youghtamund	Oweroughwough	*Werowo*	Ah-*werowo*

1. This is the only place where I suggest that we substitute a consonant. Strachey could very easily have misheard *Ashekwiski* as *Ashetwiski*, and if so, the roots fit perfectly. Indeed, he very often confused *s* and *t*, so often that one scholar has hypothesized that he had difficulty reading his own notes where those letters were concerned. See Siebert, "Resurrecting Virginia Algonquian," 293.

2. According to linguists, reduplication of a syllable as a prefix or suffix does not indicate that the root is actually different.

names begin with *ah-*, were certainly the "sisters of," and the other three could have been sisters or daughters of chiefs, depending on whether their people were matrilineal or patrilineal.

Powhatan's primary wife was understood to be a woman whom Strachey called "Winganuske." None of the chronicles tell us where she was from (though the informant Machumps said he was her brother), but a primary wife always represented an important political alliance with a relative equal. Indeed, "Winganuske" probably was a title, meaning something like, "Good Lady." The word "Wingan" definitely meant "good." The addition of the feminine marker suffix likely yielded a recognized title. Ancient Native histories often gave a queen or leading noblewoman such a universally recognized title.[28]

Nor were these women the only wives chosen for their political affiliation, or with the idea that they represented a certain type of relationship between the polities. In the cases of the neighboring Kekoughtan people as well as the Quiocohannock, we know that Powhatan was married to their ruling female chiefs (or werowansquas) and had children by them who were expected to inherit.[29] These, however, likely did not live with him for much time, if any at all. We can say, then, since Powhatan had twelve wives in residence, that at least half of the chief's currently active marriage relationships represented political alliances. And in effect, whenever he had married women *without* noble names, who were from militarily conquered tribes without rights and whose children would inherit nothing, he was simply making a different kind of political statement: he and his people had the power, and they did not.

What is more difficult to track is the extent to which these Indigenous tactics regarding the use of intermarriage as a political strategy lasted into the colonial era. We have only a tiny handful of examples of Indian-white relationships about which enough is known for us to make any kind of assessment. We have the 1614 marriage of Pocahontas to John Rolfe, together with the purported rejection on Powhatan's part of a comparable marriage for another daughter of his; the 1638 marriage of Elizabeth, daughter of the Nansemond werowance, to John Basse, son of a leading colonist; and the 1650s long-term relationship between Cockacoeske, werowansqua of the Pamunkey, and Colonel John West. Helen Rountree, who did an exhaustive search, also found a 1655 case of the Nanticoke "emperor's daughter" having a long-term liaison with an Englishman, as well as a 1688 case of an indentured Indian servant girl being allowed to marry the white man who had made her pregnant.[30] (Then in 1691, marriage on the part of whites to anyone of Indian or African descent was made illegal.) In neither of these additional cases is there enough known for us to deduce anything about Indian thinking in the matter, so we are left with our three instances. Although the analyzable sample is small, it is highly illuminating.

Pocahontas was the daughter of a politically unimportant mother; her mother was not the sister of a sitting chief, and thus she herself stood to inherit nothing, even though Powhatan was her father. Her first husband, an Indian, was a warrior, not a chief; it was just the kind of marriage we would have expected for her, according to theory. Of course, the English did not understand this, and envisioned her as a princess. They proposed to Powhatan that she marry one of their own after she had been kept among them as a prisoner for a year, and he assented. What he was assenting to, in his mind, probably was not a grand union, in which a daughter of his who carried great political power in her person became the wife of an equally ranked chief. Rather, an expendable daughter who had become a prisoner of war was being given the usual option of such prisoners when they won the affections of one of the enemy warriors:

she could marry and save herself from a life of misery. If in addition the English believed she was a woman of great standing, a crucial chip in a peace negotiation, so much the better. When, soon after, the English asked for another daughter, a favored daughter of the important wife named Winganuske, Powhatan declined in no uncertain terms. That daughter, he said, was already affianced to an important chief in Tsenacomoco, several days' walk away.[31] Her children were destined to inherit power, and it was essential to him that she ally herself strategically. It would have been unthinkable to have allowed her son, who was to be a chief, to be raised by the English, to be used by the English, to be, in essence, English.

By 1638, times had changed somewhat. The rebellion of 1622—I ask readers to allow me to use that problematic term for lack of a better one, even though the Indians had never consented to English governance—had brought English power into relief. Ultimately, the initial Indigenous triumph for a few days in March had caused the English to strengthen themselves. The Nansemonds, just south of the James River, were in danger of utter destruction. At this point, marriage with the English on the part of a woman of the noble line had become an astute move rather than an unthinkable one. In table 1, we see that Powhatan was married to a Nansemond woman who was as likely to have been the daughter as the sister of the current chief: she did not carry the *ah-* or *ahp-* ("sister" or "sibling of") prefix in her name. The Nansemonds, then, may well have been patrilineal. The daughter of the werowance, in that case, could carry on his political line if necessary. When she married, it would be important.

A daughter of the reigning Nansemond chief had taken the Christian name Elizabeth and had married John Basse, the son of Nathaniel Basse, who had extensive neighboring landholdings and who would later be a member of the House of Burgesses. This was no example of hypergamy, however, in which a subordinate people give up a beloved daughter to their political superiors, knowing that they cannot protect her and can hope for nothing for her children, that they must simply lose her. No, Elizabeth was given a church marriage. She was taken "in Holy Baptism and in Holy Matrimonie" on the fourteenth day of August 1638 and was entered into the Basse family prayer book that had come from England. Her children implicitly were successors to the family name and property. (The prayer book remained in their family's hands until at least the end of the twentieth century.) The Nansemonds also vested themselves in her person and in the persons of her heirs; some Nansemond lands became her children's lands and her grandchildren and great-grandchildren still considered themselves Nansemond and married with Indians. They continued to live in the area until the early eighteenth century, when they moved to the Great Dismal Swamp. "Elizabeth" did not simply disappear into her English family. Like the Aztecs of old, Nathaniel Basse probably hoped for hypergamy when he consented to let his son marry the girl, but because of the ability of the Nansemonds to assert themselves, he got isogamy.[32]

The situation of Cockacoeske appears to be at all puzzling at first, but when we apply a Native lens, the picture in this case, too, resolves itself most logically. Cockacoeske was a Pamunkey noblewoman. Her first husband, Totopotomoy, who ruled as chief, had apparently been her cousin; they were both descendants of Opechancanough. When Totopotomoy was killed fighting alongside the English against mutual Indian foes, power should technically have passed to his sister or her son. Apparently, there was no such person available and fit to rule, for as his female cousin (it did not matter that she was also his widow) Cockacoeske stepped in. She ruled for thirty years, from the time of her husband's death in 1656 to her own death in 1686. Early in her widowhood, she entered into a union with Colonel John West, an important English colonist, a grandson of the former governor Sir Thomas West, Lord De La Warr. By him she bore a son, also named John West.[33]

We know relatively little of John West's upbringing, but it is clear that his father saw to it that he was exposed to Anglo ways. The child was very publicly his namesake, recognized as such by people in the English world. He learned to speak English, and to write at least the alphabet (possibly more) in a clear, strong hand. Later, at the time of the signing of an important treaty, other Indians (including the boy's mother) received such gifts as lined robes and scarlet stockings, but the English officials involved recommended that young John West be given in addition to the usual garments a white beaver hat, a finely embroidered belt, a sword and filigreed pistols; they assumed he would be an astute judge of English goods.[34]

In the 1670s, as the tensions that would culminate in Bacon's Rebellion percolated, John West the son served as his mother's interpreter in her political relations with the colonials. Though she spoke some English, he could speak better, and he could explain not only phrases she did not understand but probably also the more mysterious aspects of English culture. With his help and support, she successfully negotiated her way through what were—for Indians—the horrors of Bacon's Rebellion.

Although the son was indeed useful to the mother, the events at first appear a bit incomprehensible, viewed from the perspective of Indigenous marriage relations. Why would Cockacoeske accept these terms? Colonel West did *not* marry her in any church ceremony—indeed, in about 1664, when their son would have been about eight, he chose to marry an English woman named Unity. So Cockacoeske in no sense held the position of "first wife." Her son's exposure to Anglo ways would indicate that he spent at least part of his earliest years with his father. In fact, he may have spent time with him even after his father's marriage to the English woman. (By the 1680s, according to an extant legal document, Colonel John West and Unity were "parted and lived asunder."[35])

In a pattern reminiscent of ancient hypogamy, young John was at least partly raised by his more powerful parent and his people, thus establishing personal allegiance to them to some degree. Cockacoeske's children were supposed to inherit power—so what did she think she was doing? Only a few years later, Aphra Behn would write a play about Cockacoeske entitled *The Widow Ranter or, the History of Bacon in Virginia* (1690). Echoing English assumptions about Pocahontas's motivations for everything she did, Behn had Cockacoeske sigh and say about Nathaniel Bacon, "I adore this General!" She added that despite her "endeavors to destroy her love" for this Englishman, she could not. But we know better than to accept any such assessment of her motivations, and must ask how and why Cockacoeske would have accepted such arrangements for her people's future chief?

The answer is that she did not. When she died in 1686, the English must have been stunned by the turn of events. For years they had been dealing with John West the younger as though he represented his people, or soon would. But it turned out he only held power, with authority to sign treaties, as long as he was his mother's deputy. At her death, it was not Cockacoeske's son John or any of his progeny who took up the chiefly line, but Cockacoeske's sister's child, a woman named Betty. The English learned that "Ye Pamunkey Indians did desire that ye late Queen's niece upon [whom] ye right of Government of that Indian nation doe devolve, might succeed."[36] This was perfectly legitimate within the matrilineal Pamunkey frame of reference, if Cockacoeske and her people agreed that she herself had not borne an appropriate ruler. Nearly eighty years had passed since the colonists had first arrived, and many cataclysmic changes had ensued, but the significance of various types of marriages had apparently not yet shifted in many Powhatan minds.

Pocahontas, Elizabeth, Cockacoeske: none left us a single diary entry or letter. Yet if we immerse ourselves in their language and cultural assumptions, as well as those of their neighbors, their full context becomes clearer to us, along with many of the choices they made. Our sources tell us more about their thoughts than we once thought they did.

Notes

1. For my past efforts to "read between the lines" of English sources, see my book *Pocahontas and the Powhatan Dilemma* (New York: Hill & Wang, 2004). Chapter 7 ("Pocahontas and John") addresses the question of her marriage. In this essay my goal is quite different.
2. The best presentation of this material is found in the museum at Historic Jamestowne. For more information, consult David Givens, senior staff archaeologist. Not only was Indigenous-style food being prepared on a regular basis, but even more significantly, traditional Native white beads, such as those used to celebrate marriage, were being produced within the confines of the fort.
3. Marquis de Flores to Philip III of Spain, August 1612, in Alexander Brown, *Genesis of the United States* (1890; New York: Russell & Russell, 1964), 572–73. The Spanish ambassador is furnishing spy reports from Jamestown that tell of the complaints made by an unnamed minister. The two possible candidates would be Richard Buck and Alexander Whitaker; it was almost certainly the latter. Kathleen Brown has analyzed the ways in which English colonists sexualized Indian women from a very early period, more so, in fact, than they did African women, probably because of earlier proximity. See her "Native Americans and Early Modern Concepts of Race," in *Empire and Others: British Encounters with Indigenous Peoples, 1600–1850*, ed. M. Daunton and R. Halpern (Philadelphia: University of Pennsylvania Press, 1999), 94–95.
4. Report to the Bishop of London written by a colonist, 1661, cited in David Smits, "Abominable Mixture: Toward the Repudiation of Anglo-Indian Intermarriage in Seventeenth-Century Virginia," *Virginia Magazine of History and Biography* 95, no. 2 (1987): 188–89
5. Carl Bridenbaugh, *Early Americans* (New York: Oxford University Press, 1981), 13.
6. Daniel Richter, *Facing East from Indian Country: A Native History of Early America* (Cambridge: Harvard University Press, 2001), 77–78.
7. Virginia Bernhard, "Pocahontas Was Not the Only One: Indian Women and Their English Liaisons in Seventeenth-Century Virginia," in *Searching*

for Their Places: Women in the South across Four Centuries, ed. Thomas Appleton and Angela Boswell (Columbia, MO: University of Missouri Press, 2003), 25.

8. Kelly Watson, "Mary Kittamaquund Brent, 'The Pocahontas of Maryland': Sex, Marriage and Diplomacy in the Seventeenth-Century Chesapeake," *Early American Studies* 19, no. 1 (2021): 24–63. Watson demonstrates through a careful evaluation of the evidence that the very young Mary Kitomaquund was not in control of the situation.

9. James Merrell, "Second Thoughts on Colonial Historians and American Indians," *William and Mary Quarterly* 69, no. 3 (July 2012): 451–512.

10. For an entrée into this discussion as it was formulated in the '80s, see James Clifford, *The Predicament of Culture* (Cambridge: Harvard University Press, 1988). For a sampling of scholars who have chided their peers for continuing to delight in explaining certain people's actions as a function of a singular or fixed culture, see such works as Sam Gill, *Mother Earth: An American Story* (Chicago: University of Chicago Press, 1987); Gananath Obeyesekere, *The Apotheosis of Captain Cook: European Mythmaking in the Pacific* (Princeton: Princeton University Press, 1992); Bruce Lincoln, *Theorizing Myth: Narrative, Ideology and Scholarship* (Chicago: University of Chicago Press, 1999). Scholars have turned increasingly to the concept of ethnogenesis as opposed to culture. See Eric Hinderaker and Rebecca Horn, "Territorial Crossings: Histories and Historiographies of the Early Americas," *William and Mary Quarterly* 67 (July 2010): 395–432; and Jorge Cañizares Esguerra and James Sidbury, "Mapping Ethnogenesis in the Early Modern Atlantic," *William and Mary Quarterly* 68 (April 2011): 181–208.

11. In the 1970s and '80s, the study of Indigenous people's histories transformed the history of colonial Latin American from the study of baroque arts and vice-regal politics to the study of interactions between Natives and newcomers. In the literature in Spanish, the shift was gradual and has accelerated only recently as increasing numbers of scholars have become better versed in Native languages, particularly Nahuatl, which was used as a lingua franca in many regions of the colonial Mexico. In the Anglophone world, the monumental work that both marked the moment of readiness in the field and rendered further change possible was James Lockhart's *The Nahuas after the Conquest* (Stanford: Stanford University Press, 1992).

12. Helen Rountree discusses the evidence of diminishing language use through the colonial era in her *Pocahontas's People: The Powhatan Indians of Virginia through Four Centuries* (Norman: University of Oklahoma, 1990). A few

scholars have tried to resurrect what they can of the language. The best of these is Frank Siebert, "Resurrecting Virginia Algonquian from the Dead: The Reconstituted and Historical Phonology of Powhatan," in *Studies in Southeastern Indian Languages,* ed. James M. Crawford (Athens: University of Georgia Press, 1975).

13. Thomas Harriot offers important insight into the related language spoken by the Roanoke in his *Brief and True Report of the New Found Land of Virginia* (London, 1590). John Smith also recorded language lessons he had with Pocahontas and made some vocabulary lists, published in his *Map of Virginia* (London, 1612). Most importantly, William Strachey composed what he called "A Dictionarie of the Indian Language" (see following note). Careful reading of these texts reveals more than the names of a limited list of items. Through Smith, for example, we learn that *wanches-* was the root of words for "boy." When the person kidnapped by Sir Walter Raleigh told his captors to call him Wanchese, he probably was not giving them his name at all. See Townsend, *Pocahontas and the Powhatan Dilemma,* 11.

14. Between 1609 and 1612, William Strachey worked on his manuscript, "The History of Travel into Virginia Britannia." He hoped it would be published, but it never was in his lifetime. Three copies survive: one in the British Library (often called the Bacon/ Sloan MS), one in Oxford's Bodleian Library (often called the Ashmole MS), and one at the Princeton University Library (often called the Percy MS). The names come from the people he dedicated the copies to; the handwritings vary and are clearly not all Strachey's. The first two iterations (but not the Percy MS) include an appendix Strachey called "A Dictionarie of the Indian Language." In 1849, The Hakluyt Society published the Bacon/Sloan manuscript for the first time, and in 1953, the society published the Percy manuscript. In 1955, part of the Ashmole MS was published in facsimile: John Harrington, ed., "The Original Strachey Vocabulary of the Virginia Indian Language," *Bureau of American Ethnology Bulletin 157* (Anthropological Papers No. 46. Washington, DC: Government Printing Office, 1955). A published transcription of the Dictionarie only is William Strachey, *A Dictionary of Powhatan,* edited by Frederic Gleach, American Language Reprints No. 8 (Southampton, PA: Evolution Publishers, 1999, 2005).

15. Blair Rude used the vocabulary to create Native language dialog for Terrence Malick's 2007 film. See his piece "Giving Voice to Powhatan's People: The Creation of Virginia Algonquian Dialogue for *The New World,*" *Southern Quarterly* 51, 4 (Summer 2014): 29–37. Rude's effort drew a great deal of

attention from the media. It is certainly a worthy project, but the language cannot actually be resuscitated from the surviving material (as Rude himself acknowledges, though the media failed to understand).

16. Don Domingo de San Antón Chimalpahin Quauhtlehuanitzin, *Codex Chimalpahin*, vol. 1, ed. Arthur J. O. Anderson and Susan Schroeder (Norman: University of Oklahoma Press, 1997), 120–21.

17. This was a common motif in ancient Indigenous stories: young maidens became pregnant eating powerful gems or seeds. It is present in the Andes (in the Huarochirí Manuscript) and elsewhere in Mesoamerica (in the Annals of Cuauhtitlan). For discussion, see my *Annals of Native America: How the Nahuas of Colonial Mexico Kept Their History Alive* (New York: Oxford University Press, 2016).

18. Susan Schroeder, "The First American Valentine: Nahua Courtship and Other Aspects of Family Structuring in Mesoamerica," *Journal of Family History* 23, no. 4 (1998): 341–44.

19. Pedro Carrasco, "Royal Marriages in Ancient Mexico," in *Explorations in Ethnohistory: The Indians of Central Mexico in the Sixteenth Century*, ed. H. R. Harvey and H. Press (Albuquerque: University of New Mexico Press, 1984). Carrasco brilliantly shows how the Aztecs used the delineation of types of marriage relations as a strategy to bolster their power.

20. Ann Marie Plane, *Colonial Intimacies: Indian Marriage in Early New England* (Ithaca: Cornell University Press, 2000), 25–26, 160–63. Plane comments on the ways an eighteenth-century Narragansett lawsuit reveals aspects of traditional Narragansett notions of marriage.

21. Henry Spelman, "Relation of Virginia," in *Travels and Works of Captain John Smith*, ed. Edward Arber and A. G. Bradley (Edinburgh: John Grant, 1910), cviii.

22. When the English came, Powhatan's son Tatacoope was heir to the Quiocohannock, the child's mother being their werowansqua; his son Pochins, born to a Kekoughtan noblewoman before the conquest of the chiefdom, was placed in power after their werowance's defeat. See Strachey, *History of Travel*, in *Jamestown Narratives: Eyewitness Accounts of the Virginia Colony*, ed. Edward Wright Haile (Champlain, VA: Roundhouse Press, 1998). For more on Powhatan marriage, see Margaret Holmes Williamson, *Powhatan Lords of Life and Death: Command and Consent in Seventeenth-Century Virginia* (Lincoln: University of Nebraska Press, 2003).

23. For another study of William Strachey's somewhat myopic yet ultimately useful observations, see William M. Clements, "Translating Context and Situation: William Strachey and Powhatan's 'Scornfuul Song,'" in *Born in the*

Blood: On Native American Translation, ed. Brian Swann (Lincoln: University of Nebraska Press, 2011).

24. Siebert, "Resurrecting Virginia Algonquian," 292. In some ways, on the other hand, Strachey demonstrated a sophisticated understanding of words' variable meanings and translations depending on context: under "Fall" he includes "to be like to fall"; "to fall, dropping from a tree"; and "to let any thing fall."

25. His own notes clearly often deceived him. It was not that Strachey (or his hired copyist) was using a cedilla; he was not. Nor did he often make the mistake of using a *C* before an *a, o* or *u* to express the sound of an *S*. It was apparently a question of the handwriting. The upper loop of his word-initial *S* was so large that the letter sometimes looked like a *C*, especially because his word-initial capital *C* often included a sort of crosshatch. Note that in the Percy Manuscript, the sister-monarch's name is represented as *Opossono-quonoske*, but neither of the other copies have the name this way; thus it is clearly a copyist's error.

26. Strachey, *History of Travel*, in Haile, *Jamestown Narratives*, 621–28.

27. Strachey, *History of Travel*, 619–20.

28. Winganuske is mentioned by name in Strachey (in *Jamestown Narratives*, 619–20) and discussed by Ralph Hamor in his *A True Discourse of the Present State of Virginia* (London, 1615), in Haile, *Jamestown Narratives*, 833–35. The word "Wingan" is defined as "good" in two places in Strachey's Dictionarie, under *W* and *G*. "Winganunse" is "very good." On women's titles among ancient Native nobility, see my *Annals of Native America* as well as Linda Schele, *A Forest of Kings: The Untold Story of the Ancient Maya* (New York: William Morrow, 1990).

29. See note 22.

30. Rountree, *Pocahontas's People*, 141.

31. For full discussion, see my *Pocahontas and the Powhatan Dilemma*. In the case of the latter incident, I am referring to the visit to Powhatan that Ralph Hamor claims to have made, on which occasion he says he asked for the favored daughter for Sir Thomas Dale. The story is suspect, as Dale was already married, but Hamor tells of Powhatan's rejection in such detail that I am inclined to believe that some such exchange did indeed occur.

32. See Rountree, *Pocahontas's People*, 85, 105. Rountree includes a photograph of the extant Basse family prayer book flyleaf. Note that it is possible that the Nansemonds were in fact matrilineal, and Elizabeth was actually the niece or cousin of the werowance, not the biological daughter, but considered by the English, given her position, to be his daughter; he would in fact have called such a relation, "daughter."

33. Martha McCartney first traced this remarkable woman's history through documents in the British Public Records Office. See her "Cockacoeske, Queen of Pamunkey: Diplomat and Suzeraine," in *Powhatan's Mantle: Indians in the Colonial Southeast*, ed. P. A. Wood, G. A. Waselkov, and M. T. Hatley (Lincoln: University of Nebraska Press, 1989). Bernhard put Cockacoeske in context in "Pocahontas Was Not the Only One." Ethan Schmidt has recently focused on the way being a woman worked well for her as a leader in the post-conquest era. See Schmidt, "Cockacoeske, Weroansqua of the Pamunkeys, and Indian Resistance in Seventeenth-Century Virginia," *American Indian Quarterly* 36 (Summer 2012): 288–317.

34. Multiple English sources refer to young John West by name and one even mentions his father. He and his mother are both known to have spoken English, but when they signed the Treaty of Middle Plantation, she signed with a shaky symbol vaguely similar to a *W*, presumably a mark of her own devising, whereas he signed with an unmistakable initial *W*. On the Records of the 1679 Wardrobe Accounts, see McCartney, "Cockacoekse," 252, 264.

35. Virginia Bernhard's thorough research uncovered records of John West's legal marriage—a 1665 deed from Unity's father for some land, six enslaved people, and two white indentured servants "in satisfaction of his daughter's portion as the wife of the said West"; and a mention of the dissolution of the marriage in a York County lawsuit of 1685. See Bernhard, "Pocahontas Was Not the Only One," 31n33.

36. Report to the governor, cited in McCartney, "Cockacoeske," 190. Since no legal documents explicitly mentioning young John West and dated to the early 1680s have surfaced, it is conceivable that he had died by 1686. However, that is unlikely, given his age and the colony's present state of peace, and the fact that the English seemed to feel an explanation was necessary when his mother passed the mantle to Betty. Moreover, we know that he had been married for years (see McCartney, "Cockacoekse," 256), so if he were understood to represent the royal line, his children would have been in the line of succession.

PART III

ENGAGEMENTS WITH ENGLISHNESS

POCAHONTAS'S TRIP TO ENGLAND

The View from London, 1616–1617

E. M. ROSE

In 1616, Matoaka, the daughter of the paramount chief of the Powhatans, made a celebrated visit to London and took the city by storm. Although her triumph is taken for granted today, the trip was far from an assured success. Its purpose, timing, and risks are frequently misunderstood.

Matoaka, baptized Rebecca, but better known by her nickname "Pocahontas," is usually discussed in the context of the Tsenacommacah tribal chiefdom from which she came, or of Virginia, the English settlement in which she lived after her kidnapping and later marriage. This essay considers the view from the other side of the Atlantic, the urban context in which she spent the last year of her life, and how she and her sponsors negotiated some important social and cultural boundaries.[1]

The primary focus of this study is therefore the role of Pocahontas in a very specific time and place: the commercial heart of London in the mid-Jacobean era. The thrust of much other recent work on Indigenous people in London has been on the long history of their unsurprising, but often overlooked, presence in the capital. Historians have emphasized the evolution of concepts of empire and encounter, and the particular roles of Indigenous people in the elaboration of those notions over centuries.[2] They have painted an imaginative picture with broad brushstrokes, considering the mutual and long-term impact of different cultures on one another. There is a greater appreciation today that as Pocahontas was one of a number of Indigenous Americans who came to London and confronted English natives on their own turf, she was in some ways less exceptional than she is usually portrayed.

Pocahontas appears here in an international and commercial context rather than a strictly English imperial one. Although Pocahontas was one of a number of young Christian converts brought to England in this period from around the world, her sojourn in London was remarkable in a number of ways.

The trip raised issues of politics, economics, class, race, and religion and put them squarely before a national audience on English home ground. Her departure for London accompanied by immediate family members, a large entourage of Native Americans, captured Spanish spies, Virginia settlers, well-connected colonists, and a translator was a strategic corporate decision, not a personal initiative. The trip was expensive and risky, a last-gasp effort to support a colony that was not yet a decade old. Under Company auspices, Pocahontas and her husband aimed to influence politicians and to raise contributions from the pious general public, not to woo sophisticated venture capitalists. For those who donated, the reward would be spiritual, not financial.

The trip to England was not, as many suggest, an opportunity for John Rolfe to introduce his new bride to his family, to show her an ancestral estate, to attract investors, nor to demonstrate that Virginia Natives were not savages. It was not related to Company lawsuits that were long past. Nor was it prompted by a demand for information from Pocahontas's father, the *werowance* or paramount chief Wahunsenacah, although it was of interest to him and probably one reason why he welcomed an opportunity to send other countrymen with his daughter.

Pocahontas traveled to England to lobby Parliament for aid to the colony, to raise money for a Christian mission to her people, and help establish a college for Native Virginians; the trip enabled her to demonstrate and embody the possibilities of an Anglo-Native future as well as to testify in person to the peace then existing between nations.

American historians highlight her meeting with the monarch, eager to point out that she was treated as royalty or recognized as a diplomat. They emphasize her social success, her physical appearance, dress, and accoutrements. Of equal or greater importance was her success in the sphere of religion: her meeting with the bishop of London and her modest behavior as a new member of the Church of England.

Focus on the glamorous headliner, the glowing reports, the "social whirl," and the many later reinventions of Pocahontas in American history has drawn attention away from the politics, economics, and institutions involved in the journey. Historians have glossed over some of the challenges that the marriage posed to English notions of lineage ("race and rank" in modern historiography).[3]

Context, Purpose, and Timing of the Trip

The initiative for the trip to England has been attributed to various people in Virginia: to John Rolfe, who purportedly wanted to show off his bride; to acting governor Sir Thomas Dale, who wanted to demonstrate his accomplishments; or to her father, the paramount chief Wahunsenacah, who sought information about the English. But none of these individuals had the resources, power, or motivation to arrange transatlantic travel for such a large delegation or to maintain the visitors once they arrived. The project to bring a group of this size and character to England originated in the smoke-filled rooms of London and was triggered by political developments in England.[4]

By 1616, Pocahontas was already famous, and her voyage to England that spring was unrelated to the date of her marriage. The Virginia Company of London had received news of the Anglo-Powhatan wedding in 1614 and published details of it in Ralph Hamor's *A True Discourse* more than a year before the couple arrived.[5] She was described there as one "whose fame hath even been spread in England by the title of Nonpareil of Virginia," a phrase taken from Captain John Smith's description in his *True Relation* (1608).[6] Information about the marriage was spread in manuscript as well as print and was also included in the latest version of Edmund Howe's update of Stow's *Chronicles* (London, 1615). Dale had indicated that he intended to bring Pocahontas to England, but this was a vague hope rather than a specific plan.

Matters became urgent only when rumors spread that King James would call a new Parliament. Dale's predecessor as acting governor, Sir Thomas Gates, had been rushed back to London in March 1614 to lobby the House of Commons for aid to the colony (thereby missing the famous wedding the following month). That effort ended in failure, and when the "Addled" Parliament was dissolved after just a few weeks, the Company's hopes of government support were dashed. Now another chance beckoned.

In September and again in December 1615, people believed with good cause that a new Parliament was imminent.[7] The Venetian and Spanish ambassadors confidently wrote their rulers back home that Parliament would soon meet.[8] King James had exhausted his financial options, and the Privy Council saw no other choice. After considering possible alternatives to calling an assembly, even James was persuaded that it was necessary, however undesirable, to call a new Parliament in order to secure a grant of national taxation. He complained to the Spanish ambassador that the English Parliament was nothing but "cries, shouts and confusion."[9]

When the politically astute managers of the Virginia Company realized that they might have a fresh opportunity to make their case to a national assembly, they apparently sent word to influential people in Jamestown that their presence was desperately needed in London. Sir Thomas Smythe, the leader of the Company, and Sir Edwin Sandys, who would succeed him, were experienced parliamentarians, as were many of the Company's investors.[10] They knew they were more likely to receive support from provincial members of parliament (MPs) who regarded Jamestown as a matter of national pride than from King James, who was deeply in debt and never invested a penny in the American colony but who might nevertheless be persuaded to support the enterprise in the national interest.

Although it might take months to organize a contingent from America, it was not unrealistic to hope that the Virginians would arrive in time to do some political good because, with intermittent sessions, Parliaments could last for years.[11] Many urban and industrial corporations sent representatives to Parliament to lobby and support their MPs with information and statistics.[12] The Virginia Company had to go to much greater lengths to bring representatives to Westminster to lobby on the Company's behalf, but the action was not unprecedented.

The desire to present a good show for the Privy Council and the House of Commons explains the large and varied entourage that set out from Virginia. This included individual representatives to appeal to different constituencies; captured spies to demonstrate the threat from Spain; reputable officers to indicate that the colony was in good hands; politically connected settlers to lobby their friends and families; John Rolfe to promote marketable colonial products, such as his sweet tobacco; and his wife Pocahontas, the Nonpareil convert, to confirm that missionary efforts had borne fruit and were worthy of further support. She was accompanied by an impressive group of fellow young men and women from Tsenacommacah. The ship also brought a selection of commercial goods to demonstrate Virginia's productive potential, including sassafras, tar, pitch and caviar—but samples only, no significant amounts.[13] Pocahontas, her husband, child, friends, and relatives were thus part of a large, diverse, and memorable group, but not necessarily the most important members of it in the eyes of the Londoners. Dale did not escort the Indian princess so much as the Rolfes accompanied him.

Historians imply that the group left Virginia almost by happenstance without considering how few boats had come to the colony in 1615 and how ill-advised it was to remove colonists in April at the beginning of the planting season when the colony faced chronic shortages of food.[14] Only three vessels are known to have moored in the Chesapeake in the previous year.[15] The multicultural, multilingual, and multireligious task force that sailed for England in 1616 was apparently put together in haste.

The Company's instructions, which do not survive, would have been clear and forceful, necessitating a speedy turnaround for the ship that brought the news about Parliament and requiring immediate decisions on behalf of the colonial leadership. A ship that left England at the end of December 1615 could expect to arrive at the Chesapeake by April and turn around for the return voyage within a couple of weeks.[16] Pocahontas and her family sailed on the *Treasurer*, which left Virginia the last week of April 1616 (the very week William Shakespeare died in Stratford-upon-Avon), under the command of Samuel Argall. A notably skilled captain on whom the Company frequently relied, Argall may have been the one to bring news from London in the first place, or he may have received word in Virginia from a close and trusted colleague.[17] His second-in-command was apparently the experienced Cornwall captain John Jope, who would later pilot the first vessel carrying enslaved Africans to Virginia in 1619.[18]

The directive from England must have been urgent and the instructions explicit about who was to return: men of the colony who had influence in London. Acting governor Sir Thomas Dale led the transatlantic legation back to England. He could offer detailed personal knowledge about progress of the settlement. The king had long thought highly of Dale and had recommended his employment, so his personal attendance at Parliament would have been critical.[19] Dale could point to the results of his strict policy under the *Lawes Divine, Morall and Martiall*, later condemned for their brutality, but at the time praised for their effectiveness. His superiors commended the "great and constant severity" by which he had "reclaymed almost miraculously those idle and disordered people and reduced them to labour and an honest fashion of life."[20] Dale could also explain the effectiveness of the new incentives of granting three acres of cleared ground to every male colonist, a practice which he had instituted as soon as he took over from Thomas Gates in 1614.[21]

It is often claimed that Dale was called back to London to answer for his severe administration, but there is no contemporary evidence to suggest dissatisfaction with his service in Virginia at the time.[22] The opposite was true: as recently as August 1614, King James had asked the Dutch States General, which had employed Dale in the Protestant cause on the Continent, to extend his leave for another two- or three-year tour of duty, envisaging a stay longer than the year and a half he remained in Virginia. Dale had expected to remain, but letters from England about the planned Parliament would also have included the news that Elizabeth Throckmorton, Dale's wife, was deathly ill at home in Devon, which is why he returned to nurse her rather than proceed to London with the rest of the party.[23] When eventually no Parliament took place that year, Dale was then free to go to the Netherlands to negotiate his back pay, just as Gates had earlier done in 1611 to retain his commission with the Dutch.[24]

Dale's decision to place George Yeardley in charge in the colony in his stead is ample evidence that the Company's immediate priority was to lobby politicians at home. Had he remained in the colony, Sir Francis West would have been the obvious candidate to step up in the absence of Dale, the acting governor. But West, the younger brother of the nominal governor, Baron De La Warr (still recuperating in England), a member of the colonial Council and later a governor himself, was needed in London. Instead, the colony was left in the hands of Yeardley, son of a Merchant Taylor and brother of a grocer, a competent man but one with no advantageous social connections and little influence.

Like West, other members of the returning delegation were also politically well-connected. John Martin, for example, was the brother-in-law of Sir Julius Caesar, Master of the Rolls and member of the Privy Council. Captain James Davi[e]s, who had sailed to New England and built the pinnace *Virginia* there before joining the settlers in Jamestown, was a close associate of the family of the late Sir John Popham, Lord Chief Justice and Speaker of the House of Commons. Davis had been in charge of the garrison at the new settlement at Henrico in 1616 before returning on the ship with Pocahontas. Dale also brought Diego de Molina, who had been imprisoned in Jamestown since he was captured spying on the colony in 1611. Molino's fellow spy, the "hispaniolized Englishman" Francis Limbrecke (Lymbry), was also on board but was executed for his treachery just before the ship made land in Plymouth.[25]

While the colony was still precarious, without instructions of extreme urgency it is difficult to understand what would have prompted Rolfe, whose son with Pocahontas, Thomas, was only a few months old, to venture again across the ocean. He understood better than anyone the dangers of a transatlantic journey, having lost his first wife and their newborn child immediately after his crossing from England in 1609.[26] For Rolfe, a man of modest means who had just discovered a path to prosperity by growing sweet tobacco, the call to come to England must have been pressing and persuasive.

It was an awkward time to take so many important figures away from the struggling colony leaving only Yeardley in charge, but because of its dwindling financial support, the Virginia Company had little choice. The Company planned to relaunch the colony, attract new settlers and fresh investment through a reorganization that would encourage private plantations, and reward those who paid for the transportation of others with grants of land (the "headright" system, which was implemented in the autumn of 1616). The London managers therefore instructed the colonial administrators to record certain information before departure. The surviving report of the division of settlers into farmers, laborers, and officers, was not an initiative of Rolfe's or Dale's, but that of the London Council.[27]

With the *Treasurer's* departure, only a few hundred people were left in the colony (351 were counted), spread across five settlements. Little is known about what went on in the English colony or in Tsenacommacah between Argall's departure with Pocahontas and her fellow travelers and his return to Jamestown (on the *George* with Rolfe and another large entourage) the following year.[28] Colonial farmers, however, must have been busy because in 1617 Argall, newly appointed deputy governor, found the settlement awash in tobacco; twenty thousand pounds of the leaf were exported to England that year.[29]

Pocahontas's journey should thus be placed in a larger institutional, financial, political, and group context. It was paid for with the last of the corporation's funds generated in 1615 by the sale of Bermuda to a separate Somers Island Company and by the Second Great Standing Lottery for Virginia, which was drawn in November.[30] It was only this last-minute infusion of cash that allowed the Company to equip a vessel at the end of the year. In a letter, Dale explained that the colony was "now enjoying great prosperity and peace."[31] He left for England with Pocahontas and her family because the colony was fragile and still unprofitable, not because it was finally stable and productive.

From No Profit to Nonprofit: The Change of Company Focus

Upon their arrival in England in June, the passengers on the *Treasurer* would have learned that there was to be no Parliament. James had sidestepped the need to call one by selling back to the Dutch the "cautionary towns" of Brill and Flushing at a discount for cash. James also began negotiations for a Spanish royal marriage for his son Charles, Prince of Wales, that was to include an enormous dowry from the Infanta's father, King Philip III, and he also expanded the sale of honors throughout his multiple kingdoms (the sale of an English title is documented for the first time in 1615).[32] The king of England thus was able to manage a period of "personal rule" without calling Parliament again until the end of 1620.

Since no government aid was forthcoming, Company officials changed tactics and turned the trip into a broader public relations effort focused not only on Westminster and Parliament but also on people across Britain.

Without Parliament to lobby, Pocahontas drew attention *away* from the wrapping up of the Virginia Company joint-stock in the fall of 1616 when there were no profits to distribute after seven years: investors who had put money into the company had expected to earn profits on their investment and reap rewards. The presence of Pocahontas in London assured the public that some good had come from the funds spent on the colony, which would otherwise have appeared a failure. This was a shift of emphasis from "no profit" to "nonprofit," that is, from enterprise to charity.

By this date, Londoners had seen many Indigenous people, but few had been willing converts to Christianity, despite the claims in printed broadsides advertising the lottery of 1615 suggesting that Indigenous people in Virginia welcomed missionaries.[33] Powhatan's representative Uttamatomakkin (Tomocomo), was one of the party; he never converted to Christianity and was fully prepared to discuss Native beliefs, which he did enthusiastically and at length.

Pocahontas and her husband came to London as salaried employees to raise funds for a proposed college for Native Americans. She was the face of the Company, in essence, America's first corporate spokesmodel; her husband might be considered America's first university development officer. Together they headed a capital campaign to build schools and colleges.[34] Pocahontas was no social butterfly, expected to wear glamorous and expensive court clothing with striking décolletage, but rather a demure convert, soberly attired. She aimed to impress not the fashionable elite of London but the bishop of

London—and she did. Pocahontas and her companions raised hundreds of pounds from collections in churches to establish a college in Virginia. Although fellow Indigenous people living in Virginia were baptized on this trip, Pocahontas's high profile promised more than individual converts; her status suggested that she would be the means of Christianizing her entire community, from the top down.

The promotion of Pocahontas as a model convert likely came from Virginia Company officials who were also active in the East India Company. In July 1615, Reverend Patrick Copland suggested to them that they publicly celebrate the baptism of a boy from the Bay of Bengal who had been brought to England to further his education. As his sponsor, Copland noted, "it was fit to have it publicly effected, being the first fruits of India." The Company asked the newly elected East India deputy Maurice Abbot to check with his brother George, the archbishop of Canterbury, to confirm that it would be appropriate to make the baptism a public event.[35] Virginia officials thereupon sought similar favorable publicity for the American colony. Smythe, head of the Virginia Company, was also head of the East India Company, and there were overlapping shareholders and managers of both companies (Abbot among them). Now that peace was at last arranged between Natives and newcomers in Virginia, word was sent to bring some Virginians to England, a repeated instruction to colonial leaders. They were eager to display what Samuel Purchas was to call the "first fruits of Virginian conversion."

At the same time that instructions were sent to the Chesapeake, the Company also set to work in England. Private investment and governmental support had come to naught, so the Company turned to charitable contributions. It prevailed upon the king to support an initiative to collect donations in churches to spread the gospel in America. If the Company, already overextended, raised enough through churches, it would be spared the need to underwrite the costs of a resupply ship for the colony.

In the spring of 1616, while the American contingent was still at sea, James sent a formal letter to his archbishops encouraging them to instruct their bishops to organize collections within their parishes.[36] King James urged local congregations throughout England to support "the erecting of some churches and schools for the education of the children of those barbarians." The details were put forth in a printed broadside for churchwardens and ministers that was widely distributed in April 1616, but of which only a single copy survives.[37] The printer of the sheet that urged contributions to the college for Native Americans was Thomas Snodham, who at the same time printed a short brochure for the Company, *A briefe declaration of the present state of things in Virginia, and of a division to be now made, of some part of those lands in our actuall possession.*[38] Later the same year, probably in the early winter, Snodham printed a recruiting broadside that reported the good news of Dale's arrival and the forthcoming departure of Samuel Argall in another attempt to revitalize the colony (which also survives in but a single copy).[39]

By the time the Virginia party disembarked, English parishioners throughout the country were thus already informed about a renewed corporate focus on religious conversion.[40] As instructed by the king, ministers were to preach four times during the next two years about the importance of the mission to America and to send whatever funds they collected to the head of the Company.

It seems likely that Pocahontas was present at St. Dionis in Fenchurch Street on December 22, 1616, with leaders of both the East India Company and the Virginia Company when the boy from the Bay of Bengal was baptized in the presence of a great many men from the Privy Council and the Companies.[41] The educated young convert, Peter Pope, was sent back to the Indies on a ship with Copland in hopes that, like Pocahontas, he would return and convert "others of his nation." He was to be the disciple like Peter, the first pope, upon whom Christ built his church. Pope's impressive Latin correspondence, translated into English, was later appended to a sermon preached by Reverend Copland, entitled *Virginia's God Be Thanked,* which the Virginia Company published in 1622.[42] English missionary enterprises on two sides of the world were thus explicitly linked. That summer, St. Dionis parish church buried Abraham, a Virginian who had been staying at the home of Sir Thomas Smythe, who lived nearby; it had previously buried two other Native Americans who had died in his home.[43]

Pope's public baptism took place a mere two weeks after the Virginia joint-stock wrapped up and the famous headright system with its division and allocation of land to English settlers was inaugurated. A few weeks later, Pocahontas was on her way back to Virginia. This coincidence is rarely mentioned. But the two converts, one a teenager, one not much older, probably knew each other as they waited on the docks week after week for the winds to shift to enable them to sail home to opposite sides of the world. Peter Pope sailed on the *Royal James* under the command of Captain Martin Pring. He was to be dropped off in India, after which the ship would continue to the Far East. As explained in the broadside, Captain Argall was to return the Rolfes and the

Virginians on the *George* and bring additional settlers. Pocahontas, however, died before the ship could sail out of the Thames, so only her widower returned to Virginia; their infant son Thomas, too ill to cross the Atlantic, was left to be raised in England. Pocahontas did not live to see the results of these "first fruits" and her efforts to build a school. Yet when Copland later collected money aboard the *Royal James* to support a school for Native Americans in Virginia, it may have been from mariners who had met Pocahontas, or heard directly from those who knew her.

The Pocahontas missionary initiative was part of a larger effort that extended far beyond the Atlantic world. She was but one of many young people brought to London at this time by English merchants from far-flung parts of the globe as exemplars of conversion to Christianity. Within a few short years, Sir Thomas Smythe witnessed in London, if he did not preside over them himself, the "first fruits" of English enterprise and religion worldwide. Dederj Jaquoah, a king's son from the central African coast (Liberia) was baptized in 1611 (as "John, son of a king of Guinea"); Cooree (Xore) from Southern Africa (Cape of Good Hope), who arrived in the fall of 1613, lived in Smythe's London house; and Peter Pope from India was brought to England in 1614 and baptized in 1616 under Smythe's auspices.[44] Another who belonged to this commercial community of youthful converts was John Martyn, a young man from Persia (Iran), an Armenian who served as Lord De La Warr's personal servant in England and accompanied him back to Virginia the following year.[45] Two young Japanese men sailed from London on one of Smythe's East India Company ships in February 1614, so they must have been living in England beforehand.[46] Young Totakins from Tsenacommacah was also living in Smythe's house in 1613; and maybe Eikintomino and Matahan lived there as well, two Native Americans who were drawn in St. James Park by a foreign visitor and were featured on the lottery broadside of 1615.[47] A few years later, another boy from Tsenacommacah, later baptized Georgius Thorpe shortly before his death in 1619 (possibly a member of the 1616 transatlantic crossing), served as a copyist in the home of George Thorpe. William Crashaw, "an Indian baptized" living in Virginia in 1624, was likely another of those who traveled to England, met the Company preacher of the same name, and was baptized by him.[48] Another Native American who returned to Virginia with Rolfe in 1617 may have been "Cleopatra," possibly Tomocomo's wife Mattachanna, but more likely a different relative who was baptized in London at the same time as "Mark Anthonie, a negro" at St. Olav in January 1617.[49] From English documents one can identify five men and five women from Pocahontas's tribe who sailed on the *Treasurer*. Also housed with a London merchant at this same time was a baptized Patuxet Native of the Wampanoag confederation named Tisquantum (Squanto), who had been kidnapped in 1614 by an English associate of Captain John Smith and would soon head back to New England and be there to greet the Pilgrims.[50]

No one has heretofore put Pocahontas, the most celebrated Native American of the southern states, in contact with Squanto, the most celebrated Native American of the northern states in this period (celebrated, that is, in English historiography). But they likely met in London when they were apparently living only a couple of hundred yards away from each other. The two Algonkian-speaking Natives, Pamunkey (Pocahontas) and Pawtuxet (Squanto), were both preparing for return voyages across the Atlantic. Squanto was desperate to return to his homeland; according to John Chamberlain, Pocahontas wanted to stay in England.[51] Squanto was back from a voyage to Newfoundland by the end of 1616 and was living with John Slaney, treasurer of the Newfoundland Company in the Cornhill area; after a stay in Brentford, Pocahontas and her family had probably joined Smythe's household by early 1617, immediately before their planned trip home. Slaney and Smythe were both investors in the East India Company and had conducted business together in Smythe's house on Philpot Lane that served as a corporate headquarters. If not in one of their homes, at church, or on the street, Squanto and Pocahontas—as well as Peter Pope and Georgius Thorpe—could have met in the neighboring home of Dr. Theodore Gulstone, at the nearby Leadenhall market or the recently opened emporium "Britain's Bourse," the New Exchange, or when speaking with mapmakers, mathematicians, mariners, and herbalists on Lime Street while acquiring necessary supplies for their trips. Because Squanto and Pocahontas spoke excellent English, they might even have enjoyed a performance at the Globe Theater a mere mile away, where entry cost only a penny a piece for the cheapest tickets.[52]

Such is the London context for Pocahontas, a young Algonkian mother who arrived in London with her husband in 1616. There is no evidence that they routinely socialized with princes and royal ambassadors, but there is circumstantial evidence that they associated with young Christians from abroad.[53] At this time exotic individuals, like luxury goods, were brought to London voluntarily or by trade, by coercion, or in some combination, with the intention of re-exporting them. These young people from India, Iran, south Asia, the Far

Squanto and Pocahontas in London. Detail of the Agas Map of London, with highlights. (Illustration prepared by Scott Walker, Harvard University Map Collection, based on the 1561 woodcut Agas map of London at the Map of Early Modern London project)

East, northern, southern, and central Africa, America, the Arctic, England, and Europe, who lived near one another and worshipped at the same (or a neighboring) church, were part of the same small bustling mercantile community in London.[54]

It was not necessarily a happy time and place, however; while some visitors traveled to London eagerly and voluntarily, others had been forcibly trafficked, or, like Pocahontas, made the best of their circumstances.[55] Some may have preferred life in England, others, such as Cooree and Squanto, were desperate to return. From the English Christian perspective, "success" proved elusive: the boat on which Dederj was returning to Guinea was attacked off the Barbary coast; he may have escaped by way of Morocco, as did some of his shipmates.[56] In 1614 he was back home when he met with crew members from an East India Company ship and spoke excellent English. The kidnapped Cooree was miserable in England. He was eventually returned to the Cape and ran home to his family, members of the Gorachoqua tribe of the Khoikhoi.[57] His deep ambivalence is suggested by Cooree's subsequent desire to send his son to London.[58] Peter Pope sailed home in early 1617, and after he disembarked, no more was heard of him after 1620. Pocahontas died before her ship could leave the Thames. Cooree, Squanto and Dederj all served for years as translators and intermediaries back home. Of all these people, Pocahontas has left the most traces in the historical record. Yet her entire trip has been viewed through the lens of a single documented appearance at court, which has colored all subsequent interpretations of her role. This, however, appears to have been an exceptional event.

Pocahontas's presence at the court masque on Twelfth Night, January 1617, was the culmination of months of planned appearances; she was whisked away immediately afterward. Like Eliza Doolittle at the ambassadors' ball, the American young lady, now Rebecca Rolfe, impressed all and sundry on a socially and politically important evening, the highlight of the Christmas season. The focus of the masque, Ben Jonson's *The Vision of Delight*, was James I's young favorite George Villiers, who had just been named Earl of Buckingham. That evening Villiers showed off his dancing and high leaping skills, "light and airy bounds," and danced with the queen for the first time.[59]

So far as we know, before that event, Pocahontas did not attend royal functions or routinely socialize with courtiers.[60] There is no evidence that she met the king or queen on any earlier occasion. The repeated description of Pocahontas having been formally "presented to the monarchs" is a romantic notion from a later period; such an event, had it occurred, would have been mentioned by the jealously vigilant foreign ambassadors who populated James's court. Her brother-in-law Tomocomo "denied ever to have seene the King."[61]

Nor are any English nobles known to have met her, other than Thomas West, Baron De La Warr, the first governor of Virginia, back home in England after his hurried departure from the colony in 1611.[62] By then Governor De La Warr and his family lived quietly in the provinces, too poor to participate in the social scene in London. They do not appear to have been in London for long, nor was De La Warr active in Company affairs as late as December 1616, when other noblemen signed Virginia Company correspondence directed to various municipal authorities.⁶³ It seems that the West family was brought to the capital by the Virginia Company specifically for the important celebration of Twelfth Night. It is said that the Crown was prevailed upon to include the West women in the theatrical production that evening as an easy sign of favor.⁶⁴

Pocahontas's appearance at the masque, escorted by Lord and Lady De La Warr, according to Smith, was a triumph of public relations, adumbrated in the social media of the day. Only *after* her success at the masque was her engraved portrait sold as a souvenir; copies were sent abroad, adding to her international fame. Company officials probably waited to see how she would be received before adorning her portrait with the identifying inscription "Matoaka als Rebecca, daughter of the emperor Powhatan." It is not known how many of the single-leaf prints published by Compton Holland based on a portrait by the teenage Simon van de Passe were made, but not one is known to survive. The image is known now only from reproductions made after her death and bound into volumes of collected illustrations.⁶⁵

Despite the fame of the "American Nonpareil," the Virginia Company had reason to be cautious. The trip to spearhead a mission to the Native Virginians and to establish a college for them was warmly embraced, but there were pitfalls for the Company. In bringing Pocahontas to London, the delicate issues of status and ethnicity had to be negotiated. The traits that made Pocahontas so memorable also raised the possibility that she might not be accepted in English society. Some of what could be tolerated or even welcomed across the Atlantic was more problematic in London.

Status

From the perspective of the Company, it was important to portray Pocahontas as a princess but not press her "royal" claims too far. Only after her death (and the death of her husband) was Pocahontas called a princess by the great American publicist Captain John Smith. Samuel Purchas noted that she "carried her selfe as the Daughter of a King and was accordingly respected."⁶⁶ Wahunsenacah's daughter was clearly important, but to have claimed that Pocahontas's status matched that of the daughter of King James would have been problematic because James claimed to rule Virginia. Although Pocahontas was described as the daughter of the mighty prince Powhatan, the Company was careful not to specify her precise status.

John Rolfe's wife is frequently described as "Lady Rolfe," which is the designation of the wife of a knight. But Rolfe was never knighted—he was not a "sir"—and therefore his wife was not Lady Rolfe by right of her husband; she, however, may have been called "Lady" as a courtesy title by virtue of her father's eminence.[67] Although writers assume that Rolfe accompanied his wife to the Twelfth Night masque, he is not mentioned as having been present at the Banqueting Hall that evening.[68] In a letter Captain John Smith claimed to have sent to the Queen, he explained that "her husbands estate not being able to make her fit to attend your Majestie."[69] When John Rolfe is mentioned in correspondence independent of the Company, he is dismissed as "one Rolfe."[70] At the time of his marriage to Pocahontas, Rolfe was raised in social status in the colony, but only up to a point: he became secretary and recorder of the colony only on the departure of Oxford-educated Ralph Hamor in June and was succeeded in 1619 on the arrival of Cambridge-educated John Pory, at which time he joined the Council.

Rolfe was pointedly kept in the background, and it seems that the couple was the subject of negotiations between the Company and the court. Writing in 1705, Robert Beverley first mentions King James's unhappiness about an unequal marriage. "The poor Gentleman her Husband had like to have been call'd to an Acount for presuming to marry a Princess Royal without the King's Consent: because it had been suggested that he had taken Advantage of her being a Prisoner and forc'd her to marry him. But upon a more perfect Representation of the Matter, his Majesty was pleased at last to declare himself satisfied."[71] Drawing on the same narrative, in 1747 William Stith acknowledges that there was a long tradition that the king was "highly offended" and felt Rolfe had committed a crime in marrying a princess.[72] A decade later, a Virginia minister explains in a letter to his brother in England "it was deliberated in Council, whether [Rolfe] had not committed high treason by so doing, that is marrying an Indian Princess; and had not some troubles intervened which put a stop to the inquiry, the poor man might have been hanged up . . . This put an effectual stop to all intermarriages afterward."[73] Although these concerns were dismissed by later writers, they likely weighed heavily on Pocahontas's promoters.

The marriage raised all manner of problems both social and substantive in a society deeply conscious of status. It might have led to claims that Rolfe ought to inherit some of Pocahontas's rights and privileges, perhaps even land.

This seems to be the accusation Samuel Argall tried to make (with no apparent basis) when John Rolfe returned with him to Virginia as a widower. (The firm response to Argall on the part of the Company suggests that the topic may have been discussed previously in England.)[74] Acquiring title to Native land also may have been a motivation for Dale in 1615 when he sent Hamor to ask paramount chief Wahunsenacah for the hand of another of his daughters, even though Dale had a wife back in England. Although the request produced no result, this incident was frequently illustrated in foreign editions of Hamor's work. Marrying a Native woman to acquire authority over land was also a charge laid at the feet of Captain John Smith, albeit one dismissed by his contemporary defenders.[75]

Despite the celebration of the Pocahontas marriage, there are almost no records of other such marriages between English and Native Americans from the first half of the seventeenth century (in contrast to the evidence of cohabitation). When such marriages are traceable in documents, they involve daughters of the powerful and claims to land. The marriage of Nathaniel Basse to Elizabeth, daughter of the king of Nansemond in 1638, was recorded in the Basse family Bible and resulted in Nansemond land going to their children.[76] The marriage at the age of about ten, of Mary, the daughter of the Piscataway chief Kittamaquund to the brother-in-law of the Calvert governor of Maryland, was also clearly a grab for Piscataway land, a coerced marriage that eventually ended because of inhumane treatment of the Native wife by her English husband.[77] In the letter Captain John Smith claimed to have sent the queen about Pocahontas, Smith also focuses on claims to land, "seeing this Kingdome may rightly have a Kingdome by her meanes."[78] English authorities were mindful of the claims of "royal" status, even if Native American landholding and notions of matrilineal descent were at odds with English law and tradition.

John Rolfe never claimed Powhatan land on behalf of Pocahontas. What claims he made were through the auspices of the Company: he asked for a continuation of the salary granted to him and his wife for their son in England, and in his will of 1622, he left land granted by the Virginia Company to his son by Pocahontas and to his infant daughter by his new wife Jane Peirce. Rolfe did not mention any other land. Pocahontas's son Thomas Rolfe returned to Virginia in 1635 (a trip apparently paid for by his stepmother's father, William Peirce, to judge from the headright he claimed), and six years thereafter he asked to meet his Native relatives and his aunt Cleopatra. Much later, it was said that Rolfe had inherited land that was a gift from Opechancanough (the brother of his grandfather, Wahunsenacah) and his mother's Native American family, but this is unproven and unlikely.

Anticipating objections to the apparently unequal match, the Company published Ralph Hamor's *A True Discourse of the Present State of Virginia* dedicated to Sir Thomas Smythe, which included the letters justifying the marriage and emphasizing religious duty over personal desires. The existence of a contemporary scribal copy of the Rolfe letter that was published with Hamor's *Discourse* suggests avid interest in his marriage.[79]

But this might not have been sufficient. On his arrival in England in 1616, Rolfe was encouraged to compose yet another letter directed not to the general public or investors (as is usually claimed) but specifically to the king. John Rolfe's *Relation* (as this letter is known) survives in three manuscript copies, the formal treatise to the king including corrections in his own hand. Additional copies also survive addressed to the Earl of Pembroke, who was on the Privy Council, in Rolfe's autograph manuscript, and to the Earl of Warwick, with slight differences.[80]

Rolfe's treatise may have persuaded James to welcome Pocahontas precisely by not mentioning her. It points to the peace that now existed in the colony without drawing attention to the marriage that brought it about. It hints at the possibility of finding gold and silver and mentions silkworms. In short, it touches on issues which concerned the king and assured him that English title to Virginia was good: "which places or seates are all our owne ground, not so much by conquest, which the Indians hold a just and lawfull title, but purchased of them freely, and they verie willingly selling it." It offered a justification for English dominion and indicated that land claims in Virginia were *not* to be made by marriage.

The impressive performance of the Rolfes seems to have been the basis for a decision of the Privy Council that was of great importance for the Company and colonists. In early December 1616, the Council agreed "upon a reference from his Majestie" to extend for a further year the tax exemption the Company enjoyed on goods shipped to England. With tobacco taking off as an export, this decision had significant value and provided strong motives for colonists to rush to plant because the government made clear it was only for one year, "not to bee further continewed or expected."[81] The invitation to the masque came after Rolfe's assurances and the Privy Council's endorsement that promised significant future royal revenue.

From a practical perspective as well as a rhetorical one, the trip proved successful. Immediately before their departure from London, the couple was awarded one hundred pounds by the Company to continue their missionary work.[82] But if unequal social status could be overcome in a world of nascent capitalism, the Pocahontas-Rolfe marriage risked provoking a more general unease about the mixing of peoples.

Ethnicity

In addition to concerns about marriage between partners of unequal status, the Company faced deep English ambivalence about lineage and marriage. Some people rejoiced in the union of John Rolfe and Rebecca, née Matoaka; some regarded it as miscegenation; others harbored doubts about the propriety of the union but might be open to persuasion. It was not certain that a marriage between an Englishman and a Native American—of any status—would be tolerated, not to mention welcomed or celebrated. This was the only "intermarriage" recorded during the entire Company period (1606–1624), and one of the few recorded well into the seventeenth century. In 1691, this concern was enshrined in Virginia by a law which forbade marriages between "whites" and "non-whites" (including Africans and Native Americans). Such was the contested notion of racial purity, however, that even in the twentieth century, Virginians could outlaw such marriages while at the same time praise their descent from Pocahontas as a matter of great pride.

There is a sophisticated historiography on this topic of race that cannot be summarized here. Suffice to say that the issue of English-Native marriage was debated from the earliest days of the Jamestown settlement with little consensus.[83] Whatever the personal opinions of identifiable investors, officials, preachers, and propagandists, the risks were different for a corporation than for an individual. Marriage was distinct from coupling, which archeological finds indicate was even more prevalent than texts have revealed.[84]

It is possible that Sir Thomas Gates, Dale's predecessor as deputy governor in Virginia, disapproved of such marriages. According to Hamor, Rolfe had been in love with Pocahontas for a long time but waited until Gates left the colony before proposing marriage. The union was solemnized less than a month after Gates's departure. Although he was active with the Company in later years, Gates is not mentioned in connection with the Company when Pocahontas was in England.[85] In contrast to the tacit disapproval of his superior,

Dale evidently approved of Rolfe's initiative and followed up with an offer of his own to Wahunsenacah for another of the paramount chief's daughters. Rolfe's letter to Dale requesting permission to marry was clearly written with the assumption that it would be approved quickly, and it may have been solicited with an eye to publishing it.

Despite the urging of some preachers, who saw the intermarriage of Native and English as a potential means to unite nations, many others (including Rolfe himself) pointed to a Protestant concern with the biblical injunction against taking foreign wives (Ezra 10:10). Even though Rolfe overcame his concern and notwithstanding the success of the Pocahontas-Rolfe marriage, that negative view came to predominate. English settlers married other English settlers, not Indigenous women and men. After his return to Virginia, Rolfe married the daughter of one of his fellow shipmates wrecked in Bermuda (his third wife, and her father knew both of Rolfe's previous wives and infants, as did Ralph Hamor).

No other colonists followed Rolfe's lead in taking a Native American wife and marrying her in church. Instead, to stabilize and populate the colony and to settle planters on the land, the Company organized the importation of marriageable English women who had the option to wed providing that their future husbands paid in tobacco for their passage and support (alternatively, the women could work to pay for their own passage and choose not to marry, as some did).[86] Importing wives from England—not joining with Natives in holy matrimony—was to be the way forward.

While presenting Pocahontas as a worthy woman, the Virginia Company had reason not to draw undue attention to her English husband and not to picture her with their son Thomas. All the family stories about the Rolfes are later creations: they never visited Heacham in Norfolk; Pocahontas never planted any mulberry tree there; she never wore earrings like those now marketed under her name; she never used the jug supposedly presented to her by the monarchs; she never sat for a cameo likeness; and during the seventeenth century, she was never pictured with her child.[87] Her baptismal name Rebecca, however, drew attention to the biblical verse "two nations are in your womb" (Genesis 25:23) that anticipated the offspring of two peoples.

No further marriages between English and Indigenous people were advertised or encouraged, even before the devastating attack of March 1622 ("the massacre" as it was portrayed in the English press) just a few weeks after John Rolfe's death from illness. Although it has been assumed that there was a specific program of marriages envisioned by the Company in sending a group of young people to England, this is not evident.[88] Two of the women were already married (Pocahontas to Rolfe, and Matachanna to Tomocomo) and the other Algonkians were boys and girls, young and old.

Of the Algonkians who sailed in 1616, only one other marriage is recorded and that occurred five years after their arrival in England. The governor of Bermuda was tasked with finding suitable husbands for Pocahontas's companions Mary and Elizabeth, whom the Company sent back from London in 1621 (Mary died on the way). This was no easy task, the governor explained to the Company, even with the dowry of a servant boy, but he managed to find a husband and hosted an impressive wedding celebration for Elizabeth and her spouse before sending the couple on to Jamestown. Why was it not possible, or desirable, to find a husband in England for Algonkian women? The cultural taboos in London against marrying Native Americans may have been so strong that it was advisable to look elsewhere for a spouse, in a frontier society with less rigid social mores. The couple headed back to Jamestown shortly after their marriage, but thereafter nothing more is heard of them.

After 1622, ideas of Anglo-Native marriages quickly faded. In retrospect, the Rolfe-Pocahontas marriage and its endorsement and celebration by the Virginia Company seems anomalous and even more risky than it appeared at the time.

The Aftermath

Pocahontas's trip to England was one of the more successful examples of mass marketing in the history of early America. Although everyone remembers that she and her husband and child went on the trip, there is little awareness of who else sailed with them and why they traveled. Pocahontas enabled the company to portray the colonial project as successful, peaceful, and welcome. In her erect royal carriage, her dress and conversation, in her marriage to a self-made and now successful planter, and in her new Christian identity, Pocahontas embodied English hopes—romantic, commercial, spiritual, and political. From the beginning, America was about remaking: Pocahontas as an English lady and John Rolfe as a solid and productive landed member of colonial society. That is how they are remembered. Discussions of Pocahontas's trip have centered on personal and cultural issues rather than the political and financial exigencies that underpinned it. As the Company intended and worked so hard to convey, the trip had an air of success and triumph rather than a whiff of desperation and scandal.

John Chamberlain's sneering criticism of Pocahontas as "no fayre lady" in a letter he wrote on the occasion of Rolfes' departure from London is cited repeatedly as an example of the racist, sexist, and derogatory attitude of Englishmen towards Native Americans. That comment is in keeping with those Chamberlain made about almost everybody—one reason he was such a successful correspondent: the gossip columnist everyone professes to hate, but avidly reads. The term "fayre" was increasingly associated with skin color in this period and is studied now as part of developing and intersecting discourses of race and gender.

In emphasizing the insult, however, it is easy to overlook the phrase that followed in Chamberlain's letter, one which testifies, even if offhandedly, to the achievement of the trip: "with her tricking up and high style and title you might thincke her and her worshipfull husband to be somebody."[89] In that demeaning comment, Chamberlain was especially emphasizing the notion that "Lady Rebecca" was dressing above her station. Sumptuary laws, the notion that people should not try to mimic their betters in apparel, were repeatedly proposed in Parliament and in the colonies. Queen Elizabeth had passed laws defining and restricting particular articles of clothing to individuals of high rank, specifying the fabrics and types of clothing that could be worn by people of different social strata. Although Chamberlain decried the Virginian as a social upstart, the inclusion of the Pocahontas portrait in a collection of pictures of monarchs and notables the year after her death indicates that she was widely accepted as an eminent person.[90]

Pocahontas pulled it off. Despite the ambiguities of race and class, despite the likelihood that she might be ignored or insulted, Matoaka als Rebecca achieved the near impossible, situating herself between presumption and reticence, successfully presenting herself as someone both royal and common, both English and Native. The achievement of the trip obscures the significant challenges she and the Company faced.

A fuller and more precise understanding of the circumstances surrounding the 1616 visit expands and inflects current historical thinking. By locating Pocahontas in a specific commercial, religious, and political context, placing her in the company of such figures as Squanto, Peter Pope, Cleopatra—near Thomas Dale and far from Thomas Gates, King James, and his courtiers—one gains new understanding of important facets of transatlantic engagement. The vital consideration of the broad and lasting issues of colonial encounters and the common experiences of Indigenous peoples in England should not cause one to overlook the motives rooted in immediate political and economic concerns, such as those that underlay specific initiatives connected with Pocahontas's trip. Religious considerations, moreover, in addition to commercial ones, deserve as much attention as many of the other topics now subsumed under the rubrics of the colonial and the imperial.

Notes

1. Algonkian perspectives and the agency of Native Americans in the cultural encounter are now important topics of scholarly inquiry, addressed elsewhere in this volume. For the historiographical issues involved in writing about these relations, see Jane Tompkins, "'Indians': Textualism, Morality, and the Problem of History," *Critical Inquiry* 13, no. 1 (1986), repr. in *"Race," Writing, and Difference*, ed. Henry Louis Gates Jr. (Chicago: University of Chicago Press, 1986), 59–77.

2. See, for example, Alden T. Vaughan, *Transatlantic Encounters: American Indians in Britain, 1500–1776* (Cambridge: Cambridge University Press, 2006), which focuses on 175 Indigenous Americans who came to England before the American Revolution; and Coll Thrush, *Indigenous London: Native Travelers at the Heart of Empire* (New Haven: Yale University Press, 2016), which examines travelers from around the British empire over five centuries.

3. Issues of status and ethnicity are treated separately here, although they were not easily disentangled in this period.

4. For differing views see, for example, Camilla Townsend, *Pocahontas and the Powhatan Dilemma: An American Portrait* (New York: Hill and Wang, 2004), 137; and Vaughan, *Transatlantic Encounters*. Vaughan says it took Dale almost two years to persuade the Virginia Company to assent to the trip, rather than the other way around (84). This assertion is also made by David A. Price, *Love and Hate in Jamestown: John Smith, Pocahontas, and the Heart of a New Nation* (New York: Alfred A. Knopf, 2003), 163, who explains that her trip was a publicity device for the lottery. Helen C. Rountree, *Pocahontas, Powhatan, Opechancanough: Three Indian Lives Changed by Jamestown* (Charlottesville: University of Virginia Press, 2005), 177, characterizes the trip as a voyage "subsidized" by the Virginia Company, noting "That may sound harsh, but it is true nevertheless." The phrasing intimates that it was a family trip co-opted by the Company.

5. Ralph Hamor, secretary to the colony, composed a riveting account of the courtship in a pamphlet entitled *A True Discourse of the Present Estate*

of Virginia . . . [and] The Christening of Powhatans daughter and her marriage with an English-man (London, 1615). News of the conversion and marriage were prominently displayed on the title page, so even those who did not purchase the pamphlet could learn about the events while browsing in London's bookstalls. Hamor had left the colony in June 1614, following the acting governor Thomas Gates to London. His text was entered at the Stationers' Company 20 October 1614, and published in 1615. In addition to Hamor's description of the colony, the printed text included letters from Rolfe to his superior, Deputy Governor Dale, explaining why he wanted to marry; letters from Dale to a London cleric; and from Virginia minister Alexander Whitaker to his cousin, the celebrated Puritan preacher William Gouge. The pamphlet was issued in two editions in the same year; the number of surviving copies indicates a large print run. Ralph Hamor, *A True Discourse* (London: by John Beale for William Welby, 1615) is given only a single number in the *English Short Title Catalogue* (ESTC 12736) and is not included in the European *United Short Title Catalogue* (USTC). See the facsimile edition published with an introduction by A. L. Rowse (Richmond: Virginia State Library, 1957).

6. Smith described Wahunsenacah's ten- or twelve-year-old daughter: who "not only for feature, countenance, and proportion, much exceedeth any of the rest of his people: but for wit and spirit, the only Nonpariel of his Country." She was also mentioned by William Strachey in his description of the colony dating from 1612, drawing on Smith, a work which remained in manuscript until the nineteenth century. William Strachey, *Historie of Travell into Virginia Britania* (London, 1612); facsimile edition, ed. Louis B. Wright and Virginia Freund (London: Hakluyt Society, 1953).

7. Andrew Thrush, "The Personal Rule of James I, 1611–1620," in *Politics, Religion and Popularity in Early Stuart Britain: Essays in Honour of Conrad Russell*, ed. Thomas Cogswell, Richard Cust, and Peter Lake (Cambridge: Cambridge University Press, 2002), 84, 103 at 91.

8. *Calendar of State Papers* (CSP) . . . *Venetian 1615–1617*, 89; Samuel R. Gardiner, *History of England from the Accession of James I. to the Disgrace of Chief-justice Coke. 1602–1616* (London: Hurst & Blackett, 1863), 2:368.

9. Thrush, "Personal Rule," 84.

10. Alerted most likely by sympathetic friends and fellow investors on the Privy Council, such as William Herbert, earl of Pembroke, Virginia Company officials believed, like the well-informed Spanish ambassador Diego Sarmiento, that the Privy Council had voted to proceed in mid-December.

11. If the king did call a Parliament in the new year, as everyone expected (and for which canvassing for votes had already begun), he could have prorogued

the session, as was his habit, postponing difficult decisions for as long as possible. Dr. Andrew Thrush of the *History of Parliament* kindly drew my attention to this point. Frequent prorogation was why the Parliament first called in 1604 lasted until 1610. The brief 1614 Parliament, which was not postponed but dissolved, appeared to be an anomaly.

12. Chris R. Kyle, *Theater of State: Parliament and Political Culture in Early Stuart England* (Palo Alto: Stanford University Press, 2012), 90.

13. In a letter to Sir Dudley Carleton on 22 June 1616, John Chamberlain described the disappointing lading. Norman E. McClure, ed., *The Letters of John Chamberlain* (Philadelphia: American Philosophical Society, 1939), 2:12.

14. Philip L. Barbour, *Pocahontas and Her World; A Chronicle of America's First Settlement in Which Is Related the Story of the Indians and the Englishmen, Particularly Captain John Smith, Captain Samuel Argall, and Master John Rolfe* (Boston: Houghton Mifflin, 1970), 153, for example, finds the timing of the trip of "small wonder."

15. It took more than six months for Spaniard Diego de Molina to return on "the next boat," as expected; Ambassador Diego Sarmiento de Acuña to the king of Spain, 17 October 1614, enclosing correspondence from Diego Molina in Jamestown, printed in Alexander Brown, *The Genesis of the United States* (Boston: Houghton Mifflin, 1890), 2:737, 740, 743.

16. The first expedition to Jamestown sailed from England in late December 1606 and famously arrived at the Chesapeake in mid-April 1607. After that, the Company pioneered a faster route across the Atlantic.

17. Captain Samuel Argall's movements are uncertain between November 1614, when he was in London seeking employment with the East India Company, and his departure from Virginia in April 1616. Argall is said to have sailed the *Treasurer* from England in February 1615 (Brown, *Genesis of the United States* 2:760, 816). He supposedly arrived in the colony in the summer, remaining there until April when he took the group back. More likely is that Argall made a round trip to Virginia early in 1615 and sailed there again in December on the *Treasurer* rather than staying in Virginia for most of 1616 as historians assume, following Alexander Brown.

18. E. M. Rose, "Company and Colony (1619): The Conflicted of Politics of Slavery in Early English America," (forthcoming). The name John "Hope," registered in the Port Book of Southampton, is not otherwise recorded. TNA Class E 190/820/9. Port Book. Port of Southampton., f17ro. I thank Dr. Catherine Wright for examining the manuscript with me.

19. Robert Cecil wrote to the English ambassador to The Hague, 8 April 1604, mentioning the king's gracious opinion of Captain Dale's merit. Ralph

Winwood, *Memorials of Affairs of State* (London: T. Ward, 1725), 2:18. Winwood's response acknowledging the recommendation is extant in the Cecil Papers at Hatfield House, dated from The Hague 9 April 1604: "I have received your letter which signifies his Majesty's pleasure for Capt. Dale." *Calendar of the Cecil Papers in Hatfield House*, volume 16, 1604, ed. M. S. Giuseppi (London: HMSO, 1933), 54.

20. Susan M. Kingsbury, ed., *Records of the Virginia Company* (Washington, DC: Government Printing Office, 1906), 1:267.

21. John Smith, *The Generall Historie* summarizing Hamor's *True Discourse*, printed in *The Complete Works of Captain John Smith, 1580–1631*, ed. Philip Barbour (Chapel Hill: University of North Carolina Press for the Omohundro Institute, 1986), 2:247.

22. See, for example, the explanation offered by the Library of Congress that Dale was "recalled under criticism" and wrote *A True Relation* (a text in fact authored by John Rolfe) to redeem his leadership. "The Virginia Records Timeline: 1553 to 1743," Library of Congress, https://www.loc.gov /collections/thomas-jefferson-papers/articles-and-essays/virginia-records -timeline-1553-to-1743/1610-to-1619/.

23. Despite repeated insistence by historians that Pocahontas was introduced to London society by Dale, there is contrary evidence. He is never mentioned in London but indicated on his arrival that he was headed to the Netherlands to negotiate back pay from the States General. As he later explained in a letter to Sir Dudley Carleton (printed in Brown, *Genesis*, 2:873–74), his return to the Netherlands was delayed many months while he cared for his wife.

24. See John Parker, *Van Meteren's Virginia, 1607–1612* (Minneapolis: University of Minnesota Press, 1971), 71 for Gates. Dale was in Netherlands in 1617 and with the help of a letter from King James received his back pay before sailing to Java for the East India Company the following February. Basil Morgan, "Dale, Sir Thomas (d. 1619), soldier and Administrator," *Dictionary of National Biography* (Oxford University Press, 2004), 14: 936–37.

25. Smith, *The Generall Historie*, in Barbour, *Complete Works*, 2:255. See Kimberly C. Borchard, "Diego de Molina en Jamestown, 1611–1616: Espía, prisionero, oráculo del fin del imperio," *Laberinto* 9 (2016), 33–54.

26. A member of the great fleet that sailed in 1609, Rolfe had traveled with his English wife on the *Sea Venture*, which was wrecked on the rocks surrounding Bermuda. Their daughter named Bermuda was christened there shortly after landing, but his wife and child soon died.

27. This census was included in Rolfe's *A True Relation*.

28. The months that followed the departure have been described as "having the primness of a corpse," a phrase used by Water F. Prince, "The First Criminal Code of Virginia," *Annual Report of the American Historical Association for the Year 1899* (Washington, DC: Government Printing Office, 1900), 1:309–63 at 362. This is probably based on a letter of January 1616 from George Lord Carew, who notes "The plantation att Virginia and Bermuda sleepes." John Maclean, ed., *Letters from George Lord Carew to Sir Thomas Roe, Ambassador to the Court of the Great Mogul. 1615–1617* (Westminster: Royal Historical Society, 1860), 27. For the return voyage, see below.

29. G. Melvin Herndon, *Tobacco in Colonial Virginia: "The Sovereign Remedy"* (Williamsburg: Virginia 350th Anniversary Celebration Corporation, 1957), 46.

30. E. M. Rose, "'The Real and Substantial Food of Virginia': Lottery Financing of the Early Colony, 1612–1621" (forthcoming).

31. Sir Thomas Dale to Secretary Ralph Winwood, 3 June 1616, in *Calendar of State Papers Colonial Series, America and West Indies: Volume 1, 1574–1660*, ed. W. Noel Sainsbury (London, 1860), 17.

32. For background on the sale of honors under King James I, see, most recently, E. M. Rose, "Viscounts in Virginia: A Proposal to Create American Noblemen (1619)," *Huntington Library Quarterly*, 83, no. 1 (Spring 2020), 181–98. John Chamberlain in a letter to Dudley Carleton, 11 June 1615, wrote that there is "much speach of new barons to be made for monie, which were the lesse to be misliked yf yt came to the Kings cofers" (McClure, ed., *Letters of John Chamberlain*, 1:601).

33. Christian F. Feest, "The Virginia Indians in Pictures 1612–1624," *Smithsonian Journal* 2, no. 1 (1967): 10–13; and Vaughan, *Transatlantic Encounters*, 53.

34. David R. Ransome, "Pocahontas and the Mission to the Indians," *Virginia Magazine of History* 99, no. 1 (1991): 81–94.

35. Court Minutes of the East India Company, 18 July 1615, in *Calendar of State Papers, Colonial Series, East Indies, China and Japan, 1513–1616*, ed. W. Noel Sainsbury (London: Longman, Green, Longman, and Roberts, 1862), 421.

36. Peter Walne, "The Collections for Henrico College, 1616–1618," *Virginia Magazine of History and Biography* 80, no. 3 (1972): 258–66.

37. Province of Canterbury, *To the minister and church-wardens . . . By vertue of his majesties most gracious letters, directed to the lord archbishop of Canterbury* [for collections to convert the Americans in Virginia, authorized by King James on 28 Feb. 1615 (o.s.) and implemented by G. Newman, Commissary General of Canterbury, in a letter dated 15 April 1616.] (London [T. Snodham, 1616]) The sole extant copy survives in Betherseden parish church in Kent.

38. *By His Majesties Counseil for Virginia. A briefe declaration of the present state of things in Virginia, and of a division to be now made, of some part of those lands in our actuall possession, as well to all such as have adventured their monyes, as also to those that are planters there* (London: T. Snodham, 1616). This is an eight-page text in quarto format, of which three copies are extant.

39. *By his Majesties Councell for Virginia. Whereas upon the returne of Sir Thomas Dale Knight, (Marshall of Virginia) the Treasurer, Councell, and Company of the same, have beene throughly informed and assured of the good estate of that colony* (London: Printed by Thomas Snodham). This recruiting broadside must have been published as soon as Argall received his commission as governor in November 1616.

40. Pocahontas's presence at the royal court did not first induce the king to take an interest in the education of Algonkian youngsters as suggested by Dagmar Wernitznig, *Europe's Indians, Indians in Europe: European Perceptions and Appropriations* (Lanham, MD: University Press of America, 2007), 17, following Barbour, *Pocahontas*, 173.

41. Joseph L. Chester, ed., *Register Books of St Dionis Backchurch, London* (London: Harleian Society, 1878), 96: "An East Indian was christned by the name of Peter."

42. Patrick Copland, *Virginia's God be thanked, or A sermon of thanksgiving for the happie successe of the affayres in Virginia this last yeare. Preached by Patrick Copland at Bow-Church in Cheapside, before the Honorable Virginia Company, on Thursday, the 18. of Aprill 1622. And now published by the commandement of the said honorable Company. Hereunto are adjoyned some epistles, written first in Latine (and now Englished) in the East Indies by Peter Pope, an Indian youth, borne in the bay of Bengala, who was first taught and converted by the said P.C. And after baptized by Master Iohn Wood, Dr in Divinitie, in a famous assembly before the Right Worshipfull, the East India Company, at S. Denis in Fan-Church* threele in London, December 22. 1616 (London: Printed by I[ohn] D[awson] for William Sheffard and Iohn Bellamie, 1622).

43. Two people identified as a "Virginian out Sir Thomas Smith's house" were buried in 1613 (the identical entries in the register appear on 28 October and 15 November), *St Dionis Backchurch*, 212, 213. A Virginian named Abraham was buried 6 August 1616.

44. Ian Duncan Colvin, *South Africa* (London: Caxton Publishing, 1909), 77–78, describes Cooree's legacy on his return to Africa.

45. John Martyn, "a Persian born," gave testimony in 1622 in London. See Peter Wilson Coldham, "The Voyage of the *Neptune* to Virginia, 1618–1619, and the

Disposition of its Cargo," *Virginia Magazine of History and Biography* 87 no. 1 (1979): 62.

46. Thomas Elkington took over after Captain Nicholas Downton's death in transit. "Relation of Master Elkington" in Samuel Purchas, *Hakluytus Posthumus or Purchas His Pilgrimes*, 4 vols. (London: William Stansby, 1625), vol. 1, chap. 4, 514–19.

47. Nothing more is known of these two or whether they were still living in London when Pocahontas arrived.

48. The Native American William Crashaw is listed in the Virginia muster of 1624, living on William Tucker's plantation. Rebecca Anne Goetz, *The Baptism of Early Virginia: How Christianity Created Race* (Baltimore: Johns Hopkins University Press, 2012), 91, assumes Crashaw's baptism occurred in Virginia after 1622. The English cleric and poet William Crashaw, who delivered the sermon on the departure of Lord De La Warr's fleet in 1609, was preacher at the Inner Temple, prebend of St Mary Matelon, Whitechapel from 1618; he died in 1626.

49. Imtiaz Habib, *Black Lives in the English Archives, 1500–1677: Imprints of the Invisible* (Aldershot, England: Ashgate, 2008), notes the baptism of Mark Antonie in 1616; but this should be read as 1617 [new style], three days before he was buried. The only suggestion offered about the baptism of Cleopatra, the Native American aunt whom Pocahontas's son Thomas would meet when he came to America, is that she "must have come to adopt this name after encountering an English troupe of actors, touring the colonies with Shakespeare plays"[!], for which see Wernitznig, *Europe's Indians*, 32. The more plausible scenario is that she was baptized as a young woman in England. Shakespeare's *Antony and Cleopatra* was first performed by the King's Men in 1607 and not published until 1623; but *Cleopatra*, by Queen Anne's favorite playwright Samuel Daniel, appeared in eight editions alone, with two more editions published in 1611.

50. Captain Thomas Hunt, who sailed to New England in consort with Smith in 1614, seized twenty-seven Natives, including Squanto (Tisquantum), and sold them as slaves in Spain. Squanto then made his way back to England, where he lived in the house of John Slaney before sailing back to New England with Thomas Dermer. William Bradford, *Of Plymouth Plantation, 1620–1647* (New York: Alfred A. Knopf, 1996), 80–89; John Smith, *The Generall Historie*, in Barbour, *Complete Works*, 1:294, 323, 433, 2:401, 429, 448. For the context of the kidnapping, see the traveling exhibition "Captured: 1614," part of *Our Story—A Wampanoag History* project, first held at Plymouth

Public Library in Plymouth, Massachusetts, 2014, in conjunction with the commemorations of the four hundredth anniversary of Plymouth (2020). https://www.plymouth400inc.org/our-story-exhibit-wampanoag-history/. For Squanto's legacy, see Neal Salisbury, "Squanto: Last of the Pawtuxets," in *Struggle and Survival in Colonial America,* ed. David G. Sweet and Gary B. Nash (Berkeley: University of California Press, 1981), 228–246; I thank the author for sending me an unpublished conference paper with his updated research.

51. John Chamberlain reported in January 1617 that Pocahontas was returning to America "though sore against her will." John Chamberlain to Sir Dudley Carleton, 18 January 1617, SP 14/90, f.56.

52. See E. M. Rose, "Did Squanto Meet Pocahontas, and What Might They Have Discussed?," *The Junto: A Group Blog on Early American History,* 21 November 2017, https://earlyamericanists.com/2017/11/21/did-squanto-meet-pocahontas-and-what-might-they-have-discussed/.

53. There is little evidence that the couple was "wined and dined by peers of the realm." See Francis Berkeley, "John Rolfe's Relation," in John Rolfe, *A True Relation of the State of Virginia Lefte by Sir Thomas Dale, Knight, in May Last 1616,* ed. Henry C. Taylor (New Haven: printed for H. C. T. by Yale University Press, 1951), 21–28, an opinion that is widely quoted.

54. The remarkable group of diverse individuals from around the globe is comparable to the assemblage of foreign items found in excavations of Narrow Street, Limehouse, on the outskirts of London, where many of the maritime employees of the East India Company lived in this period, an assemblage which has "no parallels in seventeenth century England." See Douglas Killock et al., "Pottery as Plunder: A Seventeenth-Century Maritime Site in Limehouse, London," *Post-Medieval Archaeology* 39, no. 1 (2005): 1–91.

55. Pocahontas had thrown in her lot with Rolfe after she had been kidnapped by Argall and her father had refused to negotiate an exchange of prisoners for her.

56. Roslyn L. Knutson, "A Caliban in St. Mildred Poultry," in *Shakespeare and Cultural Traditions,* ed. Tetsuo Kishi, Roger Pringle, and Stanley Wells (Newark, NJ: University of Delaware Press, 1994), 110–26 at 122.

57. The Gorachoqua are a tribe of the pastoral Khoikhoi people of southern Africa. Informed by Cooree, his people would later describe all English vessels as "Thomas Smythe ships."

58. Walter Peyton, "Voyage of Captain Walter Peyton to India, in 1615," in *A General History and Collection of Voyages and Travels,* ed. Robert Kerr (London: T. Cadell, 1824), 9:219–22 at 220.

59. Villiers made his debut on the masque stage at Twelfth Night 1615; he was ennobled the day before Twelfth Night 1617 as the Earl of Buckingham. For Villiers's dancing, see Jean MacIntyre, "Buckingham the Masquer," *Renaissance and Reformation* 22, no. 3 (1998): 59–81.

60. Writing well after the deaths of Pocahontas, Lord De La Warr, and Queen Anne, John Smith noted that Pocahontas was "accompanied with that honourable Lady the Lady De la Ware, and that honourable Lord her husband, and divers other persons of good qualities, *both publikely at the maskes and otherwise*" (Smith, *The Generall Historie*, in Barbour, *Complete Works*, 2:261). The oft-cited whirl of "plays, balls and other publick entertainments" she enjoyed comes from a much later interpretation based on Smith. See Robert Beverley, *The History and Present State of Virginia* (1705), ed. Susan Scott Parrish (Chapel Hill: University of North Carolina Press for the Omohundro Institute of Early American History and Culture, 2013), 34.

61. When it was explained to Tomocomo that he had indeed met the king, he famously complained, "You gave Powhatan a white dog, which Powhatan fed as himself, but your King gave me nothing, and I am better than your white dog." Smith, *The Generall Historie*, in Barbour, *Complete Works*, 2:261.

62. John Smith says "divers Courtiers and others, my acquaintances, hath gone with mee to see her," and Samuel Purchas later wrote in his *Pilgrimes* that Pocahontas met "divers particular persons of honor," but none of these are named. For De La Warr's connections with the Virginia Company, see E. M. Rose, "Lord Delaware, First Governor of Virginia and 'the Poorest Baron of this Kingdom,'" *The Virginia Magazine of History and Biography* 128, no. 3 (2020): 226–58.

63. Alexander Brown, *The First Republic in America; An Account of the Origin of this Nation* (Boston: Houghton Mifflin, 1898), 244.

64. Queen Anne's use of a masque to indicate political and social endorsements is the focus of much recent scholarship, but other than Smith, no one mentions the West family in attendance in 1617. Captain John Smith was not in London at the time.

65. The engraved portrait of Pocahontas was included in *Baziliωlogia: A Booke of Kings* (London: Printed for H: Holland, and are to be sold by Comp: Holland, 1618) and then reproduced in John Smith's *Generall Historie* (1624). Contrary to popular belief, there is no indication that the portrait was commissioned by her husband.

66. Samuel Purchas, *Purchas His Pilgrimage* (London: Henry Fetherstone, 1617), book 8, chap. 5, part 4, 946–48.

67. Writing after Pocahontas's death, Smith calls her "Lady Pocahontas alias Rebecca" (Smith, *The Generall Historie*, in Barbour, *Complete Works*, 2:261). The letter from Sir Edwin Sandys and John Wrothe to Sir Thomas Smith in the Ferrar Papers mentions "Mr John Rolfe and the Ladye Rebecka his wife, daughter of King Powhatan," printed in Ransome, "Pocahontas and the Mission to the Indians," 94. The social context of Jacobean England is frequently misunderstood. See, for example, the recent blog post by an expert on the religions of Indigenous peoples, who observed the commemoration of the four hundredth anniversary of Pocahontas's death at Gravesend in March 2017. He refers to "Lady Rolfe as an aristocrat" and *"her status as wife of an aristocratic colonist and member of the Court of King James"* (emphasis added) (Graham Harvey, "Pocahontas and Colonialism," *Contemporary Religion in Historical Perspective*, http://www.open.ac.uk/blogs/religious-studies/?p=387).

68. American historian Philip Barbour expresses surprise (with an exclamation point) that there was "not a word about her 'princely rank' or her husband!" (*Complete Works*, 260n2).

69. Smith, *The Generall Historie*, in Barbour, *Complete Works*, 2:260. Other than Smith's claim in 1624, five years after the queen's death, there is no evidence that he ever sent such a letter.

70. Chamberlain to Carleton, in McClure, *Letters of John Chamberlain*, 2:12; and Carew to Roe, in Maclean, *Letters from George Lord Carew to Sir Thomas Roe*, 36.

71. Beverley, *History and State of Virginia*, ed. Parrish, 34.

72. William Stith, *The History of the First Discovery and Settlement of Virginia: Being an Essay towards a General History of this Colony* (Williamsburg: printed by William Parks, 1747), 3:142: "There hath been indeed a constant Tradition, that the King became jealous, and was highly offended at Mr. Rolfe, for marrying a Princess. That anointed Pedant, it seems, had so high an Idea of the *Ius divinum*, and indefeasible Right, of Powhatan, that he held it a great Crime and Misdemeanor, for any private Gentleman to mingle with his Imperial Blood. And he might perhaps likewise think, consistently with his own Principles, that the Right to these Dominions would, thereby, be vested in Mr. Rolfe's Posterity. However, it passed off, without any farther bad Consequence, than a little Displeasure and Murmuring."

73. Reverend Peter Fontaine to his brother Moses, 30 March 1757, quoted in James Fontaine, *Memoirs of a Huguenot Family* (New York: G. P. Putnams, 1853), 352.

74. Kingsbury, *Records of the Virginia Company*, 2:152–53. The Company responded to Governor Argall in early 1618: "Wee cannot imagine why you should give us warninge yt Opachankano and the Natives have given their

Country to Mr Rolfe Child and that they will reserve it from all others til he comes of yeares except as we suppose as some do here report it to be a Devise of yor owne to some especiall purpose for yor selfe but whither yours or thers wee shall little esteeme of any such conveyance."

75. Barbour, *Complete Works*, 1:274.

76. Camilla Townsend, "The Pocahontas Pattern: Intermarriage as Political Strategy among Native American Women in Early Virginia" (paper delivered at the Pocahontas and Beyond Conference in London, March 2017) and developed in an essay in this volume.

77. Kelly L. Watson, "Mary Kittamaquund Brent, 'The Pocahontas of Maryland': Sex, Marriage and Diplomacy in the Seventeenth-Century Chesapeake," *Early American Studies* 19, no. 1 (Winter 2021): 24–63.

78. Smith, *The Generall Historie*, in Barbour, *Complete Works*, 2:260.

79. A manuscript copy in a scribal hand survives in Oxford, Bodleian Library, MS Ashmole 830, ff 118–119. See "Letter from John Rolfe to Sir Thomas Dale," *Virginia Magazine of History and Biography* 22, no. 2 (April 1914): 150–57.

80. The royal copy survives in the British Library. The autograph manuscript dedicated to the Earl of Pembroke (the Pembroke-[Keen]-Taylor copy), presumed to have descended in the family of Lord North, is at Yale University (Beinecke MS 567, bequeathed 1971). The copy made for Robert Rich, addressed to "my singular good frend," is preserved in the McGregor Library of the University of Virginia (MS 9202, acquired 1972). The modern edition discusses the variations: Rolfe, *A True Relation of the State of Virginia Lefte by Sir Thomas Dale, Knight, in May Last 1616*, ed. Henry C. Taylor (New Haven: printed for H. C. T. by Yale University Press, 1951). Samuel Purchas quickly summarized it in his travel compendium of 1617, but it was not otherwise "published" in 1617.

81. *Acts of the Privy Council of England, Colonial Series, I (1613–1680)*, ed. William L. Grant (London: His Majesty's Stationery Office, 1908), 14.

82. The letter from John Wrothe and Sir Edwin Sandys to Sir Thomas Smythe is printed in the appendix to Ransome, "Mission to the Indians," 94. Although it is dated 1616 (old style: the year began March 25), it was composed 10 March 1617, when Pocahontas was still alive and on the point of departure.

83. For the "formidable mental barrier," see David D. Smits, "'Abominable Mixture': Toward the Repudiation of Anglo-Indian Intermarriage in Seventeenth-Century Virginia," *Virginia Magazine of History and Biography* 95, no. 2 (1987): 157–92. For the "fantasy of intermarriage," see David Stymeist, "'Strange Wives': Pocahontas in Early Modern Colonial Advertisement," *Mosaic: A Journal for the Interdisciplinary Study of Literature* 35, no. 3 (2002): 109–26.

84. William Kelso, *Jamestown: The Truth Revealed* (Charlottesville: University of Virginia Press, 2017), 226. See also *The World of Pocahontas* exhibit at Jamestown Rediscovery Archeology Museum, Jamestown Virginia.

85. Thomas Gates may have been back in the Netherlands already by August 1614.

86. See Jennifer Potter, *The Jamestown Brides: The Story of England's Maids for Virginia* (Oxford: Oxford University Press, 2019).

87. The Jamestown-Yorktown Foundation has now sold out of its limited-edition reproduction of a small jug made c. 1590 in the Rhineland and described as "a royal gift as presented to Pocahontas by King James and Queen Anne." The Jamestown Settlement galleries also feature a blue onyx cameo of a bare-breasted woman in a huge necklace that was supposedly carved by a London jeweler during Pocahontas's time in England. They also feature a pair of mussel shell earrings set in silver and inlaid with mother of pearl—a shell found not in Virginia but on the eastern shore of the Bering Strait.

88. Mary C. Fuller, *Voyages in Print, English Narratives of Travel to America 1576–1624* (Cambridge: Cambridge University Press, 1995), 122, explains "*the proposed program of marriages* may have involved forms of coercion, deception and inequity but it was gentler than what followed" (emphasis added).

89. McClure, *Letters of John Chamberlain*, 2:56–57.

90. *Baziliωlogia: A Booke of Kings.*

WHY REBECCA?

Calvin and Indigenous Women

JAMES RING ADAMS

Names are powerful signifiers, especially when one chooses their own. Pocahontas was a childhood nickname. After her conversion, this daughter of Powhatan revealed to her English guardians that her real name was Matoaka. We
are told she had withheld this information "in a superstitious feare of hurte
by the English if her name were knowne."[1] Helen Rountree suggests that
she felt free to reveal her old secret name because she had just taken the new
and more powerful Christian name Rebecca.[2] The Simon van de Passe engraving from her trip to London identifies her as "Matoaka als Rebecca," following
the first historical mention of her secret name in Ralph Hamor's pamphlet,
A True Discourse of the Present Estate of Virginia (1614), published in connection with Virginia Company plans to bring her to England.[3] But we are concerned with her final name change, Rebecca. It seems only recently, with Helen
Rountree's note and a discussion in Camilla Townsend's excellent biography,
that this choice has received scholarly attention.[4]

Yet the name Rebecca, which Matoaka took for her baptism and marriage,
is so fraught with irony that there is little chance it was chosen lightly or without regard to its context. The biblical Rebecca was the wife of Isaac, the second
Patriarch; her story is deeply intertwined with the warnings in Genesis against
intermarriage with the daughters of the Canaanites. Abraham, the founding
Patriarch, was an immigrant to the land of Canaan. He originally came from
Ur of the Chaldees, via the plain of Haran in present-day Syria. In his last
days, he charged his chief servant to go back to his homeland and his kindred
to find a wife for his son Isaac. Abraham made his steward swear, "that thou
shalt not take a wife unto my son of the daughters of the Canaanites, among
whom I dwell."[5] The servant took the journey back to Mesopotamia and found

the young lady Rebecca, who happened to be the granddaughter of Abraham's brother. The emigration of Abraham to the new land of Canaan was a frequently cited role model for the settlement of Virginia. The analogy for an English settler in Virginia seeking marriage would be to send to England for a bride, preferably a second cousin, not to marry a daughter of the Indigenous people. By taking the name Rebecca, Matoaka turned this biblical injunction on its head.

Even more puzzling, the young divine who supervised her conversion, Alexander Whitaker, was possibly the last person in North America at that time to ignore the double and triple meanings of a biblical verse. It seems very unlikely that he would baptize his charge under this name without approving of the choice. A glimmer of his rationale emerges, however, both from a closer look at his theological background and from recent archaeology. Rebecca Rolfe was no ordinary convert, and Whitaker was no ordinary missionary.

Alexander Whitaker, Apostle of Virginia

Alexander Whitaker (ca. 1585–1617) is already a prominent figure in patriotic local histories. He has been given the sobriquet "the Apostle of Virginia." The year before he took charge of Matoaka, he published the fundraising pamphlet, *Good Newes from Virginia,* said to be the first book in English written in North America. He died at the age of thirty-two, drowned in the James River some time before May 1617, supposedly while trying to rescue an Indian woman. One wishes he had lived longer and written more.[6] Whitaker brought a notable education to Virginia. He attended Eton and received his MA from Trinity College, Cambridge, in 1604. But his family connection was even more illustrious. His father was the eminent divine William Whitaker (1547–1595), Regius Professor of Divinity and Master of St. John's College, Cambridge. Alexander was the fifth of eight offspring of the prolific theologian, who was said to have given the world a book and a child each year.[7] Although Alexander was only ten when his father died, associates of the Master remained close to the boy as he grew up. One such individual was William Crashaw (1572–1626), who earned his BA at St. John's around 1591 and remained a fellow there, receiving his BD in 1603. Before leaving for Virginia, Alexander wrote in his will, "Master Crashawe owe[s] me money."[8] A busy editor, Crashaw arranged publication of Alexander's *Good Newes from Virginia* and wrote an introduction; he also delivered a sermon of his own promoting the settlement.[9]

Interest in America ran strong in the Cambridge of the two Whitakers. As Andrew Fitzmaurice notes, an impressive number of the promoters and leaders of the Virginia Company were associated with St. John's College in the last two decades of the 1500s, when Dr. Whitaker was master. Notable figures ranged from Henry Wriothesley, Lord Southampton, patron of Shakespeare and investor of Virginia, to Samuel Purchas, the continuer of Hakluyt.[10] This influence also permeated Trinity College, the elder Whitaker's alma mater, which Alexander entered in 1602. His fellow classmates included John Winthrop, later leader of the Massachusetts Bay Colony, and John Cotton, eventually the preeminent divine in New England. (Winthrop's father, Adam, was auditor of both Trinity and St. John's. Adam's first wife was the sister of a master of Trinity. When the elder Winthrop arranged a first marriage for John, who was seventeen at the time, the service was conducted by a maternal uncle of Alexander Whitaker, Ezekiel Culverwell, who remained John Winthrop's pastor.)[11] This milieu surely contributed to young Whitaker's passion to join the Jamestown adventure.

This upbringing and intellectual ferment also shaped the theology that Whitaker brought with him, which Perry Miller has described as "almost if not quite" Puritanism.[12] Doctrinal lines were being drawn but had not yet hardened. The Separatist Brownists, later the Pilgrims of the *Mayflower* and American hagiography, were still an outlying sect, denounced by William Crashaw among others. But church discipline was beginning to tighten. In response to complaints about lax practice at Cambridge, new ecclesiastical canons in 1604 ordered the colleges to follow "the order, form and ceremonies of the Book of Common Prayer . . . without any omission or alteration." The new rules also required the wearing of the surplice, an outer draping on ecclesiastical robes and a hot item in the ongoing controversy over appropriate ceremonial vestments. Whitaker was a year short of his undergraduate degree at the time. In 1609 after earning his MA and receiving ordination, he was required to subscribe to three articles of Church discipline, including a promise to use the Book of Common Prayer "in public prayer, and administration of the sacraments, and none other."[13]

Yet at the time, a divine with doubts about High Church ritual and doctrine could still hope to remain a non-separating member of the clergy. In spite of the increasingly bitter debates over details, the dominant theology was still Calvinist, which I will discuss later. Whitaker himself played on this hope in a 1614 letter urging more clergymen to join him in Virginia: "But I much more

muse that so few of our English Ministers that were so hot against the Surplis and subscription: come hither w[h]ere neither are spoken of."[14] This jibe
might have been directed personally against his classmate John Cotton, who
remained in his Boston, Lincolnshire, parish until 1632 and emigrated to Boston in New England in 1633. Cotton and like-minded "conforming Puritans"
ultimately purged by Archbishop William Laud chose finally to go to Massachusetts Bay rather than Virginia. The first wave of this Great Puritan Migra-
tion was led by John Winthrop.

Whitaker himself seemed more motivated by a thirst for adventure, and
the glory of spreading Christian gospel, than by a need for doctrinal purity,
when after less than two years as preacher in a comfortable Yorkshire parish
he decided to emigrate to Virginia. He sailed in May 1611 with the new governor Sir Thomas Dale, planning to spend three years in Virginia. Crashaw
does not mention any doctrinal dispute in describing this decision. He emphasizes that Whitaker, "who was in as good possibility of better living as any of
his time . . . did voluntarily leave his warm nest, . . . to the wonder of his kindred and amazement of those who knew him."[15] Even though rumors were rife
in England about the hard times in Jamestown, what Whitaker found there
must have been a shock.

Women of Jamestown

Stories of the "Starving Time" and the occasional cannibalism had leaked out
in spite of the Virginia Company's strenuous efforts to suppress bad news.
But the real state of affairs is just beginning to emerge from archaeology. The
past decade and more of digging at the rediscovered site of the original Fort
James has produced thousands of artifacts showing much more interaction
between the first settlers and the local Indians than previously admitted. Specifically, the digs show extensive cohabitation with and exploitation of Native
women. The museum on the grounds of Historic Jamestowne, marvelously
named the Archaearium, displays a find of more than two thousand mussel
shell bead blanks and two stone drills used to make them, evidence that Native women lived and worked at the fort. Another exhibit recreates a domestic
scene in one of the early huts. An Indian woman prepares a dinner of turtle
while her presumptive English "master" relaxes nearby, leaving his dagger by
the bed. The tortoise carapace and the knife were preserved when the hut

caught fire and the roof caved in.[16] Later histories have been silent about the Native women of Jamestown, but there is contemporary confirmation.

A primary source on cohabitation comes from Spanish intelligence. Spain was deeply chagrined by the English intrusion into what it considered its domain. Although it lacked the military capacity to crush the colony, its ambassador to England, Don Pedro de Zuniga, maintained spies at Jamestown. In a ciphered letter from London dated August 1, 1612, he reported: "I have been told by a friend, who tells me the truth, that some of the people who have gone there, think now that some of them should marry the women of the savages of that country; and he tells me that there are already 40 or 50 thus married, and other Englishmen after being put among them have become savages, and that the women whom they took out, have also gone among the savages, and they have received and treated them well."[17] Taking this document at face value, and assuming a level of truth (albeit embellished), begs questions about where these Native women come from. Most likely, they were survivors of the neighboring tribe the Paspahegh (Pa-SPA-hay). Jamestown itself was situated on land belonging to the Paspahegh, a tributary of Powhatan's chiefdom. The tribe took the brunt of early Contact. The well justified mutual suspicion of the first days degenerated into skirmishes, hostage-taking, tense trading, and finally in August 1610 an English attack on the Paspahegh town. The seventy men led by George Percy killed fifteen to sixteen Indians (another estimate says sixty-five to seventy-six), burned the village, and cut down the corn crop.[18] One officer brought in "the Quene and her children" as prisoners but the other soldiers "murmured" because the captives' lives were spared. In a council on the boats as the force returned to Jamestown, "it was agreed upon," wrote Percy, using the bureaucratic passive voice, "to putt the children to deathe, the which was effected by Throwinge them overboard and shoteing owtt their braynes in the water."[19] The "Queen" was killed shortly after. This butchery appalled the Powhatan tribes, who considered that women and children should be preserved as war booty. The incident sparked the first Anglo-Powhatan War. It also extinguished the Paspahegh as a community.

It's a logical conclusion that at least some, if not most, of the Native women at Jamestown were survivors of the Paspahegh massacre, kept as war booty and virtual slaves. This shameful situation violated biblical injunctions, Virginia Company warnings, and even early Tudor government policy. Old Testament bans from the Babylonian captivity were harsh and explicit. "Ye shall not give your daughters unto their sons, nor take their daughters unto your sons, or for yourselves" (Neh. 13:25; see also Ezra 9:10–12). William Symonds's famous sermon at White-Chapel on April 25, 1609, admonished departing settlers, "They may not marry nor give in marriage to the heathen, that are uncircumcised. . . . The breaking of this rule, may breake the neck of all good successe of this voyage."[20]

When Henry VII issued patents to an Anglo-Azorean venture in New-foundland in 1501 and 1502, he authorized it to "chastise and punish" any of their settlers "who shall rape and violate against their will or otherwise any women of the islands or countries aforesaid." This provision paralleled Span-ish prohibitions against cohabitation in the Indies.[21]

The apparent widespread sexual exploitation in Jamestown is one of many signs of its social and moral collapse before the arrival of Governor Dale in mid-1611. Others would be the homicidal indiscipline of the troops under Percy and the archaeological and forensic evidence of cannibalism. These conditions explain the harsh discipline and extreme punishments imposed by Dale. But there has been extreme reluctance, then and later, to talk about the informal "marriage" arrangement (although one might read the frequent complaints about "idlenesse" as a coded reference to the situation). Remarkably, of the handful of explicit references that do survive, two involve Alexander Whitaker.

In Zuniga's report cited above, the ambassador's spy added a vignette about Jamestown's reaction to criticism of the "marriages": "A zealous minister of their sect was seriously wounded in many places, because he reprehended them."[22] Although not named, this zealot was almost certainly Whitaker. Shortly after arrival he was transferred to the more secure and family-friendly new settle-ment at Henrico, very likely for his own personal safety. In Whitaker's own pamphlet, *Good Newes from Virginia*, his personal anger bubbles from beneath the fund-raising homilies. A proof of God's favor toward the colony, he writes, was the effort of His Adversary to wreck it: "that the Divell is a capitall enemy against it, and continually seeketh which way to hinder the prosperitie and good proceedings of it; yea hath heretofore so farre prevailed, by his Instru-ments, the covetous hearts of many back-sliding Adventurers at home, and also by his servants here: some striving for superioritie, others by murmurings, mutinies, & plaine treasons, & others by fornication, prophanenes, idlenes, and such monstrous sinnes; that he had almost thrust us out of this kingdome." He adds, "I have shut up many things in few words."[23]

Educating Rebecca

Fornication, presumably with the daughters of the Canaanites, was Whitaker's big issue. He seems remarkably blasé about the extermination of the Paspahegh. At the conclusion of *Good Newes* he lists the "Pipsco" as one of "our eldest friends . . . who are our overthwart neighbors at *James-Towne*, and have been friendly to us in our great want."[24] But even though he denounced the cohabitation at Jamestown, he soon after was actively encouraging the romance and marriage of the Englishman John Rolfe and the daughter of Powhatan, known universally by her childhood nickname Pocahontas. This young lady, so prominent as a subteen in the early years of Jamestown, had been sent as far away from the settlement as her father could arrange and was possibly married to a warrior in a subsidiary tribe up the Potomac River. Hearing of her location, the aggressive English seacaptain Samuel Argall arranged to kidnap her and bring her to the colony as a hostage. She was placed in Whitaker's charge for Christian education in the relative security of Henrico. In 1614, he wrote that the marriage of "one Pocahuntas or Matoa daughter of Powhatan . . . to an honest and discreete English Gentlemen Maister Rolfe" and her renunciation of "her countrey Idolatry" was the best thing to happen in Virginia.[25] Obviously we are not dealing with the crude racism of later centuries. A more subtle logic is at play in Whitaker's attitude toward Indians and toward the conversion of Matoaka.

The biblical barriers to intermarriage were not based on biology or an anachronistic pseudoscience of racism; they responded to divides in language, culture, and religion. The warnings of Ezra and Nehemiah, and even the post-Exile version of the story of Rebecca, can be seen as a product of the Babylonian Captivity, when Israel struggled to maintain its national identity. The warning in Deuteronomy, "Neither shalt thou make marriages with them," is immediately explained: "For they will turn away thy son from following me, that they may serve other gods" (Deut. 7:3, 4). This religious barrier can be overcome.

It was Whitaker's job to remove this barrier, under the supervision of Governor Dale. In his brief account of the conversion, in fact, Whitaker almost obsequiously gives Dale full credit for the Christian education and baptism of Matoaka/Pocahontas. A passage published under Whitaker's name, but very likely inserted in his absence, describes the routine at Dale's residence in Henrico: "Every Sabbath day wee preach in the forenoone, and

Chatechize in the afternoon. Every Saturday at night I exercise in Sir Thomas Dale's house."[26] Whitaker's note and letters from Dale and John Rolfe were appended to a pamphlet by Ralph Hamor, *A True Discourse of the Present Estate of Virginia.* This first extended account of the courtship of Rolfe and Matoaka was published in 1615 and widely circulated in Europe in advance of their visit to England.[27]

The atmosphere of Matoaka's captivity must have been laden with far more than spiritual concerns. The sexual tension was overt in the case of John Rolfe, a recent widower who was a sometime guard and frequent visitor. The relations between Matoaka, Whitaker, and their host Governor Dale are murkier. Whitaker after all was in his late twenties, and Dale's attentions were not altogether wholesome. The already married governor later tried to wed Matoaka's younger sister, an offer Powhatan tactfully deflected. Dale, in the letter printed by Hamor, recounts that Matoaka told her brothers she "would stil dwel with the English Men, who loved her," using the plural.

However suppressed were Matoaka's ties to Dale and Whitaker, her relations with Rolfe were exposed to the world in the famous letter that Rolfe wrote to Dale explaining his decision to marry Matoaka. This tortured and tortuous letter resembles the anguished examinations of conscience so frequently written by later Puritans. Some of its most jarring passages can be read as a dialogue between Rolfe and Whitaker. Rolfe tries to deny that he was driven by "the unbridled desire of carnall affection." He acknowledges the "heavie displeasure which almightie God conceived against the sonnes of Levie and Israel for marrying strange wives." He often felt that it was a "diabolical assault" that "should provoke me to be in love with one whose education hath bin rude, her manners barbarous, her generation accursed." In this dilemma he sought "conference with honest and religious persons," among whom we can surely place Whitaker. Here he "received no small encouragement" for his growing conviction that the way out was "to indeavor to make her a Christian."[28]

We can see the hand of Whitaker at several points. Camilla Townsend notes similarities in language. Even an unpublished portion shows Whitaker's influence. The original, or a copy of it, is still extant in the Bodleian Library. It contains a section, cut by Hamor, stating Rolfe's intention to marry Matoaka even if she remained pagan. The children at least would be Christian. Rolfe bolstered this thought with a citation from Calvin's *Institutes of Religion,* very likely supplied by Whitaker. (Although an English translation of the *Institutes* was available from 1599, the citation is in the Latin style, more appropriate to Whitaker's learning.) But the real impact of Whitaker might have come in refuting the objection that Rolfe initially posed, that Matoaka was "of generation accursed."[29]

That thought, that Indians were children of the devil, fits into a recent trend to create a Black Legend of Protestant settlement in America, just as Elizabethans created a Black Legend of the Spanish empire. One hears that the Euro-American invaders demonized the Natives as children of Satan and thus justified dispossession and genocide.[30] This *histoire engagée* has plenty of material to work with, but Whitaker's theology is much more subtle and quite opposite in its conclusions.

Not Quite Puritan but All Calvinist

Whitaker and his father, as well as other Virginia Company preachers, were strong Calvinists. It is very likely that this atmosphere of "almost but not quite puritanism" enveloped the religious education of Matoaka/Pocahontas. Although the younger Whitaker was obligated to use the two-page catechism in the Book of Common Prayer, it would not be surprising if this "not unworthy son of an illustrious father" supplemented his instruction of Matoaka with the more elaborate catechism prepared by the elder Whitaker. This popular book, *A Short Sum of Christianity, Delivered by Way of Catchisme*, gave a clear and concise distillation of Calvinist doctrine.[31] And according to Calvin, we are all children of the devil. All humanity, wrote that cheery theologian, is "damned and forlorn by nature. Hath not the devil a tyrannical domination over us, from whence no man can deliver himself by his own power." Salvation comes not from human effort, "but from the peculiar mercy of God."[32] This grace comes to an Elect chosen by God, no matter how sinful or wretched their condition. The elder Whitaker emphasized in his catechism that grace could come to country folk as well to city folk, and Virginia Company preachers added that it could also come to savages in the New World. Hamor himself ended his pamphlet with the statement, "God (I hope) will raise up meanes beyond mans imagination to perfect his own glory and honour, in the conversion of those people, of whom undoubtedly (as in all other parts of the world), he hath predestined some to eternall salvation, and blessed shall those be that are the instruments thereof."[33]

Discussion of predestination is beyond the scope of this essay, and probably beyond human comprehension. Its puzzling contradictions twisted New Englanders into knots for several centuries. But no matter how many statements one compiles to the effect that Indians are "children of the divell" or "slaves to Sathan," one has to acknowledge that to a Calvinist, *all* humanity is conceived in sin and enslaved to the Devil. This theology gives no warrant for murder and dispossession.

This theology predisposed the younger Whitaker to a relatively sympathetic view of the Indians. He describes the Virginia Natives as "naked slaves of the divell" but quickly blames their condition on their awe of the Powhatan priesthood, the Quiokosoughs (an elaborate institution relatively rare in North American tribes). He compares the Quiokosoughs to English witches and reminds the reader of the benighted state of England "before the Gospell was preached in our Countrey." He calls the Indian priests "Sathan's own brood" but shows a lively curiosity about their conduct. He promises to study it further: "When I have more perfectly entered into their secrets, you shall know all."[34]

Moreover, Whitaker sees an obligation to rescue the "miserable people" under their spell. "One God created us, they have reasonable soules and intellectual faculties as well as wee: we all have Adam for our common parent: yea, by nature the condition of us both is all one, the servants of sinne and slaves of the divell."[35] Whitaker carries the argument further in a very important sentence. "Finally, there is a civill government amongst them which they strictly observe, and show thereby that the law of Nature dwelleth in them."[36] This line of thought coincides with William Crashaw's 1610 sermon before Lord de la Warr, which Whitaker probably had read.[37] It contradicts the negative depiction of Indians given by another Virginia Company propagandist, William Symonds. But most important, Whitaker gives more than an echo of a famous 1538 lecture by the Spanish jurist Francisco de Vitoria; it is a précis of Vitoria's thesis, which is now widely cited as a foundation of the modern doctrine of human rights.

Vitoria's lecture "On the Indians Lately Discovered" addressed the rights of the Indigenous peoples of the Americas in the face of Spanish conquest. It is a major surprise to those raised in the shadow of the Elizabethan "Black Legend" of Spanish cruelty to learn that Vitoria, the eminent Dominican theology professor at the University of Salamanca, defended the rights of the Indians and condemned the conquistadors. Vitoria's basic point, after a prolonged scholastic back-and-forth, was that Indians had basic political and property rights because they possessed the basic human quality of reason. He wrote, "This is self-evident, because they have some order (*ordo*) in their affairs: they have properly organized cities, proper marriages, magistrates and over-lords (*domini*), laws, industries and commerce, all of which require the use of reason; they likewise have a form (*species*) of religion, and they correctly apprehend things which are evident to other men, which indicates the use of reason."[38] It didn't matter that their government or religion sometimes sanctioned evil deeds, even human sacrifice. The capacity for organization demonstrated human reason; in Aristotelean terms, Indians were political animals and thus possessed human souls.

It is less surprising that an "almost Puritan" missionary should be citing Dominican precepts when we consider the logic of the Calvinist-influenced English colonial effort. The basic rhetorical justification for English expansion was that it brought the Word of God to the savages of the New World. Permanent settlements were necessary as bases for the spreading of the Gospel. But this effort presumed at a minimum that the savages possessed human souls capable of receiving Christianity, and with human souls came human rights. Calvinists went much further. Their preaching to Indians presupposed that scattered in this barbarous audience were souls who were predestined to conversion and membership in the Elect. As Hamor wrote in his peroration, "undoubtedly (as in all other parts of the world), [God] hath predestined some to eternall salvation, and blessed shall those be that are the instruments thereof."[39]

What Did Rebecca Think?

This emphasis on common humanity and the possibility of the in-gathering of predestined Indian members of the Elect justified Whitaker in his labors to educate Matoaka and to encourage Rolfe in proposing marriage to her. Whitaker considered their success in both endeavors to be momentous; he called the marriage and the conversion of Matoaka/Pocahontas to be "the best" of the news from Virginia.[40] But did he subject her conversion to the scrutiny later practiced in New England? Did he consider it a case of "historical faith" (the parroting of memorized words), or of "saving faith" (the true eternal salvation of the Elect)? Whitaker certainly was aware of the debate about distinguishing the two; his maternal uncle Ezekiel Culverwell later wrote a book on the subject.[41] Edmund Morgan argues that there was no requirement to prove an inward spiritual experience, a "saving faith," to join a Separatist or Puritan congregation of this period, let alone the Anglican church. Dale reported that Rebecca "openly confessed her Christian faith" but had more progress to make in knowledge of God. Still we can only surmise that the Englishmen took the conversion of Matoaka to Rebecca very seriously.[42]

But what did Matoaka herself believe? Her modern biographers emphasize that we have no firsthand testimony from her. A few decades ago, it was popular to speculate that she was merely playing to her captors or suffering from Stockholm syndrome. More recently, Camilla Townsend has emphasized Matoaka's strength and capacity to act for herself. She puts the marriage and disavowal of idolatry in the context of "time-honored" tribal custom.[43] We still don't know Matoaka's own mind. But we do have one glaring fact: for her Christian name she identified herself with Rebecca, the wife and mother of Patriarchs, the settlers of the Promised Land. She, and her mentors, saw her conversion important enough to equate her with "the mother of thousands of ten millions" (Gen. 24:60).

It is undeniable, as the material-oriented argue, that Matoaka's conversion and new life as Rebecca brought her immediate benefits. Helen Rountree observes that Matoaka's prospects in the Powhatan world, as a non-royal daughter of the polygamous chief, married off to an obscure warrior in a backwater of his domain, were rather limited. She writes, "And it was probably because of that less-than-stellar future that she was so amenable to conversion when the English captured her and treated her as a 'princess' in the permanent, European sense."[44] The political impact was direct and dramatic. If, as it appears, Matoaka and John Rolfe coordinated the announcement of their plan to marry, she telling her relatives as Rolfe released his letter to Thomas Dale, it was a masterstroke of diplomacy. The plan, quickly accepted by both authorities, defused an impending battle and produced the "Pocahontas Peace" that lasted for at least her lifetime and Powhatan's.

But these results, in her status and diplomatic impact, could have been obtained *without* her religious conversion. Rolfe expressed his intent to marry her either way. This intent, bolstered by a page citation to John Calvin's *Institutes of Religion*, was very likely supported by Whitaker. Since Rolfe mentions it in a draft of his letter to Dale, it appears that Matoaka resisted conversion until very late in her tutelage. Many biographers skim over this spiritual event, or discount it entirely, but it took place in an elaborate theological context.

What was it specifically in the Christian message, or Whitaker's version of it, that finally won her over?

From the haughty stare in Matoaka/Rebecca's one portrait during her life, one can speculate that Christian humility was not her strongest subject.[45] Her conduct in England shows no sign of the piety displayed by another convert, the Mohawk Kateri Tekakwitha, now a Roman Catholic saint. We suspect that Rebecca was much more attracted to the doctrine of the Elect, that the true converts were part of a community of Saints, predestined by God to receive salvation and escape the thrall of Satan. The Calvinist purpose in missionary work was not to make mass conversions, in the Spanish style, but to locate these predestined Saints and awaken them to their true status. For a young person caught between two worlds, the idea of belonging to a hidden elite superior to both cultures would have powerful appeal.

The special features of Powhatan society would have predisposed Matoaka/Pocahontas to accept a radical change in her status. As Rountree herself has written, "Priests were men of great power, because they had tremendous influence over the rulers they served . . . In the early seventeenth century their status was so high that they were commonly believed, along with the ruler themselves, to be demigods and to be the only people to be permitted an afterlife."[46] This dominance of a priesthood, along with religious features such as the rigorous Huskanaw training of selected youth, restricted-access temples with giant icons, and mortuary disarticulation of the elite, set the Powhatan chiefdom apart from northern Algonquian peoples; these features, among many others, led Frank Speck to call the Powhatan tribes "a marginal sub-center" of the Algonquian-speakers, mainly influenced from the outside by southeastern or Gulf culture.[47] Some recent scholars (including a tribal member) see Mississippian traces echoing Cahokia. Denied access to this priestly elite and its mysteries during her captivity, Matoaka/Pocahontas might have found it preferable to foreswear these "idolatries" in favor of membership in the Calvinist Elect and her richly layered new identity as Rebecca.

The name Rebecca already set Matoaka/Pocahontas apart from the women of Canaan, and by analogy the unfortunate Indian women, Paspahegh or other, cohabiting at Jamestown. The message might simply have been that as a convert and potential member of the Elect, "Matoaka als Rebecca" was already a member of the Christian family as the original Rebecca was already related to Abraham. But the biblical Rebecca played a major role in establishing the descendants of Abraham in their new land of Canaan. Whether at the prompting of the Rev. Whitaker or on her own, Matoaka/Rebecca was quite likely aware of the complex of resonances in the life of her new namesake. The original Rebecca suffered a difficult pregnancy and complained to the Lord: "And the Lord said unto her, two nations are in thy womb, and two manner of people shall be separated from thy bowels: and the one people shall be stronger than the other people: and the elder shall serve the younger" (Gen. 25:23). Two sons were born, Esau and Jacob. It's tricky to try to match them to the American Indian or English peoples—Esau was red but hairy; Jacob was smooth. But it's clear that Rebecca favored Jacob. She schemed to win him his dying father's blessing, in spite of Jacob's reluctance. When Esau, deprived of his rights as firstborn, threatened to slay Jacob, Rebecca heard of it and urged Jacob to leave Canaan immediately and take refuge with her relatives in Syria. She also declared to her husband Isaac that Jacob should find a wife there, dramatically expressing distaste for the women of their neighbors in Canaan. "If Jacob should take a wife of the daughters of Heth [the region around present-day Hebron], such as these which are of the daughters of the land, what good shall my life do me?" (Gen. 27:46). By scheming to give Jacob preference and then sending him back to her relatives for a wife, Rebecca became a crucial link in maintaining the tenuous Abrahamic presence in the new land of Canaan.

The extent to which Matoaka/Rebecca or Whitaker himself saw a guide to the future in the details of the life of the biblical Rebecca remains unknowable. Matoaka/Rebecca and Whitaker both died young in the same year, 1617. Matoaka/Rebecca succumbed to a possible pulmonary disease on the banks of the Thames in England; Whitaker drowned in Virginia. Rebecca bore only one son to John Rolfe, not twins, and this son remained in England for his education. The decisive conflict between the two nations of the New World erupted five years after her death. When her son Thomas returned to Virginia, he was squarely on the side of the English. Such are the confusions of biblical analogizing.

Yet Matoaka/Rebecca did come to have a role in America worthy of her namesake, the "mother of thousands of millions." Unlike the children of other Indian women of Jamestown, who disappeared from history, her descendants became famous as the First Families of Virginia. They maintained pride in their Native origin in the face of hardening racial divisions. The young Powhatan convert and bride became an icon for American identity. She might well have considered this fame her due, as the member of a spiritual elite transcending tribal divisions. But she might have been surprised, and a little annoyed, that she is remembered not by her Christian name Rebecca, but by her childhood nickname—"mischievous girl," Pocahontas.

Notes

1. William Stith, *The History of the First Discovery and Settlement of Virginia* (Williamsburg, Virginia: printed by William Parks, 1747; New York: Reprinted for Joseph Sabin, 1865; New York: Johnson Reprint Corporation, 1969 [reprint of Sabin edition with new introduction]), 136.
2. Helen C. Rountree, *The Powhatan Indians of Virginia: Their Traditional Culture* (Norman: University of Oklahoma Press, 1989), 80.
3. Raphe [Ralph] Hamor, *A True Discourse of the Present Estate of Virginia, and the Success of the Affaires there till the 18 of June, 1614*. Printed at London by John Beale for William Welby dwelling at the signe of the Swann in Paul's Church yard. 1615. Virginia State Library Publications No. 3 (Virginia State Library, Richmond: 1957), 60. Facsimile of first printing. Also accessible in *Captain John Smith: Writings with Other Narratives of Roanoke, Jamestown and the First English Settlements in America,* ed. James Horn (New York: The Library of America, 2007), 1162. Hamor himself uses the name Pocahuntas, but he appends a brief letter from Alexander Whitaker, her religious mentor, calling her "Pocahuntas or Matoa, the daughter of Powhatan." John Rolfe, in his famous letter also appended to Hamor's publication, refers to her as Pokahuntas (1164).
4. Camilla Townsend, *Pocahontas and the Powhatan Dilemma* (New York: Hill and Wang, 2004), 124–28, 202n10.
5. Gen. 24:3 (King James Version). For Rebecca, see Gen. 24:1–67, 25:20–28, 27:1–46.
6. Alexander Whitaker, *Good Newes from Virginia* (London: Imprinted by Felix Kyngston for William Welby, 1613). For biographical information, see H[arry] C[ulverwell] Porter, "Alexander Whitaker: Cambridge Apostle to Virginia," *The William and Mary Quarterly* 14, no. 3 (July 1957): 317–43; H. C. Porter, *The Inconstant Savage: England and the North American Indian 1500–1660* (London: Gerald Duckworth & Co., Ltd., 1979), 379–96.
7. William Whitaker, *A Disputation on Holy Scripture Against the Papists,* trans. and ed., William Fitzgerald (Cambridge: The University Press, 1849), x. The word play in the original Latin was *librum et liberum.*
8. Will printed in Whitaker Family Genealogy, Guildhall: 9171/23/75 and PRO: PCC PROB 11/130/95 available online at Rootsweb, accessed October 26,

2023, http://freepages.rootsweb.com/~madgenealogist/genealogy/Whitaker Desc.html.

9. Introductory letter in Whitaker, *Good Newes*, 1–15. William Crashaw, [*A New-yeeres Gift to Virginea:*] *A Sermon Preached in London before the right honorable the Lord LaWarre Governour and Captaine Generall of Virginea and others of his Majesties Councell* . . . (London: Printed for William Welby, 1610). The title, *A New Yeere's Gift*, was added by the printer to interior pages. It refers to the legal new year of the time, which started on March 25. Crashaw also transcribed and edited a number of sermons of the popular Cambridge preacher William Perkins, who was highly influential among Puritans. For Crashaw, see Porter, *Inconstant Savage*, 360–63.

10. Andrew Fitzmaurice, *Humanism and America: An Intellectual History of English Colonisation, 1500–1625* (Cambridge: Cambridge University Press, 2003), 67. Purchas included an abridged version of Whitaker's *Good Newes from Virginia* in volume 19 of his massive anthology *Hakluytus Posthumus*. Samuel Purchas, *Hakluytus Posthumus or Purchas His Pilgrimes* (Glasgow: James MacLehose and Sons, 1906), 19:334–93. Edmund S. Morgan, *The Puritan Dilemma: The Story of John Winthrop* (Glenview, Ill.: Scott, Foresman and Company, 1958), 5–7.

11. Porter, "Alexander Whitaker," 328–30.

12. Perry Miller, "The Religious Impulse in the Founding of Virginia: Religion and Society in the Early Literature," *The William and Mary Quarterly* 5, no. 4 (1948): 514. This influential article observes that "professions of Virginia adventurers sound much like those of Massachusetts Puritans" (493). Whitaker and Crashaw provide much of the source material.

13. Porter, "Alexander Whitaker," 330–31.

14. Alexander Whitaker, letter to "My Very deere and Loving cosen M[aster]. G[ouge]., minister of the B[lack]. F[riars]. in London," appended to Hamor, *A True Discourse,* 61.

15. William Crashaw, "Epistle Dedicatory," in Whitaker, *Good Newes*, 3; Porter, *Inconstant Savage*, 387.

16. "Inside the Archaearium: The World of Pocahontas, Unearthed" and "Mussel Shell Beads," Jamestown Rediscovery: Historic Jamestowne, accessed January 12, 2020, http://historicjamestowne.org/collections/exhibits/. William M. Kelso, Beverly Straube, Daniel Schmidt, eds., *2007–2010 Interim Report on the Preservation Virginia Excavations at Jamestown, Virginia* (Jamestown: Jamestown Rediscovery, March 2012), 34–36. Personal visit to Archaearium (March 2016).

17. Alexander Brown, *The Genesis of the United States* (Boston: Houghton, Mifflin and company, 1890; reissued New York: Russell & Russell Inc., 1964), 572, document ccxxiii.

18. "Timeline of Paspahegh-English Interaction: August 9, 1610," Virtual Jamestown, http://www.virtualjamestown.org/paspahegh/timeline.html.

19. George Percy, "A Trewe Relacyon of the procedeing and ocurrentes of Moment which have happened in Virginia . . ." in *Captain John Smith: Writings with Other Narratives* (New York: The Library of America, 2007), 1104–5.

20. William Symonds, *Virginia. A Sermon preached at White-Chappel, in the presence of many honourable and worshipfull, the Adventurers and Planters for Virginia, 25 April 1609. Published for the benefit and vse of the Colony, planted and to bee planted there, and for the Aduancement of their Christian Purpose* (London: Printed by I. Windet, for Eleazar Edgar and William Welby, 1609).

21. Lorraine Attreed, "Henry VII and the 'New-Found Island': England's Atlantic Exploration, Mediterranean Diplomacy, and the Challenge of Frontier Sexuality," *Mediterranean Studies* 9 (2000): 73–74.

22. Brown, *Genesis*, 572.

23. Whitaker, *Good Newes*, 32

24. Whitaker, *Good Newes*, 43.

25. Alexander Whitaker, "Letter to . . . M. G.," in Hamor, *A True Discourse*, 59–69.

26. Hamor, *A True Discourse*, 60. This account of religious routines was inserted in later printings to replace Whitaker's jibe about "Ministers . . . hot against the Surplis." On textual variants, see Virginia State Library reprint, p. viii–ix.

27. Hamor, *A True Discourse*, 61–68. A German translation appeared very quickly (Virginia State Library reprint, xii).

28. John Rolfe, "The Coppie of the Gentle-man's letter to Sir Thomas Dale, that after married Powhatan's daughter, containing the reasons that moved him thereunto," in Hamor, *A True Discourse*, 61–65.

29. Rolfe, "The Coppie of the Gentle-man's Letter to Sir Thomas Dale," in Hamor, *A True Discourse*, 64. Townsend, *Pocahontas*, 114–17, 199nn15–16. Transcription of unpublished portion of letter in Philip Barbour, *Pocahontas and Her World* (Boston: Houghton Mifflin, 1970), 247–51.

30. William Crashaw offered another way out. Although God had cursed the Canaanites, "we have no such commandement touching the Virginians." The full quotation: "it is lawfull for a Christian to have commerce in civil things even with the heathen: unlesse they bee such of whom God hath given a plaine and personal charge to the contrairie, *as he did to the Israelites of the cursed Canaanites, whome they were commanded to kill, and have nothing to do withal:*

but we have no such commandement touching the *Virginians*" (emphases in original) (*Newe-yeeres Gift*, D3v).

31. William Whitaker, *A Short Sum of Christianity, Delivered by Way of Catchisme* (London: Printed for J. E. and are to be sold by Thomas Pierrepont at his shop in Pauls Church-yard at the signe of the swan, 1651). A Book of Common Prayer, purportedly from Jamestown of this period is on display at St. George's Church in Gravesend, UK, where Rebecca Rolfe is buried. The rector, the Rev. Canon Christopher Stone, says he is confident of the dating because the book contains a prayer for Prince Henry, who died in 1612. Rector Stone graciously allowed this author to photograph the catechism. With conversion from black type and modernized spelling, it appears substantially the same as the catechism in the currently used Episcopal Book of Common Prayer.

    Catechisms proliferated in this period, along with doctrinal disputes. William Crashaw produced one of his own. It was published in London in 1617 and went through six editions by 1633. (*Milk for Babes. Or, a Countrey Catechisme* [Printed by Nicholas Okes, 1633].) The title proved highly popular. Variations were used by three other compilers, culminating in John Cotton's own *Milk for Babes, Drawn Out of the Breasts of Both Testaments*, ed. Paul Royster (London, 1646; Lincoln: DigitalCommons@University of Nebraska–Lincoln, 2013). For a history of the title, see Paul Royster's note on the text (Cotton, *Milk for Babes*, ed. Royster, 14).

32. John Calvin, *The Best of John Calvin*, comp. Samuel Dunn (London: Tegg and son, 1837; Grand Rapids, MI: Baker Book House Company, 1981), 162–63.

33. Hamor, *A True Discourse*, 47.

34. Whitaker, *Good Newes*, 33–34.

35. Whitaker, *Good Newes*, 34–35. Whitaker was also a collector of what we would call ethnological material. He reports that he sent the Virginia Council in England an image of the Powhatan god painted on one side of a toadstool. *Good Newes*, 33. Also mentioned in Samuel Purchas, *Purchas his Pilgrimage or Relations of the World and the Religions Observed in All Ages and Places*, 4th ed. (London: Printed by William Stansby for Henry Featherstone, 1626), marginal note, 765.

36. Whitaker, *Good Newes*, 35.

37. Compare Crashaw, *Newe-yeeres Gift*, "for the time was when we were savage and uncivill, and worshipped the devill, as now they do" (C4v) with Whitaker, *Good Newes*, "Oh remember (I beseech you) what was the state of *England* before the Gospell was preached in our Countrey" (33). For Whitaker's

"One God created us," compare Crashaw, "For the same God made them as well as us" (C3r). Both Whitaker and Crashaw see a rudimentary civil society among the Virginia Natives, which is a precursor for receiving Christianity. See Crashaw, "a people inclinable (as we see by some experience already), first to civility and so to religion" (C3v). Whitaker does not go as far as Crashaw in comparing the settlers in Virginia to the founders of classical Rome, but the idea of a founding certainly attends the name Rebecca.

38. Francisco de Vitoria, "De Indiis [On the American Indians]," in *Political Writings*, ed. Anthony Pagden and Jeremy Lawrance (Cambridge: Cambridge University Press, 1991), 250.

39. Perry Miller, "The Religious Impulse in the Founding of Virginia," op. cit. 517–18, quoting Hamor, *A True Discourse*, 6.

40. Hamor, *A True Discourse*, 59–60. Dale, accepting credit for the conversion, wrote "were it but the gayning of this one soule, I will thinke my time, toile and present stay well spent." Hamor, *A True Discourse*, 57–58.

41. Edmund S. Morgan, *Visible Saints: The History of a Puritan Idea* (New York: New York University Press, 1963; repr. Mansfield Center, CT: Martino Publishing, 2013), 42–43n19. Morgan quotes Culverwell's *A Treatise of Faith* (London, 1623) at several points (66–67n3, 70–71n13), and pairs him with William Perkins, the best-selling Cambridge preacher whose works were edited after his death by William Crashaw. Cf. Porter, *Inconstant Savage*, 362.

42. Hamor, *A True Discourse*, 57–58.

43. Townsend, *Pocahontas*, 118–20.

44. Rountree, *Powhatan Indians of Virginia*, 113.

45. Simon van de Passe (1595–1647), engraving "Matoaka als Rebecca," apparently made from a drawing from life now lost. According to my colleague Cecile R. Ganteaume, associate curator at the National Museum of the American Indian—Smithsonian, the engraving appeared in some editions of *Baziliωlogia: A Booke of Kings* (1618) and the frame resembles the book's portraits of British monarchs. Ms. Ganteaume curated the "Pocahontas" gallery of the museum's ongoing exhibit *Americans*. See Cecile Ganteaume, "Marking the 400th Anniversary of Pocahontas' Death," *American Indian Magazine* 18, no. 3 (Fall 2017): 28–33.

46. Rountree, *Powhatan Indians of Virginia*, 100.

47. Frank G. Speck, *Chapters in the Ethnology of the Powhatan Indians of Virginia* (New York: Museum of the American Indian—Heye Foundation, 1928), 227–28.

PART IV

VISUAL AND SENSORY RECORDS AND RECLAMATIONS

VISUAL CONSTRUCTS AND INDIGENOUS CHARACTER IN AMERICAN ORIGIN MYTHS

Pocahontas, George Washington, and the Parental Structure of Nationhood, 1820s–1870s

GRAZIELLA CREZEGUT

> The Pocahontas narrative confirms that a painless fusion of colonial and native worlds produces no synergistic social systems, but reproduces the dominant culture. As Euro-American society has reinforced conceptions of its own superiority, the Pocahontas legend has operated as a constituent of national mythologies.
>
> —Donna J. Kessler, *The Making of Sacagawea*

In their respective articles on the condition of Native women, Clara Sue Kidwell and Nancy Shoemaker point out Pocahontas's cultural pervasiveness, highlighting her presence in most schoolbooks as a key factor in the continuous dissemination of her story.[1] Dominant in this dissemination are stories of Pocahontas as the Savior of Jamestown whose role was essential to the survival of the first British colony, or as the Indian princess whose values are associated with a fantasized primitive nobility. Regardless of the nobility of her actions or status, the result is identical: she is a constructed character, whose constant characterization as a "noble Indian" from the past is constitutive of the larger myths reshaping the Contact period into a unified, national narrative.[2]

As little is known about the real life of Pocahontas, she becomes the perfect vessel for this type of mythological representation. One clear fact is that she was the daughter of a Powhatan chief, in present-day Virginia, and that her life was marked by a distinct bond with the first British settlement of Jamestown in the early seventeenth century. Because most of this connection is remembered through the account of John Smith, the only certainty is that she played the role of a mediator between Powhatans and British settlers. As such, she was progressively assimilated into British society, culminating with her conversion to Christianity and subsequent marriage to a British tobacco merchant.[3] Nevertheless, despite, or rather because of, the very scarce sources regarding her life, her story passed through time and merged into popular culture. Michelle LeMaster notes that she has become "one of white America's most familiar heroines, the subject of countless biographies, school lessons, and a Disney animated feature film."[4]

LeMaster's remark captures two key underlying issues in the representation of Pocahontas: the fragmentation of her identity and the ambiguous legacy of her story. As LeMaster describes, Pocahontas is not referred to as a Native American woman or historical figure. She is dispossessed not only of her identity but also of the legacy of her own story, being reduced to a role in a white American–owned collective memory. The characterization is interesting because it transforms the assimilation process—of a Native woman integrated into an emerging Euro-American culture—to a figurative assimilation as well, one of a Native American narrative appropriated into a white account of history. This assimilation and blurred distinction between Native American and white American components is a common theme in the literature on the subject. Elizabeth Bird describes Pocahontas as "the last white myth," while Philip Young counters that Pocahontas is "one of our few, true native myths," recalling still her liminal position inside and outside her own culture.[5]

These intertwined topics of legacy, identification, and appropriation are in fact indissociable from the image cultivated of Pocahontas in American national myth. Her role in a parental representation of the national construct emerged in the early nineteenth century and grew in importance after the so-called "Second War of Independence" against the British Empire (1812–15). This period saw the "greatest dissemination of the Pocahontas legend," according to William Rasmussen and Robert Tilton, in the ideological effort to include an Indigenous component not simply in myths of discovery, but also in myths of national origins and founding.[6] Behind this effort lay the ambition to assert the independent status of the young American Republic by appropriating Indigenous features into the creation of an American patrimony that would be distinct from the history and culture of Britain.

Visual symbols are core components of ideological attempts to create political icons and national allegories, and the nature of images is to be immediate. The capacity to encapsulate many encodings in one simple medium, which can easily be reproduced and rooted in collective memories, serves the construction of a national narrative. The construction of a singular American identity in the Early Republic also opened the way to a whole new set of representations in official and elite art. The visual material produced in this period fed the enterprise of national cohesion and the development of American cultural nationalism.

Parental structures and the concept of kinship are essential in understanding this visual mythological framework, which represents a rupture with the Old Continent and an alternative quest for a connection with the New World; a symbolic separation from the "European forefather" and adoption of a distinct "ancestry" from which the "national family" originated. The Pocahontas imagery was part of a whole schema and network of family-based representations that were constitutive of origin myths in this period, among which the most familiar image was the myth of founding fathers. George Washington benefits from a particularly rich iconography in this myth, which erected the framers of the Constitution as creators of the American Republic, adding this contractual origin as an alternative to the iconography of the British monarchy. Pocahontas, with her inscription in the distant past, would participate in this ideological effort of cultural distinction, adding a deeper historical origin to the national construct and even an alternative ancestry to the American people. The fantasized interpretation of her support of Jamestown would become foundational, transfigured into a pre-national past.

Invention of the "Rescue" Tradition and Foundational Narrative

The connection between Pocahontas and national myths in the nineteenth century was explored by Robert Tilton in his detailed analysis of the evolution of her narrative. In Tilton's reading, Pocahontas becomes the heroine of a founding episode, her actions imbued with "proto-nationalist feelings."[7] As Rayna Green has shown, the episode in which Pocahontas saves John Smith, iconically depicted with "her body flung over the head of our endangered hero," became in the antebellum period a "major scene of national myths."[8] The story was presented as the moment when the future American people were recognized by the first inhabitants of the New World as the light of civilization, thereby providing both a rationale and an anchorage for the creation of an American nation.

The mechanisms of this construct, in particular the positioning of Pocahontas as a visual icon in the broader parental structure of the founding fathers myth, merit further attention. Ann Uhry Abrams has investigated the myths of Jamestown and Plymouth in the rivalry between North and South before the outbreak of the Civil War, but she focused on the competition between the two narratives and conceptions of America's origins rather than exploring Pocahontas's inter-iconicity.[9] Rasmussen and Tilton's observation that Pocahontas was raised to the status of "female counterpart to George Washington" by southern artists in the lead-up to the Civil War invites inquiry into what made this reciprocity possible. What does Pocahontas's role in this parental structure imply about the use of Indigenous character in national foundation myths and the representation of the United States as a family entity?[10]

To further explore this connection between Pocahontas and the founding father myth, and her iconicity as giving Indigenous character to origin myths, a preliminary step is to return to and clarify the components of the visual representation of Pocahontas. Fundamental to this investigation of the connection between Pocahontas and foundational myths is the widely recognized scene of the rescue of John Smith and its integration into the visual symbols of a realigned pre-national past in the 1820s. As Tilton has shown, this popular episode of her narrative was deployed in a strategy to root the national construct in a more distant past, presenting the colonial period as a pre-national past. It also participated in a realignment of this past that downplayed the role of European settlements and emphasized the contact with seemingly noble primitive Indians as foundational material, in a strategy of cultural and historical distinction from the British Empire.

This strategy is understood in the context of the challenges experienced since the Declaration of Independence. The American Republic remained politically and militarily threatened by the British Empire, and it was threatened ideologically too, due to a lack of a singular culture and distinct past that could legitimize the constitution of a separate national entity. The effort to build a unique identity, distinct from a European legacy, and to obtain the recognition of this identity by rival powers was crucial from the beginning of the revolutionary period. The War of 1812 increased the momentum of national pride and coincided with the construction of a culture destined to represent further separation from Britain, despite the countries' similar aesthetic canons.[11]

Within this framework, specifically the production of new national and foundational symbols, the scene of Pocahontas saving John Smith became a new iconic scene of the past, or what Eric Hobsbawm calls an "invented tradition."[12] According to Hobsbawm's framework, cultural traditions are a set of ritualized practices—in this case, the repetitive exposure to a codified scene—designed to inculcate values and norms within a society. Hobsbawm argues that American nationalism in particular relied on "the invention of emotionally and symbolically charged signs of club membership rather than the statutes and objects of the club."[13] In other words, sharing the same federative symbols and traditions binds the nation together through a collective remembrance of these created signs, replacing missing features of nationalism such as an unique language.

Applying Hobsbawm's analytical framework, the scene of Pocahontas saving John Smith became part of national iconography when it was incorporated into the design of the Capitol in 1825.[14] Entitled the *Preservation of Captain Smith by Pocahontas,* Antonio Capellano's sculpture can be understood as the starting point for Pocahontas's positioning in visual symbols of reinvented foundations as she was integrated into the Capitol's depictions of the colonial period through its relief panels. This scene became a "type" that was reproduced in the period. This created a familiarity with the narrative that made it "a new tradition," a new foundational story that expressed a realigned prenational past. With a limited number of signs, the intensity of the scene is captured in what would become a typical composition in almost every repetition of it in instructive illustrations: the powerless captive lying on the ground, the rescuer standing by his side as a figure of mediation, a group of aggressors preparing for assault, and one figure of arbitration at the margins of the scene. This schematic representation is the first sign of the instrumentalization of Pocahontas's story, with the creation of a codified simple scene destined to be an immediately recognizable iconic episode.

But the strongest evidence of an invented tradition, as a new symbol in national myths, is in the choice of this episode of her narrative. Referring to Hobsbawm's definition, the process of inventing a new tradition involves representing this newly created tradition as if it was rooted in a distant past. Among other things, this inscription into the past is often achieved by adopting ancient materials, which are, in turn, reinvented in the present. Following this principle, it is already possible to identify in the visual choice of an Indian princess saving the innocent captive an echo of the European medieval folklore of knighthood and chivalry, with the brave knight rescuing the princess in her tower. But adaptation of old material in this scene is not limited to this medieval folklore; it is combined with the literary *topos* of captivity narratives in white-Indian relations, inherited from the colonial period, where stories of abductions by Indian tribes were a popular theme and source of fear.[15]

The overall result of these inter-references is that both of these deeply rooted representations are reinvented in the episode of Pocahontas saving Smith; they generate a new cultural tradition, subverting their usual construction. In this story, the noble figure rescuing the innocent in distress is not the brave knight serving a damsel but the valiant princess protecting the endangered explorer. The scene of captivity that is represented does not focus directly on the fear of Indian savagery but on the noble Indian responding to the appeal of Euro-American civilization to the point of defending it. Already, the scene resorts to ancient mental constructs to better impregnate collective memories with the new tradition, displaying Indigenous figures rescuing the future American people as an early foundational gesture.

Adding to this ancient material to shape a rejuvenated symbolic narrative of rescue, the subsequent repetition of the scene displaces the foundation of the American people to a pre-American rather than colonial past. The process exemplifies Hobsbawm's proposition that invariance and repetition are the first principles of any tradition: "Inventing a tradition . . . is essentially a process of formalization and ritualization, characterized by references to the past, if only by imposing repetition."[16] A type was indeed created from the composition of Capellano's sculpture, which produced a schematic and simplified representation of the event, already revealing what could be described as a formalization of the scene. In a very compact composition, the attention is focused on the actions and types represented. Rasmussen and Tilton see in this "simple and bold" composition the primary ambition to faithfully render, in a limited space, the representation found in the *Generall Historie* written by Smith, and in which the first mention of this episode appeared.[17] But what ultimately matters was not so much the motivations of Capellano in choosing this composition, his voluntary or involuntary choice of a minimalist representation, but rather the constitution of the type it represented and which would become invariant and systematically reproduced. Focusing on selected representations in the history and fiction books by William Croome in 1843, William Simms in 1846, and Marcius Willson in 1847, even the invariance between the scenes reinforces the process of "formalization" and "ritualization" as described by

Hobsbawm.[18] They all offered an almost identical scene in which Pocahontas was made a central character, an actress of the scene as the focal point within the composition but simultaneously made passive and submissive by her position, kneeling down by the side of the captive. In the same way, Smith and his executioner maintain their positions, the former as a defenseless victim on the ground and the latter as an aggressor whose savagery is implied by his facelessness.

Even more revealing of this invariance, to produce a monolithic federative symbol, is the reiteration, within more diversified encodings, of the same stability in the scenic composition. When taking a close look at the scenes produced by Marcius Willson, William Croome, and William Simms, different encodings are at play, but the convergence in terms of the mode of representation is indisputable. Willson played on the addition of volutes of smoke. Croome proposed the character of a mediator through the liminal position of Pocahontas, recalling the position of the Roman orator, particularly present in the political representations of the time, and thus linking the Native American oral tradition, which fascinated American artists, to that of advocacy in the American Republic.[19] Finally, Simms presented a scene that seemed to echo the issues of the Mexican War from 1846 to 1848, in which the problems relative to integration of Indigenous peoples were reactivated. However, despite these additions indicating the influence of the political context on the encoded message, and whether peaceful or belligerent white-Indian relations are emphasized, the general composition remains the same: Smith rests on the ground, Pocahontas lies over him or at least positions herself at his level, the chief presides over the scene, and two main aggressors are attacking. In the end, in the modulation of encodings, there is still invariance through a stable composition, illustrating how iconic and symbolic the image became in the period. The process of turning this "Rescue scene" into a new tradition from the European inheritance (as materialized in the recovery of the same old traditions of knighthood and chivalry) emphasized a more complex relation to the quest for cultural independence, in which a separation from European ancestry is asserted but a continuity of cultural legacy is maintained.

From Abductors to Saviors: Pocahontas and the
Indigenous Character in American Origin Myths

The creation of a ritualized, codified, and repeated symbol of foundation in the iconography of Pocahontas's rescue of Smith was informed by the evolving symbolism of primitivism in the period, and the inclusion of so-called primitive Indians in origin myths that involved constructing an alternative past to downplay the connection with Europe. Starting in the revolutionary period, myths in the United States operated as core components of nationalism. As noted by Élise Marienstras, they were "constitutive of a common culture, crystallizers of a collective identity since the end of the colonial period [and] would, after the adoption of the constitution, be unified into a coherent and active national ideology."[20] The reason for this politicization of myths lay precisely in the need to assert a political independence after the revolution, as well as to claim a culturally distinct character. To restate the well-known argument of Benedict Anderson, the specificity of American nationalism amounts to the fact no singular past, language, or culture could be isolated and used as a rationale for the nation to exist as a separate entity from the British Empire, with which it shared a common history and cultural framework.[21] Myths became therefore this necessary medium, in the ideological strategy to reinterpret history with founding episodes, national heroes, and other reinvented symbols that could evidence a singular identity, a distinct origin, and a rationale for the future national construct.

Interestingly, what this quest for an apparent distinction from British culture produced is a realignment of the relation with Indigenous peoples. Through the manifestation of a bond with the first inhabitants, unclaimed and even feared until then by the British, the figuratively young American people could associate directly with the original people of the New World, substituting European ancestry for a fantasized Indigenous link with the New World. The realignment is in fact more global; it is an addition to formerly Eurocentric myths of discovery that focused on contact with a dangerous yet appealing exotic otherness. The production of an American self, in which the focus was no longer alterity but origins, established pre-foundational episodes and proto-American figures from the contact period. If exoticism and otherness continued to feed the American imagination in the ongoing development of the myth of discovery, this additional layer of nationalism, foundations, and ancestry complicated the relation of the Indigenous character to US culture in the first half of the nineteenth century. This became especially acute when contrasting its symbolic use with the Indian policy of the Jacksonian era, which put an end to a possible "expansion with honor" as envisioned by Monroe, or the Jeffersonian ideal of peaceful relations with Indigenous peoples converted into farmers.[22] The eviction of Native populations from their land, but also from the future of the national construct in the first half of the nineteenth century, was paralleled by the inclusion of their reinvented ancestry, in the image of the noble primitive Indian.

Visually, the root of this progressive transition and integration of an Indigenous component in foundational narratives and origin myths can be identified in the inversion of the essential paradigm of captivity narratives in the representations of white-Indian relations in the first half of the nineteenth century. Focusing on the narratives of white captives detained by Indian tribes, these stories often depicted white women abducted by Indians. As part of this trope, the Indians' characterization as bloodthirsty savages was amplified by the cowardice of a crime perpetrated against women. A model text, in this respect, is Mary Rowlandson's account *The Sovereignty and Goodness of God* in 1682, based on her captivity during King Philip's War (1675–76). It was reprinted many times and remains one of the most famous captivity stories from colonial America.[23]

Captivity stories spread within all cultural media. They were translated visually in various representations and still feed the contemporary popular perception of the colonial period. In the Early Republic, the captivity motif was active not just in popular representation but also in elite art, such as the striking representations of Jane McCrea's death in 1777. Particularly notable was the representation by John Vanderlyn in 1804, which depicted her abduction by Mohawks, and was intended to illustrate Joel Barlow's American epic poem, *The Columbiad*.[24] Although the representation was targeting the alliance between certain Native tribes and the British during the Revolutionary War (rather than rehearsing a prehistory), the focus on the scene of abduction and murder—and the representation of Native characters as semi-naked, murderous savages—testifies to the continuity of the pattern inherited from colonial times.

In the Early Republic, and especially after the boost in national pride following the "Second War of Independence," a new paradigm emerged in elite and even state-sponsored national art, with captivity narratives being supplemented by rescue stories. The reactivation of stories featuring support from primitive Indians in the survival of European settlements acquired an additional national symbolism in this context. By penetrating national art and becoming connected to symbols of US independence, these stories reframed contact with Indigenous populations as a key component of the national past. This realignment can be seen in the inclusion in the Capitol in 1825 of Capellano's carving of the rescue of Smith by Pocahontas and in the simultaneous inclusion of the *Landing of the Pilgrims* by Enrico Causici as another foundational episode in the four relief panels representing the colonial past. In fact, all four relief panels were decorated with episodes involving white-Indian relations, evidencing the broad strategy, in which Pocahontas was one feature, of incorporating Indigenous figures into a variety of "new invented traditions."[25]

In this new paradigm, the relation of the settlers to the Indigenous peoples shifted, and the representation of the Indigenous figure as a categoric threat was challenged. As Jill Lepore has argued, captivity narratives inherited from the colonial era were driven by a fear of being contaminated by the savagery of the Indian way of life in settling in the New World.[26] Rescue stories, on the other hand, conveyed the idea that certain "primitive" Indians, whose courageous actions stood out from the savagery attributed to the rest of their people, offered the essential support that enabled "civilization" to survive on the continent. This new paradigm, in which so-called primitive Indians were no longer abductors but saviors, marked the incorporation of this alternative Indigenous figure into national myths. In the context of this shift, the episode of Pocahontas saving Smith is an instance of this broader realignment. Because the scene was iconic and bore the characteristics of a newly invented tradition, it enabled Pocahontas to become the quintessential example of the realignment. Yet the scene was only one instrument in the re-creation of a broader figurative bond with Indigenous culture, where Indigenous figures offered guidance and support to facilitate the birth of a new and improved American civilization. Alterity was still central to this construct, in the idea that a unique American identity originated from contact between primitive nobility and the western world. The co-optation was visually signified in the rescue of Smith by Pocahontas in the positions they occupy in the composition of Capellano's scene and by the sentimental gesture of motherly/loverly protection, which reinforces the concept of a people born from the contact between New World and Old World rather than created solely by European agency.

Yet, although the concept of a people born from the contact between primitive Indians and European settlers integrated the Indigenous character into the parental structure of nationhood, there was also a complication, namely, the nineteenth-century equation of Indians and wilderness. Inherited from the reflections on primitivism and the concept of the noble savage developed in Enlightenment philosophy, the connection between primitive nobility and the virginal, uncorrupted landscape of the New World was symptomatic of cultural nationalism in the antebellum period.[27] The association between Indigeneity and wilderness is particularly visible among early Romantic painters, especially in George Catlin's portraits, or even in paintings by Thomas Cole and the Hudson River School. Cole included Indigenous figures in majestic landscapes in his work, for instance, in his series of paintings based on Cooper's *Last of the Mohicans* (1826). Yet the association between Natives and wilderness in the representation of the origins of the new American race in fact implies an exclusion of Native ancestry, despite seeming to offer an integration of Indigenous characters into foundational myths. Because the contact was understood as noble values being transferred from Indigenous figures to the new American people, thereby rejuvenating the settlers' culture and Christian morals, the birth of the American people was not presented in a myth in which European ancestry was conjoined with Indigeneity in an equal fusion but rather depicted the new Americans as an "autochthonous" people.[28] This use of the primitive Indian character did not validate Indigenous culture but rather used it to assert a connection with the land of the New World, making the bond between people and territory the origin of the unique American people. Thus, when Young argued that Pocahontas became "the mother of us all," because "We [Americans], by our descent from her, become a new race, innocent of both European and all human origins—a race from the Earth, ... but an Earth that is made by her," he showed that her story was used not to preserve but to eradicate the Indigenous character.[29] The inclusion of Indigenous people, like Pocahontas, as saviors obliterated the European forefather, but it did not integrate an Indigenous ancestor.

The Indian Christian Princess: The Birth of an Icon and First "American"

The repeated scene of Pocahontas saving Smith positioned Pocahontas as a new origin figure, but an increased focus on the figure of Pocahontas herself, from the 1840s until the Civil War, would bring her to a higher level of iconicity and make her the center of the mythology. A key element in this development was the presentation of Pocahontas as a quasi-prototype of Americanness, found in a state of nature. Through representation of her conversion to Christianity, Pocahontas became a visible first-fruit of the contact between apparently primitive nobility and western culture, and a symbolic forerunner of exceptional American identity. Not only were her actions represented as "proto-nationalist" (Tilton), but her representation evolved over time toward assimilation: as a metaphorical ancestor, as founding hero in the Jamestown narrative, and, in certain images, as a prototypical fantasized first American.

The Americanization of the figure of Pocahontas resulted from her popularization through repeated portrayals of her role in the Jamestown narrative but also as a consequence of the rise of a pre-romantic artistic fashion for singling out noble Indians from the past in order to build an American patrimony inhabited by fantasized, appropriated Indigenous figures.[30] That Pocahontas had become an icon is evidenced by the large number of portraits of her produced in the period: she had a representative plasticity that could serve multiple political and ideological aims, including antagonistic and non-foundational ones.[31] The conventional portrayal of Pocahontas in elite art as the "Indian princess" presented a dual image, fascinating as an expression of the artistic quest to produce an "organic bond" within the nation, and as an effort to shape a certain kind of identification with what would constitute Americanness.[32] On one hand she was the "lady-like Pocahontas," the first Protestant convert among Indigenous peoples, and on the other hand she was the "forest-girl Pocahontas," a sensual princess associated with her environment and the American wilderness, albeit appropriated and tamed by Euro-American civilization.[33] Both of these representations served the national construct and the reinvention of national origins: the lady-like Pocahontas was more than a figure of first contact, she was identified as the "first aristocrat" of the nation, with her heroic behavior and virtue considered as matching her noble condition.[34] This representation of Pocahontas reflected the quest for a "natural aristocracy" in American culture, echoing Jefferson's ideal and key concept designed to oppose the corrupt hereditary aristocracy found in Europe.[35] Meanwhile the forest-girl Pocahontas served as an allegorical representation of the land. During the Revolution, the allegory of the Indian princess superseded the image of the savage "Indian queen" formerly used to represent the newly discovered America, which was perceived by Europeans to be a virginal and hostile continent. The Indian princess offered American colonists a more civilized image for their embryonic nation. Yet both Indian princess and

forest-girl types similarly blended European standards and imagined Indigeneity to form the core of Pocahontas's identity and positioned her as integrated
into US national identity. These characterizations made Pocahontas exceptional even in comparison to other appropriated Native American figures
from the past. They reveal a uniquely liminal and paradoxical figure who was
able to represent "Americanness" to a certain extent, whilst also projecting a
Euro-American ideal of Indigenousness.

The presentation of Pocahontas as a Christian figure was the key means
of differentiating her from the noble Indian of the past, as depicted by the
pre-Romantic school as a sublime but doomed character, passive and con-
templative in the vast immensity of the virginal landscape. As an idealized
prototype of Americanness, an inherent Christian, the figure of Pocahontas
invited viewers to see in her not only providential help for the survival of civilization in a foreign land but also evidence of a link between American core
values and the essence of the New World. To complicate the role of Pocahontas and what it conveys about the integration of an Indigenous component into national symbols, the focus on Christian values associated with her
narrative was in fact not new. The rescue episode had subtexts of sacrifice,
self-abnegation, even martyrdom, leading Ann Uhry Abrams to compare it
to a "quasi-religious passion play."[36] But by the 1840s, scenes of Pocahontas's
life, and especially her assimilation into the colony of Jamestown, became
more and more common, focalizing the Christian reading not on her actions
in a narrative but on her persona. The cornerstone of this shift is the inclusion in the US Capitol in 1836 of a scene representing her baptism, painted by
John Gadsby Chapman, who expressed his intention to make Pocahontas an
American "Joan of Arc."[37] The centrality of a Christian reading can be seen in
the sculpture by Joseph Mozier in 1868 (fig. 3), which Tilton describes as "a
clear attempt to follow the mid-century vogue of such American sculptors as
Randolph Rogers and Erastus Dow Palmer to provide Christian America with
suitable biblical figures and religious themes."[38] Without any other figure from
the Jamestown narrative, Pocahontas is represented in this sculpture, gazing
down on the cross she is holding in one hand, and keeping a deer on a leash
with the other.

The usurpation of an Indigenous character to create a patrimony faithful
to European cultural codes underpins this symbolic representation. The clear
attempt to challenge European artistic tradition by erecting Pocahontas as an
alternative ancestral tie to the continent is evidenced in the proximity of such

Pocahontas, Joseph Mozier, 1868. Marble. (Art Institute of Chicago; image ©2023, Photo Scala, Florence)

representations to aesthetic canons inherited from the classics. For instance, Pocahontas's clothing evokes codes of representation inherited from Ancient Greece. Even more striking, however, is the resemblance between Mozier's sculpture and the *Diana of Versailles*, a famous type depicting the Roman goddess of the hunt dominating a stag with one hand and reaching for her quiver with the other. A fifth-century exemplar of this type was made popular throughout Europe when it was displayed by the French monarchy in the seventeenth century, and it clearly inspired Mozier's sculpture.

Roman statue of Artemis, goddess of the hunt, known as "Diana of Versailles," first to second century AD. Marble, replica of a Greek original from the fourth century BC. (Louvre Museum, Paris; image © Musée du Louvre Dist. RMN-Grand Palais/Thierry Ollivier)

Despite Pocahontas's more docile appearance, the overall construction is similar, with the deer on leash replacing the controlled stag, and symbols of hunting replaced by the religious symbol of a cross. Portrayed as a lone figure, surrounded by attributes that reinforce her primitive status (wildlife, hunting, pagan goddess), Mozier's Pocahontas conveyed the idea that her Christianity was not the product of cultural contact with Jamestown, but inherent to her in a state of nature. This message undercut the connection to European Christianity, replacing it with an Americanized version of the Indian princess whose natural virtue preceded and anticipated her conversion.

It is within this understanding of Pocahontas—presented as a metaphorical first ancestor, first aristocrat, first convert, even first "Christian Indian" already possessing inherent American values—that a connection with the founding fathers myth can be established. As a result, this figure of Pocahontas became constructed as a Europeanized icon, carrying the symbol of an alternative origin within herself, which was distinct from the European past but reflected identical codes. Reaching this level of identification, Pocahontas became sufficiently Europeanized to become a founding hero for Jamestown rather than an external help. In this transfiguration, Pocahontas penetrated the parental structure so fundamental in American nationalism, being both inherently American by her Christian values and foreshadowing the founding hero role in the colonial period.

Indian Princess and Founding Father:
Inter-Iconicity, Reciprocity and Rivalry

The figure of Pocahontas bears an intriguing relation to the icon of George Washington in the mythology of the founding fathers, within the broader use of parental and kinship metaphors to strengthen the bond of American nationalism. In Hobsbawm's account, American nationalism involved "the invention of emotionally and symbolically charged signs of club membership rather than the statutes and objects of the club."[39] The emphasis on affect and emotion made a family-based metaphor particularly powerful in forging a spirit of nationhood. The parental structure in American nationalism has two aspects: generational conflict and national family. As Mary Dearborn has argued, generational conflict is a recurrent trope, from the initial rupture with the British "forefather" through the use of "paternalism" in interracial issues, to ongoing references to a country of "third generation migrants."[40] The concept of the American nation as a "family" headed by a parental authority is an image that has been used to obscure coercive or artificial elements of government. In his book, *In the Name of the Father: Washington's Legacy, Slavery, and the Making of the Nation*, for example, François Furstenberg shows how a family-based conception of American nationhood facilitated the contradiction of the preservation of slavery alongside revolutionary ideals of freedom. According to Furstenberg, slavery strengthened "a passive understanding of citizenship intertwined with an ideology of paternalism as a core feature of US nationalism."[41] It helped distill a notion of consent under the benevolent and paternalist authority of a founding father, whose role was to demonstrate the harmony and cohesiveness of the national unit. The development of a family-based network of representations, and the associated concept of consent, also played a part in the effort to break with the influence of the Old World. Imagining the whole nation as a family unit, with a founding father organizing it through the Constitution, was an additional means of presenting the United States as a nation based on consent, not constraint, and affirming the principle of equality (however imperfectly achieved), in contradistinction to the unfair aristocratic order that was built around the British monarchy.

Hence, the early nineteenth century saw the dissemination of a mythology in which George Washington embodied this parental figure, binding the national family together. The creation of the mythology involved the repetition of a national vocabulary and network of representations that used generational conflict to characterize conflict with Britain, as well as images of kinship to generate an American sense of nationhood and social cohesion via an emotional bond. Although George Washington was not the only figure in the founding fathers myth, his role as the "Father of his Country" was particularly strongly developed in narrative and iconography.[42]

Because Pocahontas represented the first convert, the first true aristocrat, and a foundational hero, her image connected with similar aspects of the founding father mythology that surrounded Washington. Heroism, self-abnegation, and Christian morals were common to both iconographies, together with the concept of an original ancestry. The figure of Pocahontas touched the essence of the family rhetoric at work in the edification of the new national culture, through her presentation as first ancestor or pre-American founding hero. Her iconography also addressed the question of how Native tribes fitted into the national construct. With the paradox of Pocahontas being both Americanized and model of Indian assimilation, her image was used not only to construct an alternative genesis but also to represent contemporary aspirations for the social formation of the United States, including the role given to Indigenous people (both past and present) in the composition of the national family.

References to Native American figures from Contact as mirroring George Washington (as quintessential founding father figure) have become fairly common in recent research. Jill Lepore, in her work on King Philip's War (1675–76), for example, draws a parallel between the dialogue of the war hero Metamora in the 1830 play of that name, describing it as being "as familiar upon the public's tongue as the name of Washington."[43] In a similar vein, Michael Witgen characterizes the representation of Louis Riel, Métis leader of the rebellions against the Canadian government at the end of the nineteenth century, as evolving "from a mixed-race savage destined to fade from history to a George Washington of Manitoba."[44] Although these comparisons are relatively superficial and serve to highlight the relative neglect of Native historical figures in comparison to prominent white figures (as epitomized by Washington) the recurring trope reveals a deeper desire to confront Indigenous and Euro-American heritage and to rebalance the American narrative. However, when Rasmussen and Tilton describe Pocahontas as "the female counterpart to George Washington," the reason is not stylistic effect or narrative realignment: they are pointing out a historically identifiable reciprocity in the iconography of these two figures.[45]

The reciprocity is primarily one of similar representative strategies and constitutive units in their respective iconic personas. Their representations express related myths of foundation (national for Washington and pre-national for Pocahontas) that raise the question of the role given to Pocahontas in nineteenth-century America, as an avatar of or alternative to the main founding father and national hero. Besides their shared ideological purpose, the visual symbolism in representations of Pocahontas and Washington built on the same network of references, and sometimes used similar modes. A striking example can be found, for instance, in the compositional parallels between Junius Brutus Stearns's The Death of Pocahontas (1848) and Life of George Washington: The Christian Death (ca. 1853).[46] The placement of Pocahontas and Washington is almost identical, and the positioning of seated and standing figures around the head of their beds follows a parallel design. Both paintings idealize the lifelong moral leadership offered by their subjects through the image of each figure's Christian death, surrounded by grieving loved ones who are paying their last respects, and both combine moral tableau with history painting. In this way, Washington and Pocahontas, despite their differences, were depicted as national heroes using overlapping symbolism. Both figures were used to present the values of the new nation as holy, familial, and anciently rooted in America.

Further evidence to confirm that Pocahontas and Washington were deployed ideologically in similar ways in the quest to endow the nation with

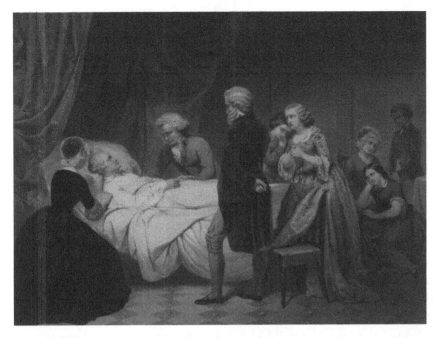

Life of George Washington: The Christian Death, Junius Brutus Stearns, ca. 1853. Lithograph by Régnier, Paris, ca. 1853. (Library of Congress)

an alternative origin can be found in the way in which their rather disparate stories were conjoined, for instance in the official biography of George Washington by John Marshall, published in 1799 after Washington's death. A biography of the first president would be "incomplete and unsatisfactory," Marshall declared, without "a narrative of the principal events preceding our revolutionary war" that helped secure the nation's founding.[47] To this end, Marshall included scenes from the story of Pocahontas, including her intervention to save Smith and her marriage to Rolfe, thereby affording her a special role as a pre-American heroine of a foundational period, whose salvific actions and commitment to the colonists foreshadowed the heroism of Washington.[48]

Correspondences in the visual modes of representing Pocahontas and Washington evolved during the nineteenth century, with sanctification as probably the most significant encoding. Washington's canonization after his death was visually expressed in John James Barralet's 1802 engraving of the apotheosis of the former president.[49] Barralet's symbolic picture of Washington, in a Christ-like pose and being escorted heavenwards by an angel, was reproduced in countless versions and copies and different media over the next two decades. Pocahontas was also increasingly represented as a holy figure in elite art, as is apparent in Chapman's representation of 1836, which Rasmussen and Tilton have compared to a scene of martyrdom by Caravaggio.[50] Nineteenth-century depictions of Pocahontas gave her an increasingly messianic role, using compositional lines to associate her with celestial intervention and incorporating symbolic rays of light, halos, and other Christian imagery. In two paintings of the episode from Smith's *Generall Historie* in which Pocahontas warns Smith of an imminent attack, one by Chapman and one by Edwin White, the nighttime setting became a means of portraying Pocahontas as an illuminated, angelic messenger sent to guide Smith (representing the American people) to their salvation.[51] In the composition of these paintings, Pocahontas stands over a reclining Smith, like the female visitant directing Washington from his deathbed to his heavenly home in Barralet's iconic image. Besides such specific reciprocities, broader connections were commonly made between founding father and Indian princess in the iconography of the new nation, as exemplified in Constantino Brumidi's fresco in the Capitol. Brumidi teamed up a cool, blonde Columbia with an affable, dark-haired Native American figure to flank a trompe l'oeil relief of a bust of Washington.[52]

Designed to celebrate and inculcate similar values in the next generation of US citizens, stories about Washington and stories about Pocahontas worked together to form a common culture. Even Parson Weems's famous tale of the young George Washington being unable to lie to his father about chopping down the cherry tree chimed, in its allusion to a natural, childlike innocence, with the representation of a young, virginal forest-dwelling Pocahontas, who embodied the innate virtues of the New World.[53] The story of Pocahontas's rescue of Smith even corresponded to the cherry tree tale on a more subversive political level, as Tilton has noted, because both depict "an act of bravery in the face of a patriarchal power" and confirm that "such acts often have positive results."[54] Moreover, the ideology of sacrifice in the name of the nation informed nineteenth-century portrayals of both figures. Pocahontas was glorified for risking her own life to protect Smith. As Alexander Lawson's 1799 *General Washington's Resignation* illustrates, Washington was glorified for sacrificing the peace of his home at Mount Vernon to the public task of organizing the nation.[55]

These similarities in modes of representations raise the question of why Pocahontas was invoked when so many of the values that she was used to affirm were already represented in the mythology of the founding fathers. One explanation is the need for roots in a more distant past. When Washington is represented as the lynchpin in the family construction of the nation, he appears as a point of origin, but only of the nation as recently established—its institutional elaboration and the pact of association that bound the new citizens together. He could not represent a long historical bond. Heroic representations of Washington focused on his military victories over the British and the drafting of the US Constitution. Pocahontas, on the other hand, enabled the national construct to be projected back into the distant past. She foreshadowed the heroism of the founding fathers, and, as a more ancient figure, she could be used to imply that the American people had a long-standing organic bond that justified the creation of the new nation, and a link with the continent that justified their occupation of it.

The significance of the complementarity in Washington's and Pocahontas's iconography appears all the deeper when ideas of kinship and consent in the Early Republic are considered. To recall François Furstenberg's argument, the image of George Washington as the father of a united national family became instrumental in a context where the practice of slavery and the fear of slave revolts were creating increasing tensions at the regional and national level, especially from the 1830s onward. Far from being abolished after the revolution, slavery became more firmly established in the Early Republic. When proslavery patriots sought to reconcile the practice of slavery with the ideal of freedom that had been promoted since the revolution, they turned to the concept of family and specifically to the idea of subjugation with consent to a benevolent parental authority. However, starting right in the post-revolutionary era and developing in the 1830s until the Civil War, the fear and reality of slave rebellions were perceived as a challenge for national cohesion. Nat Turner's revolt in 1831 triggered, in Furstenberg's words, a "paranoia" in the South.[56] Adding to political anxieties caused by the competition with Native tribes for land, slaves began to represent another potential threat to the new nation, both ideologically and politically, at the same time as they were sustaining the nation's economic development. Viewed in this light, the focus of artwork in the years 1840–60 on Washington's home life, presenting his plantation at Mount Vernon as a model Christian household, played as a metaphor for the national family.[57] At a time when white Americans increasingly perceived slavery, with the fear of insurrections, as an internal threat to national unity, Washington became a visual embodiment of appeasement and union.

If the figure of Washington was deployed to shore up the stability of the national family through the ideal of domestic paternalism, might there have been a parallel purpose in representations of Pocahontas? Whereas Washington's iconography served to accommodate slavery within the national family, Pocahontas's image offered to absorb the tensions in white-Indian relations through wifely and familial relations, by presenting an idealized image of willing subjugation and non-coercive integration. In Chapman's iconic depiction of her baptism for example, Pocahontas appears as an ideal Native American in contrast to the Indians in the foreground to the right, some of whom look belligerent or disgruntled. Pocahontas's virtuous choice of full and willing consent to Euro-American civilization is put forward symbolically as the ideal means of achieving peace. This visually encoded message was all the more significant because the political reality in 1840 was one of violence and coercion in white-Indian relations, involving the continued forced removal of Native peoples and the Second Seminole War. The role of Pocahontas in this painting was therefore not only to symbolize inherent Christianity in the New World but also to offer a visual idealization of a more honorable and peaceable assimilation of Indigenous populations into the patriarchal national family.[58]

Consent was at the heart of Chapman's presentation of Pocahontas's adoption of Euro-American culture. It was an idea that erased the brutality of the eradication of Native culture and the contemporaneous eviction of Native tribes and instead presented an idealized solution to the "Indian problem." Moreover, by emphasizing consent in their idealization of fatherly rule, the iconography of both Washington and Pocahontas also appealed to the notion of appeasement, in order to preserve unity within the (white) national family. Their visual idealizations addressed and countered contemporary racial anxieties and social tensions: both were constructed as mythic figures designed to promote the political stability of the national family, in complementary ways.

However, the looming sectional conflict that would result in the Civil War led to more regional applications of Pocahontas's image, and to a further level of appropriation of her image within a white dispute. Southern political iconography paradoxically elevated Pocahontas to the role of a founding mother, going beyond a reciprocity with the foundational heroism of George Washington and casting her as a rival origin figure. As tensions grew between North and South, Pocahontas became a sectional alternative to the image of Washington in southern propagandistic art, as distinct from—and, ultimately in opposition to—her use as a national icon in the Capitol. Henry Howe's

Historical Collections of Virginia includes a frontispiece composed of portraits of Virginia leaders, with Washington at the top, arrayed above a pedestal featuring a foundational image of Pocahontas rescuing Smith. "Peace to her gentle spirit!" Howe wrote after narrating her death, "Her memory will not perish while the commonwealth of Virginia endures, or noble and generous actions are valued by her sons."[59] This chivalric regional dedication to her image was embodied in the Civil War banner of the Fourth Virginia Cavalry (Powhatan County), which featured an idealized portrait of Pocahontas wearing a cross necklace.[60] Pocahontas was thus deployed to assert the superiority and legitimacy of the South as the true origin of the American nation. Although Washington was a southern plantation owner, he was primarily a universal figure who could not be appropriated as a sectional symbol. His lifetime commitment was too closely knitted to unification and anti-factionalism. Alternatives had to be found in less consensual images and myths that could be restricted to the South, and Pocahontas was one of them. She was a figure of national importance who belonged to Virginia's history. As a metaphorical and, to a certain extent, literal mother of the Virginia elite, Pocahontas could embody values and virtues tailored to a southern agenda.

Indeed, the raising of Pocahontas to the status of a national icon before the Civil War could be seen as partly the result of the southern loyalties of certain emerging American artists. Among the various early nineteenth-century portraits of the Indian princess, several were by the Virginian, Robert Matthew Sully. John Gadsby Chapman was also a Virginian, born in Alexandria. He painted several images of a saintly Pocahontas before creating her baptism scene for the Capitol.[61] The scene could even be interpreted regionally as "a kind of Virginia Manifesto to represent Southern interests in the entrance hall of the federal legislature."[62] Even Edwin White, who was born in Massachusetts, acquired a southern connection because he was chosen to paint a major portrait of Washington for the Maryland State House.[63] Whether the construction of Pocahontas's iconic position was the result of a local patriotism or the sign of an early rivalry between the northern and southern origin myths, the appropriation of a national symbol as a southern founding mother in the lead-up to the Civil War was paradoxical, especially given the importance of racial hierarchy in the South. Although Pocahontas's image was used to assert that the Old South was the true origin of the American nation, based on the fact that some of its elite were descended from an Indigenous woman, her mixed-race son was a notable omission from representations of scenes of her life. The veneration of an Indigenous and non-white woman was a striking anomaly in a society structured around white supremacy.

Pocahontas's transfiguration into a southern founding mother by the white South was a paradoxical culmination of her construction as an alternative founding parental figure in the early United States, which had the effect subsequently of limiting her to a regional symbol. After the loss of the Confederates in 1865, the figure of Pocahontas declined from national icon into a more vernacular and romanticized icon of exoticism. Having been appropriated to the southern cause, and de-centered by the decrease in national tension over Native Americans following the brutal removals and suppressions of the first half of the nineteenth century, Pocahontas was no longer a figure to rival and complement the founding fathers in her power to unite the nation. With Native populations evicted and marginalized, and US culture more established in its sense of Manifest Destiny and self-identification with the land, the role of the Indigenous character in origin myths had fulfilled its mission.

Surprisingly, given that she was both female and Indigenous, Pocahontas became a powerful national icon in the formative years of the United States, as she was co-opted into the parental structure of the new nation's mythology. Her pre-foundational role in the Jamestown narrative was informed by a broader structure within US origin myths that emphasized past bonds with colonial-era Indigenous figures in order to imply an autochthonous origin for the American people. In this context, the character of Pocahontas focused the realignment of the Eurocentric myth of discovery, instead revealing proto-national origins in the colonial past and marginalizing European ancestry and transatlantic cultural legacy. This realignment worked to underestimate cultural connections with Europe and to present selected noble Indians as the saviors of civilization. It thereby portrayed the newly formed American people as the unique product of the contact between primitive nobility, natural wilderness, and western culture. In this construction, the Native ancestor was subliminally identified with the land and origins, and confined to the past, rather than being truly integrated into the new national family.

Pocahontas began to stand out from the generic role of the Indigenous character in origin myths, as she was progressively transfigured into a visual icon in the antebellum period. Her role in the foundational narrative and her identification with mythological origins was developed to make her a prototype of Americanness, to the point that even her Christianity was presented as an inherent not an acquired trait. Interestingly, this process of identification relied on the cultural codes of classical and Christian art, recalling that even within this use of Pocahontas as Native ancestor, and as the first convert of the New World, she was the iconographic tool of a culture that was still profoundly Eurocentric.

Pocahontas's role developed beyond that of an Indigenous figure in origin myths, however. She achieved a level of iconicity that mirrored aspects of founding father mythology and appeared as a foreshadowing, in the distant past, of the foundational hero, George Washington. The reciprocity in the representations of this unlikely pair of American icons reveals the strong postrevolutionary emphasis on consent within the national family. Each figure offered a complementary image of cohesion: Washington the accommodation of slavery, and Pocahontas the assurance of there being an ideal, and historically precedented ideal, solution to white-Indian conflict.

The most striking feature of the interaction of Pocahontas with the parental structure of US nationhood is the paradoxical use of an Indigenous figure precisely to reject Indigeneity. Despite the flexible adaptability of representations of Pocahontas in the early nineteenth century, there was consistency in her portrayal as light complexioned (or, at least, lighter skinned than her Native companions) and as Europeanized in character. Whether participating in a revolutionary "generational conflict" over European sovereignty, or representing a "founding parental figure" in the division between North and South, Pocahontas was appropriated to white disputes over white identities. As a proto-American Christian figure, the first convert, she was positioned to counterbalance a shared European culture and past. As a foundational hero she served alongside George Washington, complementing a national narrative that needed to grow historical roots and find direction and justification in its policies regarding Native peoples. Even as a founding mother, Pocahontas's role was to oppose a rival white narrative and conception of the nation, in the wars and culture wars between Confederates and Unionists. In such contexts, Pocahontas's Indigeneity was instrumentalized as a marker of difference, but not racial difference. It was used as a tool in the formation of American national and regional identities to express the myth of opposition to what is not us, despite resembling us.

Notes

1. Clara Sue Kidwell, "Indian Women as Cultural Mediators," *Ethnohistory* 39, no. 2 (1992): 99; Nancy Shoemaker, "Native-American Women in History," in "Native Americans," special issue, *OAH Magazine of History* 9, no. 4 (Summer 1995): 10.

2. The notion of myth has to be understood both in its sociological and anthropological function here, as a mental construct explaining and justifying social relations and entities within a group, in order to produce social cohesion (sociological) and a sacred narrative aiming at laying foundations and define a set of immutable truths within a culture (anthropological). If the precise definition of myths is the subject of various interpretations, the word *myth* will be employed in this study to refer only to the concept of a sacralized narrative referring to events from the past but explaining a universal truth and therefore characterized by timelessness, echoing Levi-Strauss's own definition. Claude Levi-Strauss, "The Structural Study of Myth," *The Journal of American Folklore* 68, no. 270 (1955): 430.

3. For a brief summary see Kidwell, "Indian Women as Cultural Mediators," 99–101.

4. Michelle LeMaster, "Pocahontas: (De)constructing an American Myth," review of *Pocahontas and the Powhatan Dilemma* by Camilla Townsend, *Pocahontas, Powhatan, Opechancanough: Three Indian Lives Changed by Jamestown* by Helen C. Rountree, *Pocahontas: Medicine Woman, Spy, Entrepreneur, Diplomat* by Paula Gunn Allen, *Love and Hate in Jamestown: John Smith, Pocahontas, and the Heart of a New Nation* by David A. Price, *The William and Mary Quarterly*, 62, no. 4 (Oct. 2005): 774.

5. S. Elizabeth Bird, "Introduction: Constructing the Indian, 1830s–1990s," in *Dressing in Feathers: The Construction of the Indian in American Popular Culture*, ed. S. Elizabeth Bird (Boulder: Westview Press, 1996), 2, Philip Young, "The Mother of Us All: Pocahontas Reconsidered," *The Kenyon Review* 24, no. 3 (Summer 1962): 392.

6. William M. S. Rasmussen and Robert S. Tilton, *Pocahontas: Her Life and Legend* (Richmond: Virginia Historical Society, 1994), 7.

7. Robert S. Tilton, *Pocahontas: The Evolution of an American Narrative* (Cambridge: Cambridge University Press, 1994), 33.

8. Rayna Green, "The Pocahontas Perplex: The Image of Indian Women in American Culture," *The Massachusetts Review* 16, no. 4 (Autumn 1975): 700.

9. Ann Uhry Abrams, *The Pilgrims and Pocahontas: Rival Myths of American Origin* (Boulder: Westview, 1999).

10. Rasmussen and Tilton, *Pocahontas: Life and Legend,* 7.

11. Jaap Verheul, "'A Peculiar National Character': Transatlantic Realignment and the Birth of American Cultural Nationalism after 1815," *European Journal of American Studies* 7, no. 2 (2012), https://journals.openedition.org/ejas/9638.

12. Eric Hobsbawm, "Introduction: Inventing Traditions," in *The Invention of Tradition,* ed. Eric Hobsbawm and Terence Ranger (Cambridge: Cambridge University Press, 1983), 1–14.

13. Hobsbawm, "Inventing Traditions," 7.

14. Antonio Capellano, *Preservation of Captain Smith by Pocahontas,* 1825, sandstone sculpture, United States Capitol art collection, Washington, DC (https://www.aoc.gov/explore-capitol-campus/art/preservation-captain -smith-pocahontas-1606-relief-sculpture).

15. On captivity narratives in the representation of white-Indian relations, see Jill Lepore, *The Name of War: King Philip's War and the Origins of American Identity* (New York: Knopf, 1998), 185–90.

16. Hobsbawm, "Inventing Traditions," 4.

17. Rasmussen and Tilton, *Pocahontas: Life and Legend,* 14.

18. William Croome, "Pocahontas Rescuing Captain Smith," 1843, wood engraving, in John Frost, *The Pictorial History of the United States of America* (Philadelphia: Benjamin Walker, 1843), 1:86–106; William Gilmore Simms, "Saved by Pocahontas," in *The Life of Captain John Smith, the Founder of Virginia* (New York: G. F. Cooledge, 1846), 150; Marcius Willson, "Pocahontas Saving the Life of Captain Smith," in *History of the United States, for the Use of Schools* (New York: Mark H. Newman, 1847), 47. For more representations see also Lambert Lilly [Francis Lister Hawks], "Illustration of the Rescue Scene," engraving, in *The Early History of the Southern States: Virginia, North and South Carolina, and Georgia* (Philadelphia: Key, Mielke and Biddle, 1832); Thomas Sinclair, "Captain Smith Rescued by Pocahontas," lithograph, in James Wimer, *Events in Indian History* (Lancaster, PA, 1841); Henry Dielman, illustrated music sheet for "Pocahontas Grand March," engraving, in G. W. Custiss, *Grand March to the National Drama Pocahontas* (Philadelphia: James G. Osbourn's Music Saloon, 1836), 85.

19. For further description of the connection made between Indigenous and Roman oral traditions see, Robert F. Berkhofer, *The White Man's Indian: Images of the American Indian from Columbus to the Present* (New York: Knopf, distributed by Random House, 1978), 88.

20. Élise Marienstras, "L'imaginaire national dans les années de la Confédération," in *Nous, le peuple: Les origines du nationalisme américain* (Paris: Gallimard, 1988), 337–56, 338.

21. For further development from Hobsbawm on the specificity of American nationalism and the role and types of myths serving the national narrative, see Benedict Anderson, *Imagined Communities: Reflections on the Origin and Spread of Nationalism* (London: Verso, 1991), 10–45.

22. Brian W. Dippie, *The Vanishing American: White Attitudes and U.S. Indian Policy* (Middletown, CT: Wesleyan University Press, 1982).

23. Lepore, *Name of War*, 190.

24. Steven Blakemore, *Joel Barlow's "Columbiad"* (Amsterdam-Netherlands: Amsterdam University Press, 2007), 175–77; John Vanderlyn, *The Death of Jane McCrea*, 1804, oil on canvas, 32 ½ × 26 ½", The Wadsworth Athanaeum, Hartford, Conn.

25. Nicholas Gevelot, *William Penn's Treaty with the Indians*, 1827, sandstone sculpture, United States Capitol art collection, Washington, DC; Enrico Causici, *Conflict of Daniel Boone and the Indians, 1773*, 1827, sandstone sculpture, United States Capitol art collection, Washington, DC.

26. On the fear of contamination by Indian savagery in the colonial period, see Lepore, *Name of War*, 190.

27. For more development on the association between Indigenous populations and wilderness, as much as with the European conception of a noble savage found in the state of nature, see Berkhofer, *White Man's Indian*, 89.

28. To understand this position, based on myths as "packs of relations," among which exist overestimation or underestimation of blood relations, and the autochthonous or non-autochthonous origin of mankind, see the structure of myths proposed by Levi-Strauss, "The Structural Study of Myth."

29. Young, "The Mother of Us All," 408.

30. Jeanine Brun, review of *Les mythes fondateurs de la nation américaine: Essai sur le discours idéologique aux États-Unis à l'époque de l'Indépendance, 1763–1800*, by Élise Marienstras, *Annales. Histoire, Sciences Sociales*, 32, no. 1 (Jan.–Feb. 1977), 147.

31. Klaus Lubbers, *Born for the Shade: Stereotypes of the Native American in United States Literature and the Visual Arts, 1776–1894* (Amsterdam: Rodopi, 1994), 174.

32. *Organic bond* is understood as a bond based on the historic sharing of culture, language, and past, leading to the natural evolution of a people into a nation, in opposition to an artificial bond based on imaginary constructs, including contractual pacts of association but also myths, to form a nation. Here the function of erecting Pocahontas as a link in the distant past with Euro-American values illustrates a quest for identifying the national construct with this understanding of nationalism. For more development on the

various schools on the subject, see the synthesis of approaches in Guntram Henrik Herb and David H. Kaplan, eds., *Nested Identities: Nationalism, Territory, and Scale* (Lanham, MD: Rowman & Littlefield, 1999), 13–21.

33. Abrams, *Pilgrims and Pocahontas*, 51.

34. Young, "The Mother of Us All," cited in Green, "The Pocahontas Perplex," 700.

35. See Jefferson's letter to John Adams, October 28, 1813: "I agree with you that there is a natural aristocracy among men. The grounds of this are virtue and talents. Formerly, bodily powers gave place among the aristoi [aristocrats]. [. . .] There is also an artificial aristocracy, founded on wealth and birth, without either virtue or talents; for with these it would belong to the first class. The natural aristocracy I consider as the most precious gift of nature, for the instruction, the trusts, and government of society." *The Papers of Thomas Jefferson, Retirement Series*, ed. J. Jefferson Looney (Princeton: Princeton University Press, 2009), 6:562–68, 563.

36. Abrams, *Pilgrims and Pocahontas*, 12.

37. John Gadsby Chapman, quoted in Tilton, *Pocahontas: The Evolution of an American Narrative*, 119; John Gadsby Chapman, *Baptism of Pocahontas*, 1840, oil on canvas, United States Capitol art collection, Washinton, DC (https://www.aoc.gov/explore-capitol-campus/art/baptism-pocahontas).

38. William M. S. Rasmussen and Robert S. Tilton, *George Washington: The Man behind the Myths* (Charlottesville: University Press of Virginia, 1999), 27.

39. Hobsbawm, "Inventing Traditions," 7.

40. Mary V. Dearborn, *Pocahontas's Daughters: Gender and Ethnicity in American Culture* (New York: Oxford University Press, 1986), 72–73.

41. François Furstenberg, *In the Name of the Father: Washington's Legacy, Slavery, and the Making of the Nation* (New York: Penguin Press, 2006), 103.

42. Heike Paul, "American Independence and the Myth of the Founding Fathers," chap. 4 in *The Myths That Made America: An Introduction to American Studies* (Transcript-Verlag, 2014).

43. Lepore, *Name of War*, 192.

44. Michael J. Witgen, *An Infinity of Nations: How the Native New World Shaped Early North America* (Philadelphia: University of Pennsylvania Press, 2012), 362.

45. Rasmussen and Tilton, *Pocahontas: Life and Legend*, 7.

46. Junius Brutus Stearns, *The Death of Pocahontas*, 1848, oil on canvas, currently in private ownership, location unknown. For a reproduction, see "The Pocahontas Archive: Images," accessed November 3, 2023, https://history-on-trial.lib.lehigh.edu/trial/pocahontas/images.php?id=40; Junius Brutus

Stearns, *Life of George Washington: The Christian Death*, ca. 1853, oil on canvas; also, hand-colored lithograph by Régnier (Paris: Imprimerie Lemercier, ca. 1853), Library and Congress Prints and Photographs Division, Washington, DC.

47. John Marshall, preface to *The Life of George Washington* (1804–7), vol 1.

48. Tilton, *Pocahontas: Evolution of an American Narrative*, 34–35.

49. John James Barralet, *Apotheosis of Washington*, 1800–1802, engraving and etching, Metropolitan Museum of Art, New York; Phoebe Lloyd Jacobs, "John James Barralet and the Apotheosis of George Washington," *Winterthur Portfolio* 12 (1977): 115–37.

50. John Gadsby Chapman, *Pocahontas Saving the Life of Captain John Smith*, 1836, oil on canvas, New-York Historical Society Museum and Library; Rasmussen and Tilton, *Pocahontas: Life and Legend*, 15.

51. Chapman, *Pocahontas Saving the Life of Captain John Smith*; John Gadsby Chapman, *The Warning of Pocahontas*, ca. 1836, oil on canvas, private collection; Edwin White, *Pocahontas Informing John Smith of a Conspiracy of the Indians*, ca. 1850, oil on canvas, in private ownership. For reproduction, see Rasmussen and Tilton, 20.

52. Constantino Brumidi, *Indian Princess and Columbia Honoring George Washington*, 1855, fresco. United States Capitol, Washington, DC.

53. For further explanations of the cherry tree episode and the moral virtues attributed to Washington, see Rasmussen and Tilton, *George Washington*, 3.

54. Tilton, *Pocahontas: The Evolution of an American Narrative*, 54.

55. For more explanation of this construct, see Laura Dove, Lisa Guernsey, Scott Atkins, and Adriana Rissetto, "The Moral Washington: Creation of a Legend (1800–1920s)," George Washington, archived website, https://web.archive.org/web/20230115212329/http://xroads.virginia.edu/~CAP/gw/gwmoral.html.

56. Furstenberg, *In the Name of the Father*, 111.

57. See the development on this question by Furstenberg, *In the Name of the Father*, 37, and representations of Washington in Mount Vernon, especially Junius Brutus Stearns, *Life of George Washington: The Farmer*, ca. 1853, lith. by Régnier (Paris: Lemercier, ca. 1853), Library of Congress Prints and Photographs Division Washington, DC.

58. Chapman, Baptism of Pocahontas.

59. Henry Howe, *Historical Collections of Virginia* (Charleston, SC: Babcock, 1845), frontispiece.

60. "Guard of the Daughters of Powhatan," banner of the Powhatan Guards, Company E, Fourth Virginia Cavalry, 1860, silk with oil painted seal,

American Civil War Museum (formerly Museum of the Confederacy), Rich-mond, VA.

61. See Chapman, *The Warning of Pocahontas;* White, *Pocahontas Informing John Smith.*

62. Abrams, *Pilgrims and Pocahontas,* 1.

63. Edwin White, *Washington Resigning His Commission,* 1859, oil on canvas, Maryland State House (https://msa.maryland.gov/msa/mdstatehouse/html /stairwellrm-washington-resigning.html); White, *Pocahontas Informing John Smith.*

POCAHONTAS CHIC

CRISTINA L. AZOCAR AND IVANA MARKOVA

"Pocahontas chic" is what I jokingly dubbed the leather fringe fashion trend that I noticed the first time I visited Miami, Florida, in the early 2000s. As a young graduate student, I just thought it was weird and tacky. I hadn't heard of "cultural appropriation" at that point, although it had entered the lexicon of cultural studies more than two decades before.[1] I was a data driven social science researcher who had given up on the language of cultural studies because I didn't understand it, so I generally ignored it when I entered my doctoral program. Because cultural appropriation was not a term I encountered in my reading or classes, it was not on my radar.

Although I was appalled by sports teams that used Indian mascots and their fans that donned fake headdresses, performed tomahawk chops, and sang offensive songs, I didn't connect Pocahontas chic and the mascots as similar forms of exploitation and violence, that as an Indigenous person, I had come to expect. I am a citizen of the Upper Mattaponi Tribe. Pocahontas was Pamunkey on her father's side and Mattaponi by her mother. Pre-Virginia's tidewater tribes were matrilineal, so Pocahontas would have identified as Mattaponi. The myth of Pocahontas, and the reality of who she was, has been with me since childhood.

Pocahontas has only recently become a figure again in my life, as I had forgotten about Pocahontas chic long ago. And, until the Disney rendition of her came out in 1995, I didn't think much of her again until that walk along Ocean Drive on Miami Beach. I did not watch the film then, and I only watched it now for purposes of research. And then she popped up again in the film The New World. *I remember watching it for free in a movie theater and laughing about how ridiculous the film was, but also thinking that it was typical. Almost twenty years later, as I was researching my book* News Media and the Indigenous Fight for Federal

Recognition (2022), her name came up in almost every historical docu-
ment. I asked my Upper Mattaponi, Mattaponi, and Pamunkey relatives
about their relationship to her, and my mom's response sums up the amount
of thought that has gone into her among our tribes' women: "We used to
call her Pokie."

—Cristina L. Azocar

Unfortunately, Pocahontas chic has been a feature of Anglo-settler culture for almost two hundred years. Given the interwoven tendencies toward cultural appropriation and commodification, and subsequent efforts to appropriate and commodify Indigenous women, it's important to ask: what did Pocahontas actually wear and why? With a focus on clothes and textiles, this essay initially considers the contemporary manifestations and damage of Pocahontas chic and then contrasts that with the cultural specificity of the textiles and designs of the Indigenous clothing that Pocahontas may have worn. This essay illustrates how myriad portrayals of Pocahontas chic continue, borrow, or exploit original Indigenous textiles and practices and help perpetuate harmful stereotypes about Indigenous women.

A quick internet image search turns up seemingly endless contemporary examples of what we term Pocahontas chic. These images generally come with text that illustrates the common language used around Pocahontas and other Indigenous women, historical or not. For example, alongside the Disney-inspired Pocahontas Halloween costume, the advertiser asks the buyer to "Transform into the Powhatan Princess who loves nature and strives to restore peace between her tribe and the English settlers after falling in love with John Smith by putting on the dress and necklace included in the purchase of this ensemble."[2] The text that accompanies images like these only ever adds to the exploitation of and violence against Indigenous women, which began in popular media more than a century ago, albeit within a very different media landscape. Notably, searches of the Women's Magazine Archive, which holds well-known titles such as *Good Housekeeping, Women's Day, Seventeen, Vogue,* and *Cosmopolitan,* and a chronological range from 1800 to 2005, produced 296 search results for "Pocahontas." The results are a mix of advertisements, fashion spreads, journalism, and fiction, published between 1849 and 2004. A myth of Pocahontas is apparent throughout this 155-year span and it's worth detailing these examples to emphasize the persistence of this unfettered media representation. Through advertising and journalistic features, it's the accumulation of Pocahontas references and appropriations that generates the potency of this discussion and debate. To that end, it's worth outlining a representative, and extended, set of examples in some detail.

In advertising, Arrowhead's Pocahontas hosiery was "built for service—and style," according to an advertisement in *Good Housekeeping* in 1929;[3] in 1949 you could purchase the Famous Lovers salt and pepper shakers and sprinkle your spices from Pocahontas and John Rolfe figurines.[4] New shoes from the Belgrade Company had an interestingly worded advertisement in a 1956 edition of *Seventeen*: "paleface gladly surrender to the Indian charm of Pocahontas by Moxees . . . Pocahontas walks straight into the heart of John Smiths everywhere—with tender trap of moccasin fringe—soft, soft leather—warpaint colors. For very few beads—less than $9—at trading posts everywhere."[5] Colors include Indian maize and teepee tan. In 1980, Pocahontas "never had it so good" in a fashion spread in *Cosmopolitan*: "You're all set up with chaps and boots and other cowgirl gear, now spend some wampum on the American Indian Princess look! Squaw duds sported by Lila have *fabulous* fringe benefits. Look also for turquoise and silver jewelry, beaded headbands, laced deerskin vests, and soft, white moccasins, of *course.*"[6] In *Seventeen* magazine's 1968 fashion spread called "Let's Play Cowboys and Indians," two frightened-looking women walking among birch trees ask, " 'Why big ranchers sneak yonder in Indian hills?' 'To spy on fashion powwow. Ssh.' POW! Buckskin leather news. WOW! Fringes and bead put-ons." The two models wear a "Pocahontas buckskin wrap skirt," " 'ceremonial' beading headband," and "Heap-wide cinch, for mini-ha-ha waist, of buckskin buckled and fringed."[7] *Cosmopolitan* was into Pocahontas as a super-fashion-hero in 1999. One edition tells readers to head to page 88 for "Trends to Try: Pocahontas Power." The greatest Western-inspired wear for your wampum.[8] In 2002, a fashionista could jazz her daisy dukes up if she was "feeling like Pocahontas?" She could "wear a raw-edged pair with moccasins."[9] Another edition includes "Pocahontas Power. Go Western with tiny touches of Native American beading and Super-plush suede."[10]

Turning to journalism, a travel story in *Town and Country* from 1969 about Palm Springs is accompanied by a photo of a woman in a "Buckskin jacket with fringe swinging to make Pocahontas envious."[11] A brief for an upcoming journalistic story in 1972 *Cosmopolitan* teases, "Indian Girls Don't Laugh. What has befallen Indian maidens since Captain John Smith whisked Pocahontas away on his trusty frigate? David Shaber visits reservations to report on why liberation (and jobs, independence and fun) seems to be passing these shy, doe-eyed women by."[12] And from the story, the duality of the mythical woman: "Pocahontas incarnate, her long black hair drawn into a single braid and that hanging *girlishly* in front of her shoulder practically down to her waist, where the bottom is *seductively* tied up with a big bow of red yarn. Her tiny black eyes shift quickly about the room; on her head a jockey cap perches at a *rakish* angle, and her *lips* are made up in *flaming red*. Momma has a few things going for her, all right" (italics added).[13] Finally, *She* (London) magazine ran a series on women in history in 1986: "Savage Saviour Pocahontas, the Indian squaw who saved a colony and became an English Lady: the facts behind her legend are extraordinary enough." The third paragraph reads, "Everybody, of all races, should make a fuss of her. She offered an alternative to genocide—love, peace and intermarriage instead of hatred, war and dispossession. She was a North American Indian squaw and before she became Rebecca Rolfe, her name was Pocahontas."[14]

Throughout the history of these media representations, and especially in the final two examples above, the implicit violence of the appropriated image becomes evident. The fantasy image of Pocahontas chic preserves a white colonizer image imbued with racist ideas that support hegemonic ideologies[15] and that are perpetuated through cultural appropriation. Pocahontas has not just been subjugated through cultural appropriation, however, but both her person, her people, and her image have been victimized through the cultural commodification that accompanies the appropriation. Many forms of media, from books, to advertisements, to journalism, to social media are responsible for immortalizing Pocahontas as a hypersexual child who betrayed her people for the love of a white man. The seventeenth-century reality was, of course, very different.

Matoaka (Mah-TOH-ahkah)

Pocahontas was born Matoaka, and her mother was Pocahontas, who was Mattaponi, and her father was Wahunsenacah, better known as Powhatan because he was the paramount chief of the Powhatan nation, which consisted of many tribal groups of Algonquian-speaking people. Matoaka was given the name Pocahontas by her father when her mother passed away.[16] She most likely would not have been famous if Captain John Smith hadn't claimed, so that he could perpetuate his own status with his funders in England, that she saved him. By many accounts Pocahontas, who would have been ten or eleven at the time of the famous "saving," was an important Powhatan figure. She was becoming a gifted medicine woman and was spiritually important to the tribe.[17] Smith, who would have been twenty-seven at the time, did not have a high status, and so may have used her to gain it with King James who had chartered the Virginia Company in 1606. Other scholars have gone into much more depth than I will about Smith's dubious claims and how it supports settler-colonial beliefs,[18] but it's an unlikely story that was either created, embellished, and/or misinterpreted for a number of reasons, the most important for Smith being to gain the confidence of the English royalty to continue to finance his expeditions.[19] From the beginning, Pocahontas's identity was always and already appropriated and commodified.

Appropriation and Commodification: Violent Consequences of Sexualized Imagery in Fashion and Film

Cultural appropriation as Richard A. Rogers defined it—whereby the "use of one culture's symbols, artifacts, genres, rituals, or technologies by members of another culture—regardless of intent, ethics, function, or outcome"[20]—inevitably serves the interests of the appropriator and actively takes from the appropriated. Cultural appropriation distorts a culture in order to exploit it, corroding the reality of that culture into a stereotype that supports colonial structures.[21] Indigenous people have actively sought to ensure that others do not profit from our culture, but the rules are easy to avoid. Although the United States Indian Arts and Crafts Act of 1990 is supposed to protect tribes, its effect is limited to certain kinds of appropriation: "The United States Indian Arts and Crafts Act of 1990 is a truth-in-advertising law that prohibits misrepresentation in the marketing of Indian art and craft products within the United States. It is illegal to offer or display for sale, or sell, any art or craft product in a manner that falsely suggests it is Indian produced, an Indian product, or the product of a particular Indian or Indian tribe or Indian arts and crafts organization, resident within the United States."[22] As currently constituted, the law only protects US federally recognized tribes and their members rather than all creative arts. The Pamunkey Tribe wasn't federally recognized until 2015 and the Mattaponi are only recognized by the state of Virginia, however the Upper Mattaponi were federally recognized in 2018. And fashion designs cannot be copyrighted.[23]

Cultural appropriation and cultural commodification are two added elements in the continued violence toward Indigenous cultures. All sectors of media are responsible for practices that perpetuate stereotypes and capitalize on ignorance. Media, whether they be journalism, broadcast, social, or other, justify the ennobled and sexualized image of Native women and the destruction of Native culture.[24] According to the Justice Department (2019),[25] more than half of all American Indian and Alaska Native (AI/IN) women have experienced violence. Amnesty International has reported that one in three American Indian and Alaska Native women have been raped, which is more than twice the average for non-Native women;[26] also, AI/AN female victims of sexual violence experience violence at the hands of a non-Native perpetrator (96 percent).[27] Recently, more attention has been given to the problem of missing and murdered Indigenous women; this crisis of violence against Indigenous women is revealed in the statistics from the Bureau of Indian Affairs:

- More than 1.5 million American Indian and Alaska Native women have experienced violence in their lifetime.
- The murder rate is ten times higher than the national average for women living on reservations and is the third leading cause of death for Native women. Additionally, this group was significantly more likely to experience a rape in their lifetimes compared to other women.
- According to the National Crime Information Center, in 2016 there were 5,712 reports of missing American Indian and Alaska Native women and girls in the US Department of Justice's federal missing persons database, but the national information clearinghouse and resource center for missing, unidentified, and unclaimed person cases across the United States, called the National Missing and Unidentified Persons System (NameUs) only logged 116 of those cases.[28]

The oversexualization of Indigenous women as a contributing factor in the extent of the violence against AI/AN is exacerbated in the coexistence of media and fashion. Their images are objectified, and the static historical "costumes" are considered authentic, useful in ensuring that colonialism maintains its subjugation of and hold on Indigenous women through their dehumanization and use as sexual conveniences.[29] While seemingly a "hipster" trend, scantily clad women sporting headdresses, wearing "Navajo" panties, and drinking out of those same "Navajo" flasks are part of that savage sexualization.[30] All of this is wrapped up in the pernicious desire of white people to "play Indian," starting with the Boston Tea Party in 1773[31] and continuing today. Dressing up like Indians has allowed non-Indians to embody noble-savagery by allowing them to both hate Indians and at the same time desire to glorify them. I'm purposely switching to the term Indian here. Playing Indian performs both a physical and emotional meaning that signifies freedom and innocence. Pocahontas chic as part of women's fashion is an example of playing Indian and a continuation of the Indian princess / squaw stereotype. In this context, Pocahontas was seemingly "corrupted by the material artifacts of white culture" and "was willing to prostitute herself to white men" through appropriation.[32] Women's fashion has often been about rebelling against and owning sexuality at the same time, a dynamic that Pocahontas chic exacerbates.

Pocahontas chic is a fashion that draws on a nostalgic view of a fantasy interaction. Wrapped up in the myth of America is a mythical Pocahontas relegated to a fantasy of simplicity, purity, and wholeness: a Disney rendition of a static culture.[33] Pocahontas chic is both sexy and submissive. Pocahontas chic is a child dressed up as a woman that distorts concepts of what and how Native women actually are for the maintenance of control over the myth and to hyper-sexualize us,[34] which in turn reinforce our savageness, our femininity, and our wish to be simultaneously rebellious and colonized.

In 2012, the oversexualized short, brown-with-fringes, skimpy dress that Disney Pocahontas wore transformed into a brown-with-fringes Victoria's Secret bikini.[35] Sex "sells" so the fashion industry and other capitalist enterprises (e.g., films, television, magazines) use bodies and clothes strategically to foster desire.[36] One of the most outrageous uses of the Indigenous headdress, a cultural artifact, was when it was worn by a half-naked model at a Victoria's Secret fashion show, watched by millions of people. This appropriation of a spiritual item of clothing was a blatant act of disrespect for Indigenous culture. Headdresses are only worn by certain tribes and tribal members at specific times—not by a half-naked woman in her lingerie. Runway audiences predominantly include younger viewers—the two highest demographic groups are under eighteen years old and between eighteen and twenty-four years old[37]—for whom cultural appropriation is very influential. Stereotypes are seeded in adolescents through media and by design creators.[38] Pocahontas chic is at once primitive, noble savage, exotic, and honoring of Native culture—or so it professes to be. But each of these iterations is part of the systematic destruction of the Indigenous people; they each seek to civilize and maintain the colonial grip. "The feather headdress, the chieftain, and the dreamcatcher are all signs for exotic freedom and purity—connotations that paint the Indian as a mythological channel for the spiritual salvation of the white man."[39]

Similarly in film, Terrance Malick's *The New World* propelled an even more sexualized version of Pocahontas into the twenty-first century. This film relies on tropes that were identified with Indigenous people long before they hit the big screen. It takes all agency away from Native women, not just Pocahontas, and defines them in terms of white people while demonizing them against their own people.[40] What's most disturbing about the film, which had somewhat accurate clothing depictions, are the very sexualized scenes with actor Q'orianka Kilcher, age fourteen and Colin Farrell, who was twenty-nine at the time, and, to lesser extent, Christian Bale, who was thirty-one. Although Kilcher is the star as Pocahontas, she has very few speaking lines. When she, or any of the Native characters speak their language, it is not translated. Pocahontas is characterized as primitive until she gets to London.

The commodification of Indians through fashion, film, and media works to both civilize Indians, and to keep them in their past. The nostalgic, stoic forms of Pocahontas chic are part of the propaganda of continuing colonization. Commodification supports the hegemonic structure by removing the authenticity of Indian cultures.[41] Pocahontas was used to sell products in the nineteenth century such as cigars, perfume, and flowers. None of these benefit the current Powhatan Tribes. But most consumers of products, fashion, and media are not aware that their participation in the commodification of Pocahontas has exploited Indian identity.[42] The commodification has Americanized her myth and further appropriated her as the noble savage. And this commodification began with the Virginia Company because of its need for a story to keep pumping funds into their settlements. It has been kept alive in various media forms as a love story: "The Anglo-American story of Pocahontas has been told as a woman's story, because women's adventure stories are traditionally cast as love stories in the folk and popular narrative of England, the Continent, and following these antecedents, the United States."[43]

History and Fashion: The Material Properties of Indigenous Clothing

Pocahontas became Lady Rebecca when she was forced to go to England in 1616. She was just the best known of the likely hundreds of Indigenous women to be kidnapped and then murdered by colonists. Many portraits of her were painted, although most were not painted until the nineteenth century and by then her fate as a happily assimilated/colonized Indian woman was fixed. Her skin appears white in many of these paintings, as though she has fully become English,[44] her body made "legible for English eyes" so that her story is appropriated as an English one and not a Native one.[45] Pocahontas's story is fully American now, however, and its visibility in fashion as Pocahontas chic present in many media forms.

So what would Pocahontas have actually worn, and why? We can surmise that she was, or was becoming, a medicine woman, a Beloved Woman (even though her remembered image is generally based on the English gaze) because she is almost always pictured with white feathers.[46] Furthermore, women had a very important role in pre-colonial Powhatan society, as they were the ones working in textile cultivation and production, health management via picking herbs used to heal disease, and probably textile trade.

Obtaining information about Indigenous women's work is challenging as not only are writings about Indigenous women and their work with textiles scarce but historical writings about Indigenous populations can also be very demeaning and only from a colonial perspective. For example, the *Encyclopedia of Textiles*, second edition, published by Prentice Hall, derogatively explains the circumstances under which textiles were created during the seventeenth century: "The fabrics of that time were created out of necessity—a frantic need for clothing for household use. So, it is not surprising that American fabrics of the Colonial era did not approach the skill and sophistication of foreign materials. They are utilitarian in character, admirably adapted to the primitive surroundings in which they were created."[47]

The aesthetic part of Indigenous clothing as presented as artifacts in museums is usually culturally appropriated and mocked in the mainstream culture and fashion, but the materials they used for clothing and in their everyday lives, and still use today for ceremonies and celebrations, demonstrate a wisdom in their choice of materials that is rarely recognized. Dr. Azocar used the image of a turkey feather mantel, or cape, made by her great-grandmother

Mollie Holmes Adams in the 1930s for the cover of her book, *News Media and the Indigenous Fight for Federal Recognition,* to illustrate the persistence of culture even after centuries of colonization. The feathers have maintained their iridescence and moisture-wicking ability for almost one hundred years. Another way to consider Pocahontas chic is to consider women's clothing made out of the best materials that our natural environment has to offer, such as what animals provide through hides, fur, and feather, and plant materials such as tree bark, Spanish moss, fungi, hemp, and others. These materials take care of the environment in the process of their cultivation, use, and disposal.

Some textile scientists are seeking new, natural materials to replace the already existing natural and synthetic materials used in clothing because the fashion industry is one of the most polluting industries[48] and the processes of creating and discarding materials are contributing to climate change. One of the goals when forecasting future fashion trends is adapting to biodegradable and sustainable materials to reduce the greenhouse emissions that the production of synthetic materials (such as polyester and nylon) creates. Indigenous choices of raw materials for clothing provide unique insights into natural raw materials because of Indigenous people's relationships with the land and their understanding of preservation.

For example, part of this search for biodegradable materials led to the discovery of fungi as a viable textile. When some scientists first introduced the fungi material to use in clothing, accessories, and human living spaces, the textile community was amazed at how well it functioned and wondered why no one had thought of using fungi to create accessories or adornment before. *Scientific American* magazine published "Fabric from Fungi,"[49] revealing the wonderful fungi and how this material (specifically *Laricifomes officinalis,* also known as agarikon) has already been used by Indigenous peoples in Alaska. Suddenly, modern textile innovators could no longer take credit for being the first ones to experiment with this material.

Material scientists have been striving to develop textile materials that are not only better for the environment but also have a medicinal purpose. Indigenous peoples understand the medicinal advantages of materials very well. Continuing with the fungi example, this material was also used by Indigenous populations for medicinal purposes because it has styptic abilities to stop bleeding. And although there is no current documentation about these products being used in Powhatan Tribes, we can extrapolate what we know from other tribes. For example, the Spokane learned very early on that agarikon has styptic and purgative properties.[50] Agarikon mats were used in cradleboards to combat diaper rash.[51]

The use of Spanish moss (*Tillandsia usneoides*) by Houma and Koasati Tribes of Louisiana[52] is documented, and it grows from Texas to Virginia. The moss is an extremely difficult material to work with, but its threadlike stems grow to almost twenty-five feet long, usually hanging from trees. The entire plant has overlapping scales, which absorb water from the air, and this mechanism is what gives the fiber its special moisture-moving properties: the porous fiber structure keeps the moisture inside the pores so that it can be gradually released, while the scales on the surface of the fiber prevent fast moisture movement in and out of the fiber. Spanish moss fibers are also sanitary, odorless, resilient, and naturally mothproof.[53] Tribes used threads out of Spanish moss and wove them into cloth for centuries[54] for items such as diapers, because Spanish moss provides exactly the type of ventilation infant skin needs when covered with a material for long periods of time.

Another natural plant fiber used for clothing by Indigenous populations throughout North America is hemp. Hemp is considered to be one of the strongest cellulosic fibers used in clothing (strength in clothing is very important so that the cloth is durable). Hemp has also recently been at the forefront of environmentalism today as it could solve our problems with cultivating other materials, for example, cotton. Cotton cultivation is not sustainable as it requires enormous amounts of water and harmful pesticides and herbicides. Hemp, used as widely by Indigenous peoples as we use cotton today, is becoming more attractive for the textile industry since it is a low-impact crop that barely needs any pesticides, herbicides, or fertilizers.[55]

Indigenous peoples used a plethora of plant fibers for making cloth and other materials. The rich inventory of plants they used shows their great knowledge of plant fibers and their properties.[56] As a textile scientist, I am fascinated to see how they engaged in purposeful mixing of fibers to combine the useful properties of both fibers in one cloth. Research shows that tribes in the areas of Ohio and Arkansas mixed fibers in either single-ply (one thread) or two-ply (double thread) cords. Research (that analyzed artifacts from tribes of the Mississippi drainage and eastward) does not confirm why these specific combinations were used, but it does confirm that their use was not accidental. Some combinations of plant fibers included nettle and milkweed, blue stem grass and pawpaw, nettle and yucca, basswood and nettle, and pawpaw and yucca. Red cedar fibers and hemp fibers were found to be used by Potawatomi Tribe.[57] Tribes used many fiber types depending on what was growing in the area they lived.

As we analyze the reasons why Indigenous peoples mixed different fibers to create a cloth material, it's reasonable to wonder if there were some healing properties gained in combining particular fibers. If a cloth is made out of materials that might have nutritious or medicinal properties, those properties might be absorbed through the skin into the body ("transdermal absorption"). Since Indigenous peoples are knowledgeable about the medicinal abilities of different plants, they might have used clothing not only for protection and adornment but also for healing. For example, tree bark from the Sassafras tree, Spanish moss, and nettle plant all have healing properties and were used by Indigenous people.

Along with the aforementioned plant fibers, Indigenous populations also utilized animal products for clothing. Deerskin leather, for example, is soft and very comfortable to wear because it has a good amount of stretch. Leather-making is a complicated task, and it takes great understanding of the material in order to prepare it and cut it into a clothing piece. Unfortunately, the fringes on moccasins, leather jackets, and purses—which are very unique to Indigenous peoples—have been culturally appropriated by many fashion companies. Fringes serve an actual, practical purpose for Indigenous people: having them on an outercoat would help the wearer repel rainwater because the raindrops would travel down the tassels and away from the body.

Pocahontas would have likely worn clothing from all of these materials, and more. Unfortunately, most of what we know about Pocahontas's apparel is based on the writings of English men.

What Would Pocahontas Have Worn?

Pocahontas as a woman (not as a child) would have worn a knee-length fringed skirt, which could have been made out of plant material (possibly Spanish moss), and moccasins made out of deerskin. In colder weather, she would have worn a feather mantel, or cape, not unlike the cape made by Dr. Azocar's great-grandmother Mollie Holmes Adams. Feathers are beautiful, and they also repel water. It is very likely that Pocahontas was an active individual, delivering messages and acting as an intermediary between the settlers and her tribe, so she would have worn leggings because they were mainly worn when in the woods gathering food. For Pocahontas's coming-of-age ceremony, a huskanasquaw, her dress would have consisted of a fringed, off the shoulder dress made of deerskin, accompanied by a seashell necklace and possibly copper jewelry, given her family status. Her hair would have been adorned with turkey feathers.[58]

It must have been shocking for Pocahontas when she started wearing the clothing of the English, as English women's clothing of the time had a status-driven purpose rather than utilitarian. The clothing would not have been able to move with ease, as was the case with the clothing of her childhood. English women's clothing was constricted, heavy, and very uncomfortable to wear. Women wearing the English attire of the 1600s were not even able to fit through some doors because of the widths of their skirts, nor were they able to sit easily. It must have been particularly frustrating for Pocahontas to wear a corset that would not allow for proper air circulation (women would occasionally faint because they could not breathe).

But what would Pocahontas chic look like in the late sixteenth and early seventeenth centuries? When she was kidnapped and taken to England, she was forced to wear clothes influenced by the Queen Elizabeth I of England or Elizabethan style. Attire in England was status driven and controlled by sumptuary laws. Pocahontas is seen wearing a standing lace ruff at the neck, which was reserved for ladies of higher status. Lace ruffs represented the queen's support of English lacemaking and it also assumed a symbolic role. The lacework could also be seen on her cuffs. This high lace collar had to be supported by a metal frame or by starching, making it very uncomfortable to wear. At the end of the century (1575–1600) changes occurred in English clothing as the shape of the skirt grew wider at the top.[59] A padded roll (bum rolls) was placed around the waist in order to give skirts greater width below the waist. Steel or cane spokes fastened the topmost hoop to a waistband—it was called a wheel drum. Dresses worn over these structures had enormous skirts. In the Elizabethan style, every part of the body was constricted. The stomacher was a decorated triangular panel that filled in the front opening of a woman's gown (right above the corset). The stomacher may be boned, as part of a stay, or may cover the triangular front of a corset. Women's hair was always pulled back and heavily styled with ribbons and jewelry. In England, Pocahontas's hair was also pulled back and covered with a small top hat highlighting her importance to the English people.

When comparing Indigenous with English materials and clothing, it's impossible to avoid the contrast of the environmentally sustainable and potentially healing aspects of Indigenous clothing and material design with the excess and artifice of upper-class English designs and practices. The English, particularly the wealthy, preferred materials such as cotton and silk, neither of which are native to their land. Textile fabrics made mostly out of silk fibers were brocades, satins, velvets—these materials were costly to make, difficult to obtain, and were used for status.[60] Although in the late seventeenth century fine English woolens somewhat eclipsed the popularity of silks,[61] wool materials had long been the wardrobe of peasants. Interestingly, wool and flax materials that were used as everyday clothing by ordinary people (in England) do have some special properties. For example, flax fibers, which were used for undergarments, have a hygroscopic moisture property where the moisture is evaporated more rapidly than from other plant fibers. Wool also possesses a heat regulating ability that provides warmth.[62] However, status rather than health or healing was the focus in the selection of textile materials by English elites in the early modern period, so much so that it prompted the development of sumptuary laws. Queen Elizabeth I of England enforced new laws called the Statutes of Apparel, which were put in place to limit the expenditure of people on clothes in order to maintain the status markers of the class system.[63] In America, Indigenous design has survived through traditions and practices that have been passed down generations, though the cultural significance inherent in the healing properties of the natural materials used for Indigenous fibers may have been obscured or lost. Recently, however, material scientists have begun to develop textiles using similarly sustainable materials with qualities that, as the archaeological and other evidence has shown, were highly valued by Indigenous people.[64]

The Pernicious, Pervasive, Pocahontas Chic Problem

Brown suede material with brown suede fringes are heavily used today by many retail, leather giants (such as Coach and Gap), and Halloween retailers, which only further perpetuates stereotypes about Indigenous people. And yet, this design should not be freely used by the fashion industry without proper financial compensation because it is a protected culturally significant item. Unfortunately, in the United States, historically garment designs are usually not patentable.[65] A design patent is a special type of patent that allows a designer to protect the original shape or surface ornamentation of a useful manufactured article. But because a clothing design cannot be protected in the United States (unlike in many European countries), cultural appropriation is allowed and commodified. Copyright law applies only to fine art, but because apparel is considered a craft, it cannot be copyrighted, and so technically culturally based clothing cannot legally be protected. Many examples from magazines and fashion campaigns often depict suede.[66] Perhaps this is a place to start testing copyrighting or patenting Indigenous clothing. If suede is considered a special technological invention to manufacturing or treating fabrics or materials, it can be protected by patent. And if it can be protected as a material invented by Indigenous people, then compensation, as would be due to any fabric designer, would also be due to Indigenous people. For example, Swedish fabric giant Marimeko has protection of many simple design motifs such as stripes and poppy seed flower, and is financially compensated for their use.

Indigenous dress being "owned" by Indigenous people is crucial for our cultural survival. Moreover, as sovereign nations, Tribes have the legal right of control over both tangible and intangible aspects of their culture;[67] this includes the economic benefits of our culture, religious ceremonies and attendant costume or clothing. This control is essential if Indigenous culture heritage is to continue to thrive many generations from now.[68]

Banana Republic (Gap Inc.) launched its new Spring 2023 collection via social media platforms (such as Instagram); its marketing campaign was Pocahontas chic.[69] Pocahontas chic fashion exploits Indians for financial gain. If fashion companies feel the need to incorporate Indigenous designs into their concepts, then they need to hire Indigenous designers. No contemporary Indigenous fashion has been appropriated because it does not have the relationship with the static image of the Indian that the majority of Americans rely on. Indigenous designers like Jamie Okuma (Shoshone-Bannock and Luiseño), Bethany Yellowtail (Crow and Northern Cheyenne), and Louise Solomon (Ojibwe) challenge the stereotypes of what Indians should wear. By engaging contemporary Indigenous designers, companies will avoid appropriation and contribute to growing the economies of Indigenous people and their nations.

Notes

1. Kenneth Coutts-Smith, "Some General Observations on the Problem of Cultural Colonialism" (1976), reprinted in *The Myth of Primitivism: Perspectives on Art*, ed. Susan Hiller (London: Routledge, 1991).

2. "Disney Pocahontas Princess Cosplay Outfit for Children and Adults Halloween Costume," Costume Party World, https://www.costumepartyworld .com/disney-pocahontas-princess-cosplay-outfit-for-children-and-adults -halloween-costume.

3. Arrowhead Hosiery, advertisement, *Good Housekeeping*, February 1932, 175.

4. Ceramic Masterpieces, advertisement, *Better Homes and Gardens*, December 1949, 171.

5. Belgrade Shoe Company, advertisement, *Seventeen*, March 1956, 142.

6. "Cosmo Tells All," *Cosmopolitan*, November 1980, 62–62, 64.

7. "Let's Play Cowboys and Indians," *Seventeen*, April 1968, 144–45.

8. Table of Contents, *Cosmopolitan*, October 1999, 14.

9. *Seventeen*, May 2002, 36.

10. "Pocahontas Power," *Cosmopolitan*, October 1999, 88.

11. Robert L. Sammons, "Pastimes: Palm Springs," *Town and Country*, January 1969, 98–101.

12. "Coming in June Cosmopolitan on the News Stands May 23," *Cosmopolitan*, May 1972, 245.

13. David Shaber, "Indian Girls Don't Laugh," *Cosmopolitan*, June 1972, 150–53, 140.

14. Diana Norman, "Savage Saviour," She, August 1986, 11.

15. Jessyca Murphy, "The White Indin': Native American Appropriations in Hipster Fashion," in *Unsettling Whiteness*, ed. Lucy Michael and Samantha Schulz (Leiden: Brill, 2014), 127–38.

16. Linwood Custalow and Angela L. Daniel, *The True Story of Pocahontas: The Other Side of History* (Golden, CO: Fulcrum Pub., 2007).

17. Paula Gunn Allen, *Pocahontas: Medicine Woman, Spy, Entrepreneur, Diplomat* (San Francisco: HarperSanFrancisco, 2003); Custalow and Daniel, *The True Story of Pocahontas*.

18. Rachel Bryant, "Kinshipwrecking: John Smith's Adoption and the Pocahontas Myth in Settler Ontologies," *AlterNative: An International Journal of Indigenous Peoples* 14, no. 4 (2018): 300–308.

19. Allen, *Pocahontas*; Custalow and Daniel, *The True Story of Pocahontas*.

20. Richard A. Rogers, "From Cultural Exchange to Transculturation: A Review and Reconceptualization of Cultural Appropriation," *Communication Theory* 16, no. 4 (2006): 476.

21. B. Ziff and P. V. Rao, "Introduction to Cultural Appropriation: A Framework for Analysis," in *Borrowed Power: Essays on Cultural Appropriation*, ed. B. Ziff and P. V. Rao (New Brunswick: Rutgers University Press, 1997), 1–27.

22. The Indian Arts and Crafts Act of 1990, Pub. L. No. 101–644 (1990), U.S. Department of the Interior, https://www.doi.gov/iacb/act.

23. Denise Nicole Green and Susan B. Kaiser, "Fashion and Appropriation," *Fashion, Style & Popular Culture* 4, no. 2 (2017): 145–50.

24. Rayna Green, "The Pocahontas Perplex: The Image of Indian Women in American Culture," *The Massachusetts Review* 16, no. 4 (1975): 698–714.

25. "Department of Justice Enables Direct Tribal Access to FBI National Sex Offender Registry," United States Attorney's Office: Northern District of Oklahoma, July 11, 2019, https://www.justice.gov/usao-ndok/pr/department -justice-enables-direct-tribal-access-fbi-national-sex-offender-registry.

26. Hallie Golden, H. "US Indigenous Women Face High Rates of Sexual Violence—With Little Recourse," *Guardian*, May 17, 2022, retrieved from: https://www.theguardian.com/world/2022/may/17/sexual-violence-against -native-indigenous-women.

27. National Congress of American Indians, Policy Research Center, "Research Policy Update: Violence Against American Indian Women and Girls," February 2018.

28. "Missing and Murdered Indigenous People Crisis: Violence against Native Americans and Alaska Natives Far Exceed National Averages," U.S. Department of the Interior, Indian Affairs, accessed November 30, 2023, https:// www.bia.gov/service/mmu/missing-and-murdered-indigenous-people -crisis.

29. S. Elizabeth Bird, "Gendered Construction of the American Indian in Popular Media," *Journal of Communication* 49, 3 (1999): 61–83; Debra Merskin, "The S-Word: Discourse, Stereotypes, and the American Indian Woman," *Howard Journal of Communications* 21, 4 (2010): 345–66.

30. Tara MacInnis, "Appreciation or Appropriation," *Genteel*, September 9, 2013.

31. Philip Deloria, *Playing Indian* (New Haven: Yale University Press, 1998).

32. Rebecca Tsosie, "Reclaiming Native Stories: An Essay on Cultural Appropriation and Cultural Rights," *Arizona State Law Journal* 34, no. 1 (Spring 2002): 311.

33. "Disney Pocahontas Princess Cosplay Outfit for Children and Adults Halloween Costume."

34. MacInnis, "Appreciation or Appropriation."

35. Adrienne K., "Guess We Can Add Victoria's Secret to the List," Native Appropriations, November 9, 2012, https://nativeappropriations.com/2012/11/guess-we-can-add-victorias-secret-to-the-list.html; Jessica Misener, "Karlie Kloss Wears Native American Headdress at Victoria's Secret Fashion Show (PHOTOS, POLL) (UPDATE)," HuffPost, August 11, 2012, https://www.huffingtonpost.co.uk/entry/karlie-kloss-victorias-secret-headdress-fashion-show_n_2091958.

36. Susan B. Kaiser and N. Denise Green, *Fashion and Cultural Studies* (New York: Bloomsbury Visual Arts Publishing, 2021).

37. Emma Diehl, "What Fashion Show Viewership Means for Victoria's Secret," Civic Science, November 26, 2018, https://civicscience.com/what-viewership-means-for-the-victorias-secret-fashion-show/.

38. Media consumption continues to rise with the development of social media platforms where YouTube, TikTok, and Instagram amplify stereotypical images to become more and more harmful. Pew Research indicates that in 2022, 95 percent of teens are using YouTube. The frequency with which teens are on their social media platforms has been only increasing since its conception, and 35 percent of teens say they use at least one of the social media platforms constantly. Emily A. Vogels, Risa Gelles-Watnick, and Navid Massarat, "Teens, Social Media and Technology, 2022," Pew Research Center, August 10, 2022, accessed February 2023, https://www.pewresearch.org/internet/2022/08/10/teens-social-media-and-technology-2022/.

39. Murphy, "The White Indin," 133.

40. Tsosie, "Reclaiming Native Stories."

41. Rogers, "From Cultural Exchange to Transculturation."

42. Kent A. Ono and Derek T. Buescher, "Deciphering Pocahontas: Unpackaging the Commodification of a Native American Woman," *Critical Studies in Media Communication* 18, no. 1 (2001): 23–43; L. A. Whitt, "Cultural Imperialism and the Marketing of Native America," *American Indian Culture and Research Journal* 19, no. 3 (1995): 1–31.

43. Allen, *Pocahontas*, 59.

44. Charlotte Ickes, "The Sartorial and the Skin," *American Art* 29, no. 1 (Spring 2015): 82–105.

45. Michael Gaudio, *Engraving the Savage: The New World and Techniques of Civilization* (Minneapolis: University of Minnesota Press, 2008), 13.

46. Custalow and Daniel, *The True Story of Pocahontas*.

47. William C. Segal, *Encyclopedia of Textiles*, 2nd edition (Englewood Cliffs: Prentice Hall, 1972), 268.

48. Nattha Pensupa et al., "Recent Trends in Sustainable Textile Waste Recycling Methods: Current Situation and Future Prospects," in *Chemistry and Chemical Technologies in Waste Valorization: Topics in Current Chemistry Collections*, ed. C. Lin, (Cham, Switzerland: Springer, 2017), 189–228.

49. C. Hansen, "Fabric from Fungi: Researchers Pinpoint Mycelial Source of Museum Artifacts," *Scientific American* 324, no. 6 (June 2021): 21.

50. E. E. Hubert, *An Outline of Forest Pathology* (New York: John Wiley and Sons, 1931).

51. Robert A. Blanchette et al., "Fungal Mycelial Mats Used as Textile by Indigenous People of North America," *Mycologia* 113, no. 2 (2021): 261–67.

52. Max Carocci, "Clad with the 'Hair of Trees': A History of Native American Spanish Moss Textile Industries," *Textile History* 41, no. 1 (2010): 3–27.

53. Robert E. Martin, "Hair from Trees: . . . Spanish Moss Is New Upholstering Material," *Popular Science* 130, no. 6 (1937): 32–34.

54. Carocci, "Clad with the 'Hair of Trees.'"

55. Fieke Dhondt and Subramanian Senthikannan Muthu, *Hemp and Sustainability* (Singapore: Springer Nature, 2021).

56. A. C. Whitford, *Textile Fibers Used in Eastern Aboriginal North America* (New York: The American Museum of Natural History, 1941).

57. Whitford.

58. Custalow and Daniel, *The True Story of Pocahontas*.

59. Phyllis G. Tortora and Sara B. Marcketti, *Survey of Historic Costume*, 6th ed. (London: Bloomsbury Publishing Inc, 2015).

60. Tortora and Marcketti; Blanche Payne, *History of Costume: From the Ancient Egyptians to the Twentieth Century* (New York: Harper & Row, 1965).

61. Fernand Braudel, *The Wheels of Commerce: Civilization and Capitalism, 15th–18th Century*, vol. 2 (New York: Harper & Row, 1982).

62. Jules Labarthe, *Textiles: Origins to Usage* (New York, NY: MacMillan and Company, 1964).

63. Cristina Vallaro, "A Glimpse into Elizabethan Fashion: From Immoral Excess to Sumptuary Laws," *Journal of Literature and Art Studies* 12, no. 12 (2022): 1336–45.

64. Marie O'Mahony, *Advanced Textiles for Health and Well-Being* (New York: Thames & Hudson, 2011).

65. Elena E. Karpova, Grace I. Kunz, and Myrna. B. Garner, *Going Global: The Textile and Apparel Industry*, 4th ed. (New York: Bloomsbury Publishing, 2021).

66. Ella Alexander, "Victoria's Secret Apologises Over American Indian Outfit," *British Vogue*, November 12, 2012, https://www.vogue.co.uk/article/victorias -secret-apologises-over-american-indian-show-outfit.

67. Tsosie, "Reclaiming Native Stories."
68. Kunani Nihipali, "Stone by Stone, Bone by Bone: Rebuilding the Hawaiian Nation in the Illusion of Reality," *Arizona State Law Journal* 34, no. 1 (2002): 27–46.
69. Joanna Elizabeth, "Southwest Serenade: Banana Republic Unveils Spring 2023 Campaign," Fashion Gone Rogue, March 17, 2023, https://www.fashion gonerogue.com/banana-republic-spring-2023-campaign/.

OLD AND NEW VISUAL CULTURES

An Interview

STEPHANIE PRATT AND KATHRYN N. GRAY

The following interview takes as its starting point the initial engraving of Pocahontas after she arrived in London. From there the discussion situates this well-known print in the tradition of European portraiture, of Indigenous portraits, and portraiture of the eighteenth century, before transitioning into a wider discussion of contemporary Indigenous art and its reckoning with western traditions of portraiture and history painting. This broader understanding ultimately returns to the intersectional politics of gender and cultural identity from which the multiple aspects of Pocahontas's lived experience develop through time.

Stephanie Pratt, formerly Associate Professor (Reader) in Art History at Plymouth University, now retired, works as an independent scholar and sometime cultural consultant in many different UK organizations, art institutes, museums, etc.

KG: I'd like to begin the conversation by thinking about that original engraving that we have of the woman we know to be Pocahontas. It's produced in England at the beginning of the seventeenth century and the only image we have of her. What challenges does it present to us? Are there ways to interpret this image more or less effectively, and are there ways to misinterpret this image?

SP: It really is quite a rare image for its date in terms of a direct representation. I think the assumption is that the artist, Simon van de Passe, was able to see her. I have read in other accounts that it may be a posthumous image, but I find that difficult—If it is a posthumous image, it would suggest there was an intermediary drawing or portrait of some kind of which it was the copy, and often engravers at this date did do copies of very famous portraits.

One of the things I wanted to say about this is, number one: It's a real woman, and I think that's what shocks people. She's almost legendary, so for us to look at a seventeenth-century portrait is a rare and actually beautiful thing. There are several portraits in this seventeenth-century period, particularly one by Wenceslaus Hollar of a young man who was made captive and taken to be shown in Amsterdam. Somehow Hollar sees him in 1634–35. So, there are other images we can compare her with. She's within a kind of a visual culture of her time, dressed in courtly fashion—she is wearing *the* fashions of 1616. It's a celebrity image—it's to some extent *Hello* magazine—this is the woman-of-the-hour kind of image. She's very courtly, and she's wearing a high lace collar. We can read this as a propaganda image for the Virginia Colony and the Virginia prospectors. The people who want to make money out of the colony need to have an image which is able to give a good picture of the colony, knowing full well the colony had had a lot of trouble at the beginning, and was still, having to ask for more investment. This image was part of a publicity campaign. And secondly, it is a royal image, partly because of the fan that she's holding; it's an ostrich feather fan that looks quite like the Prince of Wales's moniker, his triple ostrich feather insignia.

In my work I think about [Indigenous] portraits as contact zones, and as a space where a person from one culture is meeting and becoming entangled with a person from the other culture, and they're forming a certain amount of middle ground: I negotiate with you, but you also must give up your image to me. This middle ground position allows us to think about Pocahontas as a real person, a person with agency who can decide what she gives away and what she doesn't. And this image, it doesn't give a lot away, she's very reserved. And everything that we have heard about her, I admit, in English texts, paints a picture of a clever person, who is able to be with others, with the colonialists and to go back to her own people. She was a respected person: she knew what was going on with the Virginia Company, she knew that they were promoting these things. I don't want to impute to her lots of intentions, because we don't know what her intentions were. Paula Gunn Allen's biography has been challenged,

"Unus Americanus ex Virginia" (An American from Virginia), Wenceslaus Hollar, 1645. Etching. (Metropolitan Museum of Art, NY; gift of Harry G. Friedman, 1956)

but her descriptions of her, "Diplomat, Spy, Medicine person," gives a sense of a person in the round. She's the individual that had to negotiate things, she had to become a Christian, maybe by force. She may have had a terrible history. The current Powhatan and Pamunkey and Mattaponi view of her is that she was stolen—she's the first murdered and missing Indigenous woman that we know of—she may have been raped, she may have got pregnant and been forced to marry. That's one way to look at this: that she was captured, she was forced, and that she was very resistant. In this middle ground space, we can allow for the possibility that, not only could she be active and own the princess role, but she could also resist and say this is not me, and you have put this all on me. And then finally, another way to read the image is through the feathers: white swan feathers are significant to Powhatan and Pamunkey women and in their women's societies. Some of John Smith's writings about his captivity with the Powhatan people mentions feathers worn by women who were coming to him with food and cleansing him and Pocahontas maybe being one of those women. Therefore, if she is allowed to hold the white feather society for the Pamunkey and she's holding it in this portrait, maybe she's reclaiming it as her Indigenous right and then self-presenting through doing that?[1] So there are multiple different ways to examine that particular portrait.

KG: Tending to these different interpretive frameworks provides fascinating reassessment of the image. It's so important to be able to establish those parameters and think about the different resonances that allow us to open up to those historical circumstances.

SP: I feel this is very important and note that we have not even bothered to care, to listen, to let people reclaim their voice, to let people reclaim their histories. We have written over her in such a terrible way. Her own people have produced their own history and it's challenged all the time. We're getting to a place where we cannot keep reasserting our power and our control of the discourse, because it's shouting over the voices of people that we need to listen to. And we need to get them talking and get them to give the stories and the histories from their perspective. And this means that even me, someone like me who is Dakota, does not have the power to claim and manipulate her story for my own purposes. So, in you interviewing me, I am speaking to you as an art historian, as a scholar, but I just want to reiterate that I do not tell her story and I do not speak for her people. I have been questioned and I have been challenged in Indian country for doing just that. These kinds of awarenesses about discourses, about the power to speak, apply to all of us, and, in saying this, I'm looking at my own position, challenging it all the time.

KG: Do we know anything about the circulation of the image (other than what you've mentioned already about the politics, the propaganda)?

SP: I would say that it probably did circulate quite a bit and certainly these sorts of images, these printed images, were sent to the colonies, and Indigenous people were becoming aware of their representation in the media of the time. I don't know the print runs, and the first states and second states of the prints, but there was another reissue in 1793, and I think that was a significant time because that's when the circulation of the image really gets going. The new United States entity is constructing its own origin stories and historical narratives, and the image is reproduced, followed by the Booton Hall portrait, a reimagining of the print as an original painting. Those are the more authentic images of her, whereas we then get all kinds of things in the nineteenth century of people imagining what Pocahontas looked like.

KG: You've accomplished a tremendous amount of work on portraiture of Native Americans in British art over the years. Does this engraving somehow fit into that tradition or not? There are different politics in play, different circumstances, different time periods that we're think-ing about, but does it fit into a similar kind of interpretive framework?

SP: I feel that it does very much fit into the history of portraiture, and British portraiture particularly, although I know Simon van De Passe is Dutch. Funnily enough, the first British painted portraits of Indig-enous individuals are done by an Anglo-Dutch artist called John Ver-elst who painted a Mohawk and Mohican delegation that came in 1710 to the court of Queen Anne, and we can put Pocahontas's face along-side these other men in the context of the middle ground: That recog-nition that the person I am actually trying to paint is not of my culture. This person is an emissary from very far away. They bring with them all the possibilities of the international contact, the international trade, the idea of alliances, and, in Pocahontas's case, intermarriage. But the portraits actually recognize that they are not Europeans, and they do that in a number of ways, but it *is* in the face. I think that Simon van de Passe—and then later John Verelst, and Willem Verelst, and even later Joshua Reynolds and Francis Parsons—who are tasked with painting these Indigenous individuals, must negotiate a portrait that has to fit the portrait paradigm. The audience would have to be able to read the portrait and say: "OK, this is so and so, they are kings, they are emperors, this is a princess" (even if this identity is misunderstood). They are trying to read it. But the portrait itself is unstable, because they don't behave like British aristocrats. Her face is not familiar—remembering the very famous comment by John Chamberlain who sees her at court and writes, she is no lady, she is "no fayre Lady."[2] What this does is upset British norms of who is a lady, and the same happens with the Mohawk delegation later. They are not kings, they are not people we really recognize. They're being presented as kings, princesses, emperors, when in fact the general British public are realizing no, there's something else going on here. These portraits are [symbolizing] the aspiration of Britain to be an empire. The portraits are like signposts on the road to British imperial control and British imperial power. If they can call this person an emperor then they're overlords of an emperor, they are overlords of a king, of a princess. These portraits embody imperial power.

As a rejoinder to that, they're in the middle ground space of encounter. Simon van de Passe and John/Jan Verelst are Dutch, and so their natural inclination is to depict what's there—that whole Dutch, Flemish Netherlandish tradition of naturalism and what reality feels like. It's a sensual reality of fur and bone and flowers and plants. And when they look at something, it's very interesting to them, and they have a scopic way of looking at things. Therefore, in her face, she's Indigenous and they are recognizing that, they are seeing it and they don't quite know how to depict it. And I think with van de Passe, he's a great artist who captures the feel of her as different—She's proud and she's dark, and there's a beauty in that. She's a beautiful, Powhatan Pamunkey Mattaponi woman. And similarly, with the Verelst portraits: they are powerful, Indigenous men with tattooing of their battle honors and the things they've done, their achievements. They are in themselves Indigenous and these Anglo-Dutch artists recognize it. The historians talk about the noble savage, but it's not a noble savage—that's a literary convention—there's something different about the engagement, entanglement in these portrait subjects, and about how we represent something we have never represented before.

KG: Moving through these centuries, we're thinking about encounter, we're thinking about ways of representing an Indigenous identity and that grappling of the Anglo-Dutch traditions, trying to find ways of doing this within the politics of the colonial Atlantic world. It strikes me that as we move into the nineteenth century, and we think of different kinds of representations, that a lot of those ideas about encounter and entanglement are starting to dissipate, especially when we move on to think about this idea of Pocahontas becoming the mother of the nation. And that narrative begins to become embedded in some of the paintings of the nineteenth century. As we move through the transition of representations, I wonder if you could say something about those nineteenth-century representations, which seem to me to be doing a whole different kind of cultural work.

SP: Yes, absolutely, we're in another paradigm: the United States republic is in formation, figuring a national identity, which is a hard thing to grapple with, especially when you're not unified. Other countries who tried to unify, particularly in the nineteenth century, had difficulties in presenting these coherent origin stories and myths. Painting has a lot to carry in these situations. I'm going to take us back a little bit to the origins of history painting because it is an academicism. It comes out of the Renaissance and there are theories which essentially have to do with composition. It's the way a painting works, like a machine. They used these pictures like tools to teach. Originating in Italy, these pictures worked to teach people in an illiterate society who needed to learn the Bible stories and the lessons of the Catholic Church about the doctrines. So that histories of ideology and pedagogy come into this. These history paintings that were commissioned for the US Capitol Building [are] a great place to tell a story and create myths and form a national identity. They were doing it early in the republic with Trumbull's paintings of the signing of the Declaration of Independence and the Constitution.

Looking back over these histories, the things that I accepted as a child, unconditionally, [are] because they were given such preeminence in the Capitol Building and the state capitol buildings. In contrast to these earlier public sculptures, my cousin, Robert Freeman [Dakota, Lakota and Rincon], who passed last year, sadly, was the first Indigenous artist to create [a] sculptural piece for the Sacramento State Capitol Building. He created a sculpture for that [which had never been represented], for Indigenous people. But we're talking about 2013/14, which is the first time (that I know of) that an Indigenous artist is invited to make an official public sculpture. You can see how history painting, sculpture, architecture are all working together to manipulate the story that this is who we are, this is our country. And in the Capitol we have the four artists who were commissioned later than Trumbull. Two of those pictures deal with the Spanish incursion by Columbus and de Soto. And the other two that are relevant to Pocahontas and New England are *Pocahontas's Baptism* (1840) by John Gadsby Chapman and the other one about the Mayflower sailing. Early in US history, these two stories become the origin myths for the whole of our country. Redecoration began after the fire in 1814, and the country wasn't unified. It wasn't what it was going to become at the end of the century. It's forcing people to look and to accept that Pocahontas is the mother of our country, that the Pilgrims are our forefathers. Yes Virginia gets a look in, but New England eventually takes the weight of the origin myths. These things become our aristocracy in the US.

What's interesting about these history paintings and sculptures in the Capitol Building is that very significantly the Native people being depicted, for instance in Chapman's painting of Pocahontas's baptism and in the relief sculpture by Enrico Causici, *Conflict of Daniel Boone and the Indians, 1773* (1827), were contemporary Indigenous people who the United States was fighting against to take their land. In the painted frieze in the Rotunda of the US Capitol building, the scene *Oglethorpe and the Indians* draws directly from contemporary portraits of Indigenous leaders from the 1820s and 1830s. The people in the Black Hawk War, the Sac and Fox, the Miami—some of those Midwestern peoples are being depicted in the Capitol as if they were resisting invasion back in the 1700s. You can see the ideological force of that is to suddenly look at the Sac and Fox: "How dare they fight against this wonderful nation that's going to be the best in the world, the most democratic, the most free." And it's such a denigration to the Indigenous people when you know what happened in the Black Hawk War, you know the truth of it. And these are the histories that the US won't tell itself. They won't go over these things. It's a horrible genocidal history which the US refuses to look at.

KG: It also strikes me that these paintings are trying to depict the past, and, as you say, it's about the present, so trying to consign a certain aspect of that nineteenth-century experience to the past. We know about these conflicts and the removals and the way that the nineteenth century does map out in the end, but it's almost like these images are trying to say this is the past, rather than now. I wondered if you have a sense of that?

SP: Yes, I think that history painting is as I say a didactic form, and you read it like a book, like yes, this is written as an event that has happened and in fact the country was still colonizing. You look at [the images of] de Soto and Columbus and you think, "yes, this is inevitable," this happened. It's like a rolling ball. They talk about Manifest Destiny in the 1840s, but these paintings are actually helping to form that. They are helping to form the inevitability of history, the idea that empire moves West. Bishop Berkeley said that, theorizing about it as early as the eighteenth century, and the whole of the Western European Anglo world is thinking about this, and these history paintings help to visualize that process of incorporating specific moments without realizing how random those moments were—the randomness of "the Pilgrims" coming. It was such a random occurrence for them to suddenly decide they were going across the Atlantic. But, maybe it wasn't so sudden because they were, in the very late sixteenth century, looking at North America as a possibility, and it was something that was growing and in Leiden was reaching a point of clarity for them. But at the same time, they could have landed somewhere else and it could have been a completely different history. But when you look at a big history painting, you think, yes of course it had to happen that way: Pocahontas had to be baptized. She had to marry and to become part of the English culture in order to save us in order to create the America that we have today. There is that inevitability because it's painted. They talk about the ennobling, the aggrandizing of stories. Well, painting does that, monumental sculpture does that, it aggrandizes it. That's why tearing a statue down, or throwing paint on something is a huge gesture because it touches that sacrosanct quality of high art. You just don't paint over a Michelangelo, you don't tear down a Sistine Chapel—and that's the way these things are looked at—the Sistine Chapel of the United States. I think history painting has a lot to answer for, for keeping these myths alive, for letting Americans have a complacent and arrogant attitude.

KG: We've talked up until now about representations of Native America, not by Indigenous artists. I'd like to move the conversation onto Indigenous art, to see a change in the way we might think about some of these ideas. In recent years, Indigenous artists, scholars, writers and readers have addressed the limitations, inaccuracies and injustices of previous representations. So I'd like to move the discussion on to more contemporary work, thinking about portraiture and history painting, visual forms that can serve as a thread through that discussion. There's been some radically new work by Indigenous artists, women and men, that have enabled powerful and original representations in all media. Given your knowledge, can you identify some recent artworks or artists that offer us important and new ways of responding to that tradition of portraiture, given that we started with portraiture (with the Pocahontas image) and self-portraiture now.

SP: Being the historian, I see the long trajectories too and that this didn't necessarily emerge completely. . . . It is very much about resistance and survivance. Indigenous cultures could have depicted the face, they just weren't interested in it. Though they were fascinated by people being interested in faces. There are all these stories about people having their portraits painted and how they were reacting, and there was a long history of engaging with the flat image. Portraits had a power; an image people carry and remember me by. Contemporary artists are starting to interrogate this, and one of the pieces I'd like to point out is James Luna's *The Artifact Piece* (1987) where he displayed himself in a cabinet case; a performance piece in the San Diego Ethnographic Museum. That image to me is a real juncture with the gaze of the colonizer, responding to the way that Native people had been represented as dead and put in a glass case was so profound. People had never seen what it felt like to be a culture that had been consigned to the glass case and the anthropological museum. There are things about the way that contemporary Native artists have engaged with this where it's a body blow, a bodily felt image, of where my identity, my culture, my language, my family, my history has been annihilated. It's quite hard to reclaim in that scenario. But I point to people like Shelly Niro's early iteration in photography, called *Mohawks in Beehives* (1991). I think it's a group of her friends, her sister, and they've got their glam on, they've got their bling, and they've got their hair done, and suddenly people are thinking, "Oh yeah, Native people can be modern, can have fun." It's like another juncture of trying to break down all of those horrible misrepresentational tropes, of the Plains person with the braids and the beads and all the beaded regalia, but then with their head hanging down: "last of their kind." At the end of the nineteenth century, they call it the termination period.

When I think of my own history—My father was born in 1916, his history reaches back to the termination period. To come out of that, out of all the assimilation, and all the misrepresentations, it's gargantuan, it's a big, big history. Another juncture was 1992, of course, which was the quincentenary of the voyage of Columbus and the landing. There was the Submuloc show which was "Columbus" backwards. People like Gerald McMaster were finding their voice. A lot of the Canadian Indigenous artists were coming forward and speaking loudly about their own positions, their own histories. In 2000 Shan Goshorn's self-portraits—the Earth Renewal series—engages with the complexity of the face not being something that the Indigenous people were necessarily fascinated with. She's wearing a ribbon skirt from the Cherokee with her moccasins and that ribbon skirt merges into the tree. Shan's photographed and double-exposed onto a tree; that's her self-portrait from 2000. She aligns with the tree. It's another worldview, another ontology, which people who are raised outside of that don't understand. It's not something I was particularly raised with but I'm coming closer and closer to understanding it, to understanding that this is a great set of knowledges, set of practices that we have totally misunderstood and totally ignored. There's one particular photograph by Nisha Supahan, called *I'm a photographer*

2001. This was a portrait at an exhibition called About Face, and she is of Northern Californian Indigenous and Celtic background, she is a person of mixed heritage, but this is truly looking back and claiming absolutely that she is the master of her image and how she wants to be seen. And I think that that moment of 2000 was another important juncture, where we have the younger artists coming out from that generation—Shan and others in photography mainly, but also performance artists, installation artists, and artists working in film and media.

Wendy Red Star stands out as a person who speaks to me. Wendy is from the Apsáalooke or Crow Nation in Montana, and I've a real appreciation for the aesthetic of the Crow and other nations of that area, the Blackfeet and others. And she just seems to get the aesthetic. She uses very bright colors, and she dresses, sometimes, in her own regalia, and yet places herself again in that scopic museum-type world, where she's got plastic animals and dioramas, and she's being the Indian, but in a knowing way, that's really reclaiming the space of encounter, like, "This is my telling of the middle ground, and this is how I want you to read it." It's very fun, but it's hard-hitting too. There's a brittleness in looking that way. You're exposed when you're being looked at all the time, and you're being examined by the anthropologists, and the ethnohistorians, and the historians, and the critics. You become brittle because you've been constantly challenged: "Show me the authentic Indian. Be the Indian." And there is no Indian! We're all very separate, individual, distinct groups with distinct heritages and distinct stories. I'd love to hear her talk about her images, particularly *Four Seasons* (2006), where she moves through the four seasons in a traditional way. But when you look at it, you think, "where is this familiar person that I hope to find?" like Pocahontas or something but she's not there, and Wendy's not going to tell you.

More recently, Cara Romero, a Chemehuevi artist from California, in one of her most powerful recent pieces, *Nikki* (2014), resists the viewer's gaze. It doesn't open itself up to your vision, to your gaze, and it's very much resistant. Another of a new generation of artists redefining the Native image, redefining it for themselves. Cara is living in the Southwest. There's a Navajo rug behind Nikki, and the long braids, which Nikki chose. And Cara has said to me personally that

Self Portrait (from the Earth Renewal Series), Shan Goshorn, 2000. Computer-generated, double-exposed black and white photo on canvas, hand-applied photo oils. (Image courtesy of the artist's estate; photo Columbia State Community College Permanent Collection, Columbia, Tennessee, gift of Constantine and Mary Vrailas)

Nikki, Cara Romero, 2014. (© Cara Romero, all rights reserved; courtesy of the artist)

she never takes a photograph without asking someone's permission, she never even starts a photo until she gets permission. She is aware of these protocols, these new ways to acknowledge that you are an ally with whoever you are working with to help bring their story out. You need to be very humble in the face of people who are telling their own personal stories, their own understandings. Cara's really aware of that.

Dana Claxton, Lakota, has a Plains aesthetic. Traditionally, Plains women's arts tend to be what they call abstract—of course we know abstract is a dangerous term because it doesn't actually mean abstract, it's just another formulation, another artistic language for signification. There's a lot of content in Lakota beadwork but people don't necessarily understand it or know how to interpret it. With Dana and with Cara, and with people like Wendy Red Star, there is an abstract level at which the Plains [or California Indigenous] aesthetic is being brought forward again but in a new media—in photography and installation, in beadwork and in 3-D design, and particularly in places like fashion. Cara talked about a work she was going to make in a swimming pool—where she has those floating women—they were used as the cover of one of the Native Spirit film festival [brochures]. . . . They are just fantastic pieces. I think she made four of them, of women falling through water. They were Indigenous Pueblo women and there was a notion of climate change, which was part of Cara's message, but working to get that image as she needed it and hearing the background to the image was just so powerful. We're going to see more and more great work coming in the future.

KG: One of the artists that you've mentioned in the past, as we think of the politics of history painting and the creation and recreation of cultural narratives, is Kent Monkman. Could you comment on the way that he responds to tradition?

SP: Ever since I've known about Kent Monkman's work I've been thrilled and fascinated [with it] and particularly his alter ego Miss Chief Eagle Testicle—I did not understand the meaning until I read on the Metropolitan Museum website that it means "Egotistical"—I didn't hear that. The Miss Chief persona gave him carte blanche to be the regal, the mischievous, trans-ish, breaking-all-boundaries kind of person. Originally, he started with these big landscape views where you would look at a Bierstadt-type of monumental landscape like they were painting in the late nineteenth century and then at the very bottom there would be these two men in congress, or in love, and a very queer and different sort of identity going on, than in a traditional western landscape. Over time, his techniques of painting just got better and better, challenging himself to make the grand machine, like we talked about from the nineteenth century, the great Salon piece. The work he did for the Met was very much going into the history books, going into art history, to feel like art history was his playground, which is how artists should look at art. Because art always reflects other art, it always has this dialogue and this conversation with it. Responding to the greatest history paintings of the Salon like Gericault's *Raft of the Medusa*, or Delacroix, or other paintings that he saw, I guess it

Miss America, Kent Monkman, 2012. Acrylic on canvas. (Image courtesy of the artist)

was Titian's Venus and Adonis. Some of these paintings are so often reproduced that we don't really look at them. That's what Kent has done—through his reclaiming, he's making us look at what those pictures were doing, and then turning that on its head.

It's then another whole maneuver, about, I think, the elevation of individual stories, the mixed stories, the trans stories, the queer stories into the monumental scale of the history painting. The ideology then changes: "Yes, of course, those are our stories" of, say, the intermarriage, the captivity stories, yes, the stories of death and destruction. But he also contemporizes this—particularly in the Met in one of those two pictures—he calls it *mistikôsiwak* in Cree, which means *wooden boat people.* He has remembered or was told that this is what the Cree people used to call the explorers, the wooden boat people, because they [Cree] had birch-bark boats, so they [wooden boats] were the others. Now we have boat people, we have people who are migrants, and he's made that really relevant. True history painting in the highest form was like [Jacques-Louis] David, we're commenting on contemporary history, we are making a statement about the conditions now. And Kent takes that on: "Let's get real, people, let's tell our histories as they really are, in a monumental scale and look very hard at our past and where we're going." He's got the whole global crisis in his mind as well. I find them tremendous. I always wanted Indigenous artists to break out of the big ghetto which is Native American art in North America. There is this kind of Indian art market element in which everyone fits in that paradigm. It's very much based in the Southwest, or you have the Toronto-Ontario group of people—again a paradigmatic sort of place where you go and study art as an Indigenous artist. But inevitably they're institutions, inevitably they behave in that way and they create an academicism, which is always a danger. I always wanted Indigenous people to break free of that. To not have to be the Indian artist, do the Indian subject. Actually to be seen on the international scale. Well done to the Met for commissioning him.

And that brings this into the US realm, because Kent is a Canadian artist. That whole dynamic, or problematic, of the 49th parallel, we need to start looking at the histories that make us—we have a joint history with Canada, and a joint history with the world. The US has always had that kind of exclusion, that exceptionalism and I think that these kinds of pictures also reveal that that is just a myth.

KG: Finishing on Kent Monkman's work is probably perfect because it opens up a global response to a global statement.

SP: He also did another set which you may or may not know. This one was the Four Continents. His *Miss America* is based on the Tiepolo (at the Würzburg Palace). This very much is about what's happening now and our determination to destroy ourselves on this planet. Kent is such an aware, intelligent, perceptive artist. We used to look at artists as the seers and the—well I won't say the prophets—but people who had to bring us round to ourselves and make us see again and make us reconsider. We've often said that the Indigenous people are now the people we need to listen to—they have experienced the world in such a different way and we've got to listen now and see about different ways to perceive where we are, where we've been, and where we're going, the whole existential crisis. We need to include them, we need to listen. We need to step back and let them take the podium right now.

Notes

1. See Paula Gunn Allen, *Pocahontas: Medicine Woman, Spy, Entrepreneur, Diplomat* (San Francisco: HarperSanFrancisco, 2003), 60–61. Pratt's reading of the portrait draws from the above biography and discussions with Dr. Max Carocci.
2. John Chamberlain, letter to Sir Dudley Carleton, February 22, 1617: "Here is a fine picture of no fayre Lady and yet with her tricking up and high stile and titles you might thincke her and her worshipfull husband to be somebody, yf you do not know that the poore companie of Virginia out of theyre povertie are faine to allow her fowre pound a weeke for her maintenance."

"LISTEN TO THE ATLANTIC"

Archives and Memory

SARAH SENSE AND KATHRYN N. GRAY

The archive can be silent on the experiences and emotions of Indigenous women. In the opening of this collection, Karenne Wood brings one of those voices back into being:

> Yes, my father said. Go. We need to know more.
> I saw Plymouth, then London. Felt its crowds press upon me, knew its
> stench. ("Amonute, 1617")

In similar ways, Sarah Sense's sculpture, *Listen to the Atlantic, It's Speaking to You*, recovers Indigenous presence. Like Wood, Sense addresses archival absences, piecing together glimpses of the past in an act of recovery and return. The sculpture is located in Plymouth, the English city that Pocahontas (referred to as Matoaka in this artwork) passed through on her visit to London. Fabricated in steel, the sculpture is imposing; a curved, tree-like supporting structure holds a parabolic dish. At the center of the concave dish is the name Matoaka, and she is surrounded by the names of her contemporaries.

The people named are North American Indigenous travelers to London, all of whom arrived between 1603 and 1630. Some of them where captives and some of them traveled for diplomatic purposes, but they all have one thing in common: they died in England and their final resting place was very far from home.

Again, Karenne Wood's poem echoes. Imagining the final thoughts of Amonute, the given name that Wood explains predates Pocahontas, Wood reinstates her subjective presence:

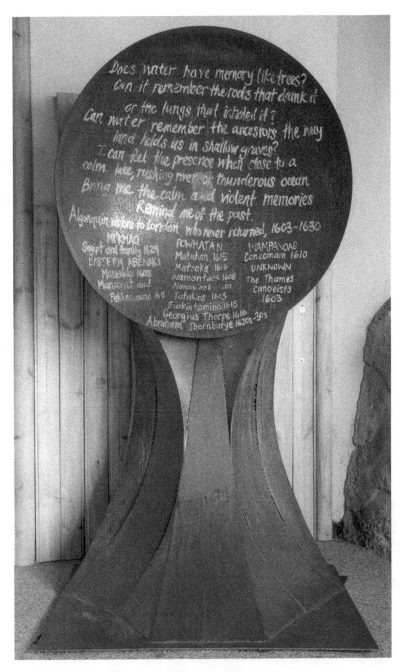

Listen to the Atlantic, It's Speaking to You, Sarah Sense, 2020. (National Marine Aquarium, Plymouth, UK; image courtesy of the artist.)

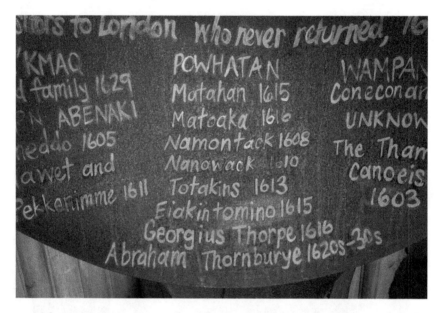

Detail from *Listen to the Atlantic, It's Speaking to You.* The artwork names and commemorates Matoaka among the other Powhatan, Mi'kmaq, Abenaki, Wampanoag, and unknown "Algonquin visitors to London who never returned, 1603–1630." (Image courtesy of the artist)

It is but the fevered dream of one who sleeps an ocean away.

Tsenacomoco.

We thought it the center of the world.

The presence of Indigenous souls and histories, sleeping an ocean away, is a central component and the essence of Sense's sculpture. This ocean in between is precisely the distance that this sculpture seeks to traverse. Reading the words on the large dish there's a haunting presence of past lives and contemporary presence. Appearing as a solid, immovable force, the sculpture feels rooted, permanent: an arboreal presence that connects and communicates through land and water.

Listen to the Atlantic, It's Speaking to You was my introduction to Sarah Sense's work, a commission completed in 2020, and her final UK-based project before her return to the United States following a six-year stay in Ireland and Britain. We begin our conversation focusing on this sculpture but quickly expand the discussion to encompass a body of work, created in Ireland, England, Europe, and the United States, that continues to generate new responses to western archives, and legacies of settler-colonialism, legacies that acknowledge the environment, shared knowledge, family, and heritage.

I ask Sarah about her research, her practice, and about the interventions her work makes in current debates:

> After learning of Coll Thrush's scholarship on Native people visiting London pre-Mayflower in his book, *Indigenous London,* and of the Algonquian people who went missing or died in Britain in the early seventeenth century, I was inspired to make a piece about this relevant British history, convinced that this would give viewers and listeners a different perspective to colonization in the early 1600s. The sound element of *Listen to the Atlantic, It's Speaking to You* seemed to be an appropriate way to connect the experience back to the Americas by way of voices traveling west over the Atlantic Ocean through the parabolic dish, with viewers and speakers participating in the sound element by using their own voice to repeat the names of the missing and murdered Algonquian people. Listed on the steel parabolic dish are the names of those who were missing or murdered or died in London in this early period of the 1600s. You can read their names aloud and their names echo back across the ocean returning them back to North America. History and space between the United Kingdom and North America is an ocean carrying stories of people moving between continents.
>
> This is the first time that I have made something incorporating sounds. Since 2004 I've been creating weavings that are 2-D, small baskets and murals. In 2019, I fabricated this sculpture and as my first installation piece. I wanted it to be interactive with the viewer and for the individual to have a direct experience with the sculpture. Doing that with sounds, speaking aloud, is a good way to draw people in. Sound moves across water easily and this whole piece is about movement across the Atlantic. This sculpture is about the space in between; it's about our imagination and sounds that could travel from Plymouth, England, all the way to North America. Maybe physically moving the bodies isn't feasible now, but we can do it verbally. And, if we can do it with our sound, in an act of talking, even if it's a whisper, we can heal.

This new exhibit adds to the many traces of Pocahontas in British spaces. In *Indigenous London,* Coll Thrush comments that, "disconnected from her own people's larger story and from the histories of other Indigenous travelers to London, the young Powhatan visitor becomes an isolated figure of tragedy, a singular anomalous presence in the urban landscape. Pocahontas is a lonely ghost."[1] But, unlike so many other references in the urban environment of London, or the literary traces that Coll Thrush identifies, in this sculpture Matoaka is remembered as part of the Powhatan people. In contrast to this isolating narrative and misremembered past, *Listen to the Atlantic* is an act of recovery that intersects with a growing body of scholarship that draws attention to the presence of many Indigenous travelers or captives in the European archives. As several historians have also demonstrated, there were many more travelers—diplomats and captives—from Indigenous America than are commonly recognized.[2]

In Europe, anniversaries of so-called discovery, early voyages, and new European settlements, provide means of remembering and redressing centuries of myth making, forgetting, obfuscation, and denial. Early American documents, especially those of the early seventeenth century, are built on Eurocentric assumptions and hierarchies, but they also contain the names of Indigenous interlocutors, translators, diplomats, warriors, mothers, fathers, children, names selectively forgotten by centuries of neglect. *Listen to the Atlantic* revives some of those names from Mi'kmaq, Eastern Abenaki, Wampanoag, and others unknown and anonymous, ensuring that this past is located again as part of a living present. The sculpture recovers the historical record and in doing so situates the legacies of the colonial past within present constructs. I ask Sarah about the anniversary in Plymouth, in 2020, four hundred years since the *Mayflower* set sail:

> When considering the *Mayflower,* I ask what has been recorded of the *Mayflower* and Native North American perspectives within the United Kingdom? For me, the idea that England, explorers, or Pilgrims didn't know very much about the people that were in North America, is not true. There were Indigenous people that were brought back to England in the early 1600s. Going through those English accounts, accurately, which Coll Thrush does in his book, is to reignite that memory. There was no accident here, it was very clearly a voyage to go somewhere where there were people already. In reality, this was about the

colonizers taking whatever they wanted, doing whatever they wanted, in whoever's name they chose.

The interconnectedness of life systems, through time and place, in the past and the present, echoes strongly in the piece, and I ask Sarah about this interconnectedness, of people and place, of environmental legacies, within her wider practice.

> I feel that the environmental issues are so deeply connected and intertwined with colonization that I see it as the same thing. At the beginning of colonial experience, the disrespect of North American land and landscapes began and continued. This was the beginning of being separated from land, removing people from their land. Those removals changed the culture and changed the landscape; they were the beginning of disrespecting the human and disrespecting the landscape. Having continued in this way for hundreds of years, very slowly, we're at a point where so many people are disconnected from environmental space. It's a huge challenge to think about how to reconnect or re-Indigenize. Coming back to the lands, coming back to that space, and recreating that relationship is incredibly important.

Thinking about family histories, and tribal histories, I ask Sarah to share how she conceptualizes memory, as a way to reconstruct the past in the present:

> Memory can become a part of your present moment. If we're dealing with historical trauma, history as it's written, versus actual history as experiences, memory is important in recalling with accuracy that lived experience. Current debates in blood memory, memory passed down to you through bloodlines, suggest that what we experience and what we feel, our own individual experience, is not just our own memory but could be a memory passed down to you. In my earlier work of weaving, and more recent work *Cowgirls and Indians* (2018), I focused on Hollywood and the changing movie posters or changing historical images of different figures that have become part of popular culture but weren't originally or supposed to be for popular culture. Particularly for me, for the Hollywood series, it was about reclaiming the woman, the women: this was white women being dressed as Native in Native regalia, not even regalia, just a feather, a pinup girl with a feather, being over-sexualized, and that happening a hundred

years ago and that happening today. Unraveling that history, or, with different Hollywood images, reclaiming power for those women, I think that's probably the first time I started working with memory and maybe history.

In *Cowgirls and Indians* (2018), Sense draws together enduring landscapes, history, and popular culture's contemporary stereotypes. In her artist statement about these works, she notes:

> Weaving these landscapes together with brightly contrasting Hollywood and pop culture imagery representing stereotypes of Native North America, questions the misconceptions of differing realities.
>
> Like photographs, stories are a recorded history, merging time and memory repeatedly both orally and visually. I use posters and personas to explore American popular culture's stereotypes of Native North America in Hollywood cinema, fashion trends and pop icons. Cowboy and Indian iconography are deeply rooted in America without recognition of the real history or the consequences of stereotypes. These generalizations are detrimental to the collective community and to the individual. *Cowgirls and Indians* explores these questions of identity, and the influence of imagery on global consciousness.[3]

In this series, and in *Weaving the Americas*, I'm intrigued by the interplay between the human, the landscape, and memory (memory as the past infiltrating the present). I ask Sarah about how interactions with specific land and landscapes form a vital feature of her work:

> With my own work I'm always looking to incorporate my own landscape photography because I want to make sure that I'm not making work about spaces or places or environments that I've never been to.

Bringing together thoughts on bloodlines, generational memory, embodied experiences of place, and a sense of connected heritage, we're drawn to consider the unique links Sarah establishes between peoples, nations, land, borders, and border crossings. Looking back at her early career, Sarah remembers:

> By 2010 I was traveling in South and Central America, working on *Weaving the Americas*. For that project, I was meeting and interviewing Indigenous artists in their communities, the research took me through

the Americas, the Caribbean, southeast Asia, and finally Europe. I first worked on a project in Ireland about the Choctaw Irish relationship through the great potato famine.

Again, in her artist statement of the time, Sarah outlines the manifold debates that are inspired and reconciled in work that remains deeply personal:

> As my travels began, landscapes grew into my work beginning with the *Weaving the Americas* series (2011), mostly landscapes of deserts, mountains and jungles; then with *Weaving Water* (2013), underwater scenes, the sun and the moon. While meeting with Indigenous communities I became intrigued with my own family again; in many ways, being that outsider encouraged me to grow closer to my origins. As travel and life merged into one, making connections between family, research, and landscape became more natural.
>
> In 2013 I was invited to have an exhibition in Bristol and stayed. Stories were unfolding to me while circumstance created new realities. When I realized that Europe would hold me for longer than I would want, I began to consider various relevant research, the most exciting was an old story that my Grandma Chilie told me long ago about the Choctaw Irish relationship and the Choctaw community gifting money to the Irish during the famine in the 1840s . . . The story goes: shortly after the Choctaw were removed and displaced in Oklahoma on the Trail of Tears, word reached the community that there was starvation in Ireland. The Choctaw gathered funds and sent the money to Ireland as a gift to help. . . . To re-write and re-record her experience is like breathing her life into her old home of Oklahoma.[4]

The scope of Sarah's interests, and her interventions, go beyond discrete transatlantic connections, and the final relation, "Choctaw Irish Relationship 16," is equally poignant, expanding the breadth and depth of common trauma and the interconnections of healing, where personal connection meets global consequence:

> This piece is the final one that I made of this series. The image is of the Croatia-Bosnia border, on the Bosnia side. This was taken the night that we left for Ireland, October 30, 2014. I was drawn to the image as a reminder of a more recent tragedy of national borders and conflict.

While the UK repression of Ireland is for the most part historical, there are still more recent histories of such tragedies such as former Yugoslavia. The image woven through it is of a water reflection in Germany from September when I was there researching my family. My Grandfather's family had to leave Germany because of WWII. This is the most conceptually devastating piece, as it speaks of war and reminds of the tragedies in North America, Germany and Bosnia, but it is probably my favorite of the 16. I like how the pattern becomes a camouflage and that a peaceful weaving brings together populations of people from different time periods and regions of the world.[5]

Turning to new projects, we discuss Sarah's recent fellowship at the Eccles Centre, at the British Library, and further research at Tulane University, the Amon Carter Museum at Fort Worth, and the University of Texas. Sarah's creative engagement with the colonial archive of maps and documents has been described by Caroline Wigginton as "a mode of reorientation" based on repurposing found material.[6] By disrupting the colonial viewpoint embodied in these materials, Sarah reorients them to accommodate Indigenous experience and to encourage new perspectives on the relationship between people and land. Throughout her work, the interlacing of Chitimacha and Choctaw practices of weaving and making, culture and resilience are a constant and evolving practice.

My research at the British Library came at a timely point in my career and at a time when I had traveled and lived abroad for around ten years. During these ten years outside of the United States I had already completed various projects in different countries, and I was eager to work on a project in the United Kingdom, a project that responded to British history. The Eccles Centre Fellowship at the British Library gave me access to contemporary research and contemporary voices, all of them reexamining the role of the British in histories of settler colonialism in the United States and Canada. It was an exciting time for me to learn about other people's research. My focus on maps of North America took me on a journey through different periods of colonization, and different parts of North America. At times, it was overwhelming. The scope, scale, and historical implications of the maps really challenged me to make connections and consider the stories that the maps embodied and revealed.

Hinushi 1, Sarah Sense, 2023. Archival inkjet prints on Hahnemuhle bamboo paper and Hahnemuhle rice paper, wax, tape. (Collection of the Choctaw Nation; image courtesy of the artist)

Given the easy access scholars and artists have to extensive digital collections, I ask Sarah about the significance of working with the material archive as part of her practice.

Working with the original maps was an important part in the making process. Working in any archive and with objects, especially baskets, involves a physical contact and a relationship with the objects or material texts. With woven baskets, my response is emotional, and its strong and powerful emotion. With maps, it's different. Often, it's surprising and exciting that the map reveals a piece of history, a perspective, evidence of actual happenings or of misunderstandings. Questions about the mapmaker, the commissioning powers, colonial or military, reveal themselves too, as part of the larger history of British settler colonialism. There are stories of removal, genocide, murder, and manipulation in the formation of these maps. Cumulatively, perhaps, is the feeling of history. Not in terms of going back in time but in recognizing the present moment as point in time as it relates to the past. The maps were centuries old, some from the eighteenth century when the United States was formed, and I was looking at the maps during my fellowship in 2019, and then working with them as part of a large commission a few years later. There's a driving historical perspective in the maps that continues into the present. The time that we're looking at a particular colonial map comes with a whole host of knowledge and experience, almost 250 years of political changes, social changes, and changes in the land too.

For me, working with the physical maps, or objects, creates an energizing space, a space to think about things or sometimes not think about things and just feel. In this context, part of the process of making, and the art that's created, is about what that space is presenting to me, what the object is presenting. My job as a maker is to tell the stories, or to retell the stories, that are created in those spaces. For me, I see this as part of wider, contemporary conversations and movements where active voices are making and reclaiming space for a revolutionary kind of inclusivity. As part of this new space for Indigenous voices and presence, Indigenous languages are being reclaimed and in special cases land returned and secured. In terms of contemporary art, this means many more exhibitions in art museums and contemporary art galleries, and many more major commissions and acquisitions for Indigenous artists.

Turning to *Power Lines*, a major project following the Eccles Centre Fellowship, Sarah shares the process of assemblage and weaving in her work, reconsidering the historical and emotional engagements with landscape as it's recorded, imagined, and recreated.

These weavings are very much about weaving the maps into my landscape and into my family practice of weaving. The photographs that I've taken are of those same locations that the maps record. By photographing these lands and weaving them into the maps is my way of decolonizing the maps, my way of undoing and reclaiming. The images are woven together, blended. It's the past of the map and present of the photograph but, for me, it's also about ancestral homelands and the close family connection in the act of weaving. The practice is emotionally blended in deeply personal ways and the final piece is an attempt to embody the experience of the archive, or the basket, for me and for the viewer.

Drawing our conversation to a close, we circle back to *Listen to the Atlantic*, and I'm struck by the ways that it works to position Indigeneity within global contexts. The parabolic dish entangles human and non-human life systems, reconnecting the past with the present, and returning agency to voices previously silenced by discriminate and partial archival practices:

> Does water have memory like trees?
> Can it remember the roots that drank it or the lungs that inhaled it?
> Can water remember the ancestors the way land holds us in shallow graves?
> I can feel the presence when close to a calm lake, rushing river or thunderous ocean
> Bring me the calm and violent memories
> Remind me of the past.

This recent UK-based commission might be a turning point, a departure, and a reorientation in a career that is actively reshaping and reimagining the legacies of settler colonialism in profound and generative ways. *Bayous Meander, Water Heals, Trees Remember, Roots Meander* (2022) sees a strengthening of practice and conviction, where settler-colonial legacies, Chitimacha and Choctaw resilience, and the living world—tree, grass, water—are interwoven. The loosening of weaving and the "fluidity of bayous, water, tree branches and roots" open up a space where Chitimacha life might emerge.[7]

The most recent work, *Power Lines*, is a timely and profound response to this contemporary moment; an opening and an intervention; incorporating a practice of weaving that generates and renews with every necessary entanglement and interaction. This artist's summary of Sarah's current work concludes this interview essay, and this collection:

> The archives of both documents and maps act as evidence to murder and genocide while the Hollywood imagery exposes an industry's power play on historical trauma to dumbify actualities that continue to persist in memory. Like blood pulsing though our bodies, or cypress tree roots drinking water from the bayou, the memory persists. Interweaving the personas with Louisiana landscapes of Chitimacha ancestral lands ties current contemporary Native life and environment, conceptually losing a gap between historical and contemporary time, much like memory. This unique rhythm spins an historical web, entangling sad realities of war and genocide while honoring ancestral basket weaving. Like webs, the spun stories swirl in circles, mirroring the portolan charts

from cartographic artists beginning with the British Library's earliest map, *Chart of the World* from the *Cape Verd Islands to the Red Sea* (1339) to more recent maps, such as the *United States Army Corps Geological Investigation of the Alluvial Valley of the Lower Mississippi River* (1944). As the pieces move through a cartographic chronology, the aesthetics of coastlines and reference points draw lines, shaping circles. Layered lines with imagery form stories, visually implying Indigenous perspective of colonial effects of climate change on community and landscapes, assimilation as marginalization, and loss of tradition and culture with loss of land. These maps along with settler's letters to the Monarchy, layered over each other with photographs, then interwoven with Chitimacha and Choctaw basket patterns re-Indigenizes the objects. Cutting the paper into strips and opening them, moving them apart to create space for differing interpretations and re-inserting Indigenous patterns from the very same locations where the ancestors were removed, taken and killed, is a process of decolonizing.[8]

A matter of months before this book went to press, the transatlantic story of Sarah's sculpture, Listen to the Atlantic, *took a surprising turn. In March 2024, the sculpture was packed up from its home in Plymouth and transported across the Atlantic to establish different roots, close to Sarah's ancestors in Oklahoma. The names of those seventeenth-century Indigenous travelers are symbolically returned to North America, continuing and evolving their historical presence in new places for new generations.*

Notes

1. Coll Thrush, *Indigenous London: Native Travelers at the Heart of Empire* (New Haven: Yale University Press, 2016), 235.
2. Thrush, *Indigenous London;* Cecilia Morgan, *Travellers through Empire: Indigenous Voyages from Early Canada* (Montreal: McGill University Press, 2017); Caroline Dodds Pennock, *On Savage Shores: How Indigenous Americans Discovered Europe* (London: Weidenfeld & Nicolson, 2023); Jace Weaver, *The Red Atlantic: American Indigenes and the Making of the Modern World, 1000–1927* (Chapel Hill: University of North Carolina Press, 2014); Alden T.

Vaughn, *Transatlantic Encounters: American Indians in Britain, 1500–1776* (Cambridge: Cambridge University Press, 2006).

3. Sarah Sense, artist's statement, *Cowgirls and Indians,* 2018, https://sarahsense.com/Artists/11571/Statements.pdf.

4. Sarah Sense, "Grandmother's Stories: Choctaw Irish Relation," March 2015, http://sarahsense.com/link/_choctawirishrelation_.

5. "Choctaw Irish Relationship 16," Sarah Sense, "Grandmother's Stories: Choctaw Irish Relation," 2015, http://sarahsense.com/link/_choctawirishrelation_.

6. Caroline Wigginton, *Indigenuity: Native Craftwork and the Art of American Literatures* (Chapel Hill: University of North Carolina Press, 2022), 201.

7. Sarah Sense, artist's notes, *Bayous Meander, Water Heals, Trees Remember, Roots Meander* (2022), https://sarahsense.com/Artists/11571/website_statements_2021-22.pdf.

8. Sarah Sense.

SELECTED BIBLIOGRAPHY

TRIBAL HISTORY

Custalow, Linwood "Little Bear," and Angela L. Daniel "Silver Star." *The True Story of Pocahontas: The Other Side of History*. Golden, CO: Fulcrum, 2007.

SOURCES AND DOCUMENTS

Barbour, Philip L., ed. *The Jamestown Voyages under the First Charter, 1606–1609*. 2 vols. Cambridge: Cambridge University Press, 1969.

Beverley, Robert. *The History and Present State of Virginia*. 1705. Edited by Susan Scott Parrish. Chapel Hill: University of North Carolina Press, 2013.

Chamberlain, John. *The Letters of John Chamberlain*. Edited by Norman E. McClure. 2 vols. Philadelphia: American Philosophical Society, 1939.

Haile, Edward Wright, ed. *Jamestown Narratives: Eyewitness Accounts of the Virginia Colony*. Champlain, VA: Roundhouse, 1998.

Hakluyt, Richard. *Discourse of Western Planting*. 1584. Edited by David B. Quinn and Alison M. Quinn. London: Hakluyt Society, 1993.

Hamor, Ralph. *A True Discourse of the Present Estate of Virginia, and the Success of the Affaires there till the 18 of June, 1614*. (London, 1615). Reprinted Richmond: Virginia State Library, 1957.

Harriot, Thomas. *Brief and True Report of the New Found Land of Virginia*. London, 1590.

Higginson, Rev. Francis. *New-Englands Plantation*. London, 1630.

Kingsbury, Susan M. *Records of the Virginia Company*. 4 vols. Washington, DC: Government Printing Office, 1906–35.

Percy, George. "A Trewe Relacyon of the procedeing and ocurrentes of Moment which have happened in Virginia . . ." In *Captain John Smith: Writings with Other Narratives*. Edited by James Horn. New York: The Library of America, 2007.

Purchas, Samuel. *Purchas His Pilgrimage*. 3rd ed. London, 1617.

Quinn, David B. ed. *The Roanoke Voyages, 1584–1590: Documents to Illustrate the English Voyages to North America under the Patent Granted to Walter Raleigh in 1584*. 2 vols. London: Hakluyt Society, Second Series, 2010.

Quinn, David B., Alison M. Quinn, and Susan Hillier, eds. *New American World: A Documentary History of North America to 1612.* 5 vols. New York: Macmillan, 1979.

Rolfe, John. "The coppie of the Gentle-mans letters to sir Thomas Dale, that after maried Powhatans daughter, containing the reasons moving him thereunto." Abridged in *A True Discourse of the Present Estate of Virginia,* Ralph Hamor, 61–68, and in full in *Jamestown Narratives,* edited by Edward Wright Haile, 850–56.

Rolfe, John. *A True Relation of the State of Virginia Lefte by Sir Thomas Dale, Knight, in May Last 1616.* Edited by Henry C. Taylor. New Haven: printed for H. C. T. by Yale University Press, 1951.

Sainsbury, W. Noel, ed. *Calendar of State Papers Colonial Series, America and West Indies: Volume 1, 1574–1660.* London, 1860.

Smith, John. *Captain John Smith: Writings with Other Narratives of Roanoke, Jamestown and the First English Settlements in America.* Edited by James Horn. New York: The Library of America, 2007.

Smith, John. *The Complete Works of Captain John Smith, 1580–1631.* Edited by Philip L. Barbour. 3 vols. Chapel Hill: University of North Carolina Press for the Omohundro Institute, 1986.

Smith, John. *The Generall Historie of Virginia, New-England and the Summer Isles.* London, 1624.

Smith, John. *Map of Virginia, with a Description of the Countrey, the Commodities, People, Government and Religion.* London, 1612.

Smith, John. *A True Relation of Such Occurrences and Accidents of Noate as Hath Hapned in Virginia.* 1608.

Spelman, Henry. *Relation of Virginia: A Boy's Memoir of Life with the Powhatans and Patawomecks.* Transcribed and edited by Karen Ordahl Kupperman. New York: New York University Press, 2019.

Strachey, William. *A Dictionary of Powhatan.* Edited by Frederic Gleach, American Language Reprints No. 8. Southampton, PA: Evolution Publishers, 1999, 2005.

Strachey, William. *Historie of Travell into Virginia Britania.* 1612. Edited Louis B. Wright and Virginia Freund. London: Hakluyt Society, 1953.

Symonds, William. *Virginia. A Sermon preached at White-Chappel, in the presence of many honourable and worshipfull, the Adventurers and Planters for Virginia.* London, 1609.

Whitaker, Alexander. *Good Newes from Virginia.* London, 1613.

SECONDARY SOURCES

Abrams, Ann Uhry. *The Pilgrims and Pocahontas: Rival Myths of American Origin.* Boulder, Westview, 1999.

Allen, Paula Gunn. *Pocahontas: Medicine Woman, Spy, Entrepreneur, Diplomat.* San Francisco: HarperSanFrancisco, 2003.

Allen, Paula Gunn. "Pocahontas to Her English Husband, John Rolfe." In *Skins and Bones: Poems 1979–87,* 8–9. Albuquerque: West End Press, 1988.

Barbour, Philip L. *Pocahontas and Her World; A Chronicle of America's First Settlement in which is Related the Story of the Indians and the Englishmen, Particularly Captain John Smith, Captain Samuel Argall, and Master John Rolfe.* Boston: Houghton Mifflin, 1970.

Barker, Joanne, ed. *Critically Sovereign: Indigenous Gender, Sexuality, and Feminist Studies.* Durham: Duke University Press, 2017.

Bernhard, Virginia. "Pocahontas Was Not the Only One: Indian Women and Their English Liaisons in Seventeenth-Century Virginia." In *Searching for Their Places: Women in the South across Four Centuries,* edited by Thomas Appleton and Angela Boswell. Columbia, MO: University of Missouri Press, 2003.

Bird, S. Elizabeth. "The Burden of History: Representations of American Indian Women in Popular Media." In *Women in Popular Culture: Representation and Meaning,* edited by Marian Meyers. Cresskill, NJ: Hampton Press, 2008.

Bird, S. Elizabeth, ed. *Dressing in Feathers: The Construction of the Indian in American Popular Culture.* Boulder, CO.: Westview Press, 1996.

Blanchette, Robert A., Deborah Tear Haynes, Benjamin W. Held, Jonas Niemann, and Nathan Wales. "Fungal Mycelial Mats Used as Textile by Indigenous People of North America." *Mycologia* 113, no. 2 (2021): 261–67.

Borchard, Kimberly C. "Diego de Molina en Jamestown, 1611–1616: Espía, prisionero, oráculo del fin del imperio." *Laberinto* 9 (2016): 33–54.

Braxton, Joanne, M. "Pocahontas' Voice." *Women's Review of Books* 21, no. 8 (2004b): 13.

Breen, T. H. *Tobacco Culture: The Mentality of the Great Tidewater Planters on the Eve of Revolution.* Princeton: Princeton University Press, 2001.

Brooks, Lisa. "Afterword: At the Gathering Place." In *American Indian Literary Nationalism,* edited by Jace Weaver, Craig Womack, and Robert Warrior, 225–54. Albuquerque: University of New Mexico Press, 2006.

Brooks, Lisa Tanya. *The Common Pot: The Recovery of Native Space in the Northeast.* Minneapolis: University of Minnesota Press, 2008.

Brooks, Lisa. *Our Beloved Kin.* New Haven: Yale University Press, 2018.

Brown, Alexander. *The Genesis of the United States.* 2 vols. Boston: Houghton Mifflin, 1890.

Brown, Kathleen. "Native Americans and Early Modern Concepts of Race." In *Empire and Others: British Encounters with Indigenous Peoples, 1600–1850,* edited by M. Daunton and R. Halpern. Philadelphia: University of Pennsylvania Press, 1999.

Bryant, Rachel. "Kinshipwrecking: John Smith's Adoption and the Pocahontas Myth in Settler Ontologies." *AlterNative: An International Journal of Indigenous Peoples* 14, no. 4 (2018): 300–308.

Cañizares Esguerra, Jorge, and James Sidbury, "Mapping Ethnogenesis in the Early Modern Atlantic." *William and Mary Quarterly* 68 (April 2011): 181–208.

Carocci, Max. "Clad with the 'Hair of Trees': A History of Native American Spanish Moss Textile Industries." *Textile History,* 41, no. 1 (2010): 3 27.

Chimalpahin Quauhtlehuanitzin, Don Domingo de San Antón. *Codex Chimalpahin.* Vol. 1. Edited by Arthur J. O. Anderson and Susan Schroeder. Norman: University of Oklahoma Press, 1997.

Clements, William M. "Translating Context and Situation: William Strachey and Powhatan's 'Scornfuul Song.'" In *Born in the Blood: On Native American Translation,* edited by Brian Swann. Lincoln: University of Nebraska, 2011.

Dearborn, Mary V. *Pocahontas's Daughters: Gender and Ethnicity in American Culture.* New York: Oxford University Press, 1986.

Deer, Jessica. "We Are Not a Costume." In *#NotYourPrincess: Voices of Native American Women,* edited by Mary Beth Leatherdale and Lisa Charleyboy. Toronto: Annick Press Ltd., 2017.

Deloria, Philip Joseph. *Playing Indian.* New Haven: Yale University Press, 1998.

Feest, Christian F. "The Virginia Indians in Pictures, 1612–1624." *Smithsonian Journal* 2, no. 1 (1967): 1–30.

Fitzmaurice, Andrew. *Humanism and America: An Intellectual History of English Colonisation, 1500–1625.* Cambridge: Cambridge University Press, 2003.

Gallivan, Martin D. *The Powhatan Landscape: An Archaeological History of the Algonquian Chesapeake.* Gainesville: University Press of Florida, 2016.

Gantaume, Cecile. "Marking the 400th Anniversary of Pocahontas' Death." *American Indian Magazine* 18, no. 3 (Fall 2017): 28–33.

Gaudio, Michael. *Engraving the Savage: The New World and Techniques of Civilization.* Minneapolis: University of Minnesota Press, 2008.

Gleach, Frederic W. "Pocahontas: An Exercise in Mythmaking and Marketing." In *New Perspectives on Native North America: Cultures, Histories, and Representations,* edited by Sergei A. Kan and Pauline Turner Strong, 433–55. Lincoln: University of Nebraska Press, 2005.

Goeman, Mishuana. *Settler Aesthetics: Visualizing the Spectacle of Originary Moments in the New World*. Lincoln: University of Nebraska Press, 2023.

Goeman, Mishuana R., and Jennifer Nez Denetdale. "Guest Editors Introduction: Native Feminisms: Legacies, Interventions, and Indigenous Sovereignties." *Wicazo Sa Review* 24, no. 2 (Fall 2009): 9–13.

Goetz, Rebecca Anne. *The Baptism of Early Virginia: How Christianity Created Race*. Baltimore: Johns Hopkins University Press, 2012.

Green, Rayna. "The Pocahontas Perplex: The Image of Indian Women in American Culture." *The Massachusetts Review* 16, no. 4 (1975): 698–714.

Jager, Rebecca K. *Malinche, Pocahontas, and Sacagawea: Indian Women as Cultural Intermediaries and National Symbols*. Norman: University of Oklahoma Press, 2015.

Justice, Daniel Heath. *Why Indigenous Literatures Matter*. Waterloo, Ontario, Canada: Wilfrid Laurier University Press, 2018.

Kelso, William. *Jamestown: The Truth Revealed*. Charlottesville: University of Virginia Press, 2017.

Kidwell, Clara Sue. "Indian Women as Cultural Mediators." *Ethnohistory* 39, no. 2 (1992): 97–107.

Kuokkanen, Rauna Johanna. *Reshaping the University: Responsibility, Indigenous Epistemes, and the Logic of the Gift*. Vancouver: UBC Press, 2007.

Kupperman, Karen Ordahl. *Pocahontas and the English Boys: Caught between Cultures in Early Virginia*. New York: New York University Press, 2019.

Kupperman, Karen Ordahl. *Roanoke: The Abandoned Colony*. 2nd ed. Totowa, NJ: Rowman and Littlefield, 2007.

Kupperman, Karen Ordahl. *Indians and English: Facing Off in Early America*. Ithaca: Cornell University Press, 2000.

Kupperman, Karen Ordahl. *The Jamestown Project*. Cambridge: The Belknap Press of Harvard University Press, 2007.

Leatherdale, Mary Beth, and Lisa Charleyboy. *#NotYourPrincess: Voices of Native American Women*. Toronto: Annick Press Ltd., 2017.

Lee, Emma, and Jennifer Evans, eds. *Indigenous Women's Voices: 20 Years on from Linda Tuhiwai Smith's "Decolonizing Methodologies."* London: Zed Books, 2021.

Lopenzina, Drew. "The Wedding of Pocahontas and John Rolfe: How to Keep the Thrill Alive after Four Hundred Years of Marriage." *Studies in American Indian Literatures* 26, no. 4 (2014): 59–77.

Lubbers, Klaus. *Born for the Shade: Stereotypes of the Native American in United States Literature and the Visual Arts, 1776–1894*. Amsterdam: Rodopi, 1994.

McCartney, Martha. "Cockacoeske, Queen of Pamunkey: Diplomat and Suzeraine." In *Powhatan's Mantle: Indians in the Colonial Southeast*, edited by P. A.

Wood, G. A. Waselkov, and M. T. Hatley. Lincoln: University of Nebraska Press, 1989.

Meissner, Shelbi Nahwilet, and Kyle Whyte. "Theorizing Indigeneity, Gender, and Settler Colonialism." In *The Routledge Companion to Philosophy of Race*, edited by Paul C. Taylor, Linda Martin Alcoff, and Luvell Anderson. New York: Routledge, 2018.

Merrell, James. "Second Thoughts on Colonial Historians and American Indians." *William and Mary Quarterly* 69 (July 2012): 451–512.

Mielke, Laura L. "A Tale Both Old and New: Jamestown at 400." *American Quarterly* 60, no. 1 (2008): 173–82.

Moreton-Robinson, Aileen. "Introduction: Gender and Indigeneity." *Australian Feminist Studies* 35, no. 106 (2020): 315–20.

Mossiker, Frances. *Pocahontas: The Life and the Legend*. New York: Knopf, 1976: Distributed by Random House.

Murphy, Jessyca. "The White Indin': Native American Appropriations in Hipster Fashion." In *Unsettling Whiteness*, edited by Lucy Michael and Samantha Schulz, 127–38. Leiden: Brill, 2014.

Oberg, Michael. *The Head in Edward Nugent's Hand: Roanoke's Forgotten Indians*. Philadelphia: University of Pennsylvania Press, 2011.

O'Brien, Jean M. "Tracing Settler Colonialism's Eliminatory Logic in *Traces of History*." *American Quarterly* 69, no. 2 (2017): 249–55.

Ono, Kent A., and Derek T. Buescher. "Deciphering Pocahontas: Unpacking the Commodification of a Native American Woman." *Critical Studies in Media Communication* 18, no. 1 (2001): 23–43.

Pennock, Caroline Dodds. *On Savage Shores: How Indigenous Americans Discovered Europe*. London: Weidenfeld & Nicolson, 2023.

Plane, Ann Marie. *Colonial Intimacies: Indian Marriage in Early New England*. Ithaca: Cornell University Press, 2000.

Potter, Jennifer. *The Jamestown Brides: The Story of England's Maids for Virginia*. Oxford: Oxford University Press, 2019.

Price, David A. *Love and Hate in Jamestown: John Smith, Pocahontas, and the Heart of a New Nation*. New York: Alfred A. Knopf, 2003.

Pulitano, Elvira. *Toward a Native American Critical Theory*. Lincoln: University of Nebraska Press, 2003.

Quinn, David B., ed. *Explorers and Colonies: America, 1500–1625*. London: The Hambledon Press, 1990.

Quinn, David B. *Set Fair for Roanoke: Voyages and Colonies, 1584–1606*. Chapel Hill: University North Carolina Press, 1985.

Ransome, David R. "Pocahontas and the Mission to the Indians." *Virginia Magazine of History* 99, no. 1 (1991): 81–94.

Ransome, David R. "Wives for Virginia, 1621." *William and Mary Quarterly*, 48, no. 1 (1991): 3–18.

Rasmussen, William M. S., and Robert S. Tilton. *Pocahontas: Her Life and Legend.* Richmond: Virginia Historical Society, 1994.

Reeds, Karen. "Don't Eat, Don't Touch: Roanoke Colonists, Natural Knowledge, and Dangerous Plants of North America." In *European Visions, American Voices*, edited by Kim Sloan, 51–57. London: British Museum, 2009.

Rennie, Neil. *Pocahontas, Little Wanton: Myth, Life and Afterlife.* London: Quaritch, 2007.

Rex, Cathy. *Anglo-American Women Writers and Representations of Indianness, 1629–1824.* Farnham: Ashgate, 2015.

Rice, James D. *Nature and History in the Potomac Country: From Hunter-Gatherers to the Age of Jefferson.* Baltimore: Johns Hopkins University Press, 2009.

Richter, Daniel. *Facing East from Indian Country: A Native History of Early America.* Cambridge: Harvard University Press, 2001.

Robertson, Karen. "Pocahontas at the Masque." *Signs* 21 (1996): 551–83.

Rose, E. M. "Lord Delaware, First Governor of Virginia and 'the Poorest Baron of This Kingdom.'" *The Virginia Magazine of History and Biography* 128, no. 3 (2020): 226–58.

Rountree, Helen C. *Pocahontas, Powhatan, Opechancanough: Three Indian Lives Changed by Jamestown.* Charlottesville: University of Virginia Press, 2005.

Rountree, Helen C. *Pocahontas's People: The Powhatan Indians of Virginia through Four Centuries.* Norman: University of Oklahoma Press, 1990.

Rountree, Helen C. *The Powhatan Indians of Virginia: Their Traditional Culture.* Norman: University of Oklahoma Press, 1989.

Rountree, Helen C. "Powhatan Indian Women: The People Captain John Smith Barely Saw." *Ethnohistory* 45 (1998): 1–29.

Rountree, Helen C., Wayne E. Clark, and Kent Mountford. *John Smith's Chesapeake Voyages, 1607–1609.* Charlottesville: University of Virginia Press, 2007.

Rude, Blair. "Giving Voice to Powhatan's People: The Creation of Virginia Algonquian Dialogue for *The New World*." *Southern Quarterly* 51, no. 4 (Summer 2014): 29–37.

Russo, Jean B., and J. Elliott Russo. *Planting an Empire: The Early Chesapeake in British North America.* Baltimore: Johns Hopkins University Press, 2012.

Salisbury, Neal. "Squanto: Last of the Pawtuxets." In *Struggle and Survival in Colonial America*, edited by David G. Sweet and Gary B. Nash, 228–46. Berkeley: University of California Press, 1981.

Schmidt, Ethan. "Cockacoeske, Weroansqua of the Pamunkeys, and Indian Resistance in Seventeenth-Century Virginia." *American Indian Quarterly* 36 (Summer 2012): 288–317.

Schwarz, Maureen. *Fighting Colonialism with Hegemonic Culture: Native American Appropriation of Indian Stereotypes.* Albany: State University of New York Press, 2013.

Sellers, Stephanie A., and Menoukha R. Case, eds. *Weaving the Legacy: Remembering Paula Gunn Allen.* Albuquerque: West End Press, 2017.

Shoemaker, Nancy. "Native-American Women in History." In "Native Americans," special issue, *OAH Magazine of History* 9, no. 4 (Summer 1995): 10–14.

Siebert, Frank. "Resurrecting Virginia Algonquian from the Dead: The Reconstituted and Historical Phonology of Powhatan." In *Studies in Southeastern Indian Languages,* ed. James M. Crawford. Athens: University of Georgia Press, 1975.

Siebert, Monika. "Historical Realism and Imperialist Nostalgia in Terrence Malick's *The New World.*" *The Mississippi Quarterly* 65, no. 1 (2012): 139–55.

Sloan, Kim, ed. *A New World: England's First View of America.* Chapel Hill: University of North Carolina Press, 2007.

Smith, Linda Tuhiwai. *Decolonizing Methodologies: Research and Indigenous Peoples.* London and New York: University of Otago Press, 1999.

Smithers, Gregory D. "The Enduring Legacy of the Pocahontas Myth." *The Atlantic.* March 21, 2017. https://www.theatlantic.com/entertainment/archive/2017/03/the-enduring-legacy-of-the-pocahontas-myth/520260/.

Smits, David D. "'Abominable Mixture': Toward the Repudiation of Anglo-Indian Intermarriage in Seventeenth-Century Virginia." *Virginia Magazine of History and Biography* 95, no. 2 (1987): 157–92.

Speck, Frank G. *Chapters in the Ethnology of the Powhatan Indians of Virginia.* New York: Museum of the American Indian—Heye Foundation, 1928.

Stith, William. *The History of the First Discovery and Settlement of Virginia: Being an Essay towards a General History of this Colony.* Williamsburg: printed by William Parks, 1747.

Stymeist, David. "'Strange Wives': Pocahontas in Early Modern Colonial Advertisement." *Mosaic: A Journal for the Interdisciplinary Study of Literature* 35, no. 3 (2002): 109–26.

Thrush, Coll. *Indigenous London: Native Travelers at the Heart of Empire.* New Haven: Yale University Press, 2016.

Tilton, Robert S. *Pocahontas: The Evolution of an American Narrative.* Cambridge: Cambridge University Press, 1994.

Tompkins, Jane. "'Indians': Textualism, Morality and the Problem of History." *Critical Inquiry* 13, no. 1 (1986). Reprinted in *"Race," Writing, and Difference,* edited by Henry Louis Gates Jr., 59–77. Chicago: University of Chicago Press, 1986.

Townsend, Camilla. *Pocahontas and the Powhatan Dilemma.* New York: Hill & Wang, 2004.

Tsosie, Rebecca "Reclaiming Native Stories: An Essay on Cultural Appropriation and Cultural Rights." *Arizona State Law Journal* 34, no. 1 (Spring 2002): 299–358.

Tuck, E., and K. W. Yang. "Decolonization Is Not a Metaphor." *Decolonisation: Indigeneity, Education and Society* 1, no. 1 (2012): 1–40.

Vaughan, Alden T. *Transatlantic Encounters: American Indians in Britain, 1500–1776.* Cambridge: Cambridge University Press, 2006.

Vitoria, Francisco de. "De Indiis [On the American Indians]." In *Political Writings,* edited by Anthony Pagden and Jeremy Lawrance. Cambridge: Cambridge University Press, 1991.

Warrior, Robert. "Native Critics in the World." In *American Indian Literary Nationalism,* edited by Jace Weaver, Craig Womack, and Robert Warrior, 179–223. Albuquerque: University of New Mexico Press, 2006.

Watson, Kelly L. "Mary Kittamaquund Brent, 'The Pocahontas of Maryland': Sex, Marriage and Diplomacy in the Seventeenth-Century Chesapeake." *Early American Studies* 19 (2021): 24–63.

Weaver, Jace. *The Red Atlantic: American Indigenes and the Making of the Modern World, 1000–1927.* Chapel Hill: University of North Carolina Press, 2014.

Wernitznig, Dagmar. *Europe's Indians, Indians in Europe: European Perceptions and Appropriations.* Lanham, MD: University Press of America 2007.

White, Richard. *The Middle Ground: Indians, Empires, and Republics in the Great Lakes Region, 1650–1815.* Cambridge: Cambridge University Press, 1991.

Williamson, Margaret Holmes. *Powhatan Lords of Life and Death: Command and Consent in Seventeenth-Century Virginia.* Lincoln: University of Nebraska Press, 2003.

Witgen, Michael J. *An Infinity of Nations: How the Native New World Shaped Early North America.* Philadelphia: University of Pennsylvania Press, 2012.

Young, Philip. "The Mother of Us All: Pocahontas Reconsidered." *The Kenyon Review* 24 (1962): 391–415.

CONTRIBUTORS

KATHRYN N. GRAY is an Associate Professor of Early American Literature at the University of Plymouth, UK. She has research interests in colonial and Indigenous literatures and cultures of the seventeenth and eighteenth century and is the author of *John Eliot and the Praying Indians of Massachusetts Bay: Communities and Connections in Puritan New England* (2013). She also edited *Transatlantic Literature and Transitivity, 1780–1850: Subjects, Texts, and Print Culture* (2017). Her recent work focuses on early American travel and natural history narratives, with a particular interest in the circulation of natural knowledge in the colonial Atlantic world.

AMY M. E. MORRIS is an Associate Professor of English at the University of Cambridge, specializing in American literature before 1800. She is the author of *Popular Measures: Poetry and Church Order in Colonial Massachusetts* (2005), and articles on topics ranging from geomythology and Indigenous-Puritan knowledge exchange, to the significance of Shakespeare's *Cymbeline* in the 1770s. She has recently published a chapter that advocates for transhistorical and transmedial comparison by interpreting the work of the colonial poet Edward Taylor through the lens of twentieth-century assemblage art. Her current project is to think about imagetext and the page in early modern English-Algonquian bilingual print.

KARENNE WOOD (MONACAN), poet, scholar, and educator, and former director of Virginia Indian Programs. Karenne's academic work and her poetry continue to influence and shape our understanding of North America's colonial and Indigenous past and its relevance to contemporary contexts. We would like to direct scholars to this memorial site to engage further with Karenne's life and work: https://virginiahumanities.org/2019/07/remembering-karenne-wood/.

KAREN ORDAHL KUPPERMAN, Silver Professor Emerita at New York University, is the author of *The Jamestown Project* (2007) and more recently, *Pocahontas and the English Boys* (2019). Previous books have won the Albert J. Beveridge Prize from the American Historical Association for the best book in American History in 1995, and the American Historical Association Prize in Atlantic History in

2001. Her current book project is an environmental and social history of North America from the first arrivals over 20,000 years ago to the time before the Europeans invaded in the fifteenth century.

HELEN C. ROUNTREE is Professor Emerita of Anthropology at Old Dominion University in Norfolk, Virginia. She began working with the modern Virginia Indians and researching their history in 1969, and she has since published over a dozen books about the Algonquian speakers of the US mid-Atlantic coast. She still works with several tribes, and through her testimony before congressional committees, she contributed significantly to the success those tribes have recently had in becoming recognized as sovereign, "federal" Indian tribes by the United States Government.

LUCINDA RASMUSSEN is a Lecturer with the University of Alberta, located on Treaty Six Territory in what is now Canada. She is a settler scholar who teaches a range of undergraduate literary studies courses, including Indigenous Literatures, Contemporary Horror, Topics in Women's Writing, and Writing Studies. Publications include journal articles and book chapters on Indigenous Literatures, postfeminism, and portrayals of ageing women in literature and visual culture.

CAMILLA TOWNSEND is Board of Governors Distinguished Professor of History at Rutgers University in New Brunswick, NJ. She is the author of numerous books, among them *Fifth Sun: A New History of the Aztecs* (2019) and *Pocahontas and the Powhatan Dilemma* (2004). A recipient of fellowships from the John Simon Guggenheim Memorial Foundation, the National Endowment for the Humanities, and the American Philosophical Society, she is also the winner of several major prizes, including the Cundill History Prize.

E. M. ROSE is a scholar of Medieval and Early Modern Europe. Rose's first book, *The Murder of William of Norwich* (2015) was named one of the "Ten Best History Books of the Year" by the *Sunday Times* of London and described by the *Wall Street Journal* as "a landmark of historical research." It won the prestigious Ralph Waldo Emerson award from the Phi Beta Kappa Association and the 2017 Albert C. Outler Prize of the American Society for Church History. Rose has taught at five universities; her articles have appeared in *Parliamentary History*, the *Huntington Library Quarterly*, the *Virginia Magazine of History*, and *Studies in the Age of Chaucer*. This essay was written while Rose was Visiting Fellow, Omohundro Institute/ Jamestown Rediscovery and Research Associate in the Department of History, Harvard University. Rose is currently a Visiting Scholar at Oxford University.

JAMES RING ADAMS is Senior Historian at the National Museum of the American Indian–Smithsonian, where he has served as managing editor of its quarterly publication American Indian magazine. He joined the Smithsonian in 2007. Previously, from 2001 to 2007, he was correspondent and then managing editor of *Indian Country Today*, at that time the leading national print newspaper written by and for American Indigenous peoples. He was previously member of the Editorial Board of the *Wall Street Journal* editorial page and author of three books on financial disasters.

CRISTINA L. AZOCAR is a citizen of the Upper Mattaponi Indian Tribe and a Professor of Journalism at San Francisco State University. She is the author of *News Media and the Indigenous Fight for Federal Recognition* (2022) and the forthcoming *Indigenous Peoples and the Media.* Her research focuses on the intersection of race and journalistic practice, particularly in the area of news coverage of Indigenous people. Dr. Azocar served as a past president of the Native American Journalists Association, was an editor of American Indian Issues for the Media Diversity Forum, and was an inaugural board member of the Women's Media Center.

IVANA MARKOVA is the author of Textile Fiber Microscopy: A Practical Approach (2019). She is an Assistant Professor in the Apparel Design & Merchandising program at San Francisco State University where her research is focused on developing innovative and sustainable practices regarding textile disposal and recycling. She has been teaching textile laboratory and other courses at SFSU for over fifteen years. Her published work includes discussions of archeological textiles from the Ancient Greek, Northern African, and Carpathian Mountain populations. Her research and teaching goal is to promote the continuity of textile science knowledge in a variety of courses in apparel undergraduate programs. This work aligns with her key focus on textile attributes and provides the greater community with an understanding of textile and fiber development over the ages.

GRAZIELLA CREZEGUT is an independent scholar based in France who specializes in eighteenth- and nineteenth-century US history. She is interested in the relations between nationalism and the visual arts. She has studied the relationship between American origin myths, identities, and Native American representations, focusing on the iconography of Pocahontas.

STEPHANIE PRATT (DAKOTA, BRITISH, AND AMERICAN), an independent scholar, was formerly Associate Professor (Reader) of Art History at Plymouth University, UK. She was first Cultural Ambassador for the Crow Creek Dakota Tribal Council, Fort Thompson, SD, where she is an enrolled member. She has published extensively on the visual and museum representations made of Indigenous American peoples from early contact to the present day. Her monograph *American Indians in British Art, 1700–1840* (2005) was the first study of its kind.

SARAH SENSE (INDIGENOUS ARTIST, US) is an internationally recognized artist from Sacramento and has lived and worked in Chile, southeast Asia, the Caribbean, Germany, Britain, and Ireland. Practicing photo-weaving with traditional basket techniques from her Chitimacha and Choctaw family, many of her commissions reveal Indigenous history as it collides with colonial pasts. In recent years, Sense has become a British Library Eccles Centre Fellow. Her most recent commissions for Florida State University (2021) and Amon Carter Museum, Fort Worth (2022) conceptually reinstate Indigeneity with traditional weaving patterns while decolonizing colonial maps.

INDEX

Italicized page numbers refer to illustrations.

Abbot, George, 125
Abbot, Maurice, 125
Abraham (biblical figure), 151–52
Abrams, Ann Uhry, 176, 185
acorns, 29
Adams, James Ring, 13, 151
Adams, Mollie Holmes, 213, 215
adoption ceremonies, 2–3, 27, 64
advertising, 7, 13, 206–7, 208. *See also* commodification; cultural appropriation
agarikon (*Laricifomes officinalis*), 213–14
Agas Map of London, *129*
agency, 14, 79–80, 211, 225, 253
agriculture, 33, 38–39, 54, 123. *See also* plantations
Ahmed, Sara, 87–88
Algonquian (Algonkian, Algonquin): language, 22, 28, 34, 102–4, 110–12nn12–15, 113n24; marriage practices, 101. *See also specific peoples, e.g., Powhatan, the*
Allen, Paula Gunn: challenges faced in literary scholarship, 11, 14, 74–84, 87–89; criticism of work, 76–78, 84, 87, 93n79; on Knowledge Keepers, 84–85; *Pocahontas,* 73, 74–75, 76–86, 87, 89; on Pocahontas's personality, 225–26; "Pocahontas to John Rolfe," 14, 76, 79–80; source use, 77, 78–79, 85, 87; "Thus Spake Pocahontas," 74, 89n3
American Civil War (1861–65), 194–96

Amonute (Pocahontas's public name), 16n12, 37, 65, 242. *See also* Pocahontas
Anderson, Benedict, 180
Anglo-Spanish War (1585–1604), 21
animal products, 215, 217–18
Anne, Queen consort of England and Ireland, 4, 145n49, 147n64
Antony and Cleopatra (Shakespeare), 145n49
Anzaldúa, Gloria, 9
appropriation. *See* cultural appropriation
Apsáalooke (Crow Nation), 235
Archaearium (Historic Jamestowne museum), 154
Argall, Samuel: kidnapping Pocahontas, 4, 33, 49, 64, 157; on Powhatan's response to Pocahontas's death, 57; on Rolfe's marriage to Pocahontas, 133; showing Bible to Iopassus, 35; on Spelman, 31; travel to England, 121, 126–27, 141n17, 148n74
aristocracy, natural, 184, 201n35
art: in Capitol buildings, 13, 177, 182, 185, 192, 194–95, 230–32; history painting, 230–33, 238–39; Indigenous, 233–35, 236, 237–40, *237, 239,* 248, 252. *See also* sculptures; *and specific artworks*
Artemis, Goddess of the Hunt, 186, *187*
Artifact Piece, The (Luna), 233–34
auto/biographical writing, 76, 80, 81–82, 191. *See also* captivity narratives
Azocar, Cristina L., 7, 13, 204–5, 212–13
Aztecs, 99–101

Babylonian Captivity, 155–56, 157
Bacon, Nathaniel, 97, 108
Bacon's Rebellion (1676–77), 107
Bale, Christian, 211
Banana Republic (clothing retailer), 218
baptism: of Cleopatra, 145n49; of
    Crashaw, 145n48; of Elizabeth (daugh-
    ter of Nansemond werowance), 106;
    of Pocahontas, 13, 33, 185, 194, 231; of
    Peter Pope, 125, 126. *See also* conver-
    sion to Christianity
Barbour, Philip, 2, 9, 148n68
Barker, Joanne, 10–11
Barlow, Joel, *The Columbiad*, 181
Barralet, John James, 191, 192
Basse, John, 105, 106–7
Basse, Nathaniel, 106–7, 133
Bavin, Thomas, 23
*Bayous Meander, Water Heals, Trees Re-
    member, Roots Meander* (Sense), 253
Baziliωlogia, 147n65, 169n45
beads, 7, 109n2, 154, 206, 237–38
Behn, Aphra, *The Widow Ranter*, 108
Belmore, Rebecca, *Vigil*, 7
Berkeley, George (Bishop), 232
Bernhard, Virginia, 97, 114n35
Betty (*werowansqua* of the Pamunkey),
    108, 114n36
Beverley, Robert, 132; *History and Present
    State of Virginia*, 13
Bible: Babylonian Captivity, 155–56, 157;
    on intermarriage, 136, 137, 164; Tupaa
    sus' interest in, 35. *See also specific Bible
    books and biblical figures, e.g., Rebecca*
biographies, 76, 80, 81–82, 89n1, 191. *See
    also* captivity narratives
Bird, Elizabeth, 6, 174
Black Elk, Nicolas, 84
Black Hawk War (1832), 231–32
Bohm, David, 83
Book of Common Prayer, 153, 159, 168n31
borders, 249
Boston (Massachusetts), 13

Boston Tea Party, 210
Braxton, Joanne, 78
Brent, Giles, 97
Bridenbaugh, Carl, 96
Brooks, Lisa, 73, 78, 85
Brumidi, Constantino, 192
Buck, Richard, 109n3
Burch, John, 77

Calvin, John, 159; *Institutes of Religion*,
    158–59, 162
Calvinism, 153, 159–61, 163
Cambridge University, 153
Canada, 75, 90n12, 240
cannibalism, 156
Capellano, Antonio, *Preservation of Cap-
    tain Smith by Pocahontas*, 177, 178, 182
Capitol buildings art, 13, 177, 182, 185, 192,
    194–95, 230–32
captivity narratives, 67–68, 178, 181–82
Carolina sassafras (*Winauk*), 24
Carrasco, Pedro, 112n19
catechisms, 159, 168n31
Catlin, George, 183
Causici, Enrico: *Conflict of Daniel Boone
    and the Indians, 1773*, 231; *Landing of the
    Pilgrims*, 182
Cayowaroco, 26
Cecil, Robert, 141n19
ceremonies and rituals, 27, 32–33, 64, 216
Chamberlain, John, 51, 128, 138, 143n32,
    146n51, 229
Chapman, John Gadsby, 13, 185, 192, 194,
    195, 231
Charles I of England, 124
Charleyboy, Lisa, *#NotYourPrincess*, 86
chiefs, 31–32, 52, 54, 99–104; wero-
    wansquas (female chiefs), 102–3, 104,
    107, 112n22. *See also specific chiefs, e.g.,
    Powhatan*
Chitimacha, the, 250, 253–54
Choctaw, the, 249

"Choctaw Irish Relationship 16" (Sense), 249–50

Christianity: Calvinism, 153, 159–61, 163; churches donating to Virginia Company, 125–26; missionary work, 120, 124, 126, 163; predestination, 159–60, 161, 163; Puritanism, 153, 154; salvation, 159, 161, 163; symbols, 185–88, 191–92. *See also* baptism; conversion to Christianity

citizenship, 10, 63, 66

Civil War (1861–65), 194–96

Claxton, Dana, 237–38

Cleopatra (Daniel), 145n49

Cleopatra (relative of Pocahontas), 127, 133, 145n49

clothing. *See* dress

Cockacoeske (Pamunkey *werowansqua*), 105, 107–8

Cole, Thomas, 183

colonists: conflict with the Powhatan, 28, 30–31, 49–50, 55, 155; dependence on Indigenous knowledge, 21, 22–23, 28–29, 49; land incursions, 39, 61n46, 181, 194, 247; marrying Indigenous women, 95, 97, 105–8, 132–33, 135–37, 155–56; marrying other colonists, 136; partnering with Indigenous people, 21, 30–31, 54, 83–84. *See also* primary material; *and specific colonists, e.g.,* Smith, John

colonization: colonial design (families vs. military model), 26, 39; and commodification, 211; decolonization, 85, 88–89, 252, 254; and environmental issues, 247; and hybrid identity, 9; and marginalization of Indigenous women, 6; in *Princess Pocahontas and the Blue Spots* (Mojica), 9. *See also* Virginia Company

Columbiad, The (Barlow), 181

Columbus, Christopher, 231, 232, 234

commodification, 7, 65–66, 79, 205–8, 211, 225. *See also* advertising; cultural appropriation

Conflict of Daniel Boone and the Indians, 1773 (Causici), 231

consent, 194, 197

consumer advertising. *See* advertising

conversion to Christianity, 22, 124, 127. *See also* baptism; Pocahontas: conversion to Christianity

Cooper, James Fenimore, *The Last of the Mohicans*, 64, 183

Cooree (Xore, Southern African convert), 127, 130, 146n57

Copland, Patrick, 125, 126–27

copyright law, 209, 217–18

Coquonasum (Appamatuck chief), 103

corsets, 216

Cosmopolitan (magazine), 206–7

cotton, 214, 217

Cotton, John, 153, 154; *Milk for Babes,* 168n31

Cowgirls and Indians (Sense), 247–48

Crashaw, William (English cleric and poet), 145n48, 152, 153, 154, 160, 166n9, 167–68nn30–31, 168n37

Crashaw, William (Indigenous Virginian), 127, 145n48

creation story, 34–35, 81

Crezegut, Graziella, 13, 173

Croome, William, 178–79

Crow, the (Apsáalooke), 235

Cuernavaca (Mexico), 99–100

cultural appropriation: definition, 208; of dress, 13, 86, 204–7, 208–10, 215, 217–18; "playing Indian," 210; of Pocahontas, 174, 184–85, 194–97; by Smith, 207–8; violence through, 207, 209–10. *See also* commodification

culture, concept of, 98

Culverwell, Ezekiel, 153, 161, 169n41

Custalow, Linwood, 15n4, 93n79

Dakota Pipeline, 7

Dale, Thomas: attempt to marry Indigenous woman, 56, 113n31, 133, 136, 158; James I on, 121–22, 141n19; and Pocahontas's conversion, 33, 49, 157–58, 162, 169n40; presumed authorship of *A True Relation of Such Occurrences,* 142n22; on Rolfe's marriage to Pocahontas, 33, 136, 158, 162; sailing for Dutch Protestant cause, 122, 142n24; severity of administration, 121, 156; travel to England, 119, 120–22, 123, 139n4, 142n23

Daniel, Angela L., 15n4, 93n79

Daniel, Samuel, *Cleopatra,* 145n49

Davis, James, 122

Davis, John, 64

Dearborn, Mary, 188

Death of Pocahontas, The (Stearns), 190

decolonization, 75–76, 85, 88–89, 252, 254

Deer, Jessica, 86

De-he-wä-mis (Mary Jemison), 63, 66–69

deities, 34–37, 56

De la Warr, Thomas West, Baron, 122, 127, 130–31, 147n60, 160

Denetdale, Jennifer Nez, 10, 17n31

Deuteronomy (Bible book), 157

Diana of Versailles, 186, 187

diseases, 24, 51–52, 57

Dodds Pennock, Caroline, 9

Doolittle, Eliza, 130

Drake, Francis, 25

dress: copyright law, 209, 217–18; cultural appropriation of, 13, 86, 204–7, 208–10, 215, 217–18; English, 216–17; feathers, 212–13, 215, 225, 227; fringe (type of trim), 13, 204, 215; headdresses, 210; lacework, 216; materials for, 212–15, 217; of Pocahontas, 13, 47–48, 186, 212, 215–16, 225; "Pocahontas chic," 13, 204–5, 210–11, 218; pollution by

fashion industry, 213; sumptuary laws, 138, 217

East India Company (EIC), 125, 128

egalitarianism, 52, 97–98

Egan, Susanna, 81

Eikintomino, 127

Elizabeth (daughter of Nansemond werowance), 105, 106–7, 114n32, 133

Elizabeth I of England, 138, 216, 217

Encyclopedia of Textiles (Segal), 212

England: American separation from, 176, 179–80, 188–89; colonial effort, 125–26, 134, 137, 161; dress, 216–17; language, 98–99, 103, 107; Parliament, 119–20, 121, 124, 140n11; tobacco smoking in, 33, 38, 134. *See also* colonists; London; Virginia Company

enslavement, 39, 189, 193–94

environmentalism and environmental politics, 7, 214, 239–40, 247

epidemics, 51–52, 57

Episkenew, Jo-Ann, 88

Esau (biblical figure), 164

Eurocentrism, 1, 3, 5, 45–46, 74–75, 86, 88, 180, 196–97, 246

"Every One" (Hanska Luger), 7

exceptionalism, American, 184, 196, 240. *See also* Manifest Destiny

exoticism, 180, 196

Fyre, Chris, 7

Ezra (Bible book), 136, 157

family: adoption ceremonies, 2–3, 27, 64; American nationhood, family-based conception of, 188–89, 193–94; kinship, 27, 96, 175, 188, 189, 193. *See also* marriage

famine, 57, 61n50, 249

Farrell, Colin, 211

fashion industry, 210, 213. *See also* dress

feathers, 212–13, 215, 225, 227

feminism, 10–11, 17n31, 76
films, 6, 211, 247–48. *See also specific films*
First Anglo-Powhatan War (1610–13), 46, 155
Fitzmaurice, Andrew, 153
flax materials, 217
food, 25, 28–29, 54
fornication, 157
Founding Families of Virginia (FFV), 63
founding fathers myth, 175–76, 188–95, 231. *See also* Washington, George
Four Continents (Monkman), 240
Freeman, Robert, 231
French and Indian War (1754–63), 67
fringe (type of trim), 13, 204, 215
fungi, 213
Furstenberg, François, 188–89, 193

Gates, Thomas, 119, 122, 135, 150n85
gender, 8, 9–10, 224. *See also* feminism; Indigenous Americans: women
General Washington's Resignation (Lawson), 192
Genesis (Bible book), 136, 151–52
gods, 34–37, 56
Goeman, Mishuana, 6, 10–11, 17n31
Goodwyn, Hugh, 26
Goshorn, Shan, 234; *Self Portrait, 236*
Goulston, Theodor, 36
Gravesend, 51–52, 62, 168n31
Gray, Kathryn N., 224, 242
Green, Rayna, 6, 65, 175
Gualtero, 26
Guiana, 25–26
Gulstone, Theodore, 128
Gunn, Meta Atseye, 84

Haile, Edward, 47
Hakluyt, Richard, *Discourse of Western Planting,* 21–22
Hall, Stuart, 75
Halloween costumes, 86, 205

Hamor, Ralph: on Dale's marriage proposal, 113n31, 133; on Pocahontas's captivity, 56; on Pocahontas's name, 165n3; on Pocahontas's role in peace negotiations, 50; on predestination, 159, 161; on Rolfe's marriage to Pocahontas, 135–36, 158; *A True Discourse of the Present Estate of Virginia,* 119, 133, 134, 139n5, 151, 158
Hanska Luger, Cannupa, "Every One," 7
Harjo, Joy, 86
Harriot, Thomas, 22, 23–24, 26, 31, 34, 38, 111n13; *A Briefe and True Report of the New Found Land of Virginia,* 23–25
headdresses, 210
hegemony: in literary scholarship, 11, 14, 74–84, 87–89; and "Pocahontas chic," 207, 211
Helms, Gabriele, 81
hemp, 214
Henry VII of England, 156
Hiakatoo (Seneca warrior, husband of Mary Jemison), 67
Higginson, Francis, 38
Hinushi 1 (Sense), *251*
Historic Jamestowne, 66, 109n2, 154
historiography, 5, 82
history painting, 230–33, 238–39
Hobsbawm, Eric, 177–79, 188
Hollar, Wenceslaus, 225; "Unus Americanus ex Virginia," *226*
Houma, the, 214
Howe, Edmund, 119
Howe, Henry, *Historical Collections of Virginia,* 194–95
Hudson River School, 183
Huitzilihuitl (Aztec high chief), 99–101
humors, 24
Hunt, Thomas, 145n50
huskanasquaw (coming of age ceremonies), 216

identity: Christian, 137, 163; commodification of, 79, 208, 211; hybrid, 9; mythic, 1, 10, 174; national, 157, 164, 176, 180, 182, 230; Native American, 76, 85, 234; queer, 238. *See also* gender; race and racism
images. *See* symbols
I'm a photographer 2001 (Supahan), 234–35
Indian romance genre, 3
Indigeneity, 10–11, 80–81, 85
Indigenous Americans: in American origin myths, 174, 176, 179, 180–85, 189–90, 194, 196; art by, 233–35, 236, 237–40, 237, 239, 248, 252; chiefs and leaders, role of, 31–32, 52, 54, 99–104; commodification of, 7, 65–66, 79, 205–8, 211, 225; conversion to Christianity, 22, 124; cultural appropriation of (*see* cultural appropriation); cultural survival, 217, 218; dress (*see* dress); egalitarianism, 52, 97–98; humanity and reason, 160–61; Indigenous life writing, 81–83; knowledge, 14, 25, 31–34, 34–37, 54, 56, 81; lack of voice in primary material, 1, 8, 46, 62, 74, 212, 242; land incursions, 39, 61n46, 181, 194, 247; legal assumptions about identity, 10; marriage practices, 53, 99–105, 104, 108, 112n22; matrilineal inheritance, 53, 101–2, 108, 114n32, 133; partnering with colonists, 21, 30–31, 54, 83–84; portraits of, 228, 233; primary material produced by, 98–99; religion, 24, 34–37, 56, 81; rules of war, 155; scholarship by, contemporary, 8, 11, 74–76, 77–78, 80–81, 83, 85, 88–89, 227–28; scholarship on, 9; travelling to London, 22, 38, 124, 127–30, 146n54, 242, 244–45. *See also* Algonquian; *and specific peoples, e.g.,* Powhatan, the
—stereotypes: captivity narratives, 67–68; children of the devil, 159–60; "noble savages," 183–84, 185, 196, 210, 211, 229–30; in popular culture, 62; primitivism, 180–83, 210, 211; wilderness, 183
—women: feminisms, Indigenous, 10, 17n31; kept as war booty, 155–56; lack of voice in primary material, 1, 8, 46, 62, 212, 242; marrying colonists, 95, 97, 105–8, 132–33, 135–37, 155–56; in *Pocahontas* (Allen), 76, 84–87; pregnancy, 100, 105, 112n17; sexualization of, 109n3, 209–10; societal importance of, 212; "squaws," 6–7; violence toward, contemporary, 6–7, 75, 86, 90n12, 209; *werowansquas* (female chiefs), 102–3, 104, 107, 112n22; work, 29, 33, 52, 54, 212
"invented traditions" (Hobsbawm), 177–78, 182
Iopassus (Patawomeck chief), 30–32, 33, 35–36, 46, 49
Ireland, 249–50
Isaac (biblical figure), 151

Jacob (biblical figure), 164
Jager, Rebecca K., 86–87
James I of England: asking churches to donate to Virginia Company, 125; calling for Parliament, 119–20, 124, 140n11; on Dale, 121–22, 141n19; did not meet Pocahontas, 51; on Rolfe–Pocahontas marriage, 132, 148n72; Rolfe's letter to (*Relation*), 134, 142n22, 149n80; on tobacco smoking, 38; Tomocomo's meeting with, 130, 147n61; Twelfth Night court masque, 130
Jamestown (Virginia): archaeological finds, 154; burning of fort (1608), 48–49; cohabitation at, 154–57; co-opting of Pocahontas, contemporary, 13; Historic Jamestowne, 66, 109n2, 154; Pocahontas's visits to fort, 27, 47–48, 185; social and moral collapse, 154, 156
Jamestown Settlement Galleries, 150n87

Jamestown-Yorktown Foundation, 150n87
Jaquoah, Dederj, 127, 130
Jefferson, Thomas, 184, 201n35
Jemison, Mary (De-he-wä-mis), 63, 66–69
jimsonweed, 29
Jonson, Ben, 4; *The Vision of Delight*, 130
Jope, John, 121
Justice, Daniel Heath, 80, 85, 88

Kekoughtan, the, 104
Kemps, 102
Kessler, Donna J., 173
Keymis, Lawrence, 26
Kidwell, Clara Sue, 173
Kilcher, Q'orianka, 211
King, John, Bishop of London, 51, 118, 124–25
King, Thomas, 81
King Philip's War (1675–76), 181
kinship, 27, 96, 175, 188, 189, 193. *See also* family
Kitomaquund, Mary (Kittamaquund), 97, 110n8, 133
knowledge: Allen on (Knowledge Keepers), 84–85; colonists' dependence on, 21, 22–23, 28–29, 49; embedded in names and titles, 37–38; expeditions, knowledge-seeking, 21–23, 25–26; forms of Indigenous knowledge, 14, 25, 31–34, 54; power relations inherent in production of, 75, 76, 84, 86, 88–89; spiritual knowledge, 34–37
Koasati, the, 214
Kocoum (first husband of Pocahontas), 4, 31, 53–54, 64, 105
Krupat, Arnold, 82
Kuokkanen, Rauna, 88
Kupperman, Karen Ordahl, 2, 12, 21; *Indians and English*, 9

lacework, 216
Landing of the Pilgrims (Causici), 182

landscapes, 183, 238, 247, 248–49, 252
Lane, Ralph, 22, 25
language: Algonquian, 22, 28, 34, 102–3, 110–12nn12–15, 113n24; English, 98–99, 103, 107; Nahuatl, 110n11; Powhatan, 98–99, 103; "strange" language used by priests, 37
Laricifomes officinalis (agarikon), 213–14
Last of the Mohicans, The (Cooper), 64, 183
Laud, William, 154
Lawes Divine, Morall and Martiall (Virginian governing document), 121
Lawson, Alexander, *General Washington's Resignation*, 192
leather, 215, 217–18
Lee, Peggy, 65
LeMaster, Michelle, 174
Lepore, Jill, 182, 190
life narratives, 76, 80, 81–82, 89n1, 191. *See also* captivity narratives
Life of George Washington (Stearns), 190, *191*
Limbrecke, Francis, 122
Listen to the Atlantic, It's Speaking to You (Sense), 242, *243*, 244, *244*, 246, 252–53, 254
literary scholarship, 11, 14, 74–84, 87–89
Lockhart, James, *The Nahuas after the Conquest*, 110n11
London: Agas Map of London, *129*; cultural taboos against marrying Indigenous women, 137; Indigenous travelers to, 22, 38, 124, 127–30, 146n54, 242, 244–45; St Dionis parish church, 126. *See also* Pocahontas: trip to London
Lopenzina, Drew, 66
"Lullaby" (Silko), 88
Luna, James, *The Artifact Piece*, 233–34
Lymbry, Francis, 122

Machumps, 102, 104
Malick, Terrence, *The New World*, 5, 65, 111n15, 204, 211

Manifest Destiny, 196, 232. *See also* exceptionalism, American

Manteo, 21–22, 23–24, 25, 34, 38

Mantoac (supernatural being), 34, 38

maps, 253–54

Marienstras, Élise, 179–80

Markova, Ivana, 13, 204

Marmon, Susie, 84

marriage: Bible on intermarriage, 136, 157, 164; between colonists, 136; between colonists and Indigenous people, 95, 97, 105–8, 132–33, 135–37, 155–56; Indigenous intermarriage, 99–105, *104*, 108, 112n22; Indigenous women's reasons for, 96, 97; and miscegenation, 4, 13, 63, 66, 135; in order to acquire land, 133. *See also* kinship; Pocahontas: marriage to Rolfe

Marshall, John, 191

Martin, John, 122

Martyn, John, 127, 144n45

masques, 4, 28, 51, 130–31, 132, 134, 147nn59–60

Matahan, 127

Matoaka (Pocahontas's sacred name): disappearance of name, 65; in *Listen to the Atlantic, It's Speaking to You* (Sense), 242, *244*; origin of name, 207–8; as private name, 16n12; withholding of name from colonists, 37, 151. *See also* Pocahontas

Mattachanna (Pocahontas's sister), 33, 127, 137

Mattaponi, the, 2–4, 204–5, 207, 209

Mayflower (ship), 231, 246

McCrea, Jane, 181

McMaster, Gerald, 234

media, 192, 205–6, 207, 209, 211, 221n38, 228, 238. *See also* popular culture

medicine, 24–25, 213–14

Meissner, Shelbi Nahwilet, 10

memory, 76, 195, 246–48, 253

Merrill, James, 98

Metamora (fictional Indigenous leader), 190

métisse (hybrid identity), 9

Mexican War (1846–48), 179

"middle ground," 9, 17n29, 225–27, 228

Mielke, Laura, 78, 87

Miller, Perry, 153

miscegenation, 4, 13, 63, 66, 135

Miss America (Monkman), *239*, 240

Miss Chief Eagle Testicle (alter ego of Monkman), 238. *See also* Monkman, Kent

Missing Matoaka (online resource), 6

missionary work, 120, 124, 126, 163

mistikôsiwak (Monkman), 239

Miyahuaxihuitl (noblewoman from Cuernavaca), 99–101

Mohawk, the, 228–29

Mohawks in Beehives (Niro), 234

Mojica, Monique, *Princess Pocahontas and the Blue Spots*, 8–9

Molina, Diego de, 122, 141n15

Monardes, Nicolas, 24

Monchalin, Lisa, 86

Monkman, Kent, 238–40; *Four Continents*, 240; *Miss America*, 239, 240; *mistikôsiwak*, 239

Monroe, James, 181

Moreton-Robinson, Aileen, 10–11

Morgan, Edmund, 161–62, 169n41

moss, 214, 215

Mossiker, Frances, 83–84, 92n33

movies, 6, 211, 247–48. See also specific movies, e.g., *New World, The*

Mozier, Joseph, *Pocahontas*, 185–87, *186*

myths: founding fathers myth, 175–76, 188–95, 231; Indigenous Americans in American origin myths, 174, 176, 179, 180–85, 189–90, 194, 196; and nationalism, 5, 175, 176–77, 179–85, 188–89, 193; on Pocahontas (*see* Pocahontas: myths); term use, 198n2

Nahuas (Aztecs), 99–101

Nahuatl (language), 110n11

names: disappearance of Pocahontas's names, 65; English names given to mixed-race children, 68, 107; Jemison retaining last name, 67; knowledge embedded in, 37–38; in *Listen to the Atlantic, It's Speaking to You* (Sense), 242, *244*, 245–46; of Powhatan's wives, 102–6, *104*; withholding of, 37, 111n13, 151. *See also specific names given to Pocahontas, e.g., Amonute*

Namontack, 27, 28, 56

Nansemond, the, 106–7, 114n32, 133

Narragansett, the, 101

National Inquiry into Missing and Murdered Indigenous Women and Girls, 90n12

nationalism, 5, 175–77, 179–85, 188–95, 197, 231

Native Americans. *See* Indigenous Americans

natural aristocracy, 184, 201n35

natural resources, 24–25, 29, 33

Nehemiah (Bible book), 156, 157

New England, 231

Newport, Christopher, 27, 28, 31, 54

New World, The (Malick), 5, 65, 111n15, 204, 211

Niro, Shelly, *Mohawks in Beehives*, 234

Oakes, Karen, 68

O'Brien, Jean, 1

Okeeus (deity), 36–37

Okuma, Jamie, 218

one-drop rule, 10, 63, 66

Opechancanough (Powhatan war chief), 38, 64, 107, 134

Opussoquonuske (*werowansqua*), 103

Orapax (Powhatan's capital), 30–31, 49

organic bonds, 184, 193, 200n32

otherness, 180, 182

painting, history, 230–33, 238–39

Pamunkey, the, 26–27, 63, 208–9

Paspahegh, the, 155, 157

Paspiha, 32–33

Passe, Simon van de, engraving of Pocahontas: Chamberlain on, 51; circulation of, 228; as direct representation, 224–25; original appearance of, 147n65, 169n45; Pocahontas's names on, 16n12, 65, 151; Pocahontas's personality, 163; portrait paradigm, 228–29; reproductions of, 131, 147n65

Patawomeck, the, 31, 34, 64. *See also* Iopassus

Peirce, William, 133

Pembroke, William Herbert, Earl of, 134, 149n80

Percy, George, 155, 156

Perkins, William, 166n9, 169n41

Philip III of Spain, 124

Pilgrims, 153, 231

Plains aesthetic, 237–38

Plane, Ann Marie, 101, 112n20

plantations, 38–39, 123

Plymouth (England), 242, 245, 246

Plymouth (Massachusetts), 13, 176

Pocahontas: age, 4, 5, 8–9, 16n13, 27–28, 47; appropriation of, 174, 184–85, 194–97; baptism, 13, 33, 185, 194, 231; captivity among the English (1613–14), 3, 4, 49–50, 53, 64, 105–6, 157–58; cartwheeling, 16n14, 27–28, 54, 80, 92n33; commodification of, 65–66, 79, 208, 211, 225; cultural pervasiveness, 173; death, 4, 38, 51, 57, 127, 130, 164; descendants, 63, 66, 86, 164, 183, 195; dress, 13, 47–48, 186, 212, 215–16, 225; fictionalized accounts on, 4–5; legacy/ afterlife, contemporary connection, 6–8; marriage to Kocoum, 4, 31, 53–54, 64, 105; name, 3–4, 37, 65, 165 (*see also specific other names of Pocahontas, e.g., Matoaka*); personality, 4, 57, 163,

Pocahontas (*continued*)
224–26; political role, 27–28, 52–53, 105; portraits of, 177, 178, 182, 184, 195, 212 (*see also* Passe, Simon van de, engraving of Pocahontas); as Powhatan's favorite daughter, 27, 48, 49, 50, 53, 56; primary material on, 8, 14, 47–49, 75, 78–80, 95, 174; as "princess," 47–48, 51, 53, 105, 131, 148n67, 162, 184, 228–29; "proto-nationalism," 13, 175, 184; rescuing Smith (*see* Smith, John: rescued by Pocahontas); sexualization of, 65–66, 207, 210–11; similarities with Mary Jemison, 68–69; skin color, 197, 212; Smith on (*see* Smith, John: on Pocahontas); stereotypes, 75, 86; symbols and imagery, 175–79, 190–92; visits Jamestown fort, 27, 47–48, 185. *See also* Amonute; Matoaka; Rolfe, Rebecca
—conversion to Christianity: and London trip, 124–25; mythical qualities of, 184–88; name change after, 151–52, 157–58; Powhatan on, 56; and release from captivity, 4; value of, for colonists, 33, 49; and Whitaker, 4, 13, 33, 157–58, 161. *See also* Rolfe, Rebecca
—marriage to Rolfe, 4; American origin myth, 191; commemoration of four-hundredth anniversary, 62, 66; ethnicity issues, 13, 66, 135–37; Hamor on, 158; James I on, 132, 148n72; land claims, 133; Powhatan on, 50, 56, 105–6; reasons for, 96, 105–6, 146n55, 162–63; status issues, 132–33, 134–35, 148n72; Whitaker on, 157–59, 161
—myths, 2–3, 5–7, 173–75; Americanness of Pocahontas, 13, 64–66, 183–88, 196; cultural appropriation of dress, 207; focus on nature, 65, 184–88, 192; founding fathers myth, 189–90, 192–97, 231; story of rescuing Smith, 3, 49, 55, 57, 175–79, 192–95

—trip to London, 4, 12, 33–34, 117–18; aftermath, 137–39; dress worn by Pocahontas, 216, 225; Londoners' interest in Uttamattomakin (Powhatans' chief priest), 34, 56; meeting important people, 50–51, 118, 124–25; meeting other converts, 126, 128–29; meeting Smith, 8, 50; Powhatan on, 57, 118; public baptism of Peter Pope, 125, 126; reasons for, 117–18, 120, 124–25, 126–27, 139; traces of, contemporary, 246; Twelfth Night court masque, 4, 28, 51, 130–31, 132, 134, 147nn59–60; Virginia Company's arranging of (*see* Virginia Company: London trip of 1616)
Pocahontas (Disney movie), 5, 65, 75, 80, 204
Pocahontas (Mozier), 185–87, *186*
Pocahontas chic, 13, 204–7, 210–11, 218
Pochins (Pocahontas's half-brother), 112n22
pollution, 213
polytheism, 34–37, 56
Pope, Peter, 125, 126, 127, 128, 130
popular culture, 62, 174, 247–48. *See also specific forms of popular culture, e.g., films*
Pory, John, 132
potato famine, 249
Potawatomi, the, 215
Power Lines (Sense), 252, 253
Powhatan (Wahunsenacah, Pocahontas's father). colonists and, 28, 30–31, 48, 83–84; on Dale's marriage proposal, 113n31, 133; death, 57; name, 41n17; nicknaming Pocahontas, 3; Pocahontas as favorite daughter, 27, 48, 49, 50, 53, 56; on Pocahontas's captivity, 49–50; on Pocahontas's conversion, 56; on Pocahontas's death, 57; on Pocahontas's marriage to Rolfe, 50, 56, 105–6; on Pocahontas's trip to England, 57, 118; power and influence, 52–55, 101–2; primary material on, 45–46; rebellion

of 1622, 106; and Smith, 27, 28, 48, 55; tribal affiliation, 15n4; wives, 52, 53, 101–5, *104*

Powhatan, the: conflict with colonists, 28, 30–31, 49–50, 55, 155; First Anglo-Powhatan War (1610–13), 46, 155; land incursions by colonists, 39, 61n46; language, 98–99, 103; matrilineal inheritance, 53, 101–2; naming practices, 37–38; Quiokosoughs (Powhatan priesthood), 160, 163; Second Anglo-Powhatan War (1622–32), 48; women's relationships with colonists, 28–29, 97, 154–57

Pratt, Stephanie, 14, 224

predestination, 159–60, 161, 163

pregnancy, 100, 105, 112n17

Preservation of Captain Smith by Pocahontas (Capellano), 177, 178, 182

Price, David A., 139n4

priests: English, 34, 36–37; Indigenous, 160, 163. *See also* Uttamattomakin

primary material: Allen's use of, 77–80, 83–84; Eurocentrism, 1, 45–46, 246; Indigenous people's lack of voice in, 1, 8, 46, 62, 74, 212, 242; making use of, 12; on Pocahontas, 8, 14, 47–49, 75, 78–80, 95, 174; produced by Indigenous people, 98–99

primitivism, 180–83, 210, 211

Princess Pocahontas and the Blue Spots (Mojica), 8–9

Pring, Martin, 126

privateering, 21

Pulitano, Elvira, 77–78

Purchas, Samuel, 32, 34, 36–37, 56, 125, 131, 149n80; *Hakluytus Posthumus*, 166n10

Puritanism, 153, 154

Quiocohannock, the, 104

Quiokosoughs (Powhatan priesthood), 160, 163

race and racism, 10, 63, 66, 86, 138, 207. *See also* miscegenation

Ralegh, Walter (Raleigh), 21–22, 24, 25–26

rape, 209

Rasmussen, Lucinda, 14, 73, 74–75

Rasmussen, William, 174, 176, 178, 190, 192

Rawhunt (Powhatan messenger), 54–55

Read, Listen, Tell (McCall et al.), 81, 82

Rebecca (biblical figure), 136, 151–52, 157, 163–64. *See also* Rolfe, Rebecca

rebellions: Bacon's Rebellion (1676–77), 107; of 1622, 106

Reder, Deanna, 82

Red Star, Wendy, 237–38; *Four Seasons*, 235

religion: Indigenous knowledge on, 34–37, 56, 81; missionary work, 120, 124, 126, 163; polytheism, 34–37, 56; priests, 34, 36–37, 160, 163. *See also* baptism; Bible; Christianity; conversion to Christianity

Rennie, Neil, 3

rescue stories, 181–82. *See also* captivity narratives; Smith, John: rescued by Pocahontas

Revolutionary War (1775–83), 67

Rich, Robert, 149n80

Richter, Daniel, 96; *Facing East from Indian Country*, 9

Riel, Louis, 190

rituals and ceremonies, 27, 32–33, 64, 216

Roanoke colony (1585–86), 21, 24, 26

Robertson, Karen, 8, 9

Rogers, Richard A., 208

Rolfe, John: death, 57; growing tobacco, 33, 123; lack of primary material on, 49–50; letter to Dale on decision to marry Pocahontas, 33, 136, 158, 162, 165n3; marriage to Pocahontas (*see* Pocahontas: marriage to Rolfe); other marriages, 123, 136, 142n26; "Pocahontas to John Rolfe" (Allen), 14, 76, 79–80;

Rolfe, John (*continued*)
on Powhatans, 34; status, 132–33, 134–35; on Thomas' illness, 51–52; travel to England, 120, 122–23; *A True Relation*, 134, 142n22, 149n80
Rolfe, Rebecca (Pocahontas's Christian name), 38, 65, 136, 151–52, 162, 163–64. *See also* Pocahontas
Rolfe, Thomas, 4; fighting with English against Indigenous peoples, 97, 164; illness, 51, 127; lack of primary material on, 50; land inheritance, 133–34; mixed race of, 13, 136, 195–96; Powhatan on, 57; travel to England (1616), 33; travel to Virginia (1635), 39, 133
Romero, Cara, *Nikki*, 235, 237–38, 237
roots, 29
Rose, E. M., 12, 117
Rountree, Helen C., 12, 45; on land incursions, 39; on *Pocahontas* (Disney movie), 5; on Pocahontas rescuing Smith, 2–3; on Pocahontas's lack of political power, 162; on Pocahontas's names, 16n12, 151; on Pocahontas's trip to London, 139n4; on Powhatan culture, 9, 110n12; on priesthood, 163; on relationships between Indigenous women and colonists, 105; source use, 83–84
Rowlandson, Mary, *The Sovereignty and Goodness of God*, 68, 181
Rude, Blair, 111n15

Sandys, Edwin, 120, 148n67, 149n82
Savage, Thomas, 27, 28, 30–31
scholarship, literary, 11, 14, 74–84, 87–89
sculptures: *Diana of Versailles*, 186, 187; by Freeman, Robert, 231; *Listen to the Atlantic, It's Speaking to You* (Sense), 242, 243, 244, 244, 246, 252–53, 254; *Pocahontas* (Mozier), 185–87, 186; *Preservation of Captain Smith by Pocahontas* (Capellano), 177, 178, 182

Seaver, James, 67–68
Second Anglo-Powhatan War (1622–32), 48
Second Seminole War (1835–42), 194
Second War of Independence (1812–15), 174, 181
Self Portrait (Goshorn), 236
Sellers, Stephanie A., 87
Seneca, the, 67
Sense, Sarah, 14–15, 242; *Bayous Meander, Water Heals, Trees Remember, Roots Meander*, 253; "Choctaw Irish Relationship 16," 249–50; *Cowgirls and Indians*, 247–48; *Hinushi 1*, 251; *Listen to the Atlantic, It's Speaking to You*, 242, 243, 244, 244, 246, 252–53, 254; *Power Lines*, 252, 253; *Weaving the Americas*, 248–49; *Weaving Water*, 249
settler colonialism, 10, 14, 78, 80, 89, 209
settlers. *See* colonists
Seventeen (magazine), 206
sexual violence, 209
Shakespeare, William: *Antony and Cleopatra*, 145n49; *The Tempest*, 22
Sharpes, Donald K., 77, 82, 84
She (magazine), 207
Shoemaker, Nancy, 173
Siebert, Monika, 5
silk, 217
Silko, Leslie Marmon, "Lullaby," 88
Simms, William, 178–79
Sinclair, Niigaanwewidam James, 73, 74, 85
Sir Gawain and the Green Knight (medieval verse), 82
Six Fingers (Lakota woman), 84–85
skin color, 197, 212
Slaney, John, 128
slavery, 39, 189, 193–94
Smith, John: captured by Pamunkey, 26–27; on feathers worn by Indigenous women, 227; fictionalized romance with Pocahontas, 4–5, 65; *Generall*

Historie of Virginia, 2, 46, 48, 54, 55, 63–64, 147n65, 178, 192; *A Map of Virginia*, 30, 48, 111n13; marrying an Indigenous woman, 133; meeting Pocahontas in London, 8, 50; military matters, 46; *New Englands Trials and Present Estate*, 2; Pocahontas sent as Powhatan's figurehead, 54–55; and Powhatan, 27, 28, 48, 55; on Powhatan food, 29; return to England, 29–30; on the role of chiefs, 52; on John Rolfe, 132; *True Relation*, 46, 47, 48, 119; unreliability of accounts, 2–3, 54–55, 58n8, 208
—on Pocahontas: age, 47; emotions, 58n8; in letter to Queen Anne, 50, 132, 133, 148n69; London visit, 147n60; love for Rolfe, 49–50; name, 148n67; personality, 4; physical looks, 140n6; rescue of Henry Spelman, 31; status, 131; unreliability of accounts, 45
—rescued by Pocahontas, 27; mythical qualities of, 3, 49, 55, 57, 175–79, 192–95; Pocahontas unable to be present, 64; *Preservation of Captain Smith by Pocahontas* (Capellano), 177, 178, 182; religious dimension of, 185; second rescue, 55, 192; unreliability of, 2–3, 48; written to receive funding, 208
Smith, Linda Tuhiwai, 75, 79, 81, 85
Smythe, Thomas, 120, 125, 127–28, 134
Snodham, Thomas, 126
social media, 221n38
Solomon, Louise, 218
Soto, Hernando de, 231, 232
Sovereignty and Goodness of God, The (Rowlandson), 68, 181
Spanish Empire, 21–22, 24, 120, 122, 155
Spanish moss (*Tillandsia usneoides*), 214, 215
Sparrow, Francis, 26
Speck, Frank, 163
Spelman, Henry (nephew), 30–32, 34–35, 36, 52; *Relation of Virginia*, 31–33, 46

Spelman, Henry (uncle), 32, 42n39
spiritual knowledge, Indigenous, 34–37, 56, 81
Spokane, the, 214
Squanto (Tisquantum), 38, 128, 130, 145n50
status, 125, 131–33, 134–35, 148n72, 216–17
Stearns, Junius Brutus: *The Death of Pocahontas*, 190; *Life of George Washington*, 190, *191*
stereotypes, 6, 75, 86, 205, 208–9, 210–11, 217–18, 247–48
Stith, William, 132
Stone, Christopher, 168n31
Strachey, William, 46; on Algonquian language, 99, 103, 111n13, 113n24; "A Dictionarie of the Indian Language," 99, 103, 111nn13–14, 113n28; editorial mistakes, 113n25; *The Historie of Travell into Virginia Britania*, 32, 99, 111n14, 140n6; on Kocoum, 53–54; on natural resources, 29; on Pocahontas cartwheeling, 16n14, 27–28, 54, 92n33; on Pocahontas's age, 16n13, 28, 47; on Pocahontas's name, 37–38; on Pocahontas's personality, 4; on Powhatans mocking colonists, 31; on Powhatan's sons and daughters, 53; on Powhatan's wives, 102–4; Spelman interview, 35
street performances, *Vigil* (Belmore), 7
suede, 217–18
Sully, Robert Matthew, 195
sumptuary laws, 138, 217
Supahan, Nisha, *I'm a photographer 2001*, 234–35
symbols, 175–79, 185–88, 190–92
Symonds, William, 156, 160

Tatacoope (Pocahontas's half-brother), 112n22
Tatonetti, Lisa, 77

Tekakwitha, Kateri, Saint, 163

Tempest, The (Shakespeare), 22

textile practices, 13, 212–13

Thorpe, George, 127

Thorpe, Georgius, 127, 128

Throckmorton, Elizabeth, 122

Thrush, Coll, 245–46

Tillandsia usneoides (Spanish moss), 214, 215

Tilton, Robert, 3, 8, 175–76, 178, 185, 190, 192

Tisquantum (Squanto), 38, 128, 130, 145n50

tobacco: grown by English, 33, 38–39, 123; Indigenous uses of, 24–25; smoking of, in England, 33, 38, 134; tax exemption for tobacco exports, 134

Tomocomo (Pocahontas's brother-in-law), 130, 137, 147n61

Topiawari, 26

Totakins (Tsenacommacah convert), 127

Totopotomoy (Pamunkey), 107

Town and Country (magazine), 206–7

Townsend, Camilla, 95, 151; on gender, 65; on *Pocahontas* (Allen), 79–81; on Pocahontas's agency, 162; on Pocahontas's names, 158; on Powhatan's wives' names, 12; research, 9; on story of Smith's rescue, 2–3

"traditions, invented" (Hobsbawm), 177–78, 182

Trumbull, John, 230

Trump, Donald, 7

Tsenacomoco (Tsenacommacah, Powhatan chiefdom), 96, 106, 127, 244

tuckahoe (root), 29

Turner, Nat, 193

United States: construction of national identity, 176–77, 179–85, 228, 230–33; exceptionalism, 184, 196, 240; Manifest Destiny, 196, 232; myths (*see* myths); nationalism, 5, 175–77, 179–85, 188–95, 197, 231; opportunities for colonists, 137; Pocahontas as prototype of Americanness, 13, 64–66, 183–88, 196; popularity of Indian romance genre, 3; separation from England, 176, 179–80, 188–89; as unpeopled landscape, 5, 183, 184–85

United States Indian Arts and Crafts Act of 1990, 208

Unity (John West's wife), 108, 114n35

university: diversity work, 87–88; literary scholarship, 11, 14, 74–84, 87–89. *See also* primary material

"Unus Americanus ex Virginia" (Hollar), 236

Uttamattomakin (Powhatans' chief priest), 33, 36–37, 50–51, 56–57, 124

Vanderlyn, John, 181

Vaughan, Alden T., 139n4

Verelst, John, 228, 229

Victoria's Secret, 210

Vigil (street performance piece by Belmore), 7

Villiers, George, 130, 147n59

violence: through cultural appropriation, 207, 209–10; toward Indigenous women, 6–7, 75, 86, 90n12, 209; sexual violence, 209

Virginia: Bacon's Rebellion (1676–77), 107; commercial goods and natural resources, 120, 134; droughts, 28–29, 57; Founding Families of Virginia (FFV), 63; Great Standing Lottery for Virginia, 123, 124, 139n4; marriage law of 1691, 135; name use, 39n1; plantations, 38, 39–40, 123; pride in connection with Pocahontas, 13, 135, 195; Racial Integrity Act (1924), 10, 63, 66; rebellion of 1622, 106; severe administration of, 121; slavery, 39; tobacco growing in, 33,

38–39, 123; as unpeopled landscape, 5. *See also* Jamestown

Virginia Assembly, 39

Virginia Company: *A briefe declaration of the present state of things in Virginia*, 126; colonial design, 26, 38–39; commodification of Pocahontas, 211, 225; control of information, 32, 42n42; financial trouble, 32, 33, 119, 123; headright system, 123, 126; receiving donations from churches, 125–26; tax exemption for tobacco exports, 134

—London trip of 1616: aftermath, 137–38; charity work, 124–26, 134–35; decided by Virginia Company, 139n4; financial reasons, 50, 118; political reasons, 119–23; Rolfes' mission grant, 51, 135; status and ethnicity issues, 131–37; visual component, 225

Vision of Delight, The (Jonson), 130

visual symbols, 175–79, 185–88, 190–92

Vitoria, Francisco de, "On the Indians Lately Discovered," 160–61

Wahunsenacah. *See* Powhatan (Wahunsenacah, Pocahontas's father)

Walsh, Susan, 68

Wanchese, 21–22, 23, 34, 111n13

Warren, Elizabeth, 7

Warrior, Robert, 77, 80, 93n79

wars: American Civil War (1861–65), 194–96; Anglo-Spanish War (1585–1604), 21; Black Hawk War (1832), 231–32; First Anglo-Powhatan War (1610–13), 46, 155; French and Indian War (1754–63), 67; Indigenous rules of war, 155; intermarriage used as means of ending/averting, 101; King Philip's War (1675–76), 181; Mexican War (1846–48), 179; Revolutionary War (1775–83), 67; Second Anglo-Powhatan War (1622–32), 48;

Second Seminole War (1835–42), 194; Second War of Independence (1812–15), 174, 181; War of 1812, 64, 176

Washington, George, 175, 176, 188–95, 197

Watson, Kelly, 110n8

weapons, 26–27

Weaver, Jace, 9

weaving, 245, 248–49, 250, 252, 253–54

Weaving the Americas (Sense), 248–49

Weaving Water (Sense), 249

Weems, Parson, 192

Wente, Jesse, 90n12

werowansquas (female chiefs), 102–3, 104, 107, 112n22

Werowocomoco (Powhatan's capital), 27, 28

West, Francis, 122

West, John (father), 105, 107–8, 114nn34–35, 130–31, 147n64

West, John (son), 107–8, 114n34, 114n36

West, Thomas, Baron De La Warr, 122, 127, 130–31, 147n60, 160

Whitaker, Alexander: background, 152–53; collecting ethnological material, 168n35; death, 164; *Good Newes from Virginia*, 152, 156, 157, 166n10; on Indigenous people, 160; and Pocahontas's conversion, 4, 13, 33, 157–58, 161; on relationships with Indigenous women, 95, 109n3, 156; on Rolfe-Pocahontas marriage, 157–59, 161; theology, 153–54, 159–62, 168n37

Whitaker, William, 152–53; *A Short Sum of Christianity*, 159

White, Edwin, 192, 195

White, John, 22, 23–24, 25, 30

Whyte, Kyle, 10

Widow Ranter, The (Behn), 108

Wigginton, Caroline, 250

wilderness, 183–84

Willson, Marcius, 178–79

Winauk (Carolina sassafras), 24

Winganuske (Powhatan's primary wife), 104, 106, 113n28

Wingina (later Pemisapan, Roanoke chief), 38

Winthrop, Adam, 153

Winthrop, John, 153, 154

Witgen, Michael, 190

women. *See* Indigenous Americans: women; *werowansquas* (female chiefs)

Women's Magazine Archive, 205

Wood, Karenne, 1, 8, 9, 14, 15, 62, 242

wool, 217

Wrothe, John, 148n67, 149n82

Xore (Cooree, Southern African convert), 127, 130, 146n57

Yeardley, George, 122, 123

Yellowtail, Bethany, 218

Young, Philip, 3, 174, 183

Zuniga, Don Pedro de, 155, 156

EARLY AMERICAN HISTORIES

To Organize the Sovereign People: Political Mobilization in Revolutionary Pennsylvania
David W. Houpt

Plain Paths and Dividing Lines: Navigating Native Land and Water in the Seventeenth-Century Chesapeake
Jessica Lauren Taylor

The Travels of Richard Traunter: Two Journeys through the Native Southeast in 1698 and 1699
Edited by Sandra L. Dahlberg

Making the Early Modern Metropolis: Culture and Power in Pre-Revolutionary Philadelphia
Daniel P. Johnson

The Permanent Resident: Excavations and Explorations of George Washington's Life
Philip Levy

From Independence to the U.S. Constitution: Reconsidering the Critical Period of American History
Douglas Bradburn and Christopher R. Pearl, editors

Washington's Government: Charting the Origins of the Federal Administration
Max M. Edling and Peter J. Kastor, editors

The Natural, Moral, and Political History of Jamaica, and the Territories thereon Depending, from the First Discovery of the Island by Christopher Columbus to the Year 1746
James Knight, edited by Jack P. Greene

Statute Law in Colonial Virginia: Governors, Assemblymen, and the Revisals That Forged the Old Dominion
Warren M. Billings

Against Popery: Britain, Empire, and Anti-Catholicism
Evan Haefeli, editor

Conceived in Crisis: The Revolutionary Creation of an American State
Christopher R. Pearl

Redemption from Tyranny: Herman Husband's American Revolution
Bruce E. Stewart

Experiencing Empire: Power, People, and Revolution in Early America
Patrick Griffin, editor

Citizens of Convenience: The Imperial Origins of American Nationhood on the U.S.-Canadian Border
Lawrence B. A. Hatter

"Esteemed Bookes of Lawe" and the Legal Culture of Early Virginia
Warren M. Billings and Brent Tarter, editors

Settler Jamaica in the 1750s: A Social Portrait
Jack P. Greene

Loyal Protestants and Dangerous Papists: Maryland and the Politics of Religion in the English Atlantic, 1630–1690
Antoinette Sutto

The Road to Black Ned's Forge: A Story of Race, Sex, and Trade on the Colonial American Frontier
Turk McCleskey

www.ingramcontent.com/pod-product-compliance
Lightning Source LLC
Chambersburg PA
CBHW030837200225
22260CB00018B/354